# A GUIDE TO INTERNATIONAL DISARMAMENT LAW

Disarmament is integral to the safeguarding and promotion of security, development, and human rights. Hundreds of millions of dollars are spent each year on disarmament operations, yet no comprehensive guide exists to explain clearly the international rules governing disarmament. This book seeks to fill that gap. It describes the international legal rules that govern disarmament and the operational, political, and technical considerations that govern their implementation. This book aims to support compliance, implementation, and further development of international disarmament law.

Traditionally, disarmament focused on weapons of mass destruction. This remains a critically important area of work. In recent decades, the scope of disarmament has broadened to encompass also conventional weapons, including through the adoption of rules and regulations to govern arms transfers and measures to eliminate specific munitions from stockpiles and to destroy explosive remnants of war. There have also been four "generations" of programmes to address small arms and light weapons at the national or sub-national level through disarmament, demobilisation, and reintegration (DDR) programmes during and following the end of armed conflict.

While an internationally accepted definition of disarmament does not yet exist, it is widely agreed that disarmament encompasses or interrelates with prohibitions and restrictions on the development, production, stockpiling, testing, and transfer of weapons and on their destruction. In addition to clarifying these elements, chapters of this guide will also consider the relationship between disarmament and the law of armed conflict, and with the United Nations Security Council, human security, public health, and non-state actors.

**Stuart Casey-Maslen** is Honorary Professor of International Law at the Centre for Human Rights in the University of Pretoria in South Africa. He holds a doctorate in the Law of Armed Conflict and master's degrees in International Human Rights Law and Forensic Ballistics. He was previously Head of Research of the Geneva Academy of International Humanitarian Law and Human Rights and has also worked for the International Committee of the Red Cross (ICRC), the United Nations Children's Fund (UNICEF), the Office of the UN High Commissioner for Human Rights (OHCHR), and several non-governmental organisations, including Norwegian People's Aid (NPA).

**Tobias Vestner** is Head of the Security and Law Programme at the Geneva Centre for Security Policy (GCSP) in Switzerland. Prior to joining GCSP, he was Research Affiliate and Global Futures Fellow at Georgetown University and Policy Advisor at the Export Control Policy Division of the Swiss State Secretariat for Economic Affairs. He also worked at the Law of Armed Conflict Section of the Swiss Federal Department of Defence, Civil Protection and Sport and serves as reserve Legal Advisor at the Swiss Armed Forces Staff. He holds a Master of Science in Foreign Service and a Master of Laws in International and European Law.

# Routledge Research in the Law of Armed Conflict

# A GUIDE TO INTERNATIONAL DISARMAMENT LAW

*Stuart Casey-Maslen and Tobias Vestner*

Routledge
Taylor & Francis Group

LONDON AND NEW YORK

First published 2019
by Routledge
2 Park Square, Milton Park, Abingdon, Oxon OX14 4RN

and by Routledge
52 Vanderbilt Avenue, New York, NY 10017

*Routledge is an imprint of the Taylor & Francis Group, an informa business*

© 2019 Stuart Casey-Maslen and Tobias Vestner

*British Library Cataloguing-in-Publication Data*
A catalogue record for this book is available from the British Library

*Library of Congress Cataloging-in-Publication Data*
Names: Casey-Maslen, Stuart, author. | Vestner, Tobias, author.
Title: A guide to international disarmament law / Stuart Casey-Maslen,
    Tobias Vestner.
Description: New York : Routledge, 2019. | Series: Routledge research in
    the law of armed conflict | Includes bibliographical references and index.
Identifiers: LCCN 2018060406 | ISBN 9780815363866 (hardback) |
    ISBN 9781351108119 (ebook)
Subjects: LCSH: Arms control. | Disarmament. | Nuclear arms
    control—Verification.
Classification: LCC KZ5624 .C37 2019 | DDC 341.7/33—dc23
LC record available at https://lccn.loc.gov/2018060406

ISBN: 9780815363866 (hbk)
ISBN: 9780815363873 (pbk)
ISBN: 9781351108119 (ebk)

Typeset in Bembo
by Apex CoVantage, LLC

# CONTENTS

# TEXT BOXES

# CASES AND MATERIALS

## Treaties

2000 Optional Protocol to the Convention on the Rights of the Child on the involvement of children in armed conflict

2001 Protocol on the Control of Firearms, Ammunition and Other Related Materials in the Southern African Development Community (SADC) Region

2003 Protocol on Explosive Remnants of War (Protocol V to the 1980 CCW)

2005 Protocol Against the Illicit Manufacturing of and Trafficking in Firearms, Their Parts and Components and Ammunition, Supplementing the United Nations Convention Against Transnational Organized Crime

2006 ECOWAS Convention on Small Arms and Light Weapons, Their Ammunition and Other Related Materials

2008 Convention on Cluster Munitions

2009 Treaty on a Nuclear-Weapon-Free Zone in Central Asia (Treaty of Semipalatinsk)

2010 Central African Convention for the Control of Small Arms and Light Weapons, their Ammunition and all Parts and Components that can be used for their Manufacture, Repair and Assembly

2013 Arms Trade Treaty

2017 Treaty on the Prohibition of Nuclear Weapons

## Directives

1998 EU Code of Conduct on Arms Exports

## Soft law instruments and Guidelines

2001 Programme of Action to Prevent, Combat and Eradicate the Illicit Trade in Small Arms and Light Weapons in All Its Aspects

2002 International Code of Conduct against Ballistic Missile Proliferation (HCoC)

2005 International Instrument to Enable States to Identify and Trace, in a Timely and Reliable Manner, Illicit Small Arms and Light Weapons

2005 Basic Principles and Guidelines on the Right to a Remedy and Reparation for Victims of Gross Violations of International Human Rights Law and Serious Violations of International Humanitarian Law

2011 OSCE Vienna Document on Confidence- and Security-building Measures. Australia Group, Guidelines for Transfers of Sensitive Chemical or Biological Items.
Wassenaar Arrangement, Initial Elements.
MTCR Guidelines for Sensitive Missile-Relevant Transfers
Nuclear Suppliers Group Guidelines.

# PREFACE

This work, the outcome of two years of research and consultation, combines the expertise of arms control and disarmament lawyers with other intersecting branches of international law. In addition to international disarmament law directly, other relevant international legal rules (*lex lata*) are identified from the law on inter-state use of force (*jus ad bellum*), the law of armed conflict (LOAC)/ international humanitarian law (IHL),[1] international criminal law, and international environmental law.

The resultant analysis reflects the sources of international law as set out in Article 38 of the 1945 Statute of the International Court of Justice (ICJ). Treaty law, custom, and general principles of law are the primary sources, while judicial decisions and the views of leading international lawyers are the subsidiary means for the determination of rules of law.[2] Since the adoption of the Statute, the ICJ has held that a unilateral declaration by a state can also be a source of binding international law, albeit only in exceptional circumstances.[3] At the same time, soft law (politically binding instruments) as well as norms elaborated by renowned experts may also be influential in identifying norms that are on the cusp of becoming customary international law. Law that is in the process of 'crystallising' as a customary rule but has not yet done so is sometimes called *lex ferenda*: law in the making.

---

1 For the purpose of this book, the two monikers are used synonymously, although some commentators argue that international humanitarian law should be restricted to provisions of the Geneva Law branch of the law of armed conflict that offers protection to those who do not, or no longer, participate directly in hostilities. See, e.g., S. Haines, 'War at Sea: Nineteenth-Century Laws for Twenty-First Century Wars?', *International Review of the Red Cross*, Vol. 98, No. 2 (2016), pp. 419–47, at 420, footnote 3.
2 See further, on the sources of international law, *infra*, para. 1.10.
3 ICJ, *Nuclear Tests Case* (*New Zealand v. France*), Judgment, 20 December 1974, paras. 45–49.

In adhering to a treaty – meaning, becoming a party to it – a state is usually required to either both sign and ratify the treaty or to accede to it (a single act that has the legal effect of signature and ratification combined). Most global disarmament treaties use what is known as the 'all states' formula. As of March 2019, the Secretary-General of the United Nations considered that this allowed a total of 197 states to become party to such a treaty: all 193 UN member states,[4] the two UN observer states (the Holy See and the State of Palestine), and two other states (Cook Islands and Niue). This list may change in the future, for example should Kosovo's secession from Serbia[5] or the existence of the Sahrawi Arab Democratic Republic (Western Sahara)[6] be recognised by the UN General Assembly, or should either be admitted as a member of a UN specialised agency.[7]

Wherever a treaty is for the first time in a chapter, the year of the adoption of the treaty is cited. (Some commentators prefer to use the date of opening for signature

---

4 The official short forms of the 193 UN member states are the following: Afghanistan, Albania, Algeria, Andorra, Angola, Antigua and Barbuda, Argentina, Armenia, Australia, Austria, Azerbaijan, Bahamas, Bahrain, Bangladesh, Barbados, Belarus, Belgium, Belize, Benin, Bhutan, Bolivia (Plurinational State of), Bosnia and Herzegovina, Botswana, Brazil, Brunei Darussalam, Bulgaria, Burkina Faso, Burundi, Cabo Verde, Cambodia, Cameroon, Canada, Central African Republic, Chad, Chile, China, Colombia, Comoros, Congo, Costa Rica, Côte d'Ivoire, Croatia, Cuba, Cyprus, Czech Republic, Democratic People's Republic of Korea, Democratic Republic of the Congo, Denmark, Djibouti, Dominica, Dominican Republic, Ecuador, Egypt, El Salvador, Equatorial Guinea, Eritrea, Estonia, Eswatini, Ethiopia, Fiji, Finland, France, Gabon, The Gambia (Republic of), Georgia, Germany, Ghana, Greece, Grenada, Guatemala, Guinea, Guinea-Bissau, Guyana, Haiti, Honduras, Hungary, Iceland, India, Indonesia, Iran (Islamic Republic of), Iraq, Ireland, Israel, Italy, Jamaica, Japan, Jordan, Kazakhstan, Kenya, Kiribati, Kuwait, Kyrgyzstan, Lao People's Democratic Republic, Latvia, Lebanon, Lesotho, Liberia, Libya, Liechtenstein, Lithuania, Luxembourg, Madagascar, Malawi, Malaysia, Maldives, Mali, Malta, Marshall Islands, Mauritania, Mauritius, Mexico, Micronesia (Federated States of), Monaco, Mongolia, Montenegro, Morocco, Mozambique, Myanmar, Namibia, Nauru, Nepal, Netherlands, New Zealand, Nicaragua, Niger, Nigeria, the Republic of North Macedonia, Norway, Oman, Pakistan, Palau, Panama, Papua New Guinea, Paraguay, Peru, Philippines, Poland, Portugal, Qatar, Republic of Korea, Republic of Moldova, Romania, Russian Federation, Rwanda, Saint Kitts and Nevis, Saint Lucia, Saint Vincent and the Grenadines, Samoa, San Marino, Sao Tome and Principe, Saudi Arabia, Senegal, Serbia, Seychelles, Sierra Leone, Singapore, Slovakia, Slovenia, Solomon Islands, Somalia, South Africa, South Sudan, Spain, Sri Lanka, Sudan, Suriname, Sweden, Switzerland, Syrian Arab Republic, Tajikistan, Thailand, Timor-Leste, Togo, Tonga, Trinidad and Tobago, Tunisia, Turkey, Turkmenistan, Tuvalu, Uganda, Ukraine, United Arab Emirates, United Kingdom of Great Britain and Northern Ireland, United Republic of Tanzania, United States of America, Uruguay, Uzbekistan, Vanuatu, Venezuela (Bolivarian Republic of), Viet Nam, Yemen, Zambia, and Zimbabwe.

5 The Republic of Kosovo is a member of the World Customs Organization (WCO).

6 The Sahrawi Arab Democratic Republic is a member of the African Union.

7 In 2015, Kosovo fell three votes short of the two-thirds majority vote it needed in the United Nations Educational, Scientific and Cultural Organization (UNESCO) General Assembly to be able to join the organisation.

of a treaty.) Thus, for instance, we refer to the 1971 (not 1972) Biological Weapons Convention[8] and the 1992 (not 1993) Chemical Weapons Convention.[9]

---

8  Convention on the Prohibition of the Development, Production and Stockpiling of Bacteriological (Biological) and Toxin Weapons and on Their Destruction; adopted at New York, 16 December 1971; entered into force, 26 March 1975.
9  Convention on the Prohibition of the Development, Production, Stockpiling and Use of Chemical Weapons and on Their Destruction; adopted at Geneva, 3 September 1992; entered into force, 29 April 1997.

# THE AIM AND LAYOUT OF THE GUIDE

Given the multiple, interconnected international instruments of, and related to, disarmament, this Guide aims to provide clarity on the contemporary international rules governing disarmament as well as on their application. As such, this book seeks to facilitate the general understanding, interpretation, and implementation of international disarmament law. The Guide's analysis of the various treaty provisions is further intended to support policymakers and diplomats in their negotiation of future disarmament instruments.

A consensual definition of disarmament does not exist in international law, though at its core it certainly involves the destruction of weapons, as the introduction will explain. Typically, however, *global* disarmament treaties – those with the specific purpose of renouncing certain weapons and which are open to adherence by all states – also incorporate prohibitions and restrictions on the development, production, stockpiling, transfer, and use of weapons. Often, the treaties also oblige states parties to assist the victims and to remediate environmental effects that the weapons cause.

This Guide provides a holistic legal and comparative legal analysis of the global disarmament treaties, namely the 1971 Biological Weapons Convention, the 1992 Chemical Weapons Convention, the 1997 Anti-Personnel Mine Ban Convention,[1] the 2008 Convention on Cluster Munitions,[2] and the 2017 Treaty on the Prohibition of Nuclear Weapons.[3] Other disarmament and disarmament-related

---

1 Convention on the Prohibition of the Use, Stockpiling, Production and Transfer of Anti-Personnel Mines and on Their Destruction; adopted at Oslo, 18 September 1997; entered into force, 1 March 1999.
2 Convention on Cluster Munitions; adopted at Dublin, 30 May 2008; entered into force, 1 August 2010.
3 Treaty on the Prohibition of Nuclear Weapons; adopted at New York, 7 July 2017; not yet in force.

multilateral treaties as well as politically binding instruments ('soft law' instruments) are elaborated when they address the particular topic of a chapter or subchapter. To facilitate ease of use of the Guide, bilateral arms control treaties, notably those between the United States of America and the Russian Federation, are briefly surveyed in the first chapters of the guide.

Chapter 1 explains the core concepts of international disarmament law. A section on disarmament and international law lists the key global disarmament treaties and summarises the nature of international law and its constituent elements. In articulating the crosscutting nature of disarmament, particular focus is placed on related arms control, non-proliferation and law of armed conflict agreements. Key definitions are expounded, notably of weapons, arms, weapons of mass destruction, conventional weapons, as well as certain specific weapons.

Chapter 2 summarizes the core elements of global disarmament treaties stockpile destruction, clearance, and destruction of the weapons that have been used, and efforts to curtail transfer and to end production, research, and development. The use of weapons is given particular attention. Positive obligations to assist victims and engage in confidence-building measures, such as transparency, have become integral components of global disarmament treaties. Verification is also covered in brief.

Chapter 3 on disarmament and security articulates the interrelationship between disarmament and other security-related processes and concepts, such as non-proliferation, arms control, and human security. It also describes the role in disarmament of the UN Security Council, the UN General Assembly, and the Conference on Disarmament, as well as state-led processes.

Chapter 4 describes how disarmament treaties prohibit the use – and occasionally also the threat of use – of weapons. Disarmament law applies at all times: during both peacetime and armed conflict. In contrast, the law of armed conflict (LOAC/ IHL) regulates use of a weapon only during a situation of armed conflict.

Chapter 5 describes what activities amount to research and development under international law and what role testing obligations and prohibitions play within the broader elements of research and development. This chapter summarises the relevant treaty obligations that govern all three.

Chapter 6 describes what constitutes a transfer under the different treaty regimes and explains the difference between export, transit, trans-shipment, and transfer. It further reviews the relevant disarmament treaty prohibitions.

Chapter 7 explains the relevant treaty obligations for stockpile destruction and describes different stockpile destruction techniques, which clearly depend on the nature of the weapon.

Chapter 8 describes how treaty regimes require forms of remediation and reparation for damage resulting from weapon use, including clearance of munitions, assistance to the victims, and environmental remediation.

Chapter 9 addresses reporting, verification, and compliance (the latter two concepts are often understood in varying terms by different actors). The chapter explains how confidence-building measures in disarmament treaties include initial and annual reporting obligations as well as, in certain circumstances, compulsory fact-finding and mechanisms to promote compliance.

Chapter 10 on operational 'micro'-disarmament (in disarmament, demobilisation, and reintegration (DDR) programmes and associated activities) explains how combatants[4] and fighters are demobilised and their weapons (typically, but not only, small arms and light weapons) are addressed. The challenges of 'fourth-generation' DDR, during counterterrorism operations in prolonged armed conflict, are specifically reviewed.

A final section summarises how disarmament law has been evolving and what challenges disarmament as a specific endeavour is facing. These challenges include artificial intelligence and autonomy as well as the ever-growing threat of cyberwarfare.

Text boxes throughout the guide cite treaty provisions that deserve closer attention. The text boxes aim to improve the understanding of the treaties' content, allow comparisons between different treaties' provisions on the same topic, and serve as examples for future treaty-making. Annex 1 provides a graphic overview of disarmament and disarmament-related treaties and soft law instruments. Annex 2 lists the key treaties and instruments, including an index of references to the treaties in the text of this work. Annex 3 offers a list of major institutions dealing with disarmament.

---

4 Strictly speaking, under the law of armed conflict combatants are members of armed forces engaged in an *international* armed conflict (where two or more states are fighting each other); the term does not formally apply in non-international armed conflict, that is to say where a state is engaged in protracted armed violence with an organised non-state armed group (or two organised non-state armed groups are fighting each other in a situation of protracted armed violence).

# ACKNOWLEDGEMENTS

Many experts in disarmament and arms control as well as in a range of branches of international law have helped to shape our work. We would particularly like to thank the following for their comments and feedback on earlier drafts of this book: Dr David Atwood, Lecturer at Paris School of International Affairs on the United Nations and Disarmament; Dr John Borrie, Chief of Research, United Nations Institute for Disarmament Research (UNIDIR); Dr Silvia Cattaneo, Attaché for Disarmament Affairs, Permanent Mission of Italy to the United Nations and Other International Organizations in Geneva; Mr Marc Finaud, Arms Proliferation Cluster Leader, Emerging Security Challenges Programme, GCSP; HE Amb. Amandeep Singh Gill, Permanent Representative of India to the Conference on Disarmament, Geneva; Dr John Hart, Senior Researcher and Head of the Chemical and Biological Security Project, Arms Control and Non-proliferation Programme, Stockholm International Peace Research Institute (SIPRI); Ms Susanne Hammer, Disarmament Expert, First Secretary, Permanent Mission of Austria to the United Nations and Other International Organizations in Geneva; Mr Peter Herby, Independent Consultant on Arms Control; Prof. Keith Krause, Head of International Relations/ Political Science Department, Graduate Institute of International and Development Studies (IHEID); Mr Richard Lennane, Executive Director, Geneva Disarmament Platform; Mr Louis Maresca, Legal Adviser, International Committee of the Red Cross (ICRC); Mr Daniel Nord, Senior Disarmament Advisor, Permanent Mission of Sweden to the United Nations and Other International Organizations in Geneva; Mr Juan Carlos Ruan, Director, Anti-Personnel Mine Ban Convention Implementation Support Unit; Ms Mallory Stewart, Principle Member of the Technical Staff, Sandia National Laboratories; and Prof. Bakhtiyar Tuzmukhamedov, Vice-President of the Russian Association of International Law. We also thank Ms Salimata Sophie Seck, Junior Programme Officer, GCSP, for her excellent project support. Further appreciation goes to the Swiss Federal Department of Foreign Affairs for its financial contribution. All involvement in the project was in a purely personal capacity, and the views expressed in the publication do not necessarily reflect those of the project's supporters or of anyone who provided input to, or commented on, earlier drafts.

# INTRODUCTION

## The rationale of disarmament

0.1   Disarmament aims to contribute to global security and stability by the elimination of weapons. By renouncing weapons, states may prevent widespread death and injury and the infliction of severe damage to infrastructure and the environment. Weapons of mass destruction (WMD) are capable of killing or injuring millions of people and devastating a huge area, and are therefore a particular focus of international disarmament law. Disarmament also contributes to international and regional stability by reducing the risk of the outbreak of armed conflict, or, when a conflict is ongoing, preventing a major escalation in the use of force during the conduct of hostilities.

0.2   Disarmament can also enhance trust between states, lessening unpredictability, miscalculation, and misperception regarding the use of force, through weapons monitoring, verification of compliance with international rules, and other confidence-building measures. Disarmament measures can also prevent costly arms races or preclude the horizontal proliferation of weapons, including to armed non-state actors.[1] General and complete disarmament – the total renunciation of all weapons – would exclude any aggressive action by states. Although the 1945 Charter of the United Nations (UN) does not foresee such an ambitious objective, the UN General Assembly and several international treaties have called for this goal to be pursued. Nevertheless, this goal is highly unlikely to be ever realised because military force remains such a powerful tool for attaining domestic and foreign policy goals.

---

1   Horizontal proliferation means the spread of particular weapons to those states (or non-state actors) that do not have them. This contrasts with *vertical* proliferation, a term that refers to an increase in the size of an arsenal of a particular weapon.

0.3   By controlling the level of armaments that states retain at a 'balanced' level, arms control may similarly enhance international stability. From a defensive perspective, deterrence is a commonly used strategic concept concerning both nuclear and conventional weapons. Some strategists argue that a balance of power between states is a stable form of order in the international system. Such equilibrium, however, requires the maintenance of an appropriate level of armaments. And given that disarmament may concern the survival of a nation, states may distrust whether agreements are being complied with, yet also be reluctant to accept external verification by other states or international institutions. Hence, disarmament has evolved, and continues to evolve, through a partial approach that addresses only specific weapons or categories of weapons.

0.4   Disarmament commitments and activities rely heavily on treaties. The law of treaties, a specific branch of international law, is of major importance to states because they require clarity as to their own engagements and a yardstick by which to measure the fulfilment of the commitments of the other parties. As a consequence, certain disarmament treaties are extremely detailed and complex, and may incorporate highly technical provisions. Unilateral commitments by the most powerful military nations, such as the renunciation of biological weapons by the United States of America in 1969, may serve as strong motivations for other states to disarm because of the lesser probability of the weapon's use against them.

0.5   Bilateral agreements between the great powers, most obviously between the United States of America (US) and the Soviet Union/Russian Federation, can underpin efforts towards global disarmament by lessening the fear of other nations that they will suffer harm. This was certainly the case in the 1970s with the Strategic Arms Limitation Talks (SALT) and the two associated treaties (SALT I and SALT II). At the same time, the level of compliance with agreements may deteriorate over time. An example is accusations and counter-accusations regarding compliance with the 1987 Intermediate-Range Nuclear Forces Treaty (INF Treaty), ultimately leading to the announcement by US President Donald Trump in October 2018 that the United States of America would withdraw from the INF Treaty (subsequently confirmed by the US Secretary of State at the beginning of February 2019).[2]

0.6   Multilateral disarmament treaties allow the interests of many states to be addressed, and generally enjoy high levels of legitimacy. Multilateral agreements are, though, hard to achieve, and even when successfully concluded, they may oftentimes be the result of major compromises. Regional disarmament treaties can be valuable intermediate steps towards global disarmament, sometimes with the potential also to prevent arms races erupting at the continental or sub-continental level.

---

2   BBC, 'Russia Nuclear Treaty: Gorbachev Warns Trump Plan Will Undermine Disarmament', 21 October 2018, at: https://bbc.in/2ODVAkt.

0.7    Commitment by states with large arsenals of the weapons being outlawed is crucial for the effectiveness of multilateral disarmament treaties. Since the end of the Cold War, however, a number of disarmament treaties have been successfully adopted even without the support of the great powers. These treaties are, notably, the 1997 Anti-Personnel Mine Ban Convention[3] and the 2008 Convention on Cluster Munitions,[4] and most recently the 2017 Treaty on the Prohibition of Nuclear Weapons[5] (not yet in force, as on 1 March 2019). This reflects an attempt to establish global norms of behaviour despite reluctance by significant states.

0.8    While treaties have advanced disarmament law by codifying new rules, the extent to which they may shape the policies of states that have not adhered to them may vary. But even where disarmament treaties are adopted by consensus and with the involvement of all the major possessor states, such as the 1971 Biological Weapons Convention[6] and the 1992 Chemical Weapons Convention,[7] this does not guarantee compliance by all the parties, as events in recent years have demonstrated.

0.9    Finally, within a country, disarmament, demobilisation, and reintegration (DDR) programmes – so-called micro-disarmament – can reduce armed violence at the domestic level. This is especially the case when small arms and light weapons (SALW) are given up by armed non-state actors. Small arms and light weapons have killed far more people than have all the WMD together. In 2015, then United Nations Secretary-General Ban Ki-moon told the UN Security Council that the widespread availability of weapons was a major factor in the more than 250 conflicts of the past decade, leading to more than 50,000 deaths each year and record high levels of displacement. 'Deny access to illegal weapons and ammunition, and you deny criminals, armed groups and extremists a central means to perpetrate violence intimidation and harm', he said.[8] In his report to the Security Council, the UN Secretary-General stated that it was 'vital that traditional arms control measures be linked and integrated with disarmament, demobilization, and reintegration and security sector reform'.[9]

---

3    Convention on the Prohibition of the Use, Stockpiling, Production and Transfer of Anti-Personnel Mines and on Their Destruction; adopted at Oslo, 18 September 1997; entered into force, 1 March 1999.

4    Convention on Cluster Munitions; adopted at Dublin, 30 May 2008; entered into force, 1 August 2010.

5    Treaty on the Prohibition of Nuclear Weapons; adopted at New York, 7 July 2017.

6    Convention on the Prohibition of the Development, Production and Stockpiling of Bacteriological (Biological) and Toxin Weapons and on Their Destruction; opened for signature at London, Moscow, and Washington, DC, 10 April 1972; entered into force, 26 March 1975.

7    Convention on the Prohibition of the Development, Production, Stockpiling and Use of Chemical Weapons and on Their Destruction; adopted at Geneva, 3 September 1992; entered into force, 29 April 1997.

8    UN, 'Human Cost of Illicit Flow of Small Arms, Light Weapons Stressed in Security Council Debate', UN doc. SC/11889, 13 May 2015, at: http://bit.ly/2PYACJF.

9    'Small Arms and Light Weapons, Report of the Secretary-General', UN doc. S/2015/289, 27 April 2015, para. 87

## Disarmament until the 1919 Treaty of Versailles

0.10    Restrictions on weapons date back hundreds of years. As far back as the fourth century BCE, the Hindu *Book of Manu* had called for the use of especially injurious weapons to be foresworn in battle, such as those with barbs or which were tipped with poison.[10] In 1139 CE, the Second Lateran Council famously outlawed the use of bows and crossbows as an anathema, though only against Christians.[11] Centuries later, an early example of a disarmament agreement in the modern era was the 1817 Rush-Bagot Pact. The 1817 Pact was an agreement between Great Britain and the United States of America to eliminate their fleets from the Great Lakes in North America (with the exception of small patrol vessels).[12] The agreement, and an associated 1818 Convention which set the international boundary between Missouri in the United States and British North America (a territory that would later become Canada) at the 49th parallel, reflected the easing of diplomatic tensions that had led to the 1812 War between Great Britain and the United States.[13]

0.11    The genesis of contemporary disarmament, however, should probably be traced back to later in the 19th century as the impact of the industrial revolution on arms production was becoming clearer. The potentially ruinous financial consequences of an arms race, in addition to the humanitarian effects of mass-produced and technically advanced weaponry, were an important motivation for Tsar Alexander II's convocation of states in St Petersburg in 1868 to outlaw the use against personnel in warfare of exploding bullets.[14] The resultant 1868 St Petersburg Declaration[15] is the first modern treaty governing the use of weapons. It is a law of armed conflict instrument rather than a disarmament treaty, but many of the objectives expressed in the preamble to the Declaration continue to inspire international law today.[16]

0.12    The St Petersburg Declaration affirms that 'the only legitimate object which States should endeavour to accomplish during war is to weaken the military

---

10  'When He Fights with His Foes in Battle, Let Him Not Strike with Weapons Concealed [in Wood], Nor with [Such As Are] Barbed, Poisoned, or the Points of Which Are Blazing with Fire', *Book of Manu*, Chapter VII, Verse 90, at: https://bit.ly/2OSf4Bk.

11  Canon 29, Tenth Ecumenical Council: Lateran II, AD 1139.

12  Office of the Historian, United States Department of State, 'Rush-Bagot Pact, 1817 and Convention of 1818', *Milestones in the History of U.S. Foreign Relations*, at: https://bit.ly/2mdwHh5.

13  Ibid.

14  See, e.g., P. Holquist, 'The Russian Empire as a "Civilized State": International Law as Principle and Practice in Imperial Russia, 1874–1878', *National Council for Eurasian and East European Research*, 2004, pp. 2–3, at: https://bit.ly/2RKyIxK.

15  Declaration Renouncing the Use, in Time of War, of Explosive Projectiles Under 400 Grammes Weight; adopted at St Petersburg, 11 December 1868; entered into force, 4 September 1900.

16  In 2002, the historian Geoffrey Best characterised the St Petersburg Declaration as 'a summary of law-of-war philosophy', the 'pithy excellence of which would never be equalled'. G. Best, *War and Law Since 1945*, Clarendon Press, Oxford, 2002, p. 46; see N. Jevglevskaja, 'St Petersburg, 1868: First International Agreement Prohibiting the Use of Certain Weapons', *Online Atlas on the History of Humanitarianism and Human Rights, IEG*, at: https://bit.ly/2yecw7c.

forces of the enemy'. This is reflected in the fundamental law of armed conflict rule of distinction, which requires that, in their military operations, parties to an armed conflict target only military objectives (military personnel or material) and not civilians or civilian objects. The preamble to the St Petersburg Declaration then affirms that for the purpose of weakening the military forces of the enemy, 'it is sufficient to disable the greatest possible number of men' – an aim that would be 'exceeded by the employment of arms which uselessly aggravate the sufferings of disabled men, or render their death inevitable'. This sentiment sustains the prohibition on the use against combatants of weapons that are 'of a nature to cause superfluous injury or unnecessary suffering'.

0.13   In 1894, six years after the adoption of the St Petersburg Declaration, states met in Brussels, once more at the initiative of Tsar Alexander II, to draft an International Declaration concerning the Laws and Customs of War.[17] Although the resultant Brussels Declaration never entered into force as binding international law – because of disputed visions among the negotiating states of what controls should be imposed on armaments[18] – many of the provisions elaborated at that 1894 conference would become international law by incorporation in the 1899 Hague Convention II and the Regulations on Land Warfare that are annexed to it.[19]

0.14   The first international instrument to regulate the arms trade in the modern era – the 1890 Brussels General Act[20] – was actually a treaty about ending the slave trade. The contracting colonial powers declared that 'the most effective means' of tackling the slave trade in Africa included restrictions on 'the importation of firearms'.[21] The colonial powers of the day were seeking generally to prohibit 'the importation of firearms, and especially of rifles and improved weapons, as well as of powder, ball and cartridges' – at least by others – into the African countries they controlled.[22]

0.15   The major powers in Europe were, though, largely unwilling to restrain the level of armaments they possessed and produced. They would countenance limited prohibitions on specific weapons as well as on the circumstances in which they could lawfully wage war. Indeed, the two Hague Peace Conferences of 1899 and 1907 gave rise to the adoption of major treaties governing the law of armed conflict as well as a number on the law on inter-state use of force (*jus ad bellum*). But the conferences did not succeed to serve as the first multilateral fora for disarmament.

---

17 Project of an International Declaration concerning the Laws and Customs of War; draft elaborated at Brussels, 27 August 1874.

18 See, e.g., Holquist, 'The Russian Empire as a "Civilized State"', pp. 2–3.

19 Convention (II) with Respect to the Laws and Customs of War on Land and Its Annex: Regulations Concerning the Laws and Customs of War on Land; adopted at The Hague, 29 July 1899; entered into force, 4 September 1900.

20 General Act on the Slave Trade and Importation into Africa of Firearms, Ammunition, and Spirituous Liquors; signed at Brussels, 2 July 1890 (1890 Brussels General Act).

21 Art. I(7), 1890 Brussels General Act.

22 Art. VIII, 1890 Brussels General Act.

0.16    The 1899 Hague Peace Conference, which was formally convened at the invitation of Russia's Minister for Foreign Affairs, Count Mikhail Nikolayevich Muravyov, had aspired to engender agreement among states on limiting the growth in the size of armed forces, along with restrictions on the deployment of new weapons. As one commentator explains, though, delegates 'failed to adopt instruments regarding the prevention of new types and calibres of rifles and naval guns. Nor were they able to agree on fixing the size of military forces and naval armaments or their budgets'.[23] The failure of the 1899 Hague Peace Conference to achieve concrete measures of disarmament was reflected in its final declaration: 'The Conference is of [the] opinion that the restriction of military charges, which are at present a heavy burden on the world, is extremely desirable for the increase of the material and moral welfare of mankind'.[24] But such aspirations notwithstanding, the large and powerful states were pitted against the small states, each with specific interests that were not altogether humanitarian.[25]

0.17    A second 'peace and disarmament' conference was summoned in 1904 at the suggestion of US President Theodore Roosevelt, but its convening was postponed because of the outbreak of war between Japan and Russia. The Second Hague Peace Conference, which was finally held in June–October 1907, was just as unsuccessful in agreeing upon disarmament measures as its predecessor had been eight years previously. The British had been hoping to prevent or limit a new arms race, but this foundered on objection by other powers. Germany in particular feared a British attempt to stop the growth of its navy.[26] In his closing address to the final plenary, the British representative proposed to the Conference the following wording for its final declaration:

> The Conference confirms the resolution adopted by the Conference of 1899 in regard to the limitation of military expenditure; and inasmuch as military expenditure has considerably increased in almost every country since that time, the Conference declares that it is eminently desirable that the Governments should resume the serious examination of this question.[27]

0.18    The legacy of the two Hague Peace Conferences for the development of the law of armed conflict was – and remains – significant.[28] But in terms of

---

23  N. Hayashi, 'The Role and Importance of the Hague Conferences: A Historical Perspective', *United Nations Institute for Disarmament Research (UNIDIR), Geneva*, 2017, p. 2, at: https://bit.ly/2Pw7LMC.

24  See, e.g., B. Baker, 'Hague Peace Conferences (1899 and 1907)', Last updated November 2009, *Max Planck Encyclopedia of Public International Law*, at: https://bit.ly/1Vl5Rv5.

25  A. Cassese, 'Current Challenges to International Humanitarian Law Introduction', in A. Clapham and P. Gaeta (eds.), *The Oxford Handbook of International Law in Armed Conflict*, Oxford University Press, Oxford, 2014, p. 6.

26  See, e.g., '1907 Second Hague Peace Conference', *Global Security*, undated but accessed 4 April 2018, at: https://bit.ly/2P1gERD.

27  Ibid.

28  Indeed, one of the two main branches of the law of armed conflict, which deals with weapons and the conduct of hostilities, is still referred to in some quarters as Hague Law. See, e.g., S. Casey-Maslen

disarmament, they must be deemed a severe disappointment. Rare opportunities to prevent a major arms race, which would lead to tremendous suffering and damage, were spurned. In less than a decade, many European nations, their soldiers, and their populace would be paying a colossal price for the unwillingness of the major powers to restrain the expansion of their armies and armaments. Moreover, as a result of the outbreak of the First World War in 1914, a third peace conference, which had been scheduled for 1915, never took place.[29] Instead, the 1919 Treaty of Versailles, the armistice that formally ended that global conflagration that claimed as many as 20 million lives, imposed unilateral disarmament on Germany in order 'to render possible the initiation of a general limitation of the armaments of all nations'.[30] The German Chancellor, Adolf Hitler, would go on to denounce the 1919 Treaty's disarmament clauses in the 1930s, using inaction on the part of the other powers as his excuse for Germany's re-armament.[31] Once again, many nations – and this time more than 50 million people – would pay dearly for the failures of the international community to achieve meaningful, global disarmament.

## Disarmament and the League of Nations

0.19    The Covenant of the League of Nations, which was concluded in 1919, had a number of provisions pertaining to disarmament. Under Article 8, the League's members 'recognise[d] that the maintenance of peace requires the reduction of national armaments to the lowest point consistent with national safety and the enforcement by common action of international obligations'.[32] They further entrusted the League 'with the general supervision of the trade in arms and ammunition with the countries in which the control of this traffic is necessary in the common interest'.[33]

0.20    Prior to the formal establishment of the League of Nations on 10 January 1920,[34] leading arms-producing nations and colonial powers agreed on the text of a Convention for the Control of the Trade in Arms and Ammunition (the 1919 Saint-Germain-en-Laye Convention). An associated protocol provided for the Convention's provisional application. This called upon states that had adhered to the Convention not to act to frustrate its object and purpose, pending its entry into force. The preamble to the Convention observed that the First World War had 'led to the accumulation in various parts of the world of considerable quantities

---

with S. Haines, *Hague Law Interpreted: The Conduct of Hostilities Under the Law of Armed Conflict*, Hart, Oxford, 2018.

29  Hayashi, 'The Role and Importance of the Hague Conferences', p. 3.

30  Arts. 159–213 (Military, Naval and Air Clauses), Peace Treaty of Versailles, at: https://bit.ly/2yD4hRc.

31  See, e.g., C.G. Fenwick, 'The Denunciation of the Disarmament Clauses of the Treaty of Versailles', *The American Journal of International Law*, Vol. 29, No. 4 (October 1935), pp. 675–78.

32  Art. 8, Covenant of the League of Nations; signed at Paris, 28 June 1919; entered into force, 10 January 1920.

33  Art. 23(d), Covenant of the League of Nations.

34  J. Goldblat, *Arms Control: The New Guide to Negotiations and Agreements*, Sage, Thousand Oaks, CA, 2002, p. 22.

of arms and munitions of war, the dispersal of which would constitute a danger to peace and public order'.[35] It was also explicitly recognised that the 1890 Brussels General Act was no longer fit for purpose.[36]

0.21    The central prohibition of the 1919 Saint-Germain-en-Laye Convention was set out in a provision by which states parties undertook

> to prohibit the export of the following arms of war: artillery of all kinds, apparatus for the discharge of all kinds of projectiles, explosive or gas-diffusing flame-throwers, bombs, grenades, machine-guns and rifled small-bore breech-loading weapons of all kinds, as well as the exportation of the ammunition for use with such arms. The prohibition of exportation shall apply to all such arms and ammunition whether complete or in parts.[37]

Notwithstanding that prohibition, states parties 'reserve[d] the right to grant, in respect of arms whose use is not prohibited by international law, export licences to meet the requirements of their Governments' or those of the other states parties, 'but for no other purpose'.[38]

0.22    The 1919 Convention did not, though, enter into force as binding international law, a consequence of the insufficient number of states that ratified it. Particularly influential was the decision of the United States of America not to become party to the treaty.[39] Six years later, however, the League of Nations tried again to agree on binding measures of disarmament. The diplomatic conference held under its auspices in Geneva from 4 May to 17 June 1925 adopted a Convention for the Supervision of the International Trade in Arms, Munitions, and Implements of War. This 1925 Convention sought to enhance the provisions of the earlier text, incorporating transparency measures on exports that sought to build confidence in its implementation among states parties. The 1925 Convention would have restricted the export of arms to those intended for the use of the government of the importing state, setting up a system of licences for all arms exported or imported. As was the case with its 1919 predecessor, however, it would not enter into force, with, notably, the United States of America, again unwilling to ratify.

0.23    The failure to disarm was at least tempered by the adoption at the 1925 Conference of an important instrument of the law of armed conflict. The 1925 Geneva Protocol[40] reaffirmed 'the prohibition on the use in war of asphyxiating,

---

35  Convention for the Control of the Trade in Arms and Ammunition, signed at Saint-Germain-en-Laye, France, 10 September 1919, first preambular paragraph.

36  1919 Saint-Germain-en-Laye Convention, third preambular paragraph.

37  Art. 1(1), 1919 Saint-Germain-en-Laye Convention.

38  Art. 1(2), 1919 Saint-Germain-en-Laye Convention.

39  See, e.g., 'Arms Manufacturers and the Public', *Foreign Affairs*, Vol. 12, No. 4 (July 1934), at: https://fam.ag/2QGvOsk.

40  Protocol for the Prohibition of the Use of Asphyxiating, Poisonous or Other Gases, and of Bacteriological Methods of Warfare; adopted at Geneva, 17 June 1925; entered into force, 8 February 1928.

poisonous or other gases, and of all analogous liquids, materials or devices' that had already been agreed at the First Hague Peace Conference in 1899,[41] and extended the existing prohibition on chemical warfare to the use of 'bacteriological methods of warfare'. This amounted to the first treaty prohibition of biological warfare. As such, it presaged the adoption of the Biological Weapons Convention in 1971 as well as of the Chemical Weapons Convention in 1992.

0.24   Also of importance was the 'Five-Power' Washington Naval Treaty of 1922. The Five-Power Treaty, signed by France, Great Britain, Italy, Japan, and the United States of America, was the 'cornerstone' of the naval disarmament programme.[42] It obligated each of the five nations to maintain a set ratio of warship tonnage: for Great Britain and the United States it was 500,000 tons; for Japan it was 300,000 tons; and for France and Italy it was 175,000 tons each. Some classes of ships were, though, omitted from regulation under the treaty. As a consequence, a new race to build cruiser ships emerged after 1922, leading the five nations to return to the negotiating table in 1927 and 1930 in an effort to close the loopholes in the treaty's regulation of naval forces.[43]

0.25   The League of Nations would make one more major push for global disarmament. The Conference for the Reduction and Limitation of Armaments, convened in Geneva in 1930–34, would prove to be the last effort that this ill-fated multilateral institution would make in disarmament and arms control. When Germany withdrew from the talks in 1933, however, the fate of the negotiations – and ultimately of the League of Nations itself – was sealed. Subsequent bilateral negotiations between Britain and Germany resulted in the conclusion of the Anglo-German Naval Agreement in 1935, permitting the development of a German navy but limiting it to one-third of the size of the British navy. Controversially, this measure of appeasement allowed Germany to violate specific terms that had been imposed upon it by the Treaty of Versailles.[44] In any event, the Anglo-German Naval Agreement was itself denounced by Adolf Hitler on 28 April 1939, prior to the outbreak of the Second World War.

## Disarmament since the establishment of the United Nations

0.26   Although the Charter of the United Nations, adopted in 1945,[45] is an important basis for disarmament, international disarmament law has developed within as well as outside the UN system. In the wake of failures to achieve disarmament within the League of Nations, the UN Charter refers to the value of promoting

---

41  Declaration (IV,2) concerning the Use of Asphyxiating or Deleterious Gases; adopted at The Hague, 29 July 1899; entered into force, 4 September 1900.

42  Office of the Historian, United States Department of State, 'The Washington Naval Conference, 1921–1922', *Milestones in the History of U.S. Foreign Relations*, at: https://bit.ly/1qCET1o.

43  Ibid.

44  'Anglo-German Naval Agreement', *Encyclopaedia Britannica*, at: https://bit.ly/2PwjxXA.

45  Charter of the United Nations; signed at San Francisco, 26 June 1945; entered into force, 24 October 1945.

'the establishment and maintenance of international peace and security with the least diversion for armaments of the world's human and economic resources'.[46] The Charter gives the UN General Assembly the authority to consider 'the general principles of cooperation in the maintenance of international peace and security, including the principles governing disarmament and regulation of armaments'.[47]

0.27　The very first resolution of the first session of the UN General Assembly in January 1946 was dedicated to disarmament, calling for the establishment of a Commission to make recommendations 'for the elimination from national armaments of atomic weapons and of all other major weapons adaptable to mass destruction'.[48] This followed the dropping of the atomic bombs, first at Hiroshima and then at Nagasaki, by the United States of America in the closing days of the Second World War. At the time, nuclear disarmament was seen as the precursor to more general disarmament.[49] In this regard, in 1968, states adopted the Treaty on the Non-Proliferation of Nuclear Weapons (NPT),[50] pledging to 'pursue negotiations in good faith on effective measures relating to cessation of the nuclear arms race at an early date and to nuclear disarmament, and on a treaty on general and complete disarmament under strict and effective international control'.[51] In its 1996 Advisory Opinion on the Legality of the Threat or Use of Nuclear Weapons, however, the International Court of Justice (ICJ) went further, determining that there existed an obligation 'to pursue in good faith and bring to a conclusion negotiations leading to nuclear disarmament in all its aspects under strict and effective international control'.[52]

0.28　Progress in nuclear disarmament advanced through arms control negotiations between the United States of America and the Soviet Union/Russian Federation. Major bilateral disarmament treaties between the two include the 1972 Anti-Ballistic Missile Treaty (ABM Treaty)[53] and its 1973 Protocol,[54] the INF Treaty

---

46 Art. 26, UN Charter.

47 Art. 11, UN Charter.

48 UN General Assembly Resolution 1(I), para. 5(c).

49 On 17 September 1959, the United Kingdom submitted a plan for 'comprehensive' disarmament to the UN General Assembly. The following day, the Soviet Union proposed a programme for complete disarmament within four years. Goldblat, *Arms Control: The New Guide to Negotiations and Agreements*, p. 44.

50 Treaty on the Non-Proliferation of Nuclear Weapons; opened for signature at London, Moscow, and Washington, DC, 1 July 1968; entered into force, 5 March 1970.

51 Art. VI, NPT. There were either 190 or 191 states parties as of writing, depending on whether the Democratic People's Republic of Korea (DPR Korea) is still bound by the treaty. The legality of its purported withdrawal in 2003 has been questioned. See, e.g., the note by the UN Office for Disarmament Affairs (UNODA), at: https://bit.ly/2yzuUGT.

52 ICJ, *Legality of the Threat or Use of Nuclear Weapons*, Advisory Opinion, 8 July 1996, dispositif F [added emphasis].

53 Treaty Between the United States of America and the Union of Soviet Socialist Republics on the Limitation of Anti-Ballistic Missile Systems (ABM Treaty); signed at Moscow, 26 May 1972; entered into force, 3 October 1972; United States' withdrawal, 2002.

54 See, e.g., US Department of State, 'Treaty Between The United States of America and The Union of Soviet Socialist Republics on The Limitation of Anti-Ballistic Missile Systems (ABM Treaty)', at: https://bit.ly/2IVgl5m.

(adopted in 1987), the 1991 Strategic Arms Reduction Treaty I (START I), the 1993 Strategic Arms Reduction Treaty II (START II), the 2002 Strategic Offensive Reductions Treaty (SORT), and the 2010 New Strategic Arms Reduction Treaty (New START). These treaties have led to major progress on the limitation and destruction of arms. They also served to improve relations between the two major powers, notably in the case of those adopted during the period of US-Soviet détente in the 1970s, as well as after the end of the Cold War. However, the United States' and Russia's mutual allegations of violations of the INF Treaty and the United States' proposed withdrawal from it, along with its earlier withdrawal from the ABM Treaty, illustrate how bilateral arms control may become subject to political tensions. As of March 2019, no talks were underway on an extension or replacement of New START, which was due to expire in 2021, while both the Russian Federation and the United States were committing substantial resources to the modernisation of their nuclear arsenals and the development of new nuclear warhead delivery systems.

0.29   Multilateral disarmament efforts in the spirit of the UN Charter led to the main global disarmament treaties – those to which any state can adhere and that require the renunciation of specific weapons. Negotiations at the Conference of the Committee on Disarmament and its successor the Conference on Disarmament, both linked to the United Nations system, led to the adoption of the Biological Weapons Convention in 1971 and the Chemical Weapons Convention in 1992. Special Sessions of the UN General Assembly dedicated to disarmament were also significant steps in consolidating views among states of disarmament actions and measures that were needed to further the cause of peace. In particular, the First Special Session of the UN General Assembly on Disarmament in 1978 was influential in its assertion that 'the accumulation of weapons, particularly nuclear weapons' constituted 'much more a threat than a protection for the future of mankind'.[55] UN member states further affirmed that the

> vast stockpiles and tremendous build-up of arms and armed forces and the competition for qualitative refinement of weapons of all kinds, to which scientific resources and technological advances are diverted, pose incalculable threats to peace.[56]

0.30   In contrast, the 1997 Anti-Personnel Mine Ban Convention (prohibiting all anti-personnel mines) and the 2008 Convention on Cluster Munitions (outlawing most types of cluster munitions), were negotiated at ad hoc diplomatic conferences convened outside UN auspices, as agreement to prohibit those weapons within the global organisation's consensus-based framework proved impossible. Indeed, achieving consensus within the United Nations has proved a major

---

55 UN General Assembly Resolution S-10/2: Final Document of the Tenth Special Session of the Assembly, 30 June 1978, para. 1.
56 Ibid., para. 11.

challenge on a number of occasions. The 1996 Comprehensive Nuclear-Test-Ban Treaty (CTBT) was drafted in the Conference on Disarmament but could not be adopted in that forum as a result of opposition by India. The text was forwarded by Australia to the UN General Assembly where it was adopted by a large majority vote.[57] It has, however, still to enter into force.[58] The 2017 Treaty on the Prohibition of Nuclear Weapons was also negotiated within the UN framework, though without the participation of the nuclear-armed states and the majority of the nuclear 'umbrella' states.

0.31 This new practice of normative initiatives is driven by states' attempt to overcome deadlocks in multilateral disarmament machinery and to advance global disarmament even without great power support. While these initiatives have produced normative progress supported by many small and middle-sized states, they have not yet prompted the major military powers to renounce the banned weapons.

---

57 Comprehensive Nuclear-Test-Ban Treaty; adopted at the UN General Assembly in New York, 10 September 1996, by 158 votes to 3 (Bhutan, India, and Libya), with 5 abstentions.

58 As on 1 March 2019, the following states named in Annex 2 had all still to ratify (or sign and ratify) the CTBT in order to trigger the treaty's entry into force: China, DPR Korea, Egypt, India, Iran, Israel, Pakistan, and the United States.

# 1

# THE CORE CONCEPTS OF INTERNATIONAL DISARMAMENT LAW

## The definition and scope of disarmament

1.1 While there is no internationally accepted definition of disarmament, it is generally agreed that disarmament entails the renunciation of weapons. Indeed, an ordinary dictionary definition of the term *disarmament* is 'the act of taking away or giving up weapons'.[1] In 1978, the process of disarmament was described in the report on the First Special Session of the United Nations (UN) General Assembly on Disarmament as 'a gradual but effective process beginning with a reduction in the present level of armaments'.[2] According to the North Atlantic Treaty Organization (NATO), disarmament 'refers to the act of eliminating or abolishing weapons (particularly offensive arms) either unilaterally (in the hope that one's example will be followed) or reciprocally'.[3] The most obvious form of such renunciation is destruction.

1.2 Disarmament usually results from the voluntary acceptance of international obligations by states. This acceptance is expressed through the conclusion of, and adherence to, treaties or other international agreements. Thus, in the 1978 report on the First Special Session of the UN General Assembly on Disarmament, UN member states declared that:

> Genuine and lasting peace can only be created through the effective implementation of the security system provided for in the Charter of the United Nations and the speedy and substantial reduction of arms and armed forces,

---

1 *Cambridge Dictionary*, 'Disarmament', at: https://bit.ly/2NF7uVW.
2 UN General Assembly Resolution S-10/2: Final Document of the Tenth Special Session of the Assembly, 30 June 1978, para. 1.
3 NATO, 'Arms Control, Disarmament and Non-Proliferation in NATO', Last updated 22 June 2018, at: https://bit.ly/2ND8I41.

by international agreement and mutual example, leading ultimately to general and complete disarmament under effective international control.[4]

1.3 The International Court of Justice (ICJ) subsequently endorsed the view that disarmament is primarily a voluntary undertaking by states:

> in international law there are no rules, other than such rules as may be accepted by the State concerned, by treaty or otherwise, whereby the level of armaments of a sovereign State can be limited, and this principle is valid for all States without exception'.[5]

That does not mean, of course, that disarmament can never be imposed: by becoming a UN member (through signature and ratification of the UN Charter),[6] a state is accepting the writ of the UN Security Council, which may order measures to be taken in case of a threat or breach of international peace and security, irrespective of the wishes of the targeted state.[7]

1.4 In addition to the requirement to destroy weapons, other measures that are widely considered to be part of disarmament are 'the balanced reduction of armed forces and of . . . armaments'[8] (also termed 'arms control'), limitations on the transfer of weapons[9] (in certain circumstances, also described as 'non-proliferation'[10]), and prohibitions or restrictions on the use of weapons.[11] Prohibitions on the use of weapons, which firmly underpin any duty of disarmament, are conceptually distinct from both arms control and non-proliferation regimes. Indeed, with the exception of the 1971 Biological Weapons Convention,[12] which

---

4 UN General Assembly Resolution S-10/2: Final Document of the Tenth Special Session of the Assembly, para. 13.

5 ICJ, *Case Concerning Military and Paramilitary Activities in and against Nicaragua (Nicaragua v. United States of America)*, Judgment (Merits), 27 June 1986, para. 269.

6 Art. 110, UN Charter.

7 The power of the UN Security Council is laid down in Article 41 of the UN Charter.

8 UN General Assembly Resolution S-10/2: Final Document of the Tenth Special Session of the Assembly, para. 22.

9 Ibid.

10 For NATO, 'non-proliferation refers to all efforts to prevent proliferation from occurring, or should it occur, to reverse it by any other means than the use of military force'. NATO, 'Arms Control, Disarmament and Non-Proliferation in NATO', citing NATO, *Comprehensive, Strategic-Level Policy for Preventing the Proliferation of Weapons of Mass Destruction (WMD) and Defending Against Chemical, Biological, Radiological and Nuclear (CBRN) Threats*. 'Non-proliferation usually applies to weapons of mass destruction, which include nuclear, chemical and biological weapons'. NATO, 'Arms Control, Disarmament and Non-Proliferation in NATO'.

11 UN General Assembly Resolution S-10/2: Final Document of the Tenth Special Session of the Assembly, para. 23.

12 Convention on the Prohibition of the Development, Production and Stockpiling of Bacteriological (Biological) and Toxin Weapons and on Their Destruction; opened for signature at London, Moscow, and Washington, DC, 10 April 1972; entered into force, 26 March 1975.

refers in its preamble to the prohibition of use during warfare laid down under the 1925 Geneva Protocol,[13] all global disarmament treaties[14] explicitly prohibit the use of the weapons being outlawed. In contrast to the law of armed conflict, however, in most cases the prohibition on use in a disarmament treaty applies not only during, and in connection with, an armed conflict, but also at all other times, including in peacetime.

1.5    Thus, 'disarmament' has often been used as a generic term for weapons-related activities, not only concerning the destruction of stockpiles, but also other forms of arms control and non-proliferation, among other activities.[15] That said, however, NATO objects to the 'inaccurate' use of disarmament 'as a synonym for arms control'.[16] This latter form of endeavour has been described by John Borrie and Tim Caughley as 'the exercise of restraint in the acquisition, deployment and use of military capabilities, including armaments, by means of international agreements among states'.[17] They point out that arms control developed 'as a method to manage arms competition, rather than reverse it' (though they concede that latterly the term 'has often been equated with disarmament').[18] Indeed, Jozef Goldblat has observed that arms control is often used interchangeably with '"arms regulation", "arms limitation", "arms reduction" or even "disarmament"'.[19] In fact, the principal distinction between arms control and disarmament is that arms control works on the basis that weapons will – and indeed should – persist as a feature of international relations.

1.6    Other measures that are integral to (or at least closely associated with) international disarmament law include prohibitions on weapons research, development, testing, and production. These measures go hand in hand with a legal prohibition on stockpiling and an obligation to destroy existing stocks. Confidence and security-building measures (CSBMs) are critical to promoting trust among states in the implementation of a disarmament treaty to which they are party.

---

13 Protocol for the Prohibition of the Use of Asphyxiating, Poisonous or Other Gases, and of Bacteriological Methods of Warfare; adopted at Geneva, 17 June 1925; entered into force, 8 February 1928.

14 Global disarmament treaties are defined in this work as those to which any state can adhere and that require the destruction of specific weapons. See, for a list of such treaties, *infra*, para. 1.10.

15 J. Kierulf, *Disarmament Under International Law*, Djof Publishing, Denmark, 2017, p. 5.

16 NATO, 'Arms Control, Disarmament and Non-Proliferation in NATO'.

17 J. Borrie and T. Caughley, 'Viewing Weapons Through a Humanitarian Lens: From Cluster Munitions to Nukes?' *Irish Studies in International Affairs*, Vol. 25 (2014), pp. 23–43. In their 2014 piece, Borrie and Caughley note that the term 'arms control' was coined in the 1950s in the context of the arms race between the United States of America and the Soviet Union.

18 Borrie and Caughley, 'Viewing Weapons Through a Humanitarian Lens: From Cluster Munitions to Nukes?' See also, *infra*, paras. 3.26–3.27.

19 Goldblat, *Arms Control: The New Guide to Negotiations and Agreements*, p. 3.

## Disarmament and international law

### The primary and subsidiary sources of international law

1.7   As noted in the Preface, the three primary sources of international law according to the 1945 Statute of the International Court of Justice[20] are *treaties;*[21] *custom;*[22]
and *general principles of law.*[23] Each of these sources plays an important role in international disarmament law, as discussed in this section. In addition to the three primary sources identified in the ICJ Statute, a binding unilateral declaration by a state
should also be considered a primary source of international law.[24] The 1974 judgment in which the ICJ held that a statement by the French president was legally
binding on France concerned a pledge never again to conduct atmospheric testing
of nuclear weapons.[25] Also of great significance to international disarmament law
are the two subsidiary means for the determination of rules of international law:
judicial decisions (case law, whether at the national, regional, or global level) and the
writings of 'publicists' (meaning the world's leading public international lawyers).[26]

### Treaty as a primary source of international law

1.8   International disarmament law is mainly treaty-based. A treaty is generally
defined in international law as 'an international agreement concluded between
States in written form and governed by international law, whether embodied in a
single instrument or in two or more related instruments and whatever its particular
designation'.[27] Thus, an agreement will be internationally legally binding when (1)
it has been made by states; (2) is in writing; and (3) in the circumstances of its negotiation and adoption, is intended to be regulated by international law. If it meets
all of these criteria, it does not matter whether a particular text is called a treaty,
a convention, a protocol, a declaration, or even a memorandum of understanding.

---

20  Statute of the International Court of Justice; adopted at San Francisco, 24 October 1945.
21  Art. 38(1)(a), ICJ Statute. The provision in the ICJ Statute refers to 'international conventions' while
   in international law, the generic term used today is 'treaty'. A 'convention' is, though, a common form
   of treaty. This is reflected in the title of the 1969 'Vienna *Convention* on the Law of *Treaties*' (emphases
   added). Both terms are used in international disarmament law, as paragraph 1.8 *infra* notes.
22  Art. 38(1)(b), ICJ Statute.
23  Art. 38(1)(c), ICJ Statute.
24  ICJ, *Nuclear Tests Case (New Zealand v. France)*, Judgment, 20 December 1974, paras. 45–49. In paragraph 46, the Court stated that:

   When it is the intention of the State making the declaration that it should become bound according to its terms, that intention confers on the declaration the character of a legal undertaking,
   the State being thenceforth legally required to follow a course of conduct consistent with the
   declaration. An undertaking of this kind, if given publicly, and with an intent to be bound, even
   though not made within the context of international negotiations, is binding.
25  ICJ, *Nuclear Tests Case (New Zealand v. France)*, Judgment, 20 December 1974, para. 53.
26  Art. 38(1)(d), ICJ Statute.
27  Art. 2(1)(a), *Vienna Convention on the Law of Treaties*; adopted at Vienna, 23 May 1969; entered into
   force, 27 January 1980 (1969 Vienna Convention on the Law of Treaties, or VCLT).

1.9    A treaty enters into force after a set number of negotiating states have indicated their consent to be bound. Multilateral disarmament treaties generally specify a threshold of ratifications necessary for entry into force and a certain period after the last ratification. Certain disarmament treaties, notably the 1996 Comprehensive Nuclear-Test-Ban Treaty (CTBT),[28] require ratification by specific states. The CTBT is not yet in force, as several of the states named in a legally binding annex have not yet ratified the treaty.[29] As soon as a treaty enters into force, its provisions bind states as soon as they become party to it (see Box 1.1).

---

## BOX 1.1   SIGNATORY STATES AND STATES PARTIES TO TREATIES

Becoming a *state party* to a treaty is normally achieved by the separate acts of signature and ratification* or by the singular act of accession. A state that ratifies or accedes to a disarmament treaty typically becomes party to it after a set period of time (as long as the treaty itself has entered into force). A state party is one that is fully bound by all of the provisions of the treaty. This is so, unless it is possible to enter 'reservations' to some of the provisions. Global disarmament treaties typically prohibit reservations.

Instruments of ratification or accession are sent to – 'deposited with' – the treaty depositary. This is often the Secretary-General of the United Nations: the UN Secretary-General is the depositary for the 1992 Chemical Weapons Convention, the 1997 Anti-Personnel Mine Ban Convention, the 2008 Convention on Cluster Munitions, and the 2017 Treaty on the Prohibition of Nuclear Weapons. The depositary may also, however, be an individual state (Switzerland is the depositary for the 1949 Geneva Conventions and their Additional Protocols) or a small group of states. For instance, the depositaries of the 1968 Treaty on the Non-Proliferation of Nuclear Weapons (NPT) and the 1971 Biological Weapons Convention are the Russian Federation (as successor state to the Soviet Union), the United Kingdom, and the United States of America.

A *signatory state* – meaning a state that has signed but not become a party to the treaty – has more limited obligations under international law. These comprise a duty to 'refrain from acts which would defeat the object and purpose' of the treaty.** These are fundamental acts, such as using a weapon that is the subject of a total prohibition under a disarmament treaty. The term signatory state is often used incorrectly to denote a state party, but legally these descriptors mean very different things.

---

28 Comprehensive Nuclear-Test-Ban Treaty; adopted at New York, 10 September 1996; not yet in force.
29 As at 1 March 2019, the following states named in an annex to the treaty had all still to ratify (or sign and ratify) the CTBT in order to trigger the treaty's entry into force: China, DPR Korea, Egypt, India, Iran, Israel, Pakistan, and the United States.

> \* Certain states, based on their domestic constitutional processes, 'approve' or 'accept' a treaty rather than ratify it. As the United Nations observes: 'The instruments of "acceptance" or "approval" of a treaty have the same legal effect as ratification and consequently express the consent of a state to be bound by a treaty. In the practice of certain states acceptance and approval have been used instead of ratification when, at a national level, constitutional law does not require the treaty to be ratified by the head of state'. See: http://bit.ly/2D5h3N7. For instance, Japan accepted the 1997 Anti-Personnel Mine Ban Convention while Slovakia approved it.
> \*\* Art. 18, 1969 Vienna Convention on the Law of Treaties.

### Key disarmament treaties

1.10   The most important global disarmament treaties – those with the specific purpose of renouncing certain weapons and which are open to adherence by all states – are the following: the 1971 Biological Weapons Convention; the 1992 Chemical Weapons Convention;[30] the 1997 Anti-Personnel Mine Ban Convention;[31] the 2008 Convention on Cluster Munitions;[32] and the 2017 Treaty on the Prohibition of Nuclear Weapons (not yet in force, as in March 2019).[33]

1.11   Major non-proliferation treaties and others limiting the transfer or testing of weapons include the following: the 1963 Partial Nuclear-Test-Ban Treaty (PTBT),[34] the NPT,[35] and the 2013 Arms Trade Treaty (ATT).[36] As noted above,[37] the CTBT is not yet in force. In fact, as of writing, the prospects of its entry into force in the short or medium term remained poor, although its adoption and very widespread ratification have been influential in curtailing explosive nuclear testing.

1.12   The following bilateral arms control treaties are especially noteworthy: the 1972 Strategic Arms Limitation Treaty (SALT I) and the 1979 Strategic Arms Limitation Treaty II (SALT II, even though it did formally not enter into force), as well as the 1972 Anti-Ballistic Missile Treaty (ABM Treaty), which is no longer in force.

---

30 Convention on the Prohibition of the Development, Production, Stockpiling and Use of Chemical Weapons and on Their Destruction; adopted at Geneva, 3 September 1992; entered into force, 29 April 1997.

31 Convention on the Prohibition of the Use, Stockpiling, Production and Transfer of Anti-Personnel Mines and on Their Destruction; adopted at Oslo, 18 September 1997; entered into force, 1 March 1999.

32 Convention on Cluster Munitions; adopted at Dublin, 30 May 2008; entered into force, 1 August 2010.

33 Treaty on the Prohibition of Nuclear Weapons; adopted at New York, 7 July 2017; not yet in force.

34 Treaty Banning Nuclear Weapon Tests in the Atmosphere, in Outer Space and Under Water; opened for signature at London, Moscow, and Washington, DC, 8 August 1963; entered into force, 10 October 1963.

35 Treaty on the Non-Proliferation of Nuclear Weapons; opened for signature at London, Moscow, and Washington, DC, 1 July 1968; entered into force, 5 March 1970.

36 Arms Trade Treaty; adopted at New York, 2 April 2013; entered into force, 24 December 2014.

37 See, *supra*, para. 1.9.

The 1976 ENMOD Convention,[38] which prohibits military or any other hostile use of environmental modification techniques that have widespread, long-lasting, or severe effects, is arguably also a form of arms control treaty.[39] Further significant arms control treaties are the 1987 Intermediate-Range Nuclear Forces Treaty (INF Treaty), the 1990 Treaty on Conventional Armed Forces in Europe (CFE Treaty), the 1991 Strategic Arms Reduction Treaty I (START I), the 1993 Strategic Arms Reduction Treaty II (START II), the 2002 Strategic Offensive Reductions Treaty (SORT), and the 2010 New Strategic Arms Reduction Treaty (New START).

1.13    Regional zones without nuclear weapons (or, in certain instances, any weapons of mass destruction) comprise the 1959 Antarctic Treaty, the 1967 Outer Space Treaty,[40] the 1971 Seabed Treaty,[41] and the 1979 Moon Treaty,[42] as well as the 1967 Treaty on the Prohibition of Nuclear Weapons in Latin America and the Caribbean (Treaty of Tlatelolco),[43] the 1985 South Pacific Nuclear Weapons Free Zone Treaty (Treaty of Rarotonga),[44] the 1995 Treaty on the Southeast Asia Nuclear-Weapon-Free Zone (Bangkok Treaty),[45] the 1996 African Nuclear-Weapon-Free Zone Treaty (Pelindaba Treaty),[46] and the 2006 Treaty on a Nuclear-Weapon-Free Zone in Central Asia (CANWFZ; Treaty of Semipalatinsk).[47]

## Soft law instruments

1.14    All global disarmament instruments which impose legally binding restrictions on weapons are in the form of treaties. In contrast, 'soft law' instruments are political declarations or agreements that do not have the legal status or direct binding effect of a treaty, but may nonetheless be influential in setting or changing

---

38  Convention on the Prohibition of Military or Any Other Hostile Use of Environmental Modification Techniques (ENMOD); adopted at New York, 10 December 1976; entered into force, 5 October 1978.

39  The International Committee of the Red Cross (ICRC), however, describes it as an instrument of international disarmament law. See '1976 Convention on the Prohibition of Military or any Hostile Use of Environmental Modification Techniques', *Fact Sheet*, ICRC, Geneva, January 2003.

40  Treaty on Principles Governing the Activities of States in the Exploration and Use of Outer Space, Including the Moon and Other Celestial Bodies; opened for signature at London, Moscow, and Washington, DC, 27 January 1967; entered into force, 10 October 1967.

41  Treaty on the Prohibition of the Emplacement of Nuclear Weapons and Other Weapons of Mass Destruction on the Sea-Bed and the Ocean Floor and in the Subsoil Thereof; opened for signature at London, Moscow, and Washington, DC, 11 February 1971; entered into force, 18 May 1972.

42  Agreement Governing the Activities of States on the Moon and Other Celestial Bodies; opened for signature at New York, 18 December 1979; entered into force, 11 July 1984.

43  Treaty for the Prohibition of Nuclear Weapons in Latin America and the Caribbean; opened for signature at Mexico City, 14 February 1967; entry into force for each state individually.

44  South Pacific Nuclear Free Zone Treaty; signed at Rarotonga, 6 August 1985; entered into force, 11 December 1986.

45  Treaty on the Southeast Asia Nuclear-Weapon-Free Zone; opened for signature at Bangkok, 15 December 1995; entered into force, 27 March 1997.

46  African Nuclear Weapon Free Zone Treaty (Treaty of Pelindaba); opened for signature at Cairo, 11 April 1996; entered into force, 15 July 2009.

47  Treaty on a Nuclear-Weapon-Free Zone in Central Asia (CANWFZ); opened for signature at Semipalatinsk, 8 September 2006; entered into force, 21 March 2009.

policy or identifying trends in the practice of states. Some soft law instruments call for disarmament or limitations on armaments and their transfer. Examples include the 1987 Missile Technology Control Regime (MTCR), the 2001 UN Programme of Action on Small Arms and Light Weapons (PoA), and the 2002 International Code of Conduct against Ballistic Missile Proliferation. A further example is the 2015 Joint Comprehensive Plan of Action (JCPOA), better known colloquially as the Iran Nuclear Deal. Arguably, though, the most important soft law arms control instrument, which applies to the European continent, is the Organization for Security and Co-operation in Europe (OSCE) Vienna Document, which establishes a set of politically binding CSBMs.

1.15    A principal advantage of soft law instruments is that they are easier to negotiate than treaties. This is because there is less political cost or burden to their adoption and states may therefore be willing to show greater flexibility than they would in a diplomatic conference negotiating a legally binding instrument. Enforcement is also not a core feature of a soft law instrument. Soft law instruments may also apply to other actors beyond states, such as non-state armed groups, corporations, and non-governmental organisations. The obvious disadvantage of a soft law instrument is of course that they do not have the force of 'hard law' at international or domestic level.[48] That said, however, a soft law instrument may precede the adoption of a treaty. Certain provisions in soft law instruments may also become legally binding on all states by becoming customary international law.

### Customary international law

1.16    Customary international law applies to states irrespective of whether they are party to a treaty codifying a particular norm. For a rule of customary law to exist, specific conduct ('state practice') must be widespread among states and must be supported by a belief that the practice is obligated by a rule of international law (*opinio juris*). To attain the level of custom, a rule needs general consistency among all states, including 'specially affected states', but does not need to reflect the views or actions of every single one.[49] It is also widely argued that in limited circumstances, a state or small group of states can hold 'persistent objector' status to a rule of customary law, meaning that such states are not bound by the rule if they

---

48  G.C. Shaffer, M.A. Gregory, and M. Pollack, 'Hard vs. Soft Law: Alternatives, Complements, and Antagonists in International Governance', *Minnesota Law Review*, Vol. 94 (June 2009), pp. 706–99. See also: K. Abbott and D. Snidal, 'Hard and Soft Law in International Governance', *International Organization*, Vol. 54, No. 3 (2000), pp. 421–56.

49  In the *1969 North Sea Continental Shelf Cases*, the ICJ explained the criteria necessary to establish state practice: widespread and representative (though not necessarily universal) participation by states, but including states that were specially affected by the proposed customary rule. ICJ, *North Sea Continental Shelf Cases* (*Germany/Denmark* and *Germany/The Netherlands*), Judgment, 20 February 1969, para. 73.

consistently objected to it during its formation and if they sustain their objection thereafter.[50]

1.17   A detailed study of customary international disarmament law has not yet been conducted. In its 1996 Advisory Opinion on the legality on the threat or use of nuclear weapons, the ICJ found, by an 11 to 3 majority, that no comprehensive and universal prohibition of the threat or use of nuclear weapons existed 'as such' in customary international law.[51] However, the Court also held unanimously that there 'exists an obligation to pursue in good faith and bring to a conclusion negotiations leading to nuclear disarmament in all its aspects under strict and effective international control'.[52] This is a rare instance of the identification of a rule of customary international disarmament law by a judicial authority.

1.18   Far more customary international legal rules exist in the realm of the law of armed conflict. The International Committee of the Red Cross (ICRC) dedicated ten years of research to identify the rules of customary international humanitarian law (IHL, the other term used to describe the law of armed conflict). The ICRC concluded that biological and chemical weapons may not be used in any armed conflict. The ICRC study further identified customary prohibitions on the use, during armed conflict, of poison, expanding bullets, exploding bullets, and blinding laser weapons.[53]

1.19   Despite widespread adherence to the 1997 Anti-Personnel Mine Ban Convention and the 2008 Convention on Cluster Munitions (as of writing, 164 states and 106 states parties, respectively), continued employment of anti-personnel mines and cluster munitions by a number of major military powers indicate that treaty prohibitions on the use of these weapons have not yet crystallised in customary international law. To amount to a customary rule, there must be general support for it within state practice, including among 'specially affected' states. While a prohibition on the use of anti-personnel mines is becoming customary law (*de lege ferenda*), the opposition (and continued use) of anti-personnel mines by China, Russia, and the United States is legally significant. With regard to landmines, however, a customary rule identified by the ICRC demands that the location of emplacement of landmines be recorded and that they be removed or neutralised at the end of hostilities.[54]

50  See, e.g., H. Thirlway, 'Sources of International Law', in M.D. Evans (ed.), *International Law*, 4th Edn, Oxford University Press, Oxford, 2014, p. 103; and M.N. Shaw, *International Law*, 8th Edn, Cambridge University Press, Cambridge, 2017, p. 67.
51  ICJ, *Legality of the Threat or Use of Nuclear Weapons*, Advisory Opinion, 8 July 1996, dispositif B.
52  Ibid., dispositif F.
53  ICRC Study of Customary IHL, Chapter IV, at: https://bit.ly/2QNAbly.
54  Ibid., Rules 82 and 83.

## General principles of disarmament law

1.20    General principles of law comprise principles of international and domestic law that are found in most states.[55] The international legal duty on states to respect treaties to which they are party (termed *pacta sunt servanda*), and the allied principle of good faith in the interpretation and application of treaty obligations, underpin all treaties,[56] including those governing disarmament. These general principles of law support the functioning of the international legal system. While most general principles apply to the entire international legal system, some are related to particular branches of international law, for example the principle of humanity in the law of armed conflict.[57]

1.21    Given the very technical nature of disarmament and states' emphasis on its codification by international treaties, few general principles of law exist within international disarmament law. One such general principle may be the right of states to participate in disarmament negotiations. This was included in the outcome document of the first Special Session of the UN General Assembly on Disarmament in 1978 and has since been asserted by states on numerous occasions.[58] Another such principle could be the duty of reasonable transparency: to build confidence that they are complying with international disarmament law, states must be transparent in their conduct, at least to the extent that national security allows.

## The notions of 'jurisdiction' and 'control'

1.22    Jurisdiction is an important concept in international disarmament law. Jurisdiction under international law generally concerns the scope of legal power or competence of the state: 'the power of the state under international law to regulate or otherwise impact upon people, property and circumstances'.[59] In international disarmament law, jurisdiction also governs the extent of the disarmament obligations upon states. This is expressed in one of three main ways: geographically (with respect to territory), materially (with respect to the weapons themselves), and individually (with respect to persons or legal undertakings to be encompassed by prohibitions and restrictions).

1.23    Control is sometimes used in conjunction with 'jurisdiction' in international disarmament law, especially (but not only) with respect to foreign territory,

---

55 See, e.g., J. Crawford, *Brownlie's Principles of Public International Law*, 8th Edn, Oxford University Press, Oxford, 2012, p. 37; Shaw, *International Law*, pp. 73–78.

56 See Art. 26 ('*Pacta sunt servanda*'), VCLT: 'Every treaty in force is binding upon the parties to it and must be performed by them in good faith'. See also, e.g., Shaw, *International Law*, p. 77.

57 M. Kohen and B. Schramm, 'General Principles of Law', *Oxford Bibliographies*, Last updated 26 August 2013, at: https://bit.ly/2BwybtD.

58 UN General Assembly Resolution S-10/2: Final Document of the Tenth Special Session of the Assembly, 30 June 1978, para. 28. It should be noted, though, that the Conference on Disarmament (CD) has consistently refused to admit new members since 1999.

59 Shaw, *International Law*, p. 483.

although the concept is not defined in the relevant treaties. In international law on the responsibility of states and under the law of armed conflict, 'control' can also pertain to state control over auxiliary forces. The military term 'command and control' refers to the authority by a commander over forces in the accomplishment of the mission[60] (thus including items such as weapons).

1.24 The ordinary definition of control is 'to be in charge of something [or someone] and have the power to make decisions relating to them'.[61] This definition and the recurrent use of the term in conjunction with 'jurisdiction' in disarmament treaties suggest that 'control' means a state's de facto authority over territory or weapons that may arise in practice without the jurisdiction that results from sovereignty or ownership. This might arise, for instance, in foreign occupation or in multinational operations when forces take control of another state's stockpiles (see Box 1.2).

---

### BOX 1.2 THE NOTION OF CONTROL IN INTERNATIONAL LAW

The notion of 'control' in international law extends the disarmament obligations of a state to foreign territory. Such extraterritorial application is typical under a disarmament treaty. It means that where a state – for example, through its armed forces – is in effective control of an area under the jurisdiction of another state, it may be obligated to conduct clearance and/or destroy stockpiles of weapons it encounters.

With respect to stockpile destruction, however, it is sometimes critical to distinguish between control of an area and control of the weapons themselves. This may apply territorially as well as extraterritorially. The 1992 Chemical Weapons Convention, for instance, obligates states parties to destroy chemical weapons that are located *in any place* under its jurisdiction or control. In contrast, the corresponding obligation in the 1997 Anti-Personnel Mine Ban Convention is to destroy or ensure the destruction of all stockpiled anti-personnel mines that are under its jurisdiction or control. The change signifies that mines that are in a state party's territory but which are held in a military base by a foreign power under a Status of Forces Agreement may be exempted from the duty of destruction. This distinction was made even more explicit in the 2008 Convention on Cluster Munitions which required that a state party have both jurisdiction and control over the weapons for a duty of destruction to apply.

---

60 See notably the definition in US *Department of Defense Dictionary of Military and Associated Terms*, September 2018, p. 43, at: http://bit.ly/2qbOvcj. Command and control is linked to 'operational control' and 'tactical control'.

61 *Cambridge English Dictionary*, 'Control', at: http://bit.ly/2D3i9ZX.

> The 2017 Treaty on the Prohibition of Nuclear Weapons provides that each state party that controls nuclear weapons (whether territorially or extraterritorially) must immediately remove them from operational status, and destroy them as soon as possible but not later than the deadline determined by the first meeting of states parties.

## Geographical jurisdiction

1.25    Jurisdiction under international law is primarily territorial.[62] Thus, a state has primary jurisdiction over all of its sovereign territory, which includes not just landmass but also the airspace above that land and the territorial seas (typically extending 12 nautical miles from the coastal baseline).[63] The Treaty of Rarotonga, for example, specifies that for the purposes of the Treaty, '"territory" means internal waters, territorial sea and archipelagic waters, the seabed and subsoil beneath, the land territory and the airspace above them'.[64] Jurisdiction also applies to vessels that fly the flag of the state on the high seas or in the air and a state's foreign embassies.[65]

1.26    Disarmament treaties typically set out their jurisdictional reach, in particular their geographical scope. Usually, this includes the national territory of a state party. For treaties dealing with specific geographical regions or dimensions, the delimitations are specifically mentioned. Thus, for example, the 1959 Antarctic Treaty applies to Antarctica, prohibiting any nuclear explosions and disposal of radioactive waste material anywhere on the landmass, the waters adjacent, and the ice shelf south of 60° south latitude.[66] Specific regions are laid down for the scope of the nuclear-weapons-free zones.[67] Outer space is not defined in the 1967 Outer

---

62  Shaw, *International Law*, p. 483.

63  C. Staker, 'Jurisdiction', in Evans, *International Law*, p. 316.

64  Art. 1(b), Treaty of Rarotonga.

65  It is, though, a popular myth that embassies are the sovereign territory of the foreign state. This is not the case. See A. Clapham, *Brierly's Law of Nations*, 7th Edn, Oxford University Press, Oxford, 2012, p. 207.

66  Arts. V(1) and VI, The Antarctic Treaty; adopted at Washington, DC, 1 December 1959; entered into force, 23 June 1961. According to Article VI, the treaty applies to 'the area' south of 60° south latitude, 'including all ice shelves'.

67  The Treaty of Tlatelolco, for example, states in its Article 4(2) that, upon the fulfilment of certain events, 'the zone of application of this Treaty shall also be that which is situated in the western hemisphere within the following limits (except the continental part of the territory of the United States of America and its territorial waters): starting at a point located at 35° north latitude, 75° west longitude; from this point directly southward to a point at 30° north latitude, 75° west longitude; from there, directly eastward to a point at 30° north latitude, 50° west longitude; from there, along a loxodromic line to a point at 5° north latitude, 20° west longitude; from there directly southward to a point 60° south latitude, 20° west longitude; from there, directly westward to a point at 60° south latitude, 115° west longitude; from there, directly northward to a point at 0 latitude, 115° west

Space Treaty, although a widely accepted 'working definition' is that it begins at the Kármán Line, set at 100 kilometres above the earth's sea level.[68]

## Material jurisdiction

1.27   With respect to the duty to destroy stockpiles of weapons, disarmament treaties usually set out their material reach. Thus, for example, the 1992 Chemical Weapons Convention obliges each state party to 'destroy chemical weapons it owns or possesses, or that are located in any place under its jurisdiction or control'.[69] This is extremely broad, encompassing chemical weapons that are owned or possessed by a state party anywhere and extending to chemical weapons that are owned or possessed by a foreign state but are located on a state party's territory.

1.28   The PTBT operates on the basis that a state party will always have jurisdiction or control over its own nuclear weapons ('at any place under its jurisdiction or control'), even if this occurs in the atmosphere, in outer space, or underwater, including beneath the high seas. A far narrower obligation is contained in the 2008 Convention on Cluster Munitions, wherein each state party is obliged to destroy all cluster munitions that are simultaneously under *both* its jurisdiction *and* its control.[70]

## Personal jurisdiction

1.29   The implementation of disarmament treaties often requires the adoption of penal sanctions for violations of the prohibited activities. Thus, for example, the 1992 Chemical Weapons Convention obliges each state party to:

> Prohibit natural and legal persons anywhere on its territory or in any other place under its jurisdiction as recognised by international law from undertaking any activity prohibited to a State Party under this Convention, including enacting penal legislation with respect to such activity.[71]

A natural person is a human being. A legal person is a corporate entity ('body corporate') or other legal undertaking, such as a partnership or charitable foundation. This notion would not apply to a non-state armed group, although the members of such groups would fall within the domestic criminal law that governs the acts of natural persons.

---

longitude; from there, along a loxodromic line to a point at 35° north latitude, 150° west longitude; from there, directly eastward to a point at 35° north latitude, 75° west longitude'. See similarly Annex 1 to the Treaty of Rarotonga.

68  This is where an aircraft would have to travel at a speed greater than orbital velocity to get enough lift from its wings to stay in the air. Institute of Physics, 'A Brief History of Space', undated but accessed on 14 December 2017, at: http://bit.ly/2Rbsdmk.

69  Art. I(2), 1992 Chemical Weapons Convention.

70  Art. 3(1) and (2), 2008 Convention on Cluster Munitions.

71  Art. VII(1)(a), 1992 Chemical Weapons Convention.

## Key definitions

1.30 This section sets out certain key definitions, first of weapons/arms and certain categories thereof and then of specific weapons/arms.

### Weapons and arms

1.31 There is no generally agreed definition of what constitute either arms or weapons. The definition of a weapon is, though, widely understood to be broader in scope than is the notion of arms or armaments. So all arms are weapons, but not all weapons are arms. Arms are limited to weapons, including weapons systems, which are produced in a factory, especially when they are destined for the military.[72]

1.32 Weapons, though, include also tools or materials that are adapted or improvised in the field. One suggested definition of a weapon is the following:

> Any device constructed, adapted, or used to kill, harm, disorient, incapacitate, or affect a person's behaviour against their will, or to damage or destroy buildings or *matériel*. A weapon acts through the application of kinetic force or of other means, such as the transmission of electricity, the diffusion of chemical substances or biological agents or sound, or the direction of electromagnetic energy. The term 'weapon' includes offensive cyber operations that damage or interrupt the normal operation of computer systems and networks or result in physical harm to people or objects.[73]

1.33 The law of armed conflict uses the term 'means of warfare', which can be defined as all weapons, weapons platforms and associated equipment used directly to deliver force during hostilities.[74] In this context, weapons can be defined as an 'offensive capability' that can be applied to a military object or enemy combatant.[75] The ICRC refers to 'weapon bearers', by which it means regular armed forces, police forces, paramilitary groups, armed opposition groups, and private military and security companies.[76]

1.34 Munitions are a type of weapon, typically, but not always, containing explosive. One useful definition is of 'a complete device charged with explosives; propellants; pyrotechnics; initiating composition; or chemical, biological,

---

72 With the emergence of 3D printing, however, arms may also be produced outside of factories.

73 S. Casey-Maslen (ed.), *Weapons Under International Human Rights Law*, Cambridge University Press, Cambridge, 2014, p. xx.

74 W. Boothby, *Weapons and the Law of Armed Conflict*, 2nd Edn, Oxford University Press, Oxford, 2016, p. 4.

75 J. McClelland, 'The Review of Weapons in Accordance with Article 36 of Additional Protocol 1', *International Review of the Red Cross*, Vol. 850 (2003), p. 397.

76 ICRC, 'The ICRC and weapon bearers', 29 October 2010, at: http://bit.ly/2q8Maiq.

radiological, or nuclear material for use in operations including demolitions'.[77] In English, the term 'ammunition' is often used as a synonym for 'munition'.[78] In French, there is only the term *munition*.[79]

## Weapons, military equipment, and dual-use items

1.35    Weapons can be distinguished from military equipment that does not possess offensive capabilities. Military trucks or soldiers' personal protective equipment are examples of such equipment. Military equipment is not banned by any global disarmament treaty,[80] but the distinction is relevant in arms control and non-proliferation measures. Equipment and systems that are used for reconnaissance, surveillance, navigation, or communication, as well as technologies that enable and support the use of weapons, such as computer software, may be considered as parts and components of weapon systems.

1.36    Weapons and their parts and components are distinguished from so-called dual-use items by their specific design for a military purpose. Dual-use items and technologies mean equipment and parts and components that are designed for peaceful use but can also be used for weapons or weapon systems. Ordinary production items that are also used for weapons production, such as machine tools, are similarly considered dual-use.

1.37    The distinction between weapons and dual-use items is particularly important for the implementation and, notably, the non-proliferation aspects of disarmament treaties regarding weapons of mass destruction (WMD). This is because biological toxins, chemical agents, and nuclear material and related equipment can oftentimes be used for either peaceful purposes or the development of weapons. While global disarmament treaties explicitly exclude activities and items for peaceful purposes from their scope, the export control regimes (notably the Nuclear Suppliers Group, Australia Group, MTCR, and Wassenaar Arrangement) and the UN Security Council Resolution 1540 establish guidelines and information exchange regarding international transfers of dual-use items.

## Weapons of mass destruction

1.38    There is no formally agreed definition of what constitute WMD under international law, but the term is generally taken to mean biological weapons, chemical

---

77 US Department of Defense (DoD), *DoD Dictionary of Military and Associated Terms*, September 2018, p. 159.

78 See Art. 3, Arms Trade Treaty; adopted at the UN General Assembly in New York, 2 April 2013; entered into force, 24 December 2014; and S. Parker, 'Commentary on Article 3', in S. Casey-Maslen, A. Clapham, G. Giacca, and S. Parker, *The Arms Trade Treaty, A Commentary*, Oxford University Press, Oxford, 2016, paras. 3.21–3.22.

79 Art. 3, ATT.

80 Anti-handling devices fitted to mines and the dispensers of explosive bomblets, for instance, are considered as integral parts of landmines and cluster munitions, respectively.

weapons, nuclear weapons, and weapons dispersing radiation. The US Department of Defense has defined WMD as: 'Chemical, biological, radiological, or nuclear weapons capable of a high order of destruction or causing mass casualties, and excluding the means of transporting or propelling the weapon where such means is a separable and divisible part from the weapon'.[81] This definition would exclude, for instance riot control agents, such as tear gas. While WMD are most often possessed for strategic purposes, they could also be used at the tactical level.

### Conventional weapons

1.39    Conventional weapons are, in turn, generally understood to mean all weapons other than WMD. This was the approach taken by the United Nations in 1948;[82] this understanding has been endorsed more recently by the US Department of Defense.[83] Traditionally, individual conventional weapons inflicted considerably less damage than weapons of mass destruction, and many were 'designed for offensive or defensive use at relatively short range with relatively immediate consequences'.[84] The United Nations Register of Conventional Arms, a non-legally binding transparency mechanism, defines seven categories of heavy weapons. Although these definitions are outdated and incomplete, the 2013 Arms Trade Treaty refers to this categorisation in defining its scope of application. Small arms and light weapons are complementary to heavy weapons. It is not settled whether cyberweapons are to be considered as conventional weapons or whether they represent a new and distinct third category.

## Treaty definitions

### Weapons of mass destruction

#### Biological weapons

1.40    The 1971 Biological Weapons Convention (BWC) effectively defines 'bacteriological (biological) and toxin weapons' as 'microbial or other biological agents, or toxins whatever their origin or method of production, of types and in quantities that have no justification for prophylactic, protective or other peaceful purposes'.[85] Also prohibited under the BWC are 'weapons, equipment or means of delivery designed to use such agents or toxins for hostile purposes or in armed conflict'.[86]

---

81 US Department of Defense, *DOD Dictionary of Military and Associated Terms*, September 2018, p. 248.
82 Report of the Conventional Armaments Commission, UN doc. S/C.3/32/Rev.1, 18 August 1948.
83 US Department of Defense, *DOD Dictionary of Military Terms*, as amended through 31 October 2009, p. 122. The dictionary has not repeated the definition in its more recent editions, although there is a narrower definition applied to 'conventional forces' in the September 2018 edition as: 'Those forces capable of conducting operations using nonnuclear weapons'. *DOD Dictionary of Military and Associated Terms*, September 2018, p. 53.
84 *Encyclopedia Britannica*, at: https://bit.ly/2O0xlZu (accessed 15 February 2018).
85 Art. I(1), 1971 Biological Weapons Convention.
86 Art. I(2), 1971 Biological Weapons Convention.

Potentially, a flea or a rat could be a means of delivery for 'microbial or other biological agents'.

## Chemical weapons

1.41    Under the 1992 Chemical Weapons Convention (CWC), chemical weapons mean the following: toxic chemicals and their precursors; munitions and devices specifically designed to cause death or other harm through the toxic properties of those toxic chemicals; and equipment specifically designed for use directly in connection with the employment of those munitions and devices.[87] This includes use of toxic chemical agents outside an armed conflict, as seemingly occurred in the 2018 attack in Salisbury in the United Kingdom, for instance. Excluded from the scope of the definition are toxic chemicals where they are intended for purposes not prohibited under the CWC, 'as long as the types and quantities' of those chemicals 'are consistent with such purposes'.[88]

## Nuclear weapons

1.42    There is no universally agreed definition of a nuclear weapon under international law. Neither the NPT nor the 2017 Treaty on the Prohibition of Nuclear Weapons (TPNW) includes a definition of nuclear weapons for the purpose of the respective treaty. Common dictionary definitions are 'a bomb or missile that uses nuclear energy to cause an explosion' and 'any weapon that derives its destructive force from nuclear reactions'.[89] The *Glossary of Key Nuclear Terms* elaborated by the five permanent members of the UN Security Council (the P5) defines nuclear weapons as a 'weapon assembly that is capable of producing an explosion and massive damage and destruction by the sudden release of energy instantaneously released from self-sustaining nuclear fission and/or fusion'.[90] According to the 1967 Treaty of Tlatelolco, a nuclear weapon is

> any device which is capable of releasing nuclear energy in an uncontrolled manner and which has a group of characteristics that are appropriate for use for warlike purposes. An instrument that may be used for the transport or propulsion of the device is not included in this definition if it is separable from the device and not an indivisible part thereof.[91]

---

87  Art. I(1), 1992 Chemical Weapons Convention.

88  Art. I(1)(a), CWC.

89  Oxford Dictionaries, undated but accessed 13 December 2017 at: http://bit.ly/2PKZt3D; Nuclear Weapon Law and Legal Definition', *US Legal*, undated but accessed 13 December 2017 at: http://bit.ly/2CulXlK.

90  P5 Working Group on the Glossary of Key Nuclear Terms, *P5 Glossary of Key Nuclear Terms*, Atomic Energy Press, Beijing, 2015, p. 6; see *A Prohibition on Nuclear Weapons: A Guide to the Issues*, UN Institute for Disarmament Research (UNIDIR) and International Law and Policy Institute (ILPI), Geneva, February 2016, p. 30, Box E.

91  Art. 5, Treaty of Tlatelolco. See also Art. 1(c), Bangkok Treaty.

1.43    These definitions would encompass both atomic (fission) and more powerful hydrogen/thermonuclear (fission and fusion) weapons. They would exclude
radiological dispersion devices, since conventional explosives are used therein to
diffuse radioactive substances into the air without a nuclear chain reaction.[92] These
devices are also known colloquially as 'dirty bombs' when used by non-state actors.
Aircraft and submarines used to launch nuclear weapons would not be encompassed as they are not 'an indivisible part thereof'.

1.44    'Other nuclear explosive devices', a term included in both the NPT
and the TPNW, is also not defined in either treaty. It is generally understood that
the notion similarly covers both fission and thermonuclear devices but describes
objects which have not been weaponised, for example because they are too large or
too heavy. According to the Treaty of Rarotonga, 'nuclear explosive device'

> means any nuclear weapon or other explosive device capable of releasing
> nuclear energy, irrespective of the purpose for which it could be used. The
> term includes such a weapon or device in unassembled and partly assembled
> forms, but does not include the means of transport or delivery of such a
> weapon or device if separable from and not an indivisible part of it.[93]

Article V of the NPT implicitly allows 'peaceful applications of nuclear explosions'. Such explosions were used for mining, among other activities. All nuclear
detonations are prohibited by the CTBT and the TPNW.

## Conventional weapons

### Anti-personnel mines

1.45    Anti-personnel mines are defined in two treaties. The 1996 Amended Protocol II to the Convention on Certain Conventional Weapons (CCW), to which
105 states were party as of writing, defines anti-personnel mine as 'a mine *primarily*
designed to be exploded by the presence, proximity or contact of a person and
that will incapacitate, injure or kill one or more persons'.[94] Subsequently, the 1997
Anti-Personnel Mine Ban Convention (APMBC), to which 164 states were party

---

92  Domestic legislation may, though, be broader. This is the case, for instance, in the United States.
   According to 18 USCS §832, 'nuclear weapon' means any weapon that contains or uses nuclear
   materials. Nuclear material is defined as 'material containing any: (A) plutonium; (B) uranium
   not in the form of ore or ore residue that contains the mixture of isotopes as occurring in nature;
   (C) enriched uranium, defined as uranium that contains the isotope 233 or 235 or both in such
   amount that the abundance ratio of the sum of those isotopes to the isotope 238 is greater than the
   ratio of the isotope 235 to the isotope 238 occurring in nature; or (D) uranium 233'. [18 USCS
   §831(f)(1).]
93  Art. 1(c), Treaty of Rarotonga.
94  Art. 2(2), Protocol on Prohibitions or Restrictions on the Use of Mines, Booby-Traps and Other
   Devices as amended on 3 May 1996 (Amended Protocol II), annexed to the Convention on Prohibitions or Restrictions on the Use of Certain Conventional Weapons Which May Be Deemed to Be

as of writing, defines anti-personnel mines as 'a mine designed to be exploded by the presence, proximity or contact of a person and that will incapacitate, injure or kill one or more persons'.[95]

1.46   The Anti-Personnel Mine Ban Convention definition clarifies that mines 'designed to be detonated by the presence, proximity or contact of a vehicle as opposed to a person, that are equipped with anti-handling devices, are not considered anti-personnel mines as a result of being so equipped'.[96] This clarification sought to remove the ambiguity introduced by the word 'primarily' in the Amended Protocol II definition, which was introduced to reflect the position of certain states that a mine detonated by a person would not be considered anti-personnel if its primary design purpose was said to be anti-materiel or anti-vehicle.

## Cluster munitions

1.47   The 2008 Convention on Cluster Munitions (CCM) defines a cluster munition as 'a conventional munition that is designed to disperse or release explosive submunitions each weighing less than 20 kilograms, and includes those explosive submunitions'.[97] Cluster munitions are typically deployed by aircraft or artillery with a canister or dispenser that disperse explosive submunitions. The Convention applies also to explosive bomblets that are specifically designed to be dispersed or released directly from dispensers fixed to aircraft.[98]

1.48   All mines are excluded from the scope of the Convention on Cluster Munitions,[99] as are munitions or submunitions designed to dispense flares, smoke, pyrotechnics, or chaff,[100] munitions 'designed exclusively for an air defence role',[101] and munitions or submunitions designed to produce electrical or electronic effects.[102] A specific exclusion from the definition is also incorporated for a particular form of autonomous weapon. This is one that is designed to detect and engage a single target object, where the munition contains fewer than ten explosive submunitions; where each such submunition weighs more than four kilograms; and where all of the submunitions are equipped with an electronic self-destruction mechanism and an electronic self-deactivating feature.[103]

---

Excessively Injurious or to Have Indiscriminate Effects; adopted at Geneva, 3 May 1996; entered into force, 3 December 1998 (emphasis added).

95  Art. 2(1), 1997 Anti-Personnel Mine Ban Convention.

96  Ibid. Article 2(3) stipulates that an anti-handling device is 'a device intended to protect a mine and which is part of, linked to, attached to or placed under the mine and which activates when an attempt is made to tamper with or otherwise intentionally disturb the mine'.

97  Art. 2(2), 2008 Convention on Cluster Munitions.

98  Art. 1(2), 2008 Convention on Cluster Munitions.

99  Art. 1(3), 2008 Convention on Cluster Munitions.

100  Art. 2(2)(a), 2008 Convention on Cluster Munitions.

101  Ibid.

102  Art. 2(2)(b), 2008 Convention on Cluster Munitions.

103  Art. 2(2)(c), 2008 Convention on Cluster Munitions.

## Small arms and light weapons

1.49   Small arms and light weapons (SALW) are defined not in a treaty but in a soft law instrument, the 2005 International Tracing Instrument (ITI).[104] Under the ITI, SALW encompasses

> any man-portable lethal weapon that expels or launches, is designed to expel or launch, or may be readily converted to expel or launch a shot, bullet or projectile by the action of an explosive, excluding antique small arms and light weapons or their replicas.[105]

1.50   The ITI goes on to explain that small arms are, 'broadly speaking, weapons designed for individual use'. This category includes revolvers and self-loading pistols, rifles, and carbines, sub-machine guns, assault rifles, and light machine guns.[106] With respect to light weapons, the ITI notes that they are, 'broadly speaking, weapons designed for use by two or three persons serving as a crew, although some may be carried and used by a single person'. This category includes heavy machine guns, hand-held under-barrel and mounted grenade launchers, portable anti-aircraft guns, portable anti-tank guns, recoilless rifles, portable launchers of anti-tank missile and rocket systems, portable launchers of anti-aircraft missile systems, and mortars of a calibre of less than 100 mm.[107]

1.51   Not covered by the ITI definition, hand grenades are sometimes understood as SALW.[108] In an earlier report by the UN Panel of Governmental Experts on Small Arms, the following had been covered:

### a   Small arms

i     Revolvers and self-loading pistols;

ii    Rifles and carbines;

iii   Sub-machine-guns;

iv    Assault rifles;

v     Light machine-guns.

---

104 International Instrument to Enable States to Identify and Trace, in a Timely and Reliable Manner, Illicit Small Arms and Light Weapons, adopted by the UN General Assembly on 8 December 2005.

105 Section II, ITI. The section goes on to state that antique small arms and light weapons and their replicas 'will be defined in accordance with domestic law. In no case will antique small arms and light weapons include those manufactured after 1899'.

106 S. II(a), ITI.

107 S. II(b), ITI.

108 The Role of Parliaments in Strengthening Control of Trafficking in Small Arms and Light Weapons and Their Ammunition, Resolution adopted by the 114th Assembly of the Inter-Parliamentary Union, Nairobi, 12 May 2006.

## b   Light weapons

i     Heavy machine-guns;
ii    Hand-held under-barrel and mounted grenade launchers;
iii   Portable anti-aircraft guns;
iv    Portable anti-tank guns, recoilless rifles;
v     Portable launchers of anti-tank missile and rocket systems;
vi    Portable launchers of anti-aircraft missile systems;
vii   Mortars of calibre of less than 100 mm.

## c   Ammunition and explosives

i     Cartridges (rounds) for small arms;
ii    Shells and missiles for light weapons;
iii   Mobile containers with missiles or shells for single-action anti-aircraft and anti-tank systems;
iv    Anti-personnel and anti-tank hand grenades;
v     Landmines;
vi    Explosives.[109]

---

109 'Report of the Panel of Governmental Experts on Small Arms', Annex to UN doc. A/52/298, 27 August 1997, para. 26, at: http://bit.ly/2ORrUQX.

# 2

# THE CORE ELEMENTS OF DISARMAMENT TREATIES

2.1   This chapter summarises the core elements found in international disarmament treaties. This concerns the following measures: stockpile destruction, the clearance and destruction of weapons that have been used, transfer prohibitions or restrictions, the ending of weapons production and the destruction or dismantling of production facilities, prohibitions on development, and prohibitions or limitations on the testing of weapons (where this activity is addressed separately from development).

2.2   Specific prohibitions on the use of weapons are also discussed, as are the positive obligations to assist the victims of the use of weapons that have been included in recent disarmament treaties. The chapter, which also considers the outlawing of assisting others to conduct prohibited activities, ends with a summary of transparency and verification measures. For information as to which activities are covered by which global disarmament treaties, see Tables 2.1 and 2.2 at the end of the chapter.

## Stockpile destruction

2.3   Central to a disarmament treaty is the obligation to destroy stockpiles of the weapon being prohibited under the treaty. A stockpile is an accumulation of stored weapons that have not been used. There is no minimum quantity necessary to constitute a stockpile: possession of one nuclear weapon, for example, will of course amount to a stockpile. Often, stockpiles exist where there are accumulations of critical parts or components or integral material rather than of assembled weapons. For example, in the case of munitions, detonators will often be stored separately from explosive material, for reasons of safety and security.

2.4   It is common in disarmament treaties to include a general prohibition on stockpiling[1] and then to fix the modalities for the destruction of some or all of the weapons held in a stockpile. These modalities will typically involve a deadline for each state party, which may or may not be capable of extension, depending on the treaty. The respective deadlines for stockpile destruction under the 1971 Biological Weapons Convention (BWC)[2] and the 1997 Anti-Personnel Mine Ban Convention (APMBC)[3] are fixed and may not be extended.

2.5   In contrast, under the 1992 Chemical Weapons Convention (CWC),[4] states parties were permitted to extend their deadlines, by agreement, for five years up to 2012.[5] The deadline for stockpile destruction under the 2008 Convention on Cluster Munitions[6] may also be extended by each concerned state party, subject to the agreement of the other states parties. The first stockpile destruction treaty deadlines under the Convention on Cluster Munitions expired in 2018 but no concerned state party requested an extension. Unusually, the 2017 Treaty on the Prohibition of Nuclear Weapons[7] (TPNW; not yet in force, as on 1 March 2019) leaves the question of the deadline for destruction – including whether it may be extended – to a decision to be taken by the first meeting of the states parties. The First Meeting of States Parties will be held within one year of the TPNW's entry into force.

## Destruction of used weapons

2.6   Two global disarmament treaties require the clearance and destruction of weapons that have been used: the 1997 Anti-Personnel Mine Ban Convention and the 2008 Convention on Cluster Munitions.[8] Both treaties require that destruction be completed within ten years of their entry into force for the affected

---

1   Exceptions to the general prohibition are included in certain global disarmament treaties, for instance in the case of the treaties prohibiting anti-personnel mines and explosive submunitions, in order to permit the development of clearance and destruction techniques.
2   Convention on the Prohibition of the Development, Production and Stockpiling of Bacteriological (Biological) and Toxin Weapons and on Their Destruction; adopted at New York, 16 December 1971; entered into force, 26 March 1975.
3   Convention on the Prohibition of the Use, Stockpiling, Production and Transfer of Anti-Personnel Mines and on Their Destruction; adopted at Oslo, 18 September 1997; entered into force, 1 March 1999.
4   Convention on the Prohibition of the Development, Production, Stockpiling and Use of Chemical Weapons and on Their Destruction; adopted at Geneva, 3 September 1992; entered into force, 29 April 1997.
5   As discussed in Chapter 7, the 1992 Chemical Weapons Convention obligated states parties to destroy their chemical weapons within ten years of the Convention's entry into force, meaning by 2007. However, it was permitted to request an extension of the destruction deadline, once only, by up to five years, until 2012, subject to the approval of other states parties.
6   Convention on Cluster Munitions; adopted at Dublin, 30 May 2008; entered into force, 1 August 2010.
7   Treaty on the Prohibition of Nuclear Weapons; adopted at New York, 7 July 2017; not yet in force.
8   Art. 5, 1997 Anti-Personnel Mine Ban Convention; Art. 4, 2008 Convention on Cluster Munitions.

state, although in both cases it is possible to request extensions to the deadline.[9] Clearance or destruction of weapons is also required by the 1996 Amended Protocol II on mines, booby-traps, and other devices[10] and by the 2003 Protocol V on Explosive Remnants of War to the 1980 Convention on Certain Conventional Weapons (CCW).[11] These are, however, generally viewed as law of armed conflict rather than disarmament treaties.[12] In one disarmament treaty – the 2017 Treaty on the Prohibition of Nuclear Weapons – the 'remediation' of affected areas is required, irrespective of whether environmental impact results from the use of a nuclear explosive device or as a result of its detonation in testing.[13]

## Transfer

2.7    Other than the duty of stockpile destruction, the most common element in any disarmament treaty is a prohibition (or restriction) on the transfer of the weapons that fall within its scope. This is the case in, for instance, the Biological Weapons Convention, the Chemical Weapons Convention, the Anti-Personnel Mine Ban Convention, the Convention on Cluster Munitions, and the Treaty on the Prohibition of Nuclear Weapons. Prohibitions on transfer are also included in Amended Protocol II and Protocol IV on blinding laser weapons[14] to the Convention on Certain Conventional Weapons. A prohibition on transfer of nuclear weapons to non-state actors as well as to non-nuclear-weapon states by the five nuclear-weapon states the treaty designates is incorporated in the 1968 Treaty on the Non-Proliferation of Nuclear Weapons (NPT).[15]

2.8    The definition of transfer differs from treaty to treaty, and oftentimes is also rather unclear. In some cases, for example, the concept comprehends export but not import, while in others it requires both movement into the territory of another state and transfer of title to it. In the 2013 Arms Trade Treaty (ATT) – which is

---

9  Art. 5(3)–(6), 1997 Anti-Personnel Mine Ban Convention; Art. 4(5)–(8), 2008 Convention on Cluster Munitions.

10  Protocol on Prohibitions or Restrictions on the Use of Mines, Booby-Traps and Other Devices as amended on 3 May 1996 (Protocol II, as amended on 3 May 1996) annexed to the Convention on Prohibitions or Restrictions on the Use of Certain Conventional Weapons which may be deemed to be Excessively Injurious or to have Indiscriminate Effects; adopted at Geneva, 3 May 1996; entered into force, 3 December 1998.

11  Convention on Prohibitions or Restrictions on the Use of Certain Conventional Weapons which may be deemed to be Excessively Injurious or to have Indiscriminate Effects; adopted at Geneva, 10 October 1980; entered into force, 2 December 1983.

12  Protocol on Explosive Remnants of War (Protocol V to the 1980 CCW Convention); adopted at Geneva, 28 November 2003; entered into force, 12 November 2006.

13  Art. 6(2), 2017 Treaty on the Prohibition of Nuclear Weapons.

14  Additional Protocol to the Convention on Prohibitions or Restrictions on the Use of Certain Conventional Weapons which may be deemed to be Excessively Injurious or to have Indiscriminate Effects (Protocol IV, entitled Protocol on Blinding Laser Weapons); adopted at Vienna, 13 October 1995; entered into force, 30 July 1998.

15  Art. I, Treaty on the Non-Proliferation of Nuclear Weapons; opened for signature at London, Moscow, and Washington, DC, 1 July 1968; entered into force, 5 March 1970.

treated by some states as a trade treaty but considered by the United Nations as a disarmament treaty[16] – transfer is defined as export, import, transit, trans-shipment, and brokering.[17]

## Production

2.9   Disarmament treaties typically include a comprehensive prohibition on the production of the weapon being outlawed. This is so in the Biological Weapons Convention, the Chemical Weapons Convention, the Anti-Personnel Mine Ban Convention, the Convention on Cluster Munitions, and the Treaty on the Prohibition of Nuclear Weapons. A limited prohibition on production is also included in the Amended Protocol II to the Convention on Certain Conventional Weapons (but not the original Protocol II on mines, booby-traps, and other devices of 1980).

2.10   The term 'production' is not defined in a disarmament treaty, but is generally understood to include not only manufacture (i.e. production in a factory) but also local improvisation or adaptation of weapons. Certain treaties, such as the Chemical Weapons Convention,[18] encompass an obligation also to destroy production facilities. Under the Anti-Personnel Mine Ban Convention, states parties are required to report on the 'status of programmes for the conversion or decommissioning of anti-personnel mine production facilities'.[19]

## Development

2.11   A prohibition on developing a weapon is typically included in a global disarmament treaty. This is the case in the Biological Weapons Convention, the Chemical Weapons Convention, the Anti-Personnel Mine Ban Convention, the Convention on Cluster Munitions, and the Treaty on the Prohibition of Nuclear Weapons. Development is not defined in any disarmament treaty but refers to the stage of research prior to formal production of the weapon in question. In the context of the Chemical Weapons Convention, to '"develop" is said to be, by virtue of its purpose, the preparation of the production of chemical weapons as distinct from permitted research'.[20] The concept would appear to include testing of prototypes and even, in certain circumstances, computer modelling or simulations.

---

16 The ATT is, for instance, listed as a disarmament treaty on the UN Treaty Section website. In addition, in 1996 the UN Disarmament Commission issued Guidelines for international arms transfers. 'Guidelines for international arms transfers in the context of General Assembly resolution 46/36 H of 6 December 1991: Report of the Disarmament Commission', UN General Assembly, UN doc. A/51/42, 1996.

17 Art. 2(2), ATT.

18 Art. I(4), 1992 Chemical Weapons Convention.

19 Art. 7(1)(e), 1997 Anti-Personnel Mine Ban Convention.

20 See W. Krutzsch and R. Trapp, *A Commentary on the Chemical Weapons Convention*, Martinus Nijhoff, The Netherlands, 1994, p. 13.

## Testing

2.12 Testing of a weapon means its use in controlled conditions as opposed to hostile use against an adverse party, particularly in an armed conflict. The testing of a weapon would normally be considered as part of its development, but in a number of disarmament or arms control agreements it is treated as a distinct element, while in the case of the Partial Nuclear-Test-Ban Treaty[21] and the Comprehensive Nuclear-Test-Ban Treaty[22] prohibiting testing is the object and purpose of the treaty.

2.13 In the case of weapons of mass destruction, particularly nuclear weapons, testing has major safety and environmental implications. In the case of banned conventional weapons, continued testing may be permitted under certain circumstances, such as for the development of techniques in the clearance and destruction of landmines or cluster munition remnants.[23]

## Use

2.14 Use of a weapon means, at the least, its employment against an adverse party to an armed conflict or other target both outside as well as within a situation of armed conflict. It is thus broader than a prohibition under the law of armed conflict, which, as is recalled in Chapter 1, governs only use within and associated with an armed conflict. It has also been discussed – notably in the context of the 1997 Anti-Personnel Mine Ban Convention – that the prohibition on use may also extend to outlawing the act of taking operational advantage of the presence of anti-personnel mines that were previously emplaced by another state or even by a non-state actor.[24]

2.15 In the case of one disarmament treaty, the Biological Weapons Convention, use is not explicitly prohibited. This is in large part due to the fact that use of bacteriological weapons as a method of warfare had already been outlawed in the 1925 Geneva Protocol.[25] It also reflected the distinction, rigidly respected at the time, between the law of armed conflict and disarmament law. In the Chemical Weapons Convention, use of certain chemical agents for the purpose of law enforcement is not prohibited, whereas the use (of riot control agents) as a method of warfare is explicitly outlawed.[26]

---

21 Treaty Banning Nuclear Weapon Tests in the Atmosphere, in Outer Space and Under Water; opened for signature at London, Moscow, and Washington, DC, 8 August 1963; entered into force, 10 October 1963.

22 Comprehensive Nuclear-Test-Ban Treaty; adopted at New York, 10 September 1996; not yet in force.

23 Art. 3(1), APMBC; Art. 3(6), CCM.

24 Maslen, *Commentary on the 1997 Anti-Personnel Mine Ban Convention*, paras. 1.22–1.27.

25 Protocol for the Prohibition of the Use of Asphyxiating, Poisonous or Other Gases, and of Bacteriological Methods of Warfare; adopted at Geneva, 17 June 1925; entered into force, 8 February 1928.

26 Arts. I(5) and II(9)(d), 1992 Chemical Weapons Convention.

## Victim assistance

2.16   Where harm results from the use of a weapon, the victims – the survivors and potentially also family members of those killed and even the broader community – will need a range of support and assistance measures. These include medical care and rehabilitation, reintegration, and compensation, among others. This challenge is increasingly addressed as a set of positive obligations to assist victims. The Anti-Personnel Mine Ban Convention, the Convention on Cluster Munitions, and the Treaty on the Prohibition of Nuclear Weapons all include specific provisions on victim assistance. To date, the most detailed provisions are those set out in Article 5 of the Convention on Cluster Munitions.

## Information exchange and transparency

2.17   Information exchange among states and measures of transparency are designed to increase the level of information on particular activities among states parties and to facilitate the verification of compliance. Thus, information exchange and transparency measures aim to build confidence among states parties to a disarmament treaty. Often, measures will include annual reporting, along with regular conferences or meetings of states parties that enable discussion of issues arising from the annual reports.

## Verification

2.18   Verification is a means of checking whether states are complying with the obligations in disarmament treaties to which they are party. It is often a sensitive issue among states, particularly when it concerns the possibility of other states or treaty bodies conducting fact-finding on sovereign territory with a view to confirming whether an alleged violation of international law has occurred. Verification was a primary reason for the decades of discussions and negotiations that were needed to achieve the adoption of the Chemical Weapons Convention. The complexity of the verification procedures laid down by the Convention helps to explain its length (some 160 pages). In fact, the Convention has the most sophisticated verification system of any global disarmament treaty; indeed, a dedicated institution – the Organisation for the Prohibition of Chemical Weapons (OPCW) – was created by the Convention to oversee implementation of its obligations.

## Assisting prohibited activities

2.19   Global disarmament treaties typically outlaw assisting or encouraging others to commit prohibited acts. In the Chemical Weapons Convention, for instance, it is prohibited 'to assist, encourage or induce, in any way, anyone to engage in any activity prohibited' to a state party under the Convention. Similar provisions are contained in the Anti-Personnel Mine Ban Convention, the Convention on Cluster Munitions, and the Treaty on the Prohibition of Nuclear Weapons.

2.20  The precise scope of the prohibition on assisting, encouraging, or inducing is debated. It is, though, undoubtedly wide: in the context of the Chemical Weapons Convention, for instance, it is claimed that the undertaking 'never under any circumstances' to 'assist, encourage or induce, in any way, anyone' outlaws 'any action which contributes to prohibited activities'.[27] It is not finally settled whether the scope of the provision in the Convention extends to curtailing the financing of prohibited activities or to outlawing the transit of weapons across the sovereign territory of a state party. In certain other treaties, these activities are explicitly prohibited.

## Treaty withdrawal

2.21  Most treaties allow withdrawal by states parties in certain circumstances.[28] This is typically the case in both bilateral and multilateral disarmament treaties (see Box 2.1). According to the law of treaties, the withdrawal of a party may take place only where the treaty implicitly or explicitly allows it, such as where there is a material breach by another party, or with the consent of all the other states parties.[29]

2.22  Withdrawal means that a state is no longer bound by the provisions of the treaty[30] and is no longer considered a party to it. Withdrawal does not, however, 'affect any right, obligation or legal situation of the parties created through the execution of the treaty prior to its termination'.[31] Thus, for example, financial obligations accrued by a state while it was party to a treaty cannot be avoided by withdrawing, nor can an investigation that was initiated while the state was bound by the treaty.

2.23  If the withdrawing state had signed and ratified the treaty, it not only ceases to be a party, it is not even considered a signatory (see Box 1.1). It will, though, continue to be bound by any customary rules of international law that are codified in the treaty.[32] This is made explicit in the Anti-Personnel Mine Ban Convention whose Article 20(4) stipulates that: 'The withdrawal of a State Party from this Convention shall not in any way affect the duty of States to continue fulfilling the obligations assumed under any relevant rules of international law'.

27  Krutzsch and Trapp, *A Commentary on the Chemical Weapons Convention*, p. 15.
28  For instance, the UN Charter has no provision that allows a UN member state to withdraw from the Charter (and hence the United Nations).
29  Arts. 42, 54, and 56, Vienna Convention on the Law of Treaties; adopted at Vienna, 23 May 1969; entered into force, 27 January 1980 (1969 Vienna Convention on the Law of Treaties).
30  Art. 70(1)(a) and (2), 1969 Vienna Convention on the Law of Treaties.
31  Art. 70(1)(b) and (2), 1969 Vienna Convention on the Law of Treaties.
32  Art. 43, 1969 Vienna Convention on the Law of Treaties.

2.24    One of the most contentious withdrawals from a global weapons treaty in recent years has been that of the Democratic People's Republic of Korea (DPRK) from the NPT. On 10 January 2003, the DPRK announced that it was withdrawing from the NPT 'effective immediately' (despite the treaty's requirement for three months' notice), and that its withdrawal from the Treaty left it free from the binding force of its Safeguards Agreement with the International Atomic Energy Agency (IAEA).[33] In 1993, one day before the expiration of the three months' notice period, the DPRK had suspended its withdrawal from the NPT. As the UN Office for Disarmament Affairs observes, 'States parties to the Treaty continue to express divergent views regarding the status of the DPRK under the NPT'.[34]

2.25    In 2002, the United States of America withdrew from the 1972 Anti-Ballistic Missile Treaty (ABM Treaty) it had concluded with the erstwhile Soviet

---

### BOX 2.1    WITHDRAWAL FROM DISARMAMENT TREATIES

Each State Party to this Convention shall in exercising its national sovereignty have the right to withdraw from the Convention if it decides that extraordinary events, related to the subject matter of the Convention, have jeopardised the supreme interests of its country. It shall give notice of such withdrawal to all other States Parties to the Convention and to the United Nations Security Council three months in advance. Such notice shall include a statement of the extraordinary events it regards as having jeopardised its supreme interests.

*Article XIII(2), 1971 Biological Weapons Convention*

Each State Party shall, in exercising its national sovereignty, have the right to withdraw from this Convention if it decides that extraordinary events, related to the subject-matter of this Convention, have jeopardised the supreme interests of its country. It shall give notice of such withdrawal 90 days in advance to all other States Parties, the Executive Council, the Depositary and the United Nations Security Council. Such notice shall include a statement of the extraordinary events it regards as having jeopardised its supreme interests.

*Article XVI(2), 1992 Chemical Weapons Convention*

---

33 See, e.g., F.L. Kirgis, 'North Korea's Withdrawal from the Nuclear Nonproliferation Treaty', *Insights*, Vol. 8, No. 2 (24 January 2003), at: http://bit.ly/2D6Iru8.
34 UNODA, 'Democratic People's Republic of Korea: Accession to Treaty on the Non-Proliferation of Nuclear Weapons (NPT)', at: http://bit.ly/2CvGW7Q.

Each State Party shall, in exercising its national sovereignty, have the right to withdraw from this Convention. It shall give notice of such withdrawal to all other States Parties, to the Depositary and to the United Nations Security Council. Such instrument of withdrawal shall include a full explanation of the reasons motivating this withdrawal.

Such withdrawal shall only take effect six months after the receipt of the instrument of withdrawal by the Depositary. If, however, on the expiry of that six- month period, the withdrawing State Party is engaged in an armed conflict, the withdrawal shall not take effect before the end of the armed conflict.

The withdrawal of a State Party from this Convention shall not in any way affect the duty of States to continue fulfilling the obligations assumed under any relevant rules of international law.

*Article 20(2) to (4), 1997 Anti-Personnel Mine Ban Convention*

Each State Party shall, in exercising its national sovereignty, have the right to withdraw from this Convention. It shall give notice of such withdrawal to all other States Parties, to the Depositary and to the United Nations Security Council. Such instrument of withdrawal shall include a full explanation of the reasons motivating withdrawal.

Such withdrawal shall only take effect six months after the receipt of the instrument of withdrawal by the Depositary. If, however, on the expiry of that six-month period, the withdrawing State Party is engaged in an armed conflict, the withdrawal shall not take effect before the end of the armed conflict.

*Article 20(2) and (3), 2008 Convention on Cluster Munitions*

Each State Party shall, in exercising its national sovereignty, have the right to withdraw from this Treaty if it decides that extraordinary events related to the subject matter of the Treaty have jeopardised the supreme interests of its country. It shall give notice of such withdrawal to the Depositary. Such notice shall include a statement of the extraordinary events that it regards as having jeopardised its supreme interests.

Such withdrawal shall only take effect 12 months after the date of the receipt of the notification of withdrawal by the Depositary. If, however, on the expiry of that 12-month period, the withdrawing State Party is a party to an armed conflict, the State Party shall continue to be bound by the obligations of this Treaty and of any additional protocols until it is no longer party to an armed conflict.

*Article 17(2) and (3), 2017*
*Treaty on the Prohibition of Nuclear Weapons*

Union.[35] In 2018, the Trump administration declared that the United States would also be withdrawing from the 1987 Intermediate-Range Nuclear Forces Treaty (INF Treaty),[36] which had similarly been concluded with the Soviet Union.[37] According to Article XV(2) of the INF Treaty, the United States may withdraw if it decides that 'extraordinary events related to the subject matter of the treaty' have 'jeopardized its supreme interests'. It is obligated to give six months' notice in writing prior to withdrawal and to detail in a statement the extraordinary events that have led to its decision. It gave this notice in early February 2019, followed by Russia, meaning that the INF Treaty would effectively cease to exist in August 2019 unless their withdrawal was revoked.

**TABLE 2.1** Prohibitions in global disarmament treaties

| Treaty | Development | Production | Stockpiling | Transfer | Use | Assisting prohibited activities | Withdrawal notice period |
|--------|-------------|------------|-------------|----------|-----|---------------------------------|--------------------------|
| BWC | Yes | Yes | Yes | Yes | No | Yes | 3 months |
| CWC | Yes | Yes | Yes | Yes | Yes | Yes | 90 days |
| APMBC | Yes | Yes | Yes | Yes | Yes | Yes | 6 months★ |
| CCM | Yes | Yes | Yes | Yes | Yes | Yes | 6 months★ |
| TPNW | Yes | Yes | Yes | Yes | Yes | Yes | 12 months★ |

★ Or the end of the armed conflict, if on the expiry of the period the withdrawing state is engaged in an armed conflict.

**TABLE 2.2** Positive obligations in global disarmament treaties

| Treaty | Stockpile destruction | Destruction of used weapons | Environmental remediation | Victim assistance | Implementing legislation |
|--------|-----------------------|-----------------------------|---------------------------|-------------------|--------------------------|
| BWC | By 1975 | No | No | No | Yes |
| CWC | By 2012 | No | No | No | Yes |
| APMBC | 4 years from becoming party | Yes | No | Yes | Yes |

(*Continued*)

35  See, e.g., US Department of State, 'Treaty Between The United States of America and The Union of Soviet Socialist Republics on The Limitation of Anti-Ballistic Missile Systems (ABM Treaty)', at: https://bit.ly/2IVgl5m. The Russian Federation is bound as the state that continued the legal personality of the Soviet Union (as 'successor state').

36  Treaty Between the United States of America and the Union of Soviet Socialist Republics on the Elimination of Their Intermediate-Range and Shorter-Range Missiles; signed at Washington, DC, 8 December 1987; entered into force, 1 June 1988. The Russian Federation is bound as the successor state to the Soviet Union.

37  BBC, 'Russia Nuclear Treaty: Gorbachev Warns Trump Plan Will Undermine Disarmament', 21 October 2018, at: https://bbc.in/2ODVAkt.

**TABLE 2.2** (Continued)

| Treaty | Stockpile destruction | Destruction of used weapons | Environmental remediation | Victim assistance | Implementing legislation |
|---|---|---|---|---|---|
| CCM | 8 years from becoming party | Yes | No | Yes | Yes |
| TPNW | To be set by First Meeting of States Parties | No | Yes | Yes | Yes |

# 3
# DISARMAMENT, ARMS CONTROL, AND SECURITY

## Introduction

3.1 Disarmament is traditionally an element of both international and national security but also aims to strengthen individual 'human' security. This chapter articulates the context and role of disarmament in security affairs and its interrelationship with related processes, such as arms control and non-proliferation, as well as restrictions on the use of weapons during armed conflict. The chapter also describes the role of the United Nations (UN) system in disarmament and the global organisation's disarmament machinery.

## Arms races

3.2 States continue to rely on armaments to fulfil their security needs, often referring to their inherent right to self-defence, which is reflected in Article 51 of the 1945 UN Charter. While war can be caused by multiple factors, such as power transitions in the international system, domestic political factors, and/or the characteristics of decision-makers, debate continues as to whether arms acquisitions contribute to stabilising international relations among states or are themselves a cause of conflict and insecurity. According to the security dilemma, as long as states are armed and cannot easily distinguish between offensive and defensive military preparations, other states fear being attacked. Thus, the spiral model of war explains that states continue to arm themselves, thereby incentivising other states to increase their own armament efforts, thereby leading to an arms race. And when the means of warfare that states possess favour offensive strategies over defensive postures, arms races may be intensified.[1] Such militarisation and mutual fear may ultimately lead

---

1  See, e.g., K.A. Lieber, 'Grasping the Technological Peace: The Offense-Defense Balance and International Security', *International Security*, Vol. 25, No. 1 (Summer 2000), pp. 71–104.

to the outbreak of war between states involved in an arms race.[2] The First World War, which is generally characterised as an inevitable war that nobody actually wanted, is often cited as an example of such a scenario.

3.3    Disarmament and related measures can limit arms races by prohibiting the possession, acquisition, and supply of certain weapons and requiring their elimination. Thereby, the likelihood of conflict erupting may be reduced and the high financial costs associated with arms races can be obviated, while the potential for destruction in the event war does occur may be limited. While partial disarmament cannot fully achieve all these results, disarmament and arms control treaties have helped to limit the availability of weapons needed for surprise attacks (as evidenced by the 1987 Intermediate-Range Nuclear Forces Treaty (INF Treaty) between the then Soviet Union and the United States of America);[3] weapons systems that may alter the strategic context (such as the 1972 Anti-Ballistic Missile Treaty: the ABM Treaty);[4] and particularly destructive weapons (such as the 1971 Biological Weapons Convention[5] and the 1992 Chemical Weapons Convention[6]).

## Balance of power and deterrence

3.4    It is also argued that international stability may be achieved by maintaining a balance of power among states as well as through deterrence. The concept of balance of power foresees that unchecked states are inclined to attack other states.[7] Not only do they have the capacity to do so, but they also have an interest in fostering their national security and prosperity by enlarging their international influence. The outbreak of the Second World War is sometimes explained by the fact that Germany was not balanced by other, equally powerful states. Similarly, deterrence is the defence strategy that aims to prevent an attack by raising its costs so high that any rational decision-maker will refrain from an attack.[8] Effective deterrence relies on appropriate capabilities to respond to an attack, the credibility that an attack will

---

2  See, e.g., R. Jervis, 'Cooperation Under the Security Dilemma', *World Politics*, Vol. 30, No. 2 (January 1978), pp. 167–214.

3  Treaty Between the United States of America and the Union of Soviet Socialist Republics on the Elimination of Their Intermediate-Range and Shorter-Range Missiles; signed at Washington, DC, 8 December 1987; entered into force, 1 June 1988.

4  Treaty Between the United States of America and the Union of Soviet Socialist Republics on the Limitation of Anti-Ballistic Missile Systems (ABM Treaty); signed at Moscow, 26 May 1972; entered into force, 3 October 1972; United States withdrawal, 2002.

5  Convention on the Prohibition of the Development, Production and Stockpiling of Bacteriological (Biological) and Toxin Weapons and on their Destruction; opened for signature, 10 April 1972; entered into force, 25 March 1975.

6  Convention on the Prohibition of the Development, Production and Stockpiling of Development, Production, Stockpiling and Use of Chemical Weapons and on their Destruction; adopted at Geneva, 3 September 1992; entered into force, 29 April 1997.

7  See, e.g., D.H. Nexon, 'The Balance of Power in the Balance', *World Politics*, Vol. 61, No. 2 (2009), pp. 330–59.

8  See, e.g., T. Schelling, *Arms and Influence*, Yale University Press, New Haven, 1966.

be defended or retaliated against, and sustained command, control, and communication that convince a potential adversary of defensive readiness.

3.5   Deterrence may be applied to conventional weapons as well as to weapons of mass destruction (WMD). Nuclear deterrence foresees that an attack will be followed by retaliatory nuclear strikes. During the Cold War, US and Soviet policies foresaw mutually assured destruction (MAD) and nuclear brinkmanship. Current nuclear doctrines encompass 'graduated deterrence', with the use of nuclear weapons foreseen as a last resort, although the potential to inflict massive destruction on an enemy remains at the core of nuclear policies.[9] Given the complexities of developing or acquiring nuclear weapons, chemical weapons were oftentimes referred to as the poor man's deterrent.

3.6   According to this logic, weapons may actually have a stabilising effect on international relations and ensure states' national security. However, the appropriate balance of power and requisite level of deterrence are hard to assess and establish in practice. Moreover, misperceptions, miscalculations, and technical errors may still escalate crises and lead to the outbreak of war. In addition, WMD, in particular, may proliferate to states and non-state actors, potentially leading to new instability and threats. In this context, disarmament treaties allow states to reduce their holdings of particular weapons at an equal or otherwise agreed rate, thereby avoiding a perception of stockpile destruction amounting to a threat to their security. The full renunciation of certain types of weapons also precludes their proliferation. WMD-free zones are designed to eliminate the logic of a balance of power and deterrence in the context of WMD. Prior to its suspension as a result of US withdrawal, the ABM Treaty prohibited the development of weapons that could undermine nuclear deterrence by putting into doubt the effectiveness of retaliatory strikes.

## Humanitarian disarmament and human security

3.7   While strategies based on the potential to inflict massive destruction and suffering may be rational, they raise both security and ethical concerns. The suffering caused by vesicant (blistering) gases in the First World War, for example, led to a popular outcry against the entire class of chemical weapons. The nuclear bombing of Hiroshima and Nagasaki gave a sense of the devastation that such weapons could cause. In light of this context, disarmament seeks to assure that certain weapons are never used, even against soldiers. Disarmament treaties can also contribute to preventing human suffering by eliminating weapons, such as anti-personnel mines, which are indiscriminate or inflict excessive injuries when compared to the military utility.

3.8   In recent years, a number of states and non-governmental organisations (NGOs) have been promoting the concept of 'humanitarian disarmament', which

---

9   See, e.g., M. Kroenig, *Logic of American Nuclear Strategy: Why Strategic Superiority Matters*, Oxford University Press, Oxford, 2018.

is explicit about the moral impulse for disarmament based on the effects that result from a weapon's use.[10] Typically involving small and medium-power states, disarmament is seen as a means to codify and change the norms and standards for all states, with the ultimate aim of stigmatising certain weapons in the public conscience. To achieve this, states and NGOs seek to counter narratives related to the possession of certain weapons, such as the international prestige some states feel they garner by virtue of having acquired nuclear weapons.

3.9    Yet, since the end of the 20th century, inter-state armed conflict has become rare. Most conflicts are fought within states, and most violent deaths tend to occur outside conflict settings. In this context, human security emerged in the 1990s as a paradigm linking the security and safety of individuals to socio-economic development and respect for fundamental human rights.[11] Although this concept is difficult to operationalise without clear policy prescriptions,[12] a number of states and NGOs argue that human security is enhanced by banning weapons.[13] As such, disarmament can contribute to conflict prevention and resolution by limiting access to certain weapons that may fuel intra-state conflicts and enable terrorism and other human rights abuses. In war-torn societies, disarmament, demobilisation, and reintegration (DDR) programmes, discussed in Chapter 10, endeavour to facilitate the transition to peace by disarming former fighters and offering them peaceful social, economic, and even political alternatives.

## Conditions for disarmament

3.10    At the international level, disarmament generally requires cooperation, reciprocity, and a minimum level of trust. International disarmament law, whether through treaties or politically binding (soft law) agreements, is a valuable tool for establishing and maintaining these conditions. Confidence- and security-building measures, notably information exchange, which are usually enshrined in disarmament instruments, aim to counter states' fear of deception by other parties. New disarmament treaties may emerge for a range of reasons: because weapons or weapons systems are not, or cease to be, militarily useful; they are not technically feasible to develop or use; their costs of acquisition or maintenance are unaffordable; or insofar as they inflict harm that is widely deemed to be unacceptable.

---

10 See, e.g., M. Finaud, '"Humanitarian Disarmament": Powerful New Paradigm or Naive Utopia?', Research Series No. 21/17, Geneva Centre for Security Policy (GCSP), Geneva, at: http://bit. ly/2zc4n2q. See also UNIDIR's programme on 'Disarmament as Humanitarian Action: Making Multilateral Negotiations Work', at: http://bit.ly/2yFxBHM.
11 The term was popularised by the UN Development Programme (UNDP), which first coined the term in 1994 in its Human Development Report, *New Dimensions of Human Security*, at: http://bit. ly/2D9fOfL.
12 See, e.g., R. Paris, 'Human Security: Paradigm Shift or Hot Air?' *International Security*, Vol. 26, No. 2 (Fall 2001), pp. 87–102.
13 K. Boyle and S. Simonsen, 'Human Security, Human Rights and Disarmament', *Disarmament Forum*, No. 3 (2004), p. 11, at: http://bit.ly/2RjrW0U.

3.11   Traditionally, the conclusion of disarmament treaties was led and managed by the great powers. The disarmament regimes under the League of Nations and the UN Charter, for instance, were largely designed by the leading states of the given period. But over time, other states have increasingly sought to influence disarmament. In 1978, the Special Session of the UN General Assembly encouraged states to 'seek security in disarmament', affirming that 'enduring international peace and security cannot be built on the accumulation of weaponry by military alliances nor be sustained by a precarious balance of deterrence or doctrines of strategic superiority'.[14] The Assembly recommended 'the speedy and substantial reduction of arms and armed forces, by international agreement and mutual example'.[15]

3.12   Since the mid-1990s, transnational civil society networks have been active in advocating the development of new disarmament treaties.[16] Campaigns to ban anti-personnel mines, cluster munitions, and nuclear weapons have resulted in the negotiation and adoption of new treaties, primarily at the behest of coalitions of small and mid-ranking military powers, with the great powers largely absent from the process.

## Disarmament and the UN system

### United Nations Charter

3.13   Disarmament law in the modern world continues to be closely linked to and influenced by, as well as largely implemented with the support of, the UN system. One of the main purposes of the United Nations according to its Charter is to maintain international peace and security.[17] Thus, one of items on the agenda of the UN General Assembly's First Special Session on Disarmament was to review and appraise 'the present international situation in the light of the pressing need to achieve substantial progress in the field of disarmament, the continuation of the arms race and the close interrelationship between disarmament, international peace and security and economic development'.[18] Under the contemporary international legal order, primary responsibility for the maintenance of international peace and security is given to the UN Security Council,[19] with a supporting role accorded to the General Assembly.[20]

---

14 'Final Document of the Tenth Special Session of the Assembly', UN General Assembly Resolution S-10/2, 30 June 1978, para. 13.

15 Ibid.

16 See, e.g., C. Carpenter, 'Vetting the Advocacy Agenda: Network Centrality and the Paradox of Weapons Norms', *International Organization*, Vol. 65, No. 1 (2011), pp. 69–102.

17 Art. 1, UN Charter.

18 Agenda Item 9, UN General Assembly First Special Session on Disarmament, 1978.

19 Art. 24, UN Charter.

20 Art. 11, UN Charter.

## UN Security Council

3.14   The Security Council is specifically tasked with formulating plans, to be submitted to UN member states, for 'the establishment of a system for the regulation of armaments' with a view to promoting 'the establishment and maintenance of international peace and security with the least diversion for armaments of the world's human and economic resources'.[21] This 'system' has not yet been established, although the Council has adopted many measures that regulate armaments on a piecemeal basis, especially through arms embargoes vis-à-vis specific targets.

3.15   According to Chapter VII of the UN Charter, the Security Council

> may decide what measures not involving the use of armed force are to be employed to give effect to its decisions, and it may call upon the Members of the United Nations to apply such measures. These may include complete or partial interruption of economic relations.'[22]

As of 2018, mandatory arms embargoes were in place with respect to the governments of the Central African Republic,[23] Eritrea,[24] Iran,[25] Libya,[26] the Democratic People's Republic of Korea,[27] Somalia,[28] South Sudan,[29] and Sudan (for the Darfur region).[30] Further arms embargoes are imposed on non-state actors in a number of countries.[31]

3.16   The UN Charter also called for the creation of a Military Staff Committee (MSC) to advise and assist the Security Council on all questions relating to the Security Council's 'military requirements for the maintenance of international peace and security, the employment and command of forces placed at its disposal, the regulation of armaments, and possible disarmament'.[32] Although it is the longest standing subsidiary body of the Security Council, it is dormant. As the United Nations has itself observed,

---

21 Art. 26, UN Charter.
22 Art. 41, UN Charter.
23 UN Security Council Resolution 2127 of 5 December 2013.
24 UN Security Council Resolution 1907 of 23 December 2009.
25 UN Security Council Resolution 1737 of 23 December 2006.
26 UN Security Council Resolution 1970 of 26 February 2011.
27 UN Security Council Resolution 1718 of 14 October 2006.
28 UN Security Council Resolution 733 of 23 January 1992.
29 UN Security Council Resolution 2428 of 13 July 2018.
30 UN Security Council Resolution 1556 of 30 July 2004.
31 For a list of embargoes in place under European Union auspices, see, e.g., Stockholm International Peace Research Institute (SIPRI), 'SIPRI Databases: Arms Embargoes', undated but accessed 28 October 2018, at: http://bit.ly/2qhmqR2. See also *infra* para. 3.23.
32 Art. 47, UN Charter.

Cold War dynamics and the early rejection of an autonomous, permanent UN military force prevented the MSC from fulfilling its intended purpose of serving as the UN's global defence department. This evolutionary process has left the MSC in an advisory-only capacity with respect to the work of the Security Council.[33]

3.17 The Department of Peace Operations (DPO), the Department of Operational Support (D=S), and the Department of Political and Peacebuilding Affairs (DPPA) have placed the UN Secretariat, rather than the MSC, at the centre for the UN's military management activities. More important for disarmament activities is the Office for Disarmament Affairs (UNODA). Headed by the Under-Secretary-General and High Representative for Disarmament Affairs, UNODA supports negotiations, analysis, and implementation of disarmament treaties at the UN offices in New York, Geneva, and Vienna, as well as from regional centres in Kathmandu, Lima, and Lomé. Associated, but with a degree of autonomy from the UN, the Institute for Disarmament Research (UNIDIR) aims to contribute to international disarmament policy with expert research.[34]

## UN General Assembly

3.18 The General Assembly is authorised under the UN Charter to 'consider the general principles of cooperation in the maintenance of international peace and security, including the principles governing disarmament and the regulation of armaments'. The Assembly 'may make recommendations with regard to such principles to the Members or to the Security Council or to both'.[35] To date, the General Assembly has held three Special Sessions on disarmament (in 1978, 1982, and 1988), and since 1995 there have been calls for a fourth to be convened, most recently in Resolution 65/66 of 8 December 2010.[36] A number of disarmament treaties have been adopted by the UN General Assembly or under its auspices, including, in recent years, the 2013 Arms Trade Treaty[37] and the 2017 Treaty on the Prohibition of Nuclear Weapons. The work in its First Committee dedicated to 'Disarmament and International Security', traditionally throughout the entire month of October, serves as permanent and continuous basis for political dialogue and action among UN member states. The First Committee generally deals with around 50 to 70 draft resolutions, most of them recurring regularly, typically annually.

---

33 'United Nations Military Staff Committee', undated but accessed 17 December 2017, at: http://bit. ly/2EQaDTM.
34 See: http://unidir.org.
35 Art. 11(1), UN Charter.
36 The resolution was adopted by 178 votes to nil, with 5 abstentions.
37 Arms Trade Treaty; adopted at New York, 2 April 2013; entered into force, 24 December 2014.

### Conference on Disarmament

3.19    The Conference on Disarmament (CD), formerly the Committee on Disarmament (set up in 1979),[38] was designated as the principal multilateral disarmament negotiating forum by UN General Assembly Resolution S-10/2 of 30 June 1978.[39] It had 65 member states as of 2019,[40] with a further 45 observers in its 2018 session. The CD has a special relationship with the United Nations, adopting its own rules of procedure and agenda, but taking into account recommendations by the UN General Assembly. The CD is serviced by UNODA from the regular UN budget and reports annually to the General Assembly. The CD's permanent broad agenda (the Decalogue) was agreed upon in 1978 at the Assembly's first Special Session devoted to disarmament.[41] At each session, however, the CD is required to adopt a specific agenda based on the recommendations of the previous session of the UN General Assembly.[42] The CD conducts its work by consensus.

3.20    The CD and its predecessors negotiated the 1968 Treaty on the Non-Proliferation of Nuclear Weapons (NPT),[43] the 1976 ENMOD Convention,[44] the

---

38  It was renamed pursuant to General Assembly Resolution 37/99K of 13 December 1982.

39  The Conference succeeded the ten-state Committee on Disarmament (1960), the 18-state Committee on Disarmament (1962–68), and the Conference of the Committee on Disarmament (1969–78).

40  Algeria, Argentina, Australia, Austria, Bangladesh, Belarus, Belgium, Brazil, Bulgaria, Cameroon, Canada, Chile, China, Colombia, Cuba, the Democratic People's Republic of Korea, the Democratic Republic of Congo, Ecuador, Egypt, Ethiopia, Finland, France, Germany, Hungary, India, Indonesia, Iraq, Ireland, the Islamic Republic of Iran, Israel, Italy, Japan, Kazakhstan, Kenya, Malaysia, Mexico, Mongolia, Morocco, Myanmar, the Netherlands, New Zealand, Nigeria, Norway, Pakistan, Peru, Poland, the Republic of Korea, Romania, the Russian Federation, Senegal, Slovakia, South Africa, Spain, Sri Lanka, Sweden, Switzerland, the Syrian Arab Republic, Tunisia, Turkey, Ukraine, the United Kingdom, the United States, Venezuela, Viet Nam, and Zimbabwe. Since 1982, requests for membership have been received from 27 states (in chronological order): Greece, Croatia, Kuwait, Portugal, Slovenia, Czech Republic, Costa Rica, Denmark, The former Yugoslav Republic of Macedonia (now renamed the Republic of North Macedonia), Cyprus, Lithuania, Ghana, Luxembourg, Uruguay, the Philippines, Azerbaijan, Libya, Armenia, Thailand, Georgia, Jordan, Estonia, Latvia, Malta, Serbia, Moldova, and Qatar. 'Report of the Conference on Disarmament to the General Assembly of the United Nations', Doc. CD/2112, 22 September 2017, para. 24.

41  The permanent agenda includes the following issues: nuclear weapons in all aspects, other weapons of mass destruction, conventional weapons, reduction of military budgets, reduction of armed forces, disarmament and development, disarmament and international security, collateral measures, confidence-building measures, effective verification methods in relation to appropriate disarmament measures, acceptable to all parties, and a comprehensive programme of disarmament leading to general and complete disarmament under effective international control. A tenth issue relating to chemical weapons was removed following the conclusion of the Chemical Weapons Convention in 1992.

42  For the 2018 session, see Document CD/2116, at: http://bit.ly/2z7DkFH.

43  Treaty on the Non-Proliferation of Nuclear Weapons; opened for signature at London, Moscow, and Washington, DC, 1 July 1968; entered into force, 5 March 1970.

44  Convention on the Prohibition of Military or Any Other Hostile Use of Environmental Modification Techniques (ENMOD); adopted at New York, 10 December 1976; entered into force, 5 October 1978.

1971 Seabed Treaty,[45] the 1971 Biological Weapons Convention, the 1992 Chemical Weapons Convention, and the 1996 Comprehensive Nuclear-Test-Ban Treaty (CTBT).[46] Since the conclusion of the negotiation of the CTBT, however, when consensus within the Conference proved impossible to achieve, the CD has had a troubled history. There have been minimal deliberations on substance in the subsequent two decades, and widespread disagreement as to priorities, with certain states blocking discussions by seeking to link progress in one area to parallel progress in others.[47] Despite apparent new momentum, no consensus was reached on a programme of work for the 2017 session.[48] Expectations for the CD in 2019 and beyond, however, remained low.

### Disarmament and non-state actors

3.21   Disarmament of non-state actors has largely occurred through either peace agreements or by voluntary 'micro' disarmament of individuals associated with a non-state armed group, especially within DDR programmes. Such programmes are often promoted by the UN Security Council. For example, in 2017, with respect to disarmament of Boko Haram and Islamic State, Resolution 2349 encouraged governments in the Lake Chad Basin Region to

> develop and implement a regional and coordinated strategy that encompasses transparent, inclusive, human rights-compliant disarmament, demobilisation, de-radicalisation, rehabilitation and reintegration initiatives, in line with strategies for prosecution, where appropriate, for persons associated with Boko Haram and ISIL, drawing upon regional and international best practice and lessons learned.[49]

3.22   At the same time, arms embargoes, particularly those adopted by the UN Security Council, have sought to preclude horizontal proliferation by preventing non-state actors from acquiring new weapons. Mandatory arms embargoes imposed by the Security Council with respect to non-state actors and which remained in force as of 2018 were in respect of non-state actors operating in the following states:

---

45 Treaty on the Prohibition of the Emplacement of Nuclear Weapons and Other Weapons of Mass Destruction on the Sea-Bed and the Ocean Floor and in the Subsoil Thereof; opened for signature at London, Moscow, and Washington, DC, 11 February 1971; entered into force, 18 May 1972.

46 UN, 'Conference on Disarmament: An Introduction to the Conference', undated but accessed 17 December 2017 at: http://bit.ly/2EPqaDm.

47 NTI, 'Conference on Disarmament (CD)', Last updated 10 January 2018, at: http://bit.ly/2z7BxjN.

48 'Report of the Conference on Disarmament to the General Assembly of the United Nations', Doc. CD/2112, 22 September 2017, para. 20.

49 UN Security Council Resolution 2349, 31 March 2017, para. 29.

the Democratic Republic of Congo,[50] Iraq,[51] Lebanon,[52] and Yemen,[53] as well as the Taliban.[54] The embargoes generally require, at a minimum, the taking of the 'necessary measures to prevent the direct or indirect supply, sale or transfer of arms and any related material' to the designated armed groups and individuals.

3.23    The treaty regime prohibiting armed non-state actors' access to weapons of mass destruction and related material is fragmented. As a general rule, disarmament treaties do not apply directly to non-state actors. As a result of particular concern on the part of the United States of America, on 28 April 2004 the Security Council, acting under Chapter VII of the UN Charter, unanimously adopted Resolution 1540. The Resolution, which affirmed that the proliferation of nuclear, chemical, and biological weapons and their means of delivery constitute a threat to international peace and security, obligated all states to: 'refrain from providing any form of support to non-State actors that attempt to develop, acquire, manufacture, possess, transport, transfer or use nuclear, chemical or biological weapons and their means of delivery'.[55]

3.24    Under Resolution 1540, the Security Council also decided that:

> all States, in accordance with their national procedures, shall adopt and enforce appropriate effective laws which prohibit any non-State actor to manufacture, acquire, possess, develop, transport, transfer or use nuclear, chemical or biological weapons and their means of delivery, in particular for terrorist purposes, as well as attempts to engage in any of the foregoing activities, participate in them as an accomplice, assist or finance them.[56]

In total, the Resolution creates more than 200 legally binding obligations for each state, including reporting on measures undertaken.[57] A 1540 Committee, functioning as a subsidiary body of the Council, was established to promote effective implementation of the Resolution. Its current mandate was due to expire in 2021.[58]

---

50  UN Security Council Resolution 1493 of 28 July 2003. The arms embargo relates to 'all foreign and Congolese armed groups and militias operating in the territory of North and South Kivu and of Ituri, and to groups not party to the Global and All-inclusive agreement' (para. 20).
51  UN Security Council Resolution 661 of 6 August 1990, para. 3(c).
52  UN Security Council Resolution 1701 of 11 August 2006, para. 15.
53  UN Security Council Resolution 2216 of 14 April 2015, para. 14.
54  UN Security Council Resolution 1390, 16 January 2002.
55  UN Security Council Resolution 1540, 28 April 2004, para. 1. Means of delivery are defined 'for the purpose of this resolution only' as 'missiles, rockets and other unmanned systems capable of delivering nuclear, chemical, or biological weapons, that are specially designed for such use'.
56  UN Security Council Resolution 1540, para. 2.
57  The resolution reserves the 'rights and obligations' of the states parties to the main disarmament treaties, in particular the NPT. This has been interpreted by the five NPT nuclear-weapon states as authority to manufacture nuclear weapons (including by resorting to non-state actors, particularly private contractors).
58  Its mandate was extended first for two years by Security Council Resolution 1673 (2006) and then for a further three years by Resolution 1810 (2008). On 20 April 2011, the Council adopted Resolution 1977, which extends the mandate of the 1540 Committee for a period of ten years to

3.25   In 2013, the Security Council adopted Resolution 2117, its first thematic resolution on the issue of small arms and light weapons (SALW). The resolution focused on the illicit transfer, destabilising accumulation, and misuse of SALW, recognising that their use 'has resulted in grave crimes'. The Council reaffirmed the relevant provisions of the 2005 World Summit Outcome Document regarding the protection of civilians in armed conflict, including the responsibility to protect populations from genocide, war crimes, ethnic cleansing, and crimes against humanity.[59]

## Disarmament and arms control

3.26   Arms control is the managed limitation of armaments, especially bilaterally between major powers or rival military alliances, with a view to enhancing mutual security.[60] Confidence-building measures are at the core of arms control as they aim to reduce surprises, miscalculations, and misperceptions. Kierulf defines arms control in very broad terms as 'international agreements on measures to limit the effect and capacity of weapons, and the testing, production, storage, deployment, transfer, and use of weapons'.[61] In United States, Russian, and other states' literature, arms control is often used as a generic term meaning both disarmament and arms control.

3.27   Jozef Goldblat, in his 2002 treatise on arms control, describes it as encompassing a wide range of measures, including those intended to:

- Freeze, limit, reduce, or abolish certain categories of weapons
- Ban the testing of certain weapons
- Prevent certain military activities
- Regulate the deployment of armed forces
- Proscribe transfers of some militarily important items
- Reduce the risk of accidental war
- Constrain or prohibit the use of certain weapons or methods of war[fare]
- Build up confidence among states through greater openness in military matters.[62]

This is a very broad understanding of what arms control is, and certainly one that is broader than the approach taken in this book. 'Abolition' of weapons falls within

---

2021. The Resolution provides for two comprehensive reviews, one in 2016 and a second before the end of the mandate 'prior to the renewal of its mandate'. See, e.g., S. Casey-Maslen, 'Armed non-state actors and "nuclear terrorism"', Chap. 17 in G. Nystuen, S. Casey-Maslen, and A. Golden Bersagel (eds.), *Nuclear Weapons under International Law*, Cambridge University Press, Cambridge, 2014, p. 426ff.

59 UN Security Council Resolution 2117, 16th preambular paragraph.

60 See, on the definition of arms control, *supra* paras. 1.4 and 1.5.

61 J. Kierulf, *Disarmament under International Law*, Djof Publishing, 2017, p. 6.

62 J. Goldblat, *Arms Control: The New Guide to Negotiations and Agreements*, Sage, Thousand Oaks, CA, 2002, p. 348.

the realm of disarmament, while the use of weapons or methods of warfare is specifically addressed by the law of armed conflict.

3.28    Modern arms control emerged as a moniker to describe certain aspects of the relationship between the United States and the Soviet Union/Russia with regard to weapons. Arms control on conventional weapons – the 1990 Treaty on Conventional Armed Forces in Europe (CFE Treaty)[63] and the Vienna Document (both discussed below) – also included their European allies. US and Soviet officials initiated negotiations on nuclear arms control in the late 1960s. Nuclear arsenals already had reached such high levels that leaders came to the conclusion that mutual constraints advanced their interests, the policy of deterrence notwithstanding. The goal was to limit the risks and costs of unrestrained accumulation of weapons without hampering the 'balance of terror'.

3.29    Bilateral negotiations on the restrictions of strategic nuclear arsenals started in 1969 as Strategic Arms Limitation Talks, eventually leading to the adoption of the ABM Treaty in 1972. The 1972 SALT Interim Agreement (SALT I) paved the way for the 1979 US-Soviet Treaty on the Limitation of Strategic Offensive Arms (SALT II Treaty), which set ceilings for both parties on intercontinental ballistic missile (ICBM) launchers, submarine-launched ballistic missiles, heavy bombers, and long-range air-to-surface ballistic missiles. Although never ratified, the SALT II Treaty was effectively implemented until 1986 when the United States equipped a new heavy bomber with long-range cruise missiles.

3.30    The continuous development and deployment of intermediate- and short-range missiles led to the conclusion of the INF Treaty in 1987, which required the elimination of an entire category of weapons. It led to the removal from Europe and destruction of, in particular, Cruise and Pershing missiles by the United States and the multiple-warhead SS20 intermediate-range missiles by the Soviet Union. In 1991, the Treaty on the Reduction and Limitation of Strategic Offensive Arms (START I Treaty) and related documents led to reductions in the US and Soviet stockpiles of strategic offensive arms to mutually comparable levels. As such, it reduced their potential to launch a nuclear attack and established unprecedented measures of verification (while permitting qualitative improvements in nuclear arms technology). The 1993 US-Russia Treaty on Further Reduction and Limitation of Strategic Offensive Arms (START II Treaty) and its related documents established equal quantitative ceilings for the deployment of strategic nuclear weapons, but the treaty never entered into force due to the United States' refusal to ratify it.

3.31    Even though the United States withdrew from the ABM Treaty in 2002, Russia and the United States signed the Treaty on Strategic Offensive Reductions (SORT) that year. While the SORT Treaty reduced the risk of unauthorised or accidental nuclear war due to the reduction in the number of their nuclear warheads, it allowed both parties to rearrange or even produce new warheads and delivery systems. In February 2011, the SORT Treaty was superseded by the Treaty

---

63 Treaty on Conventional Armed Forces in Europe (CFE Treaty); signed, 19 November 1990; entered into force, 17 July 1992.

on Measures for the Further Reduction and Limitation of Strategic Offensive Arms (New START). This Treaty reduces the numbers of strategic nuclear missile launchers by each side and establishes new verification mechanisms. While the New START was expiring in 2021, at time of writing, no negotiations had begun on its extension or on the elaboration of any agreement between Russia and the United States to replace it. The following sections summarise some of the most significant arms control treaties.

## Treaty on Conventional Armed Forces in Europe

3.32   The CFE Treaty is an agreement that was negotiated during the final years of the Cold War and signed on 19 November 1990.[64] Once termed the 'cornerstone of European security', the Treaty eliminated the overwhelming numerical advantage the erstwhile Soviet Union enjoyed in conventional weapons, by setting equal limits on the amount of tanks, armoured combat vehicles, heavy artillery, combat aircraft, and attack helicopters that the North Atlantic Treaty Organization (NATO) and the Warsaw Pact could deploy on the European continent. The CFE Treaty was designed to prevent a lightning offensive that could have triggered the use of nuclear weapons in response.[65]

3.33   The CFE Treaty obligated, inter alia, that both NATO and the Warsaw Pact limit their forces across Europe to 20,000 battle tanks, 30,000 armoured combat vehicles, 20,000 artillery pieces, 6,800 combat aircraft, and 2,000 attack helicopters.[66] Weapons systems not in active units were required to be placed in designated permanent storage sites.[67] States parties were given the right to conduct inspections and were required to accept such inspections, in accordance with a Protocol on Inspection.[68] The Treaty also established a Joint Consultative Group to address questions relating to compliance with the Treaty.[69] Despite the end of the Cold War, states parties to the CFE Treaty (which number 30, although, as noted below, Russia has suspended its implementation of the agreement for more than a decade)[70] had stressed its continued value in setting weapons limits and providing for an inspection regime, 'which provides an unprecedented degree of transparency on military holdings'.[71]

---

64   Some commentators describe the CFE Treaty as an arms control agreement, while others deem it to be a disarmament treaty.
65   D. Kimball and K. Reif, 'The Conventional Armed Forces in Europe (CFE) Treaty and the Adapted CFE Treaty at a Glance', *Fact Sheet*, Arms Control Association, August 2012, at: http://bit.ly/2SqD1i6.
66   Art. IV(1), CFE Treaty.
67   Ibid.
68   Art. XIV, CFE Treaty.
69   Art. XVI, CFE Treaty.
70   Armenia, Azerbaijan, Belarus, Belgium, Bulgaria, Canada, the Czech Republic, Denmark, France, Georgia, Germany, Greece, Hungary, Iceland, Italy, Kazakhstan, Luxembourg, Moldova, the Netherlands, Norway, Poland, Portugal, Romania, the Russian Federation, Slovakia, Spain, Turkey, Ukraine, the United Kingdom, and the United States.
71   Kimball and Reif, 'The Conventional Armed Forces in Europe (CFE) Treaty and the Adapted CFE Treaty at a Glance'.

3.34    An adapted version of the Treaty was adopted at a conference in Istanbul in 1999, reflecting the reality of the dissolution of the Warsaw Pact, but the Adapted Treaty has never entered into force. At the same conference, Russia pledged, in the Istanbul Commitments, to withdraw its remaining military forces and equipment from Georgia and Moldova. NATO members refused to ratify the 1999 Adapted Treaty until Russia complied with those commitments. In December 2007, Russia announced it was suspending its implementation of the original Treaty. On 22 November 2011, the United States announced that, along with its NATO allies, Moldova and Georgia, it was ceasing to carry out certain obligations under the original CFE Treaty with regard to Russia.[72] As of writing, the CFE Treaty appeared moribund.

### Anti-Ballistic Missile Treaty

3.35    The 1972 ABM Treaty, which the United States and the Soviet Union concluded with a view to restraining their nuclear weapons arms race, is no longer in force. The Treaty barred Washington and Moscow from deploying nationwide defences against strategic ballistic missiles to ensure the continuation of the capabilities for mutually assured destruction by the two superpowers. The logic behind the Treaty was to prevent an arms race in seeking to attain numbers of weapons intended to overwhelm missile defences. The Treaty entered into force on 3 October 1972, but on 13 June 2002 – almost 30 years later – the United States withdrew from it. The United States claimed that the Treaty prevented US defences against terrorist or 'rogue state' missile attacks. US President George W. Bush argued that Washington and Moscow no longer needed to base their relationship on their ability to destroy each other.[73] Russia objected to US research and development of new anti-ballistic missile systems, however, and its concerns were behind the development of new nuclear-weapon systems. In June 2015, Russian President Vladimir Putin said that the unilateral US withdrawal from ABM Treaty was pushing Russia towards a new arms race.[74]

### Intermediate-Range Nuclear Forces Treaty

3.36    Signed by US President Ronald Reagan and Soviet leader Mikhail Gorbachev in 1987, the INF Treaty was, for a time, the only Cold War-era US-Soviet arms control agreement that remained in full force.[75] The Treaty required the United

---

72  NTI, 'Treaty on Conventional Armed Forces in Europe (CFE)', Last updated 29 September 2017, at: http://bit.ly/2qhmQXy.

73  D. Kimball and K. Reif, 'The Anti-Ballistic Missile (ABM) Treaty at a Glance', *Fact Sheet*, Arms Control Association, August 2012, at: http://bit.ly/2PmA8jN.

74  'Putin: Unilateral US Withdrawal from ABM Treaty Pushing Russia Toward New Arms Race', *RT*, 19 June 2015, at: http://bit.ly/2OTOt7V.

75  A. Panda, 'The Uncertain Future of the INF Treaty', Council on Foreign Relations, 25 October 2017, at: http://bit.ly/2Q0Y9tz.

States and the Soviet Union to eliminate all nuclear and conventional ground-launched ballistic and cruise missiles with ranges of between 500 and 5,500 kilometres. This was the first time the superpowers had agreed to reduce their nuclear arsenals, eliminate an entire category of nuclear weapons, and employ extensive on-site inspections for verification of compliance. As a result of the Treaty, the two parties destroyed a total of 2,692 short-, medium-, and intermediate-range missiles by the treaty's implementation deadline of 1 June 1991.[76] In October 2018, however, US President Donald Trump publicly announced that the United States of America would withdraw from the Treaty, citing violations by Russia and the absence – from a bilateral agreement between the United States and Russia – of China.[77] China's growing nuclear and conventional missile arsenal is mostly composed of weapons in the range prohibited by the INF Treaty.[78]

3.37   Prior to the US announcement of its intended withdrawal, the United States and Russia had, over the course of several years, each alleged material breaches of the INF Treaty by the other. In 2014, the US Department of State alleged that Russia had violated the obligation not to 'possess, produce, or flight-test' missiles prohibited by the treaty, though at the time it did not offer details of the alleged violation. In late November 2017, however, a senior US national security official stated that the Novator 9M729, a land-based cruise missile, was the weapon that constituted the violation.[79]

3.38   In mid-December 2017, NATO issued a public statement affirming that the Treaty had 'contributed to strategic stability and reduced the risk of miscalculation leading to conflict'. As such, the organisation noted, 'full compliance with the INF Treaty is essential' and it affirmed that it remained 'fully committed to the preservation of this landmark arms control treaty'. At the same time, it observed that 'a situation whereby the United States and other parties were abiding by the treaty and Russia were not – would be a grave and urgent concern'.[80]

3.39   For its part, Russia had alleged that the United States had violated the Treaty by deploying, in Romania, a component of a missile defence system – the Mark 41 Vertical Launch System (VLS) – that is capable of launching offensive missiles. It has also claimed that the United States had used prohibited missiles in defence tests and that some US armed drones were effectively unlawful cruise missiles.[81]

---

76 D. Kimball, 'The Intermediate-Range Nuclear Forces (INF) Treaty at a Glance', *Fact Sheet*, Arms Control Association, Updated October 2018, at: http://bit.ly/2EzzzPf.

77 BBC, 'Russia Nuclear Treaty: Gorbachev Warns Trump Plan Will Undermine Disarmament', 21 October 2018, at: https://bbc.in/2ODVAkt.

78 Ibid.

79 D. Majumdar, 'Novator 9M729: The Russian Missile that Broke INF Treaty's Back?', *The National Interest*, 7 December 2017, at: http://bit.ly/2P7C3bI.

80 Statement by the North Atlantic Council on the Intermediate-Range Nuclear Forces (INF) Treaty, Press Release (2017) 180, Issued 15 December 2017, at: http://bit.ly/2OzJFnY.

81 Kimball, 'The Intermediate-Range Nuclear Forces (INF) Treaty at a Glance'.

### Vienna Document and Treaty on Open Skies

3.40   The Vienna Document is a soft law instrument that was elaborated within the Organization for Security and Co-operation in Europe (OSCE). Originally concluded in 1990 in parallel to the CFE Treaty, and subsequently revised several times, the latest iteration of the Vienna Document is from 2011. This politically binding agreement, which is said to be the most important confidence- and security-building measure in the OSCE arena, provides for the exchange and verification of information about armed forces and military activities. It requires the 'Participating States' to provide each other annually with information on their military forces, including with respect to manpower and major conventional weapon and equipment systems as well as deployment plans and budgets. The Participating States must also notify each other in advance about major military activities such as exercises; accept up to three inspections of their military sites per year (though some sensitive areas are excluded); and consult and cooperate in case of unusual military activity or increasing tensions. The Vienna Document encourages Participating States to, for example, voluntarily host military visits with a view to dispelling any concerns that may exist among the concerned states.[82]

3.41   The 1992 Treaty on Open Skies[83] also establishes confidence and security-building measures among member states of the OSCE. The Treaty allows states parties to conduct short-notice, unarmed reconnaissance flights over other states' entire territories to collect data on military forces and activities. The treaty allows participation in overflights by other states than the overflying state. While all of a state party's territory can be overflown, no territory can be declared off-limits by the host nation.[84]

## Disarmament and non-proliferation

3.42   Non-proliferation seeks to prevent the spread of weapons, particularly weapons of mass destruction.[85] Non-proliferation also 'refers to all efforts to prevent proliferation from occurring, or should it occur, to reverse it by any other means than the use of military force'.[86] Proliferation is generally described as being either horizontal or vertical. Horizontal proliferation concerns the spread of weapons, materials, and technologies to states or non-state actors that did not previously possess them. Vertical proliferation refers to increases in the number, quality, or

---

82  See, e.g., OSCE, 'Ensuring Military Transparency – The Vienna Document', at: http://bit.ly/2F0YTOz.

83  Treaty on Open Skies; signed, 24 March 1992; entered into force, 1 January 2002.

84  D. Kimball, 'The Open Skies Treaty at a Glance', Fact Sheet, Arms Control Association, Updated October 2012, at: http://bit.ly/2G7AmYD.

85  NATO, 'Arms Control, Disarmament and Non-Proliferation in NATO', last updated 22 May 2017.

86  NATO's Comprehensive, Strategic-Level Policy for Preventing the Proliferation of Weapons of Mass Destruction (WMD) and Defending Against Chemical, Biological, Radiological and Nuclear (CBRN) Threats, 1 September 2009, at: http://bit.ly/2OcxY1c.

destructive capacity of existing arsenals of weapons.[87] Prevention and reversal of vertical proliferation is a main objective of disarmament.

3.43   The most significant horizontal non-proliferation treaty is the NPT, which, as discussed below, prohibits the five nuclear-weapon states designated under the Treaty from transferring nuclear weapons (or other nuclear explosive devices) to anyone. In turn, the non-nuclear-weapon states parties undertake not to acquire such weapons or devices. Also legally binding (at least on UN member states) is UN Security Council Resolution 1540, cited above, which obliges all member states to establish appropriate export controls to prevent the proliferation of WMD with a view to preventing non-state actors from getting hold of such weapons. With respect to conventional weapons, the 2013 Arms Trade Treaty establishes legally binding standards regarding transfers, seeking to prevent the supply of a very broad range of conventional weapons to those who would or might use them unlawfully.

3.44   The politically binding export control regimes of the Nuclear Suppliers Group and the Australia Group support the implementation of the BWC, the CWC, and the NPT by coordinating national export controls of dual-use items that may be used to develop WMD. The 1987 Missile Technology Control Regime (MTCR) limits access to technologies that are necessary for the construction of delivery systems. Also politically binding is the Wassenaar Arrangement regime, which helps to coordinate export controls on conventional weapons and dual-use items among the major exporting states.

### Nuclear Non-Proliferation Treaty

3.45   The NPT is the principal international treaty designed to limit the spread of nuclear weapons beyond the five 'nuclear-weapon states' (see below). Since its entry into force in 1970, the Treaty has become almost universal in application, comprising 190 states parties (or 191 if one includes DPR Korea, which on 10 January 2003 announced its withdrawal in circumstances that continue to be contested). Of the other UN member states, only India, Israel, Pakistan, and South Sudan have, to date, not adhered to the NPT.

3.46   The five nuclear-weapon states recognised by the NPT – China, France, Russia, the United Kingdom, and the United States – are not prohibited from acquiring the material necessary for their nuclear weapons programmes from non-nuclear-weapon states. The Treaty does not address the operational deployment of nuclear weapons. Yet, according to Article 6 of the NPT, all states parties are obliged to 'pursue negotiations in good faith on effective measures relating to cessation of the nuclear arms race at an early date and to nuclear disarmament, and on a treaty on general and complete disarmament under strict and effective international control'. The interpretation and application of this provision is the subject of dispute between the nuclear-weapon states and many non-nuclear-weapon states.

---

87 Kierulf, *Disarmament under International Law*, p. 6.

3.47   Under the NPT, non-nuclear-weapon states parties are prohibited from ever acquiring or developing nuclear weapons. They do have the right to research, develop, and use nuclear energy for peaceful purposes as well as to receive related information and material from all other states to that end. The NPT mandates the International Atomic Energy Agency (IAEA) to inspect non-nuclear-weapon states' facilities in order to verify their compliance with the Treaty. For this purpose, safeguards agreements covering plutonium and uranium and other fissile material along with equipment for their processing, use, or production are concluded between the non-nuclear-weapon states and the IAEA. The more intrusive IAEA Additional Protocol expands the confidence that material is not being diverted to the production of nuclear weapons. In 1995, the states parties to the NPT decided to indefinitely extend the duration of the Treaty, which had initially been limited to 25 years.

### Nuclear Suppliers Group and the Zangger Committee

3.48   The Nuclear Suppliers Group (NSG),[88] which first met in London in 1975, is a group of 48 nuclear supplier nations[89] that seek to prevent proliferation of nuclear weapons through implementation of two sets of guidelines for nuclear exports and nuclear-related exports.[90] The NSG was established after India's first testing of a nuclear explosive device in May 1974 and serves to support the implementation of the NPT. The NSG Guidelines contain the 'Non-Proliferation Principle', adopted in 1994, whereby a supplier authorises a transfer only when it is satisfied that it would not contribute to the proliferation of nuclear weapons. The Principle 'seeks to cover the rare but important cases' where adherence to the NPT or to a Nuclear-Weapon-Free Zone Treaty 'may not by itself be a guarantee that a State will consistently share the objectives of the Treaty or that it will remain in compliance with its Treaty obligations'.[91] The Permanent Mission of Japan to the International Organisations in Vienna, acting as a Point of Contact, provides practical support to the NSG.

3.49   The earlier Zangger Committee, an informal intergovernmental group meeting in Vienna and whose establishment in 1971 preceded the NSG,[92] defined

---

88  See: http://bit.ly/2QUjGEq.

89  The 48 supplier states are: Argentina, Australia, Austria, Belarus, Belgium, Brazil, Bulgaria, Canada, China, Croatia, Cyprus, the Czech Republic, Denmark, Estonia, Finland, France, Germany, Greece, Hungary, Iceland, Ireland, Italy, Japan, Kazakhstan, the Republic of Korea, Latvia, Lithuania, Luxembourg, Malta, Mexico, the Netherlands, New Zealand, Norway, Poland, Portugal, Romania, the Russian Federation, Serbia, Slovakia, Slovenia, South Africa, Spain, Sweden, Switzerland, Turkey, Ukraine, the United Kingdom, and the United States of America.

90  Nuclear Suppliers Group, 'About the NSG', at: http://bit.ly/2qhp49q.

91  Ibid.

92  The Committee was set up because of France's decision, at the time, not to adhere to the NPT. W. Burr, 'The Making of the Nuclear Suppliers Group, 1974–1976', Wilson Center, 16 April 2014, at: http://bit.ly/2Avpsa0.

which transfers of 'especially designed or prepared equipment or material for the processing, use or production of special fissionable material' covered by Article III(2) of the NPT were to be controlled. It also ensured that items transferred to non-nuclear-weapon states would remain subject to IAEA safeguards. Although both institutions remain formally distinct, the NSG – of which all states of the Zangger Committee are members – has effectively taken over the Committee's activities.

## Australia Group

3.50   The Australia Group, which usually meets in Paris (even though its Secretariat is based in Australia), is a politically binding regime which, through the harmonisation of export controls, seeks to ensure that exports do not contribute to the development of biological or chemical weapons.[93] As such, it aims to support the implementation of the Biological and Chemical Weapons Conventions. The Australia Group was established after the use of chemical weapons in the Iran-Iraq war in the 1980s. The 43 members of the Group (42 states and the European Union) aim to ensure that legitimate trade in sensitive dual-use goods and technology is not diverted to biological or chemical weapons production.[94] All participants have licensing measures on 63 chemical weapons precursors. Participants also require licences for the export of specific dual-use chemical manufacturing facilities, equipment, and related technology; plant pathogens; animal pathogens; biological agents; and dual-use biological equipment and related technology.[95]

## Missile Technology Control Regime and the Hague Code of Conduct

3.51   Established in April 1987, the MTCR[96] aims to limit the spread of ballistic missiles and other unmanned delivery systems that could be used for biological, chemical, or nuclear attacks.[97] The non-legally binding regime urges its 35 participating states – known as 'Partners'[98] – which include most of the major missile

---

93 See: http://bit.ly/2CNuWyJ. The following states are members: Argentina, Australia, Austria, Belgium, Bulgaria, Canada, Croatia, the Republic of Cyprus, the Czech Republic, Denmark, Estonia, Finland, France, Germany, Greece, Hungary, Iceland, India, Ireland, Italy, Japan, Latvia, Lithuania, Luxembourg, Malta, Mexico, the Netherlands, New Zealand, Norway, Poland, Portugal, Romania, Slovakia, Slovenia, South Korea, Spain, Sweden, Switzerland, Turkey, Ukraine, the United Kingdom, the United States, and the European Union.
94 Statement by the Chair of the 2017 Australia Group Plenary, 30 June 2017, at: http://bit.ly/2Rkm8El.
95 Australia Group, 'Activities', at: http://bit.ly/2z5YuE6.
96 See: http://bit.ly/2yCbSAq.
97 K. Davenport, 'The Missile Technology Control Regime at a Glance', Fact Sheet, Updated July 2017, at: http://bit.ly/2yLAOFV.
98 Argentina, Australia, Austria, Belgium, Brazil, Bulgaria, Canada, the Czech Republic, Denmark, Finland, France, Germany, Greece, Hungary, Iceland, India, Ireland, Italy, Japan, Luxembourg, the Netherlands, New Zealand, Norway, Poland, Portugal, Russia, South Africa, South Korea, Spain, Sweden, Switzerland, Turkey, Ukraine, the United Kingdom, and the United States.

manufacturers, to restrict their exports of missiles and related technologies. There is no formal secretariat for the MTCR, although France serves as its point of contact. The MTCR Guidelines define the purpose, overall structure and elements to guide member states' export control decisions related to all items covered by the Equipment, Software, and Technology Annex.

3.52   The MTCR identifies five factors that Partners should take into account when evaluating a possible export of controlled items: whether the intended recipient is pursuing or has ambitions for acquiring weapons of mass destruction; the purposes and capabilities of the intended recipient's missile and space programmes; the potential contribution the proposed transfer could make to the intended recipient's development of delivery systems for weapons of mass destruction; the credibility of the intended recipient's stated purpose for the purchase; and whether the potential transfer conflicts with any multilateral treaty.[99]

3.53   The Equipment, Software, and Technology Annex is divided into 'Category I' and 'Category II' items, with the first of the two categories demanding more restraint in transfer than the second. Category I items include 'complete rocket systems (including ballistic missiles, space launch vehicles and sounding rockets) and unmanned air vehicle systems (including cruise missiles systems and target and reconnaissance drones) with capabilities exceeding a 300 km/500 kg range/payload threshold; production facilities for such systems; and major sub-systems including rocket stages, re-entry vehicles, rocket engines, guidance systems, and warhead mechanisms. Category II items, which include complete rocket systems (including ballistic missiles systems, space launch vehicles, and sounding rockets) and unmanned air vehicles (including cruise missile systems, target drones, and reconnaissance drones) not covered in item I, capable of a maximum range equal to or greater than 300 km. Also included is a wide range of equipment, material, and technologies, most of which have uses other than for missiles capable of delivering WMD.[100]

3.54   The Hague Code of Conduct against Ballistic Missile Proliferation (HCoC), an initiative of the MTCR Partners, was established on 25 November 2002 to prevent the proliferation of ballistic missiles capable of carrying WMD. The HCoC establishes transparency and confidence-building instruments: member states commit themselves politically to provide pre-launch notifications (PLNs) on ballistic missile and space launch vehicle launches (SLVs) and test flights. States also commit themselves to submit an annual declaration (AD) of their country's policies on ballistic missiles and space launch vehicles.[101] In contrast to the MTCR, the HCoC does not limit its membership to exporting states. At time of writing, 139 states had joined HCoC. Austria serves as the Immediate Central Contact

---

99 Davenport, 'The Missile Technology Control Regime at a Glance'.

100 Missile Technology Control Regime, 'MTCR Guidelines and the Equipment, Software and Technology Annex', at: http://bit.ly/2RlbEo5.

101 The International Code of Conduct against Ballistic Missile Proliferation, at: http://bit.ly/2PrAsO9.

(Executive Secretariat), which coordinates the information exchange and organises the annual meetings of member states.

## Arms Trade Treaty

3.55   The Arms Trade Treaty (ATT), which is variously considered a non-proliferation and an arms control regime, was adopted on 2 April 2013 by the UN General Assembly. The ATT sets standards for the regulation of international arms transfers. The Treaty aims to reduce human suffering caused by irresponsible and illegal arms transfers, to improve international and regional security and stability, and to promote transparency regarding conventional arms transfers. A core obligation under the ATT is the establishment of national authorities that control international transfers of conventional weapons.[102] Similarly, states need to maintain national lists of items that are subject to transfer control.[103]

3.56   The ATT prohibits certain arms transfers[104] and establishes criteria that need to be fulfilled for authorising weapons exports.[105] The Treaty also provides mechanisms for the prevention and combating of diversion, notably unauthorised re-exports and illicit trafficking of weapons.[106] In addition to requirements for recording, the ATT obliges states parties to report on their measures to implement the Treaty as well as to submit annual reports on weapon imports and exports or authorisations for such imports or exports.[107]

## Wassenaar Arrangement

3.57   The Wassenaar Arrangement on Export Controls for Conventional Arms and Dual-Use Goods and Technologies is a multilateral export control regime with 42 'Participating States', including all the major exporters of conventional weapons. The Wassenaar Arrangement arose out of the end of the Cold War. The Coordinating Committee for Multilateral Export Controls (CoCom) was the informal multilateral organisation through which the United States of America and its allies sought to coordinate national controls over export of strategic materials and technology to the Communist world. Following the end of the Cold War, CoCom's members recognised that the institution was no longer fit for purpose and that a new mechanism was needed to address risks 'related to the spread of conventional weapons and dual-use goods and technologies'.[108]

---

102 Art. 5(2), ATT.
103 Ibid.
104 Art. 6, ATT.
105 Art. 7, ATT.
106 Art. 11, ATT.
107 Art. 13, ATT.
108 Wassenaar Arrangement, 'Genesis of the Wassenaar Arrangement', 3 October 2015, at: http://bit. ly/2zbcXPj.

3.58    Formal agreement to establish the Wassenaar Arrangement was reached at a meeting on 19 December 1995. Agreement was reached to site the secretariat in Vienna. At the inaugural plenary meeting on 2–3 April 1996, the founding members adopted the 'Initial Elements', including the List of Dual-Use Goods and Technologies and the Munitions List,[109] which became active on 1 November 1996. Best practice, such as 'Elements for Objective Analysis and Advice concerning Potentially Destabilising Accumulations of Conventional Weapons' and 'Best Practices for Effective Legislation on Arms Brokering', guides the implementation of national export controls and export decisions by participating states. All Wassenaar Arrangement documents are adopted by the plenary meeting, which convenes every year in December in Vienna. Guiding documents are developed and updated by the General Working Group, which generally meets twice a year.

3.59    The Munitions List and the List of Dual-Use Goods and Technologies are regularly updated by the Expert Group. Military items are divided into 22 categories, ranging from small arms to heavy weapons systems and ammunition. Nine categories are covered by the List of Dual-Use Goods and Technologies: (1) Special Materials and Related Equipment, (2) Materials Processing, (3) Electronics, (4) Computers, (5) Telecommunications (Part 1) and 'Information Security' (Part 2), (6) Sensors and 'Lasers', (7) Navigation and Avionics, (8) Marine, and (9) Aerospace and Propulsion. Some of the items contained in the nine categories are listed on a 'Sensitive List' while others are included on a 'Very Sensitive List', which require 'a more vigilance' approach prior to any export.[110]

## Disarmament and the law of armed conflict

3.60    Traditionally, disarmament law and the law of armed conflict were strictly separated, with the law of armed conflict addressing the *use* of weapons and disarmament law stipulating the measures that would lead to the elimination of particular weapons (e.g. a prohibition on development, production, and transfer combined with an obligation to destroy existing stockpiles).[111] The law of armed conflict (LOAC), also widely known as international humanitarian law (IHL), governs acts committed during and in connection with armed conflicts, imposing limits on the destruction and suffering that may be wrought by the parties to an armed conflict. There are both general and specific prohibitions on use of weapons under the rules on the 'conduct of hostilities' (the term used in the law of armed conflict/IHL to describe

109  The latest versions of the Wassenaar Arrangement 'List of Dual-Use Goods and Technologies' and 'Munitions List' are at: http://bit.ly/2OWA6j5.

110  See, e.g., Ambassador Philip Griffiths, Head of Secretariat, Wassenaar Arrangement on Export Controls for Conventional Arms and Dual-Use Goods and Technologies, 'Updates from the Wassenaar Arrangement', SMi Twelfth Annual Conference, Defence Exports, Rome, 27–28 September 2017, at: http://bit.ly/2CL4lCa.

111  In a number of cases, however, disarmament treaties have built on and expanded existing law of armed conflict treaty prohibitions on the use of a weapon as a means or method of warfare. This is the case with the 1992 Chemical Weapons Convention, for instance.

the fighting), as detailed in Chapter 4. The requirement under the law of armed conflict to conduct legal reviews of weapons is discussed in Chapter 5.[112] An important law of armed conflict treaty addressing conventional weapons, discussed at the end of this chapter, is the 1980 Convention on Certain Conventional Weapons.[113]

## Classification of armed conflicts

3.61   Two classifications of armed conflict exist under LOAC/IHL: international armed conflict[114] and non-international armed conflict.[115] A valuable and widely cited[116] general definition of these two categories was offered by the Appeals Chamber of the International Criminal Tribunal for the former Yugoslavia (ICTY) in a 1995 decision in the *Tadić* case:

> an armed conflict exists whenever there is a resort to armed force between States [i.e. international armed conflict] or protracted armed violence between governmental authorities and organized armed groups or between such groups within a State [i.e. non-international armed conflict].[117]

Political science definitions of armed conflict, such as the one used by Uppsala University,[118] have no basis in international law.

---

112  See *infra* para. 5.21.

113  See *infra* paras. 3.71–3.72.

114  The notion was first reflected in Article 2 common to the 1949 Geneva Conventions, which, as discussed below, provides as follows:

> the present Convention shall apply to all cases of declared war or of any other armed conflict which may arise between two or more of the High Contracting Parties, even if the state of war is not recognized by one of them. . . . The Convention shall also apply to all cases of partial or total occupation of the territory of a High Contracting Party, even if the said occupation meets with no armed resistance.

115  The term was first employed in Article 3 common to the 1949 Geneva Conventions but was not defined.

116  See, e.g., US Department of Defense, *Law of War Manual*, June 2015, updated December 2016, §3.4.2.2 note 74, at: http://bit.ly/2JlHY7C; United Kingdom (UK) Ministry of Defence, *The Manual of the Law of Armed Conflict*, Oxford University Press, Oxford, 2005, §3.3; French Ministry of Defence, *Manuel de Droit des Conflits Armés*, 2012, pp. 33, 34, at: http://bit.ly/2Dbsm6H.

117  ICTY, *Prosecutor v. Tadić (aka 'Dule')*, Decision on the Defence Motion for Interlocutory Appeal on Jurisdiction (Appeals Chamber) (Case No. IT-94-1), 2 October 1995, para. 70, at: http://bit.ly/2JkqZ5z. See also International Committee of the Red Cross (ICRC), 'How Is The Term "Armed Conflict" Defined in International Humanitarian Law?', ICRC Opinion Paper, March 2008, at: http://bit.ly/2CLr9Sc; and S. Vité, 'Typology of Armed Conflicts in International Humanitarian Law: Legal Concepts and Actual Situations', *International Review of the Red Cross*, Vol. 91, No. 873 (March 2009), pp. 69–94, at: http://bit.ly/2Aw8TLm.

118  The Uppsala Conflict Data Program defines an armed conflict as

> a contested incompatibility that concerns government and/or territory over which the use of armed force between the military forces of two parties, of which at least one is the government of a state, has resulted in at least 25 battle-related deaths each year.

3.62   Article 2 common to the four 1949 Geneva Conventions applies to declared war or 'any other armed conflict' between two or more states parties, 'even if the state of war is not recognized by one of them'. These are both forms of *international armed conflict*. Common Article 2 further stipulates that the Conventions also apply to all cases of partial or total occupation of the territory of a state party, 'even if the said occupation meets with no armed resistance'. Such foreign military occupation is also a form of international armed conflict.[119] An additional scenario for an international armed conflict is when, in effect, one state attacks another by means of a proxy armed group operating under its 'effective control', rather than with its own armed forces.

3.63   To amount to a *non-international armed conflict*, any given situation must involve regular and intense armed combat either between state armed forces and an organised non-state armed group, or between two or more organised non-state armed groups. All non-international armed conflicts are regulated by Common Article 3 to the 1949 Geneva Conventions and customary law rules on the conduct of hostilities. The 1977 Additional Protocol II to the Geneva Conventions also regulates the use of force in certain non-international armed conflicts where the armed opposition group controls territory within a state party.

3.64   The intensity of the violence is the first criterion to assess in any situation of armed violence. Non-international armed conflicts are not 'situations of internal disturbances and tensions, such as riots, isolated and sporadic acts of violence and other acts of a similar nature'.[120] In cases before the ICTY, the Tribunal tended to consider especially the number and severity of clashes in deciding whether armed violence had been sufficiently intense for an armed conflict to exist. In its judgment in the *Mrkšić* case, for instance, an ICTY trial chamber referred to 'the seriousness of attacks and potential increase in armed clashes, their spread over territory and over a period of time'.[121] In its judgment in the *Haradinaj* case, the ICTY stated that indicative factors for an armed conflict include 'the number, duration and intensity of individual confrontations'.[122] This notion of combat – direct conflict between two opposing armed groups – is particularly important, helping to distinguish a situation of armed conflict from one of other armed violence.[123]

---

Definitions, sources and methods for Uppsala Conflict Data Program Battle-Death estimates, Uppsala Conflict Data Program, Department of Peace and Conflict Research, Uppsala University, Sweden, at: http://bit.ly/2z7GTLV.

119  The Elements of Crimes established under the International Criminal Court (ICC) provide that 'the term 'international armed conflict' includes military occupation'. ICC, 'Elements of crimes', UN doc. PCNICC/2000/1/Add.2 (2000), note 34.

120  See, e.g., Art. 1(2), Protocol Additional to the Geneva Conventions of 12 August 1949, and Relating to the Protection of Victims of Non-International Armed Conflicts (Protocol II), of 8 June 1977 (1977 Additional Protocol II to the Geneva Conventions).

121  See, e.g., ICTY, *Prosecutor v. Mile Mrkšić, Miroslav Radić, and Veselin Šljivančin*, Judgment (Trial Chamber II) (Case No. IT-95–13/1-T), 27 September 2007, para. 407, and sources cited in note 1592.

122  ICTY, *Prosecutor v. Haradinaj*, Judgment (Trial Chamber) (Case No. IT-04–84-T), 3 April 2008, para. 49.

123  *The War Report* argued that the requirement that there be actual combat was a third criterion for a non-international armed conflict to exist. Here it is subsumed into the criterion of intensity, as

3.65   To be party to an armed conflict, the armed group or groups engaged in the fighting must be sufficiently 'organised'. This means that such groups are a military or paramilitary force with a martial-style hierarchy, and that some of the members are equipped with, at the very least, firearms. They must be capable of mounting military operations, but they do not need to possess uniforms, nor do they ordinarily need to control territory.

## Principles of the law of armed conflict

3.66   The law of armed conflict is suffused by a number of general principles that underpin the rules. Most notably, these include the principle of humanity and the principle of military necessity.[124] With respect to the conduct of hostilities, the core general principles (which are also customary rules) include distinction and proportionality in attack as well as the prohibition on the use of means or methods of warfare that are of a nature to cause superfluous injury or unnecessary suffering (the unnecessary suffering rule).

3.67   The principle of humanity prescribes that under all circumstances persons must receive humane treatment, even when no specific rule of the law of armed conflict is applicable. This is reflected in the Martens Clause, which is contained in the 1977 Additional Protocol I, stating that 'civilians and combatants remain under the protection and authority of the principles of international law derived from established custom, from the principles of humanity and from the dictates of public conscience'.[125] While there is no direct application of the Martens Clause to weapons,[126] some argue that weapons which are contrary to the public conscience, namely ethical concerns, should be prohibited.

3.68   The principle of military necessity is largely a permissive principle, which allows destructive actions that are required to achieve a legitimate military purpose in an armed conflict. Any destruction beyond that necessity will be unlawful. The principles of humanity and military necessity combine in the unnecessary suffering rule. It is widely agreed that prohibitions on the use of poison, expanding bullets, exploding bullets, and blinding laser weapons as means of warfare, among others, reflect this rule.

3.69   The principle of distinction obligates parties to an armed conflict to distinguish between combatants and civilians as well as between military objectives

---

per the approach of the ICTY. See S. Casey-Maslen (ed.), *The War Report: Armed Conflict in 2013*, Oxford University Press, Oxford, 2014, p. 19.

124  J. Pictet, *Development and Principles of International Humanitarian Law*, Martinus Nijhoff, Geneva, 1985, p. 59.

125  Preambles of Hague Convention No. II of 1899, Hague Convention No. IV of 1907 and the CCW. The clause is also reflected in GC I–IV, Arts 63/62/142/158 and Art. 1(2), 1977 Additional Protocol I; and fourth preambular paragraph to the 1977 Additional Protocol II.

126  However, see the claim made by the International Court of Justice in its 1996 Advisory Opinion on the Legality of the Threat or Use of Nuclear Weapons, that the Martens Clause 'has proved to be an effective means of addressing the rapid evolution of military technology'. International Court of Justice, *Legality of the Threat or Use of Nuclear Weapons*, Advisory Opinion, 8 July 1996, para. 78.

and civilian objects in all their military operations and to attack only combatants and military objectives. Weapons that cannot distinguish according to the principle of distinction (indiscriminate weapons) are unlawful. Besides WMD, anti-personnel mines and cluster munitions have been prohibited by disarmament treaty because of their indiscriminate effects.

3.70    The principle of proportionality requires that, even when the attack targets a legitimate military objective, expected incidental civilian harm (death or injury or damage to civilian objects and the environment) should not be excessive when compared to the concrete and direct military advantage anticipated.[127]

## Convention on Certain Conventional Weapons

3.71    The Convention on Certain Conventional Weapons[128] (also known as, by some, as the Inhumane Weapons Convention), prohibits or restricts the use of specific types of weapons that may cause unnecessary suffering to combatants or have indiscriminate effects, putting civilians at risk.[129] The Convention on Certain Conventional Weapons is a framework agreement that allows for flexibility over time. While the Convention only contains general provisions, the respective Protocols prohibit or restrict the use of specific weapons. To adhere to the Convention, a state must ratify both the Convention and at least two of the Protocols. Currently covered are weapons whose primary effect is to leave 'undetectable' fragments in the human body (Protocol I); mines, booby-traps, and other devices (Protocol II and Amended Protocol II); incendiary weapons (Protocol III); blinding laser weapons (Protocol IV); and explosive remnants of war (Protocol V).

3.72    Membership of the Convention on Certain Conventional Weapons includes most of the world's major weapons producers and users. All meetings related to the Convention are convened by the UN Office at Geneva and supported by the Geneva branch of UNODA.[130] Further protocols on specific weapons may be negotiated by the states parties to the Convention. Discussions – but not formal negotiations – have concerned anti-vehicle mines, the use of explosive weapons in populated areas, the use of improvised explosive devices, and lethal autonomous weapons systems.

127 See Art. 51(5)(b), 1977 Additional Protocol I.
128 Convention on Prohibitions or Restrictions on the Use of Certain Conventional Weapons Which May Be Deemed to Be Excessively Injurious or to Have Indiscriminate Effects; adopted at Geneva, 10 October 1980; entered into force, 2 December 1983; and amended on 21 December 2001 to apply also to non-international armed conflict.
129 UN Office at Geneva (UNOG), The Convention on Certain Conventional Weapons, at: http://bit.ly/2O9InuF.
130 See, e.g., UNOG, 'Disarmament', at: http://bit.ly/2O9IBSx.

# 4

# USE AND THREAT OF USE

## Introduction

4.1    This chapter explains how disarmament treaties address the use of weapons. Prohibitions under the law of armed conflict (LOAC)/international humanitarian law (IHL) apply to the conduct of hostilities during situations of armed conflict.[1] Disarmament law, however, typically outlaws use of weapons at all times: during peacetime[2] and during armed conflict. The chapter also describes the exceptional cases in which disarmament treaties have addressed, in some form, threat of use of weapons.

4.2    In most instances, global disarmament treaties – those that prohibit the development, production, stockpiling, and transfer of a weapon and require its destruction – also outlaw directly the weapon's use by the state and its agents (and require its use by any person under its jurisdiction or control to be made illegal by a state party's domestic law). A ban on use may be explicitly included even if

---

1   See Chapter 3 for a discussion of the scenarios and criteria that exist under international law for the existence of an armed conflict.

2   Peacetime is not formally defined in international law, although the 1949 Geneva Conventions imply that it means all situations other than armed conflict. Article 2 common to the Geneva Conventions stipulates, in part, that:

> In addition to the provisions which shall be implemented in peacetime, the present Convention shall apply to all cases of declared war or of any other armed conflict which may arise between two or more of the High Contracting Parties, even if the state of war is not recognized by one of them.

Peacetime seemingly encompasses 'situations of internal disturbances and tensions, such as riots, isolated and sporadic acts of violence and other acts of a similar nature', as the 1977 Additional Protocol II notes that they are not armed conflicts. Art. 1(2), Protocol Additional to the Geneva Conventions of 12 August 1949, and Relating to the Protection of Victims of Non-International Armed Conflicts (Protocol II), of 8 June 1977 (1977 Additional Protocol II to the Geneva Conventions).

an existing prohibition exists under the law of armed conflict/IHL, because a prohibition on use in a disarmament treaty is usually broader in scope, applying also during peacetime or to operations during an armed conflict that do not amount to the conduct of hostilities. This means, in particular, that the prohibition will apply to use of the weapon during a law enforcement operation. This is certainly the case with respect to the 1997 Anti-Personnel Mine Ban Convention[3] and the 2008 Convention on Cluster Munitions.[4] In contrast, the 1992 Chemical Weapons Convention[5] allows use of certain chemical agents, such as riot control agents (e.g. pepper spray, tear gas), in law enforcement. Often, a prohibition on use in a disarmament treaty will be underpinned by measures of verification and enforcement.[6]

4.3    Not all disarmament treaties explicitly prohibit use, however. The 1987 Intermediate-Range Nuclear Forces (INF) Treaty[7] required the United States and the Soviet Union to 'eliminate' all nuclear and conventional ground-launched ballistic and cruise missiles with ranges of between 500 and 5,500 kilometres and 'not have such systems thereafter'. As is the case with the 1971 Biological Weapons Convention[8] (see below), the INF Treaty does not contain an explicit prohibition on use, although this may be implied by virtue of the prohibition on possession or retention.[9]

4.4    Non-proliferation treaties do not, directly at least, regulate use of weapons. But by preventing regimes or terrorists gaining access to weapons or related technologies, such treaties can help to prevent the use of the weapons they cover. This is certainly the case with the 1968 Treaty on the Non-Proliferation of Nuclear Weapons (NPT),[10] which seeks to prevent all but the five nuclear-weapon states

---

3  Art. 1(1)(a), Convention on the Prohibition of the Use, Stockpiling, Production and Transfer of Anti-Personnel Mines and on their Destruction; adopted at Oslo, 18 September 1997; entered into force, 1 March 1999.

4  Art. 1(1)(a), Convention on Cluster Munitions; adopted at Dublin, 30 May 2008; entered into force, 1 August 2010.

5  Convention on the Prohibition of the Development, Production, Stockpiling and Use of Chemical Weapons and on their Destruction; adopted at Geneva, 3 September 1992; entered into force, 29 April 1997.

6  Verification is a term that denotes the range of methods used to assess whether a state party to a treaty is complying with its obligations. Verification may be intrusive or non-intrusive. Compliance means respect by a state party to a treaty with its obligations under that treaty (or under broader international law). Enforcement means coercive measures to promote compliance by a state party to a treaty with its international obligations.

7  Treaty Between the United States of America and the Union of Soviet Socialist Republics on the Elimination of Their Intermediate-Range and Shorter-Range Missiles; signed at Washington, DC, 8 December 1987; entered into force, 1 June 1988.

8  Convention on the Prohibition of the Development, Production and Stockpiling of Bacteriological (Biological) and Toxin Weapons and on their Destruction; opened for signature, 10 April 1972; entered into force, 25 March 1975.

9  Russia apparently disputes this interpretation, believing that use while destruction was ongoing would have been lawful. Information provided orally and in writing by Professor Bakhtiyar Tuzmukhamedov, Vice-President of the Russian Association of International Law, Geneva, 18 September 2018.

10  Treaty on the Non-Proliferation of Nuclear Weapons; opened for signature at London, Moscow, and Washington, DC, 1 July 1968; entered into force, 5 March 1970.

designated under the treaty from acquiring any nuclear explosive devices.[11] The 2013 Arms Trade Treaty[12] may also be said to indirectly prevent use of weapons contrary to international human rights law or the law of armed conflict/IHL.[13]

## The definition of use

4.5   Several, but not all, global disarmament treaties prohibit use, though none defines it. New employment of a prohibited weapon in the conduct of hostilities – for example by dropping a bomb or firing a missile or a rocket against an enemy target – is clearly at the heart of the notion. Employment of a prohibited weapon during a law enforcement operation also falls within the notion of use.

4.6   Use may, however, be broader in scope, at least with respect to certain weapons. As noted in the introduction to this Guide, for instance, it has been argued in the context of the 1997 Anti-Personnel Mine Ban Convention that the treaty prohibition on use encompasses not only new employment by a state party but may also extend to the act of taking operational advantage of the presence of anti-personnel mines that were laid at an earlier stage. This is so, even if the original emplacement was by the forces of another state or even by a non-state actor.[14]

4.7   At the same time, however, state practice suggests that employment under controlled conditions with a view to enhancing clearance or remediation approaches is either not to be considered use at all or it is not a prohibited use. Such eventualities are foreseen in the Anti-Personnel Mine Ban Convention and the Convention on Cluster Munitions.[15] There is also the challenge of distinguishing the testing of a weapon from its use, especially when the activation of the weapon occurs extraterritorially. In particular, the effects of a weapon of mass destruction could seriously affect the territory of another state. This issue is discussed further in Chapter 5.

## Global disarmament treaties' prohibitions on use

4.8   The first global disarmament treaty concluded by states was the Biological Weapons Convention in 1971. The preamble to the Convention had noted the determination of the states parties, 'for the sake of all mankind, to exclude

---

11 See, *supra*, paras. 3.44–3.46.

12 Arms Trade Treaty; adopted at New York, 2 April 2013; entered into force, 24 December 2014.

13 See Arts. 6 and 7, 2013 Arms Trade Treaty.

14 S. Maslen, *Commentary on the 1997 Anti-Personnel Mine Ban Convention*, Oxford University Press, Oxford, 2003, paras. 1.22–1.27.

15 Art. 3(1), 1997 Anti-Personnel Mine Ban Convention; Art. 3(6) and (8), 2008 Convention on Cluster Munitions. Paragraph 8 of Article 3 of the Convention on Cluster Munitions obligates states parties that retain or acquire cluster munitions or explosive submunitions for the purpose of 'the development of and training in cluster munition and explosive submunition detection, clearance or destruction techniques, or for the development of cluster munition counter-measures' to 'submit a detailed report on the planned and actual *use* of these cluster munitions and explosive submunitions and their type, quantity and lot numbers' (emphasis added).

completely the possibility of bacteriological (biological) agents and toxins being used as weapons', along with their conviction 'that such use would be repugnant to the conscience of mankind and that no effort should be spared to minimise this risk'. The Convention's operative provisions, though, do not include an explicit prohibition on use.

4.9    Under Article I of the Convention, states parties undertake 'never in any circumstances' to 'develop, produce, stockpile or otherwise acquire or retain' biological weapons.[16] In 1996, states parties included in the Final Declaration of the Convention's fourth review conference the affirmation that use is 'effectively prohibited under Article I of the Convention'.[17] During the Conference, Iran had put forward a proposal to amend the Biological Weapons Convention to explicitly prohibit use.[18] In December 2017, states parties to the 1998 Rome Statute of the International Criminal Court (ICC) amended the Statute to give the Court potential jurisdiction over the war crime of using biological weapons.[19]

### Chemical weapons

4.10    The use in warfare of asphyxiating or poisonous gases,[20] such as chlorine or sulphur mustard, was first prohibited in the 1899 Hague Declaration (IV,2),[21] a law of armed conflict treaty applicable in international armed conflict (see below). Despite the prohibition, chemical weapons were widely used against combatants during the First World War. In 1925, a new protocol was negotiated at a conference held in Geneva under the auspices of the League of Nations. The preamble to what is generally known as the 1925 Geneva Protocol noted the intention of its

16  Use is mentioned in a number of instances in the preamble to the Convention, among others by reference to the 1925 Geneva Protocol (see below). In that protocol, states parties agreed to extend an existing prohibition on the use of chemical warfare to 'the use of bacteriological methods of warfare'. Protocol for the Prohibition of the Use of Asphyxiating, Poisonous or Other Gases, and of Bacteriological Methods of Warfare; adopted at Geneva, 17 June 1925; entered into force, 8 February 1928 (1925 Geneva Protocol).

17  Fourth Review Conference of the Parties to the 1971 Biological Weapons Convention, Geneva, 25 November–6 December 1996, UN doc. BWC/CONF.4/9, Final Declaration, Commentary on Article I, para. 3.

18  'A proposal for amending the Convention to incorporate therein the explicit "Prohibition of the Use of Biological Weapons", Submitted by the Islamic Republic of Iran, 1996, at: http://bit.ly/2Qa0zWI. The Final Declaration of the Fourth Review Conference took note of the proposal and recommended it for consideration by states parties.

19  The amendments apply to both international armed conflict (Art. 8(2)(b)(xxvii), ICC Statute) and non-international armed conflict (Art. 8(2)(e)(xvi)).

20  The United States Department of Defense classifies chemical agents as 'persistent', 'non-persistent', or 'dusty'. Based on their effects on the body, there are six major types of chemical agent: nerve, blood, blister, choking, psychochemical, and irritants. US Department of Defense, *Field Manual 3–3 – Chemical and Biological Contamination Avoidance*, 1992, Chap. 3 (Chemical Agents), at: http://bit.ly/2Q2qMXv.

21  Declaration (IV,2) concerning the Use of Asphyxiating or Deleterious Gases; adopted at The Hague, 29 July 1899; entered into force, 4 September 1900.

states parties to ensure that the pre-existing prohibition of the use of 'asphyxiating, poisonous or other gases, and of all analogous liquids materials or devices' would become 'universally accepted as a part of International Law, binding alike the conscience and the practice of nations'. However, subsequent reservations by more than 20 states parties largely reduced the Protocol to a ban only on first use.

4.11    It took a further 67 years to transform the law of armed conflict prohibition on use of the most toxic chemical weapons into the global disarmament treaty – the 1992 Chemical Weapons Convention – that prohibits all use of chemical weapons in the conduct of hostilities.[22] According to Article I(1)(b) of the Convention, each state party 'undertakes never under any circumstances' to 'use chemical weapons'. But while the use of riot control agents, such as tear gas, is specifically prohibited as a method of warfare, the Convention allows use of chemical agents for law enforcement ('including domestic riot control'), 'as long as the types and quantities are consistent with such purposes'.[23]

4.12    Despite Syria's accession to the Chemical Weapons Convention in October 2013, chemical weapons (specifically chlorine and sarin, a nerve agent)[24] have continued to be used on many occasions during the manifold armed conflicts that, as of writing, had persisted across Syria.[25] In May 2018, the Fact-Finding Mission of the Organisation for the Prohibition of Chemical Weapons (OPCW), which verifies compliance with the Convention, reported that chlorine had been used as a chemical weapon on 4 February 2018 in Saraqib in Idlib governorate. The OPCW Fact-Finding Mission determined that chlorine was released from cylinders by mechanical impact in a neighbourhood in Saraqib.[26]

## Anti-personnel mines

4.13    Since 1980, the use of all landmines during armed conflict has been governed by the Protocol II to the 1980 Convention on Certain Conventional Weapons, a

---

22 Their use as a method of warfare in armed conflict is also prohibited under customary international law. Furthermore, use of chemical weapons is a war crime for which potential jurisdiction is given to the ICC through the prohibition of 'employing asphyxiating, poisonous or other gases, and all analogous liquids, materials or devices'. Art. 8(2)(b)(xviii) and 8(2)(e)(xiv), ICC Statute.

23 Arts. I(5), II(1)(a), and II(9), 1992 Chemical Weapons Convention.

24 At the end of June 2017, for example, a report by the Organisation for the Prohibition of Chemical Weapons (OPCW) confirmed that sarin had been diffused on 4 April 2017 in the Khan Shaykhun area of Idlib province. 'OPCW Fact-Finding Mission Confirms Use of Chemical Weapons in Khan Shaykhun on 4 April 2017', OPCW, 30 June 2017, at: http://bit.ly/2qjdH0p.

25 The Independent International Commission of Inquiry on the Syrian Arab Republic confirmed at least 34 chemical attacks in 2013–18, many of which used chlorine or sarin, and were conducted by the Syrian government. S. Almukhtar, 'Most Chemical Attacks in Syria Get Little Attention: Here Are 34 Confirmed Cases', *The New York Times*, 13 April 2018, at: http://bit.ly/2Q3c2rl. For a timeline of chemical weapons in Syria over the past seven years, see, e.g., 'Timeline of Syrian Chemical Weapons Activity, 2012–2018', Arms Control Association, at: http://bit.ly/2Sqa5Xv.

26 OPCW, 'OPCW Fact-Finding Mission Confirms Likely Use of Chlorine in Saraqib, Syria', Press release, 16 May 2018, at: http://bit.ly/2Roqw5r.

law of armed conflict treaty.[27] In 1996, an Amended Protocol II was adopted by states parties to the Convention,[28] a response to the 'epidemic' of landmine injuries[29] occurring in many nations long after the end of armed conflict.[30] In what was at the time a rare departure from established practice for the law of armed conflict, the Amended Protocol prohibits not only the use of certain anti-personnel mines that are deemed unacceptable, but also their transfer.[31] The prohibitions address hard-to-detect anti-personnel mines as well as remotely delivered anti-personnel mines (e.g. those fired by artillery or dropped from aircraft) that fail to meet the technical specifications for self-destruction and self-deactivation, which are set out in a technical annex.[32]

4.14    On 3 May 1996, at the closing assembly of the UN diplomatic conference that adopted the Amended Protocol, Canada announced that it would host a meeting of like-minded states in Ottawa to discuss how to achieve a total ban on anti-personnel mines. This meeting, in October 1996, resulted in the initiation of a stand-alone, fast-track negotiation of a comprehensive prohibition of anti-personnel mines outside UN auspices, known as the Ottawa Process. The process culminated with the adoption in Oslo in September 1997 of the Anti-Personnel Mine Ban Convention, the first global disarmament treaty outlawing a conventional weapon.

4.15    The core of the new disarmament treaty was based primarily on wording adapted from the Chemical Weapons Convention. Article 1 prohibits all use, development, production, acquisition, stockpiling, retention, and transfer of anti-personnel mines. In contradistinction to the Chemical Weapons Convention, however, there was no pre-existing treaty prohibition of the use of anti-personnel mines as a means or method of warfare. This is reflected in the fact that the first

27 Convention on Prohibitions or Restrictions on the Use of Certain Conventional Weapons Which May Be Deemed to Be Excessively Injurious or to Have Indiscriminate Effects; adopted at Geneva, 10 October 1980; entered into force, 2 December 1983 (Convention on Certain Conventional Weapons).

28 Protocol on Prohibitions or Restrictions on the Use of Mines, Booby-Traps and Other Devices as amended on 3 May 1996 (Amended Protocol II), annexed to the Convention on Certain Conventional Weapons; adopted at Geneva, 3 May 1996; entered into force, 3 December 1998.

29 See, e.g., ICRC, 'Stopping the Landmines Epidemic: From negotiation to action', 1 July 1996, at: http://bit.ly/2qgo7hq.

30 See, e.g., R.M. Coupland and R. Russbach, 'Victims of Antipersonnel Mines: What Is Being Done?', *Medicine & Global Survival*, Vol. 1 (1994), p. 18.

31 All anti-personnel mines produced after 1 January 1997 must

> incorporate in their construction a material or device that enables the mine to be detected by commonly-available technical mine detection equipment and provides a response signal equivalent to a signal from 8 grammes or more of iron in a single coherent mass.

CCW Amended Protocol II, Technical Annex, para. 2(a).

32 No more than 1 in 10 activated mines may fail to self-destruct within 30 days after emplacement, and each mine shall have a back-up self-deactivation feature with the result that, in combination with the self-destruction mechanism, 'no more than one in one thousand activated mines will function as a mine 120 days after emplacement'. 1996 Amended Protocol II, Technical Annex, para. 3(a).

sub-paragraph of Article 1(1) of the Anti-Personnel Mine Ban Convention obligates each state party never under any circumstances to use anti-personnel mines. This prohibition on use applies at all times, not merely during armed conflict, and in all circumstances, including during law enforcement or in self-defence, even to an act of aggression.

## Cluster munitions

4.16   This new comprehensive prohibition on use of a conventional weapon under international law was replicated in 2008 in the Convention on Cluster Munitions. Without an existing prohibition on their use under the law of armed conflict, each state party undertakes 'never under any circumstances' to use cluster munitions.[33] As

---

### BOX 4.1   GLOBAL DISARMAMENT TREATIES AND PROHIBITIONS ON USE

#### Explicit prohibitions on use

Each State Party to this Convention undertakes never under any circumstances: . . . (b) To use chemical weapons. . .
*Article I(1), 1992 Chemical Weapons Convention*

Each State Party undertakes never under any circumstances: . . . a) To use anti-personnel mines. . .
*Article 1(1), 1997 Anti-Personnel Mine Ban Convention*

Each State Party undertakes never under any circumstances to: . . . (a) Use cluster munitions. . .
*Article 1(1), 2008 Convention on Cluster Munitions*

Each State Party undertakes never under any circumstances to: . . . (d) Use or threaten to use nuclear weapons or other nuclear explosive devices. . . .
*Article 1(1), 2017 Treaty on the Prohibition of Nuclear Weapons*

#### Implicit prohibition on use

Each State Party to this Convention undertakes never in any circumstances to develop, produce, stockpile or otherwise acquire or retain. . .
*Article I, 1971 Biological Weapons Convention*

---

33 Art. 1(1)(a), 2008 Convention on Cluster Munitions.

with the Anti-Personnel Mine Ban Convention, the corresponding treaty prohibition on the use of cluster munitions applies at all times, including peacetime, and in all circumstances, including in self-defence, even when cluster munitions are used against a state party by an adversary.[34] This is so whether or not the user state is also a party to the Convention on Cluster Munitions.

### Nuclear weapons

4.17    In its 1996 Advisory Opinion on the Threat or Use of Nuclear Weapons, the International Court of Justice (ICJ) held, by 11 votes to 3, that no comprehensive and universal prohibition of the use of nuclear weapons 'as such' existed in customary international law.[35] By the most slender majority,[36] the Court did find, however, that the use of nuclear weapons 'would generally be contrary to the rules of international law applicable in armed conflict, and in particular the principles and rules of humanitarian law'.[37]

4.18    In the 2017 Treaty on the Prohibition of Nuclear Weapons (not yet in force, as of writing),[38] each state party undertakes never under any circumstances to use nuclear weapons or other nuclear explosive devices.[39] In the preamble to the Treaty, states parties consider 'that any use of nuclear weapons would be contrary to the rules of international law applicable in armed conflict, in particular the principles and rules of international humanitarian law'.[40]

4.19    It has also been proposed in the UN General Assembly on a number of occasions that a treaty on the non-use of nuclear weapons be elaborated as a precursor to comprehensive nuclear disarmament. India, which has submitted resolutions to the Assembly in this sense, has declared it is 'ready to join multilateral negotiations to endorse its commitment to no-first-use and non-use of nuclear weapons against non-nuclear weapons states in legally binding agreements'.[41] Such a step-by-step approach, which underpins the 'taboo' on first use of nuclear weapons, has been suggested as one way to bring the nuclear weapons powers towards a process of nuclear disarmament.[42] On 4 December 2017, the UN General Assembly adopted Resolution 72/38 in which it called upon the nuclear-armed states,

---

34 Mines are excluded from the purview of the Convention: Art. 1(3), 2008 Convention on Cluster Munitions.

35 ICJ, *Legality of the Threat or Use of Nuclear Weapons*, Advisory Opinion, 8 July 1996, dispositif B.

36 The result was 7 votes to 7, adopted with the president's casting vote.

37 ICJ, *Legality of the Threat or Use of Nuclear Weapons*, Advisory Opinion, 8 July 1996, dispositif E.

38 Treaty on the Prohibition of Nuclear Weapons; adopted at New York, 7 July 2017; not yet in force.

39 Art. 1(1)(d), 2017 Treaty on the Prohibition of Nuclear Weapons.

40 Tenth preambular paragraph, 2017 Treaty on the Prohibition of Nuclear Weapons.

41 Permanent Mission of India to the UN in New York, 'India and United Nations: Disarmament', at: http://bit.ly/2JmGzhg.

42 A. Gill, 'Taking the Path of Delegitimization to Nuclear Disarmament', Working Paper, Centre for a New American Security, Stanford, April 2009, at: http://bit.ly/2OZg8UX.

'pending the achievement of the total elimination of nuclear weapons, to agree on an internationally and legally binding instrument on a joint undertaking not to be the first to use nuclear weapons'.[43]

## General regulation of use of weapons under the law of armed conflict

4.20   The law of armed conflict governs the conduct of hostilities by the parties to an armed conflict. As noted above, in some cases, a disarmament treaty has built on an existing law of armed conflict treaty prohibition of the use of a weapon as a means or method of warfare during armed conflict. Both general and specific prohibitions apply to the use of weapons under the rules on the conduct of hostilities.

### Indiscriminate weapons

4.21   The rule of distinction (also termed a principle in light of its importance) is the most fundamental of the rules governing the conduct of hostilities. It holds that all parties to any armed conflict, whether state or non-state, must direct their military operations only against lawful military objectives (military personnel or objects of concrete military value)[44] and never against the civilian population, individual civilians, or civilian objects. The rule of distinction in attack was first unequivocally expressed by treaty law in the 1977 Additional Protocol I (which applies in international armed conflicts).[45] The basic rule, as set out in the Protocol, is as follows:

> In order to ensure respect for and protection of the civilian population and civilian objects, the Parties to the conflict shall at all times distinguish between the civilian population and combatants and between civilian objects and military objectives and accordingly shall direct their operations only against military objectives.[46]

---

43  UN General Assembly Resolution 72/38 adopted on 4 December 2017 by 119 votes to 41, with 20 abstentions, para. 9.

44  According to Article 52(2) of the Protocol Additional to the Geneva Conventions of 12 August 1949, and Relating to the Protection of Victims of International Armed Conflicts (Protocol I), of 8 June 1977 (hereafter, 1977 Additional Protocol I):

> In so far as objects are concerned, military objectives are limited to those objects which by their nature, location, purpose or use make an effective contribution to military action and whose total or partial destruction, capture or neutralization, in the circumstances ruling at the time, offers a definite military advantage.

45  See, in particular, Arts. 48–57, 1977 Additional Protocol I.

46  Art. 48, 1977 Additional Protocol I.

## BOX 4.2   SELECTED SPECIFIC LAW OF ARMED CONFLICT TREATY PROHIBITIONS ON USE

The Contracting Parties engage mutually to renounce, in case of war among themselves, the employment by their military or naval troops of any projectile of a weight below 400 grammes, which is either explosive or charged with fulminating or inflammable substances.

*1868 St Petersburg Declaration*

The Contracting Powers agree to abstain from the use of projectiles the sole object of which is the diffusion of asphyxiating or deleterious gases.

*1899 Hague Declaration (IV,2) on the*
*Use of Asphyxiating Gases*

The Contracting Parties agree to abstain from the use of bullets which expand or flatten easily in the human body, such as bullets with a hard envelope which does not entirely cover the core or is pierced with incisions.

*1899 Hague Declaration (IV,3) concerning Expanding Bullets*

Whereas the use in war of asphyxiating, poisonous or other gases, and of all analogous liquids, materials or devices, has been justly condemned by the general opinion of the civilized world; and Whereas the prohibition of such use has been declared in Treaties to which the majority of Powers of the world are Parties;

That the High Contracting Parties, so far as they are not already Parties to Treaties prohibiting such use, accept this prohibition, agree to extend this prohibition to the use of bacteriological methods of warfare and agree to be bound as between themselves according to the terms of this declaration.

*1925 Geneva Protocol*

It is prohibited in all circumstances to use any mine, booby-trap or other device which is designed or of a nature to cause superfluous injury or unnecessary suffering.

It is prohibited to use mines, booby-traps or other devices which employ a mechanism or device specifically designed to detonate the munition by the presence of commonly available mine detectors as a result of their magnetic or other non-contact influence during normal use in detection operations.

*Article 3(3) and (5), 1996 Amended Protocol II*
*to the Convention on Certain Conventional Weapons*

> It is prohibited to employ laser weapons specifically designed, as their sole combat function or as one of their combat functions, to cause permanent blindness to unenhanced vision, that is to the naked eye or to the eye with corrective eyesight devices. The High Contracting Parties shall not transfer such weapons to any State or non-State entity.
>
> *Article 1, 1995 Protocol IV on Blinding Laser Weapons*
> *to the Convention on Certain Conventional Weapons*

4.22    In addition to restricting the use of weapons in all military operations, whether offensive or defensive in nature,[47] the rule of distinction means that the use of any weapon that is 'incapable' of distinguishing between military targets and civilian objects is unlawful. The ICJ described this as a 'cardinal' principle in its 1996 Advisory Opinion on the Legality of the Threat or Use of Nuclear Weapons.[48] In 2005, the International Committee of the Red Cross (ICRC)'s study of customary international humanitarian law concluded that 'the use of weapons which are by nature indiscriminate is prohibited'.[49] This customary rule is applicable in all armed conflicts.[50]

4.23    Thus, consonant with the 1977 Additional Protocol I, a means or method of warfare that either cannot be directed at a specific military objective or whose effects cannot be limited as required by law of armed conflict rules are inherently indiscriminate and their use is prohibited. This encompasses a weapon that cannot be targeted with sufficient accuracy or whose effects spread too far beyond the target in time and space in an uncontrolled manner.[51] Any weapon that is indiscriminate may not be used in an armed conflict, irrespective of whether its use as a means of warfare is specifically prohibited by treaty.[52]

4.24    But although the rule is not contentious per se, its application to specific weapons is. In its discussion of the customary law rule, the ICRC cites a number of conventional weapons and weapons of mass destruction that have been alleged to be of an indiscriminate nature but observes that there is 'insufficient consensus . . . to conclude that, under customary international law, they all violate the rule prohibiting the use of indiscriminate weapons'.[53]

---

47  See Art. 49(1), 1977 Additional Protocol I ('Definition of attacks and scope of application'): '"Attacks" means acts of violence against the adversary, whether in offence or in defence'.

48  ICJ, *Legality of the Threat or Use of Nuclear Weapons*, Advisory Opinion, 8 July 1996, para. 78.

49  ICRC Study of Customary IHL, Rule 71, at: http://bit.ly/2zaMT6O.

50  Ibid. See also W.H. Boothby, *Weapons and the Law of Armed Conflict*, Oxford University Press, Oxford, 2009, p. 82.

51  'It is prohibited to employ weapons which cannot be directed at a specific military objective or the effects of which cannot be limited as required by Additional Protocol I and consequently are of a nature to strike military objectives and civilians or civilian objects without distinction'. UK Ministry of Defence, *The Manual of the Law of Armed Conflict*, para. 6.4.

52  The only exception to this general rule is when an otherwise unlawful weapon is used in a lawful reprisal, with a view to stopping serious violations of the law of armed conflict by the enemy.

53  ICRC Study of Customary IHL, Rule 71: 'Weapons That Are by Nature Indiscriminate'.

4.25  Weapons whose effects cannot be limited as required by law of armed conflict rules are of an indiscriminate nature. This is so on the basis that although they can be directed at a specific military objective, their effects go far and beyond that objective, often harming civilians. Biological weapons are a generally accepted example of such a weapon.

### The rule of proportionality in attack

4.26  If an attack is targeted at a lawful military objective in accordance with the rule of distinction, the decision to launch the attack must also comply with the rule of proportionality.[54] According to this customary rule, an attack against a lawful target will be unlawful where it 'may be expected' to cause incidental civilian harm that is 'excessive' compared with the projected 'concrete and direct military advantage'.[55] Civilian harm is explicitly defined as encompassing deaths or injuries to civilians, destruction of or damage to civilian objects, 'or a combination thereof'. Proportionality thus has 'nothing to do with injury to combatants or damage to military objectives', except insofar as they amount to the expected 'concrete and direct military advantage'.[56]

4.27  Weapons are not 'inherently' disproportionate. The contextualisation that is part and parcel of the rule of proportionality in attack prohibits this classification operating in the same way that the rule of distinction applies to inherently indiscriminate weapons. In practice, however, the less accurate the weapon, the more likely it is that civilian harm should be expected to occur in the proportionality assessment, especially in urban areas. Precautionary measures are required by the law of armed conflict both in attack and in defence.[57]

### The superfluous injury rule

4.28  One of the very few rules protecting combatants while they are fighting is the prohibition on means and methods of warfare that are 'of a nature to cause superfluous injury or unnecessary suffering'. The 1868 St Petersburg Declaration, which prohibited the use of exploding bullets (in international armed conflict), incorporated the observation that since the only 'legitimate object' that states should endeavour to accomplish through warfare is 'to weaken the military forces of the enemy', this objective 'would be exceeded by the employment of arms which uselessly aggravate the sufferings of disabled men, or render their death inevitable'.[58]

---

54 Both rules are also termed principles of international humanitarian law; see, *supra*, paras. 3.66 and 3.69–3.70.

55 The ICRC has expressed the customary law of armed conflict/IHL rule as follows:

> Launching an attack which may be expected to cause incidental loss of civilian life, injury to civilians, damage to civilian objects, or a combination thereof, which would be excessive in relation to the concrete and direct military advantage anticipated, is prohibited.

56 Y. Dinstein, *The Conduct of Hostilities under the Law of International Armed Conflict*, 2nd Edn, Cambridge University Press, Cambridge, 2010, p. 129.

57 Arts. 57 and 58, 1977 Additional Protocol I.

58 Declaration Renouncing the Use, in Time of War, of Explosive Projectiles Under 400 Grammes Weight; adopted at Saint Petersburg, 11 December 1868; entered into force the same day.

4.29    In 1899, the regulations on land warfare annexed to the Hague Convention II (1899 Hague Regulations) stipulated that 'it is especially prohibited. . . [t]o employ arms, projectiles, or material of a nature to cause superfluous injury'.[59] Today, the rule prohibiting the use of weapons causing superfluous injury or unnecessary suffering is a customary norm applicable to all parties to any armed conflict.[60] In its 1996 Nuclear Weapons Advisory Opinion, the ICJ defined unnecessary suffering as 'harm greater than that unavoidable to achieve legitimate military objectives'.[61] Its application to specific weapons is, however, frequently contested. For instance, it is not settled whether to kill or seriously injure combatants by deliberately burning them out in the open (using napalm or a flamethrower), to deliberately blind them (using a laser), or to kill them slowly through the irremediable effects of radiation (using a nuclear weapon) is a violation per se of the customary rule.

4.30    The ICRC has asserted that the following means of warfare are unlawful under the unnecessary suffering rule:

- Explosive bullets and projectiles filled with glass
- Bullets which easily expand or flatten in the human body
- Poison and poisoned weapons, as well as any substance intended to aggravate a wound
- Asphyxiating or deleterious gases
- Bayonets with a serrated edge and lances with barbed heads.[62]

## Specific prohibitions of the use of weapons during armed conflict

4.31    In a number of other instances, the use of specific weapons has been prohibited as a means of warfare by law of armed conflict treaty. As noted above, in 1925, the Geneva Protocol in fact contained a new prohibition on the use of biological (bacteriological) weapons in international armed conflicts, while reiterating the already existing prohibition on chemical weapons. In 1996, Protocol IV to the Convention on Certain Conventional Weapons outlawed the use in international armed conflicts of laser weapons specifically designed to cause permanent blindness to the naked eye (see Box 4.2).

## Weapons and international criminal law

4.32    International criminal law lays down individual criminal responsibility for international crimes such as aggression, genocide, crimes against humanity, and war crimes. Consonant with the general understanding of a crime under domestic law,

---

59  Art. 23(e), Regulations concerning the Laws and Customs of War on Land annexed to Convention (II) with Respect to the Laws and Customs of War on Land. The Hague, 29 July 1899.
60  ICRC Study of Customary IHL, Rule 70 ('Weapons of a Nature to Cause Superfluous Injury or Unnecessary Suffering'), at: http://bit.ly/2Az2Vcz.
61  ICJ, *Legality of the Threat or Use of Nuclear Weapons*, Advisory Opinion, 8 July 1996, para. 78.
62  ICRC Commentary on the 1977 Additional Protocols, para. 1419.

to secure any conviction for an international crime it needs to be proven, beyond a reasonable doubt, that an individual suspect had the requisite culpable state of mind (mens rea) at the time he or she committed the relevant culpable act (actus reus).

4.33   War crimes are serious violations of the law of armed conflict that also entail individual criminal responsibility under international law. These crimes are defined in law of armed conflict treaties, notably the 1899 and 1907 Hague Regulations, the 1949 Geneva Conventions, the 1954 Hague Convention on Cultural Property, and the 1977 Additional Protocols. The crimes are also set out in the ICC Statute and under customary international law.[63]

4.34   The ICC Statute accords the Court potential jurisdiction over an individual belonging to a party to an armed conflict who employs:

- Poison or poisoned weapons
- Asphyxiating, poisonous or other gases, and all analogous liquids, materials or devices
- Bullets which expand or flatten easily in the human body, such as bullets with a hard envelope which does not entirely cover the core or is pierced with incisions.[64]

Since December 2017, these provisions apply to both international and non-international armed conflict alike.[65]

4.35   War crimes regarding the use of weapons that are committed during the conduct of hostilities are hard to prosecute successfully. In the *Gotovina* case, an ICTY Trial Chamber had found that, on 4 and 5 August 1995, during Operation Storm, Croatian army artillery units fired artillery shells and rockets at four towns in the Serb Krajina region of Croatia. After comparing the evidence on the locations of impacts in these towns with the locations of possible military targets, it concluded that the Croatian forces had targeted certain areas that did not contain military objectives. As such, the Chamber found that the Croatian forces had conducted an indiscriminate attack on the towns and an unlawful attack on civilians and civilian objects.

4.36   The controversial elements of the judgment concerned the focus on an ex post facto impact assessment as evidence of violations to be judged at the time of launch, and especially that strikes more than 200 metres away from a possible military objective were unlawful. This conclusion by the Trial Chamber was of concern to a number of law of armed conflict experts. They submitted an amicus curiae ('friend of the court') brief to the Appeals Chamber, arguing that 200 metres was an 'unrealistic operational standard' and suggesting use of a 400-metre standard instead for artillery.[66]

---

63 See ICRC Study of Customary International Humanitarian Law, Rule 156.

64 Art. 8(2)(b)(xvii–xiv), ICC Statute.

65 The amendments apply to both international armed conflict (Art. 8(2)(b)(xxvii)) and non-international armed conflict (Art. 8(2)(e)(xvi)).

66 Application and Proposed Amicus Curiae Brief Concerning the 15 April 2011 Trial Chamber Judgment and Requesting that the Appeals Chamber Reconsider the Findings of Unlawful Artillery Attacks during Operation Storm, p. 21.

4.37    In its judgment in the appeal, the ICTY Appeals Chamber noted that the Trial Chamber had not explained the basis on which it arrived at the 200-metre margin of error.[67] The Appeals Chamber held that a 200-metre standard for artillery and rocket attacks in populated areas did not exist in the law. But the Chamber failed to articulate what the correct standard was.[68] The international legal standard for accuracy of targeting under the law of armed conflict therefore remains unsettled.

## Weapons and the law on inter-state use of force (*jus ad bellum*)

4.38    *Jus ad bellum* – the law on the inter-state use of force – is the branch of international law that governs when one state may lawfully use force against or on the territory of another state. It is not weapon-specific, and does not per se outlaw the use of any weapon. The UN Charter is the foundation of modern *jus ad bellum*. A serious violation thereof amounts to aggression. *Ad bellum* rules apply in parallel and in addition to the rules *in bello* that apply under the law of armed conflict.

### The general prohibition of inter-state use of force

4.39    The cornerstone of the UN Charter provisions concerning *jus ad bellum* is the general rule set out in Article 2(4), whereby:

> All Members shall refrain in their international relations from the threat or use of force against the territorial integrity or political independence of any state, or in any other manner inconsistent with the Purposes of the United Nations.

Although originally directed to UN member states, the general prohibition on use of force extends to all states under customary international law.

4.40    It is argued by one leading commentator that the correct interpretation of the provision is that any use of inter-state force by (at least) UN member states 'for whatever reason' is unlawful, 'unless explicitly allowed by the Charter'.[69] Article 2(4) does not, though, preclude use of force on the territory of another state when express consent is secured, without duress, from the government of that state.[70]

4.41    Article 51 of the UN Charter preserves a state's 'inherent' right of self-defence in response to an armed attack, though the principles of necessity and

---

67  ICTY, *Prosecutor v. Gotovina and Markač*, Judgment (Appeals Chamber), 16 November 2012, para. 58.

68  Ibid., Dissenting Opinion of Judge Fausto Pocar, paras. 8–9; see also Dissenting Opinion of Judge Carmel Agius, paras. 7–10.

69  Y. Dinstein, *War, Aggression and Self-Defence*, 5th Edn, Cambridge University Press, Cambridge, 2017, p. 90.

70  C. Gray, *International Law and the Use of Force*, 4th Edn, Oxford University Press, Oxford, 2018, pp. 75–119.

proportionality constrain what action in self-defence will be lawful. In *jus ad bellum*, the principles of necessity and proportionality have a distinct meaning that differs from that under other branches of international law, such as the law of armed conflict/IHL or international human rights law. Necessity *ad bellum* means that other measures short of the use of force, such as political pressure and sanctions, have been unsuccessful in resolving the issue or would be doomed to failure. Proportionality holds that the force used may be sufficient to repel the threat but cannot rise to the level of regime change, a measure that is not acceptable in self-defence and which violates the general prohibition on the use of force.

4.42   With a view to restraining war, the UN Charter set up and mandated the UN Security Council with a primary responsibility for maintaining international peace and security. When it has determined 'the existence of any threat to the peace, breach of the peace, or act of aggression' the Council can authorise measures short of war, such as sanctions and arms embargoes, and the interruption of diplomatic relations.[71] Should the Council consider that such measures 'would be inadequate or have proved to be inadequate', however, it may authorise 'such action by air, sea, or land forces as may be necessary to maintain or restore international peace and security'.[72] The authorisation to states to use all necessary means – Security Council language that is taken to authorise the use of force – to liberate Kuwait following its invasion by Iraq in 1990 is an example thereof.

### The prohibition of threat of force

4.43   Very few disarmament treaties address the threat of use of a weapon. Under the UN Charter there is a general prohibition imposed on all UN member states of the threat of using force 'against the territorial integrity or political independence of any state, or in any other manner inconsistent with the Purposes of the United Nations'.[73] There is, however, no accepted definition of what amounts to threat of force under international law. Ian Brownlie has defined the notion as 'an express or implied promise by a government of a resort to force conditional on non-acceptance of certain demands of that government'.[74] The extent of the meaning of the prohibition remains debated. A wide understanding is that any type of threats of force is prohibited by the UN Charter, including the possibly lawful use of force.[75] In its Advisory Opinion on the Threat or Use of Nuclear Weapons, the ICJ affirmed that 'if the envisaged use of force is itself unlawful, the stated readiness to use it would be a threat prohibited under Article 2, paragraph 4'.[76] This suggests a much narrower view of the prohibition.

---

71 Arts. 39 and 41, UN Charter.
72 Art. 42, UN Charter.
73 Art. 2(4), UN Charter.
74 I. Brownlie, *International Law and the Use of Force by States*, Oxford University Press, Oxford, 1963, p. 364.
75 N. Stürchler, *The Threat of Force in International Law*, Cambridge University Press, Cambridge, 2007.
76 ICJ, *Legality of the Threat or Use of Nuclear Weapons*, Advisory Opinion, 8 July 1996, para. 47.

## Threat of use of weapons of mass destruction

4.44   Under the 1992 Chemical Weapons Convention, each state party has the right to request assistance and protection against the use 'or threat of use of chemical weapons' if it considers that it is 'threatened by actions or activities of any State that are prohibited for States Parties by Article I'.[77] The Director-General of the OPCW is required to 'immediately forward' the request to states parties that can provide 'humanitarian assistance in case of serious threat of use of chemical weapons or serious threat of use of riot control agents as a method of warfare'.[78]

4.45   In a relative innovation for a disarmament treaty, under the 2017 Treaty on the Prohibition of Nuclear Weapons, each state party undertakes never under circumstances to 'threaten to use nuclear weapons or other nuclear explosive devices'.[79] The precise scope of this prohibition is not settled yet. In general, Dubuisson and Lagerwall affirm the following to qualify as a threat:

> demonstrations of force must be accompanied by particular circumstances showing that these demonstrations amount to political pressure in order to obtain something from the targeted state by declaring a willingness to react if certain events occur. . . . Implicit terms should not, in principle, be considered as threats of force, . . . unless particular circumstances so justify.[80]

## Threat of use of nuclear weapons and security assurances

4.46   Especially relevant concerning the threat of use of nuclear weapons are security assurances. In 1978, in the UN General Assembly Resolution on the first Special Session on Disarmament, member states noted that 'effective arrangements . . . to assure non-nuclear-weapon States against the use or the threat of use of nuclear weapons could strengthen the security of those States and international peace and security'.[81] The Assembly urged nuclear-weapon states 'to pursue efforts to conclude' effective arrangements of negative security assurances (NSAs).[82] The first legally binding NSAs had been provided a decade earlier, in Additional Protocol II of the 1967 Treaty of Tlatelolco, which established the nuclear-weapon-free zone in Latin America and the Caribbean.

---

77 Art. X(8), CWC.

78 Art. X(9), CWC.

79 Art. 1(1)(d), 2017 Treaty on the Prohibition of Nuclear Weapons.

80 F. Dubuisson and A. Lagerwall, 'The Threat of the Use of Force and Ultimata', Chap. 42 in M. Weller (ed.), *The Oxford Handbook of the Use of Force in International Law*, Oxford University Press, Oxford, 2015, p. 915 (footnotes omitted).

81 UN General Assembly Resolution S-10/2: Final Document of the Tenth Special Session of the Assembly, 30 June 1978, para. 32.

82 Ibid., para. 59.

4.47   In 1979, the Conference on Disarmament (CD), which was created by the General Assembly's first Special Session on Disarmament, included in its annual agenda the issue of NSAs. No specific provision on security assurances to non-nuclear-weapon states had been included in the NPT, despite calls for it to do so. Work therefore began to promote the provision of guarantees by the five nuclear-weapon states recognised by the NPT not to use or threaten to use nuclear weapons against states that have formally renounced them.[83]

4.48   In April 1995, the five declared nuclear-weapon states made unilateral pledges on NSAs to the non-nuclear-weapon states parties to the NPT. These declarations were reflected in UN Security Council Resolution 984.[84] France, Russia, the United Kingdom, and the United States reaffirmed that nuclear weapons would not be used against non-nuclear weapons states parties to the NPT when they were in compliance with the Treaty, except if one of the nuclear-weapons states were attacked by a non-nuclear weapons in 'association or alliance' with another nuclear-weapons state. The United States of America's 2018 *Nuclear Posture Review* repeated existing US negative security assurances by stating that it 'will not use or threaten to use nuclear weapons against non-nuclear weapons states that are party to the NPT and in compliance with their nuclear non-proliferation obligations'.[85] At the same time, it reiterated that 'the United States would only consider the employment of nuclear weapons in extreme circumstances to defend the vital interests of the United States, its allies, and partners. Extreme circumstances could include significant non-nuclear strategic attacks'.[86] Only China has persistently declared that it will never use or threaten the use of nuclear weapons against a non-nuclear weapon state or a nuclear-weapon-free zone.

4.49   UN Security Council Resolution 984 also welcomed the intention of certain states to support and assist any non-nuclear-weapon state that became a victim or was threatened by acts of aggression in which nuclear weapons were used – so-called positive security assurances. All of the five recognised nuclear-weapon states declared that they would take appropriate measures to provide humanitarian, medical, scientific, and technical assistance if so requested by a state that had suffered aggression or was threatened with the use of nuclear weapons. Due regard would also be given to compensation.

83 UN Office for Disarmament Affairs (UNODA), 'The Conference on Disarmament and Negative Security Assurances', *Fact Sheet*, July 2017, at: http://bit.ly/2SI9VL0.

84 UN Security Council Resolution 984: 'Security assurances against the use of nuclear weapons to non-nuclear-weapon States that are Parties to the Treaty on the Non-Proliferation of Nuclear Weapons', adopted on 11 April 1995.

85 US Department of Defense, *Nuclear Posture Review*, February 2018, p. 21, at: http://bit.ly/2AzQ4Hb.

86 Ibid.

# 5

# DEVELOPMENT AND TESTING

## Introduction

5.1    It is common for global disarmament treaties to prohibit the development of the weapon that is being outlawed. This chapter summarises the relevant treaty obligations, describing which research activities amount to prohibited development under international law and the role of specific prohibitions on testing within that broader concept. There is then discussion of the disarmament treaties that prohibit testing of nuclear weapons both because of the harmful effects of such testing and with a view to preventing their further proliferation.

5.2    Notwithstanding the disarmament treaty prohibitions on weapons testing, however, the law of armed conflict imposes a duty to assess the legality of weapons prior to their deployment. Article 36 of the 1977 Additional Protocol I stipulates that:

> In the study, development, acquisition or adoption of a new weapon, means or method of warfare, a High Contracting Party is under an obligation to determine whether its employment would, in some or all circumstances, be prohibited by this Protocol or by any other rule of international law applicable to the High Contracting Party.[1]

This provision does not explicitly require that a weapon be tested before its 'employment', but – at least for the 174 states parties to the Protocol (as of writing)[2] – compliance with this treaty obligation would be likely to be enhanced by some

---

1    A High Contracting Party is a state party to the Protocol. This different language is often used in law of armed conflict treaties, but does not vary the legal effect of adherence.
2    See the list maintained by the International Committee of the Red Cross (ICRC) at: http://bit. ly/2Oe2Iin.

form of testing. The International Committee of the Red Cross (ICRC) has affirmed that the requisite determination should take place at various stages of development: before entering the production phase, before the weapon system is acquired, and at the earliest possible stage of modifications.[3] The process of review, the organisation recommends, should involve experts from various disciplines in order to cover all relevant empirical information, including the weapon's technical description, its actual performance, and the effects on health and the environment.[4]

## Definitions

### 'To develop'

5.3    The notion of development of a weapon is not defined in any disarmament treaty, but is a broad concept. In everyday parlance, to develop something is to 'work out the possibilities of' or to 'create or produce especially by deliberate effort over time';[5] to 'invent something or bring something into existence';[6] or to 'design' a 'new product'.[7] When applied to weapons, the ordinary meaning of the phrase encompasses a range of activities. Associated research and testing certainly form part of the broader process of development, so computer modelling and simulations are covered, as is the construction of a prototype. When a weapon is designed for sale or use, however, typically this would fall outside the prohibition of development and within any corresponding prohibition on production or manufacture.[8]

5.4    Usually, the formulation in global disarmament treaty is an undertaking by states parties never under any circumstances 'to develop' the respective weapon that is being prohibited. But despite this common wording, the scope of prohibited development sometimes varies to a certain extent. For instance, in the context of the 1992 Chemical Weapons Convention (CWC), '"develop" is, by virtue of its purpose, the preparation of the production of chemical weapons as distinct from permitted research'.[9] This is because research and other forms of development

---

3    *Guide to the Legal Review of New Weapons, Means and Methods of Warfare*, ICRC, Geneva, 2006, s. 2.3.1; see in relation to legal reviews of weapons N. Weizmann, 'Armed Drones and the Law of Armed Conflict', Chap. 4 in S. Casey-Maslen, M. Homayounnejad, H. Stauffer, and N. Weizmann, *Drones And Other Unmanned Weapons Systems Under International Law*, Brill, Boston, MA, August 2018.

4    *Guide to the Legal Review of New Weapons, Means and Methods of Warfare*, ICRC, Geneva, 2006, s. 1.3.

5    *Merriam-Webster online dictionary*, 'Develop', definition 2(a) and (b), accessed 31 December 2017, at: http://bit.ly/2PwKTQk.

6    *Cambridge Dictionary online*, 'Develop (start)', accessed 31 December 2017, at: http://bit.ly/2Ofjdee.

7    *Collins Dictionary online*, 'Develop', definition 11, accessed 31 December 2017, at: http://bit.ly/2PnMisH.

8    Thus, for example, Norway's explanatory note to national implementing legislation for the 2008 Convention on Cluster Munitions stated that 'it is presumed that the development of cluster munitions covers the process up to production'. Proposition No. 7 (2008–2009) to the Odelsting on a Bill relating to the implementation of the Convention on Cluster Munitions in Norwegian law, 17 October 2008, §4.2.2.

9    W. Krutzsch and R. Trapp, *A Commentary on the Chemical Weapons Convention*, Martinus Nijhoff, The Netherlands, 1994, p. 13.

of chemical agents may use toxic chemicals or their precursors for purposes not prohibited under the Convention, such as industrial, agricultural, medical, pharmaceutical, or other peaceful purposes, or for law enforcement.[10] Arguably, however, the ambit of the 2008 Convention on Cluster Munitions[11] is broader, covering a prohibition on indirect as well as direct development.[12] Such a prohibition would outlaw construction or procurement of parts and components with a view to their incorporation in the weapon and also offshore licensing arrangements.

## Research

5.5    Research forms an integral part of the international legal concept of development. This is notwithstanding the fact that, in both the military and corporate world, the term R&D (research and development) suggests that the two have an autonomous existence. It is therefore necessary to define research. As a noun, ordinarily it means 'the systematic investigation into and study of materials and sources in order to establish facts and reach new conclusions'.[13] In turn, to research something is to investigate it systematically.[14] It is a scientific process that looks at materials, substances, and technologies. In contrast to development, research serves the identification of elements, structures, mechanisms, and options but not necessarily the creation of solutions to further a specific aim. Permitted research into toxic chemicals and their precursors for peaceful purposes is distinguished from their development for prohibited purposes in the CWC,[15] though this does not affect the breadth of the notion of 'to develop'.

## Testing

5.6    Under the 1963 Partial Nuclear-Test-Ban Treaty (PTBT),[16] states parties undertake 'to prohibit, to prevent, and not to carry out any nuclear weapon test explosion'.[17] In the 1996 Comprehensive Nuclear-Test-Ban Treaty (CTBT),[18] a treaty not yet in force as in March 2019, each state party undertakes 'not to carry

---

10  Art. II(9), Convention on the Prohibition of the Development, Production, Stockpiling and Use of Chemical Weapons and on their Destruction; adopted at Geneva, 3 September 1992; entered into force, 29 April 1997.

11  Art. 1(1)(b), Convention on Cluster Munitions; adopted at Dublin, 30 May 2008; entered into force, 1 August 2010.

12  V. Wiebe, Commentary on Article 1, in G. Nystuen and S. Casey-Maslen (eds.), *The Convention on Cluster Munitions: A Commentary*, Oxford University Press, Oxford, 2010, para. 1.36.

13  'Research' as defined in the *Oxford English Dictionary*.

14  Ibid.

15  See, e.g., Arts. X(2) and XI(2), 1992 Chemical Weapons Convention.

16  Treaty Banning Nuclear Weapon Tests in the Atmosphere, in Outer Space and Under Water; opened for signature at London, Moscow, and Washington, DC, 8 August 1963; entered into force, 10 October 1963.

17  Art. I(1), PTBT.

18  Comprehensive Nuclear-Test-Ban Treaty; adopted at the UN General Assembly in New York, 10 September 1996.

out any nuclear weapon test explosion or any other nuclear explosion'. In the 1979 Moon Treaty,[19] it is stipulated that the 'testing' of any type of weapons on the Moon shall be forbidden.[20] This reflects the language of the earlier 1967 Outer Space Treaty.[21] In the most recent global disarmament treaty, the 2017 Treaty on the Prohibition of Nuclear Weapons (TPNW), each state party undertakes never under any circumstances to test nuclear weapons or other nuclear explosive devices.[22]

5.7    To test a product is ordinarily defined by the *Oxford English Dictionary* 'to take measures to check the quality, performance, or reliability (of something), especially before putting it into widespread use or practice'.[23] Under this understanding, a prototype of the weapon may exist. Correspondingly, a test is 'a procedure intended to establish the quality, performance, or reliability of something, especially before it is taken into widespread use'. The example of usage given by the *Oxford English Dictionary* is 'both countries carried out nuclear tests in May'.[24]

5.8    Indeed, the testing of nuclear weapons is the most obvious example of an element of weapons development that is singled out for specific prohibition under disarmament law. Under the PTBT, for example, test explosions are prohibited, inter alia, in the atmosphere; beyond its limits, including outer space; and underwater, including in territorial waters or the high seas.[25] Testing is not defined in the treaty, but its use in the phrase 'nuclear weapon test explosion' clarifies that the ban is limited to a functioning nuclear explosive device and does not cover other forms of testing, such as sub-critical testing or computer simulations.

## The prohibition of development

5.9    As noted above, global disarmament treaties typically prohibit the development of the weapon that is the subject of the treaty prohibition. This is the case with the 1971 Biological Weapons Convention,[26] the 1992 Chemical Weapons Convention,[27] the 1997 Anti-Personnel Mine Ban Convention,[28] the 2008

---

19 Agreement Governing the Activities of States on the Moon and Other Celestial Bodies; opened for signature at New York, 18 December 1979; entered into force, 11 July 1984.

20 Art. 3(4), 1979 Moon Treaty.

21 Art. IV, Treaty on Principles Governing the Activities of States in the Exploration and Use of Outer Space, including the Moon and Other Celestial Bodies; opened for signature at London, Moscow, and Washington, DC, 27 January 1967; entered into force, 10 October 1967.

22 Art. 1(1)(a), 2017 Treaty on the Prohibition of Nuclear Weapons.

23 'Test (verb)' in *Oxford English Dictionary*.

24 'Test (noun)', Definition 1, in *Oxford English Dictionary*.

25 Art. I(1)(a), PTBT.

26 Art. I, Convention on the Prohibition of the Development, Production and Stockpiling of Bacteriological (Biological) and Toxin Weapons and on their Destruction; opened for signature at London, Moscow, and Washington, DC, 10 April 1972; entered into force, 26 March 1975.

27 Art. I(1)(a), 1992 Chemical Weapons Convention.

28 Art. 1(1)(b), Convention on the Prohibition of the Use, Stockpiling, Production and Transfer of Anti-Personnel Mines and on Their Destruction; adopted at Oslo, 18 September 1997; entered into force, 1 March 1999.

Convention on Cluster Munitions,[29] and the 2017 Treaty on the Prohibition of Nuclear Weapons.[30] This is consistently phrased as an undertaking by states parties never under any circumstances to 'develop' the prohibited weapon (see Box 5.1).

5.10   All acts that amount to, or are directed towards, development of the weapon or its integral parts and components are prohibited. Other research activities are not outlawed. Under the Convention on Cluster Munitions, the development of multi-use components with intent that 'the designs of such components be used in cluster munitions' would violate the Convention, though clearly, 'such development raises difficult evidentiary challenges in proving the requisite intent'.[31]

---

**BOX 5.1   GLOBAL DISARMAMENT TREATY PROHIBITIONS ON WEAPONS DEVELOPMENT**

Each State Party . . . undertakes never in any circumstances to develop . . . microbial or other biological agents, or toxins whatever their origin or method of production. . . [or] weapons, equipment or means of delivery designed to use such agents or toxins for hostile purposes or in armed conflict.

*Art. I, Biological Weapons Convention*

Each State Party . . . undertakes never under any circumstances: . . . To develop . . . chemical weapons. . . .

*Art. I(1)(a), Chemical Weapons Convention*

Each State Party undertakes never under any circumstances: . . . To develop . . . directly or indirectly, anti-personnel mines. . . .

*Art. 1(1)(b), Anti-Personnel Mine Ban Convention*

Each State Party undertakes never under any circumstances: . . . To develop . . . directly or indirectly, cluster munitions. . . .

*Art. 1(1)(b), Convention on Cluster Munitions*

Each State Party undertakes never under any circumstances to: . . . Develop . . . nuclear weapons or other nuclear explosive devices

*Art. 1(1)(a), Treaty on the Prohibition of Nuclear Weapons*

---

29 Art. 1(1)(b), 2008 Convention on Cluster Munitions.
30 Art. 1(1)(a), Treaty on the Prohibition of Nuclear Weapons; adopted at New York, 7 July 2017; not yet in force.
31 Wiebe, Commentary on Article 1, in Nystuen and Casey-Maslen, *The Convention on Cluster Munitions: A Commentary*, para. 1.38.

5.11 The Biological Weapons Convention prohibits the development of 'microbial or other biological agents, or toxins whatever their origin or method of production, of types and in quantities that have no justification for prophylactic, protective or other peaceful purposes' and 'weapons, equipment or means of delivery designed to use such agents or toxins for hostile purposes or in armed conflict'.[32] Thus, the prohibition is on developing the biological agents as well as on their subsequent weaponisation.

5.12 In the Chemical Weapons Convention, each state party undertakes never under any circumstances to develop chemical weapons. Chemical weapons are any of the following: toxic chemicals and their precursors (for purposes prohibited under the Convention); munitions and devices specifically designed to cause death or other harm through the release of the toxic properties of such toxic chemicals; and equipment specifically designed for use directly in connection with the employment of such munitions and devices.[33] In turn, toxic chemicals are defined as any chemical 'which through its chemical action on life processes can cause death, temporary incapacitation or permanent harm to humans or animals', while precursors are 'any chemical reactant which takes part at any stage in the production by whatever method of a toxic chemical. This includes any key component of a binary or multicomponent chemical system'.[34]

## *Permitted development*

5.13 Several global disarmament treaties make specific provision for permissible activities that might otherwise be captured by the general prohibition on development. Thus, for example, while the general prohibition on research and development of chemical agents in the Chemical Weapons Convention is very broad in scope, it is significantly tempered by the designation of purposes 'not prohibited' under the Convention. These are the following:

a    Industrial, agricultural, research, medical, pharmaceutical or other peaceful purposes;
b    Protective purposes, namely those purposes directly related to protection against toxic chemicals and to protection against chemical weapons;
c    Military purposes not connected with the use of chemical weapons and not dependent on the use of the toxic properties of chemicals as a method of warfare;
d    Law enforcement including domestic riot control purposes.[35]

This excludes from the scope of the prohibition, among others, all research and development of chemicals and their precursors for peaceful purposes.

---

32 Art. I(a) and (b), 1971 Biological Weapons Convention.
33 Art. II(1), CWC.
34 Ibid.
35 Art. II(9), CWC.

5.14   It is further stipulated that nothing in the Chemical Weapons Convention 'shall be interpreted as impeding the right of any State Party to conduct research into, develop . . . means of protection against chemical weapons', as long as they are for purposes not prohibited under the Convention.[36] It is also decreed that states parties shall have 'the right, individually or collectively, to conduct research with' and 'to develop' chemicals.[37]

5.15   The preamble to the Treaty on the Prohibition of Nuclear Weapons emphasises that nothing in the Treaty 'shall be interpreted as affecting the inalienable right of its States Parties to develop research, production, and use of nuclear energy for peaceful purposes without discrimination'. This language draws on a provision in the 1968 Treaty on the Non-Proliferation of Nuclear Weapons (NPT).[38]

5.16   One of the items specifically highlighted for the annual meetings of states parties under the 1997 Anti-Personnel Mine Ban Convention is the 'development of technologies to clear anti-personnel mines'.[39] The provision is mirrored in the 2008 Convention on Cluster Munitions.[40] These activities are explicitly allowed as exceptions to the prohibition on retention and stockpiling of the respective weapons, but might also involve activities that would otherwise be captured by the prohibition on development.

## The prohibition of testing

5.17   A generic prohibition on the testing of all weapons was first included in the 1959 Antarctic Treaty.[41] Article I(1) stipulates that Antarctica 'shall be used for peaceful purposes only'. Specifically prohibited by the Treaty is 'the testing of any type of weapons'. This Treaty served as a model, in its approach and even in its specific provisions, for later treaties that 'excluded nuclear weapons from outer space, from Latin America, and from the seabed'.[42] Indeed, as noted above, both the 1967 Outer Space Treaty[43] and the 1979 Moon Treaty[44] prohibit the 'testing of any type of weapons' on the moon (or other celestial bodies).

5.18   Other treaties specifically prohibit the testing of nuclear weapons. States parties to the PTBT undertake 'to prohibit, to prevent, and not to carry out any

---

36 Art. X(2), CWC.

37 Art. XI(2)(a), CWC.

38 'Nothing in this Treaty shall be interpreted as affecting the inalienable right of all the Parties to the Treaty to develop research, production and use of nuclear energy for peaceful purposes without discrimination and in conformity with Articles I and II of this Treaty'. Art. IV(1), Treaty on the Non-Proliferation of Nuclear Weapons; opened for signature at London, Moscow, and Washington, DC, 1 July 1968; entered into force, 5 March 1970.

39 Art. 2(1)(d), APMBC.

40 Art. 2(1)(d), CCM.

41 The Antarctic Treaty; adopted at Washington, DC, 1 December 1959; entered into force, 23 June 1961.

42 US Department of State, 'Antarctic Treaty', Bureau of Arms Control, Verification and Compliance, undated but accessed 1 January 2018, at: http://bit.ly/2QkjYEQ.

43 Art. IV, 1967 Outer Space Treaty.

44 Art. 3(4), 1979 Moon Treaty.

nuclear weapon test explosion'.[45] Similarly, under the CTBT (a treaty not yet in force, as in March 2019),[46] each state party undertakes 'not to carry out any nuclear weapon test explosion or any other nuclear explosion'. The adoption of the PTBT followed evidence that atmospheric testing between 1945 and 1980 – amounting to 428 megatons of TNT, the equivalent of more than 29,000 'Hiroshima' yield bombs[47] – was causing significant and widespread harm to health and the environment.

5.19 The Preparatory Commission for the CTBTO (Comprehensive Nuclear-Test-Ban Treaty Organization) observes that it is difficult to assess the number of deaths attributable to radiation exposure from nuclear testing.[48] It cites an estimate by Arjun Makhijani that cancer fatalities due to the global radiation doses from the atmospheric nuclear testing programmes of the five nuclear-weapon states might amount to hundreds of thousands of people by the end of the 21st century.[49]

---

## BOX 5.2  DISARMAMENT TREATY PROHIBITIONS ON WEAPONS TESTING

There shall be prohibited, inter alia, . . . the testing of any type of weapons.

*Art. I(1), 1959 Antarctic Treaty*

The Moon and other celestial bodies shall be used by all States Parties to the Treaty exclusively for peaceful purposes. The . . . testing of any type of weapons . . . shall be forbidden.

*Art. IV, 1967 Outer Space Treaty*

The . . . testing of any type of weapons . . . on the Moon shall be forbidden.

*Art. 3(4), 1979 Moon Treaty*

Each of the Parties to this Treaty undertakes to prohibit, to prevent, and not to carry out any nuclear weapon test explosion, or any other nuclear explosion, at any place under its jurisdiction or control:

---

45 Art. I(1), PTBT.
46 Comprehensive Nuclear-Test-Ban Treaty; adopted by the UN General Assembly in New York, 10 September 1996; not yet in force.
47 CTBTO Preparatory Commission, 'General Overview of the Effects of Nuclear Testing', undated but accessed 1 January 2018, at: http://bit.ly/2OmfMCu.
48 Ibid.
49 Ibid., citing A. Makhijani, 'A Readiness to Harm: The Health Effects of Nuclear Weapons Complexes', *Arms Control Today*, 1 July 2005, at: http://bit.ly/2zkUgso.

a   in the atmosphere; beyond its limits, including outer space; or under
    water, including territorial waters or high seas; or
b   in any other environment if such explosion causes radioactive debris to be
    present outside the territorial limits of the State under whose jurisdiction
    or control such explosion is conducted.

*Art. I(1), 1963 Partial Nuclear-Test-Ban Treaty*

Each State Party undertakes not to carry out any nuclear weapon test
explosion or any other nuclear explosion, and to prohibit and prevent
any such nuclear explosion at any place under its jurisdiction or control.

*Art. I(1), 1996 Comprehensive Nuclear-Test-Ban Treaty*

Each State Party undertakes never under any circumstances to: . . .
Develop, test . . . nuclear weapons or other nuclear explosive devices

*Art. 1(1)(a), Treaty on the Prohibition of Nuclear Weapons*

5.20   The Treaty on the Prohibition of Nuclear Weapons is unusual for a global
disarmament treaty insofar as it prohibits not only the development but also, explicitly, the testing of nuclear weapons and other nuclear explosive devices. As set out
in Box 5.2, the undertaking by states parties is never under any circumstances to
develop or test nuclear weapons or other nuclear explosive devices. This can be
taken to imply that only testing of a completed weapon is explicitly prohibited
by the specific notion of testing and not also prior computer simulations or sub-
critical testing, as some states had advocated during the negotiations. That said,
such non-explosive testing is unlawful under the corresponding prohibition on
development.[50]

5.21   The Treaty on the Prohibition of Nuclear Weapons further obligates each
state party, with respect to areas under its jurisdiction or control that are contaminated as a result of the testing of any nuclear explosive devices, to take 'necessary and appropriate measures towards the environmental remediation of areas so
contaminated'.[51]

---

50 See, e.g., G. Oestern (ed.), *Nuclear Weapons Ban Monitor*, Norwegian People's Aid, New York, October 2018, pp. 26–27, at: http://bit.ly/2Q1eOgA.
51 Art. 6(2), TPNW.

# 6

# TRANSFER

## Introduction

6.1 A common element in disarmament or non-proliferation agreements is a prohibition on the transfer of the weapon or weapons that fall within its scope. The definition of 'transfer', though, differs materially from treaty to treaty, and oftentimes its scope is unclear. There are also important definitional and other issues contained in key resolutions of the United Nations (UN) Security Council, in particular Resolution 1540 (2004) on the non-proliferation of weapons of mass destruction.

6.2 This chapter explains and discusses the different meanings of the term *transfer*. It also describes the prohibition of transfer in the different treaties, including where exceptions limit the scope of the prohibitions. Regulation of transfer under the 2013 Arms Trade Treaty[1] and the subjects of UN Security Council embargoes are outlined. The chapter concludes with a summary of politically binding regimes' restrictions on transfers.

## Definitions of transfer

6.3 The definition of transfer of a weapon sometimes means only its export. The same may be true with respect to the export of parts and components or of weapons-related technology. Even when the two terms 'transfer' and 'export' are synonyms, though, their meaning may be unclear in certain respects. It is uncontested that physical movement of the weapon from one state to another accompanied by transfer of title over the weapon from the exporting state to the importing state satisfies the definition. But what if only one of those two acts occurs? If one state

---

1 Arms Trade Treaty; adopted at the UN General Assembly in New York, 2 April 2013; entered into force, 24 December 2014.

moves the weapon into the territory – and possession – of another state while retaining ownership of it, according to one interpretation, this physical movement of the weapon alone will not suffice for a transfer/export to have occurred. In such a scenario, transfer/export is defined so as to exclude loans and leases of weapons since transfer of title does not occur, only that of possession. Another issue concerns whether a transfer/export requires a sale (i.e. some form of payment or other 'consideration'). If that is not the case, gifts will be excluded from the definition.

6.4   In some treaties, as discussed below, the term transfer is not defined. In rare cases, however, the notion of transfer is explicitly defined in especially broad terms. Notably, this is the case of the 2013 Arms Trade Treaty, where transfer is explicitly defined as comprising the export, import, transit, trans-shipment, and brokering (of conventional weapons).[2]

### The meaning of transfer in disarmament treaties governing WMD

6.5   In none of the global treaties governing weapons of mass destruction (WMD) is the term 'transfer' formally defined. The 1968 Treaty on the Non-Proliferation of Nuclear Weapons (NPT)[3] sought to restrict the availability of nuclear weapons to those designated under the Treaty as nuclear-weapon states.[4] The five nuclear-weapon states parties to the NPT (in practice, the five permanent members of the UN Security Council)[5] undertake not to 'transfer to any recipient whatsoever nuclear weapons or other nuclear explosive devices or control over such weapons or explosive devices directly, or indirectly'.[6] This prohibits China, France, Russia, the United Kingdom, and the United States of America from transferring any nuclear explosive devices to anyone else, whether state or non-state. The separate prohibition on the transfer of *control* over all nuclear explosive devices implies that, under the NPT, transfer of any such device means passing *both* title *and* possession to another.

6.6   The corresponding provision binding non-nuclear-weapon states parties to the NPT was in the form of an undertaking 'not to receive the transfer from any transferor whatsoever of nuclear weapons or other nuclear explosive devices or of control over such weapons or explosive devices directly, or indirectly'.[7] The context

---

2   Art. 2(2), 2013 Arms Trade Treaty.

3   Treaty on the Non-Proliferation of Nuclear Weapons; opened for signature at London, Moscow, and Washington, DC, 1 July 1968; entered into force, 5 March 1970 (NPT).

4   In 1961, at the urging of Ireland, the UN General Assembly had adopted Resolution 1665 (XVI) on the prevention of the wider dissemination of nuclear weapons. The resolution, which passed by consensus, called on all states to conclude an agreement in which 'the nuclear States would undertake to refrain from relinquishing control of nuclear weapons' and states not possessing nuclear weapons would undertake not to 'acquire control of such weapons'. UN General Assembly Resolution 1665 (XVI), adopted without a vote on 4 December 1961, para. 1.

5   This is because Article IX(3) of the NPT defines a nuclear-weapon state as one that had manufactured and detonated a nuclear explosive device prior to 1 January 1967.

6   Art. I, NPT.

7   Art. II, NPT.

of the negotiation and adoption of the treaty makes it clear that the prohibitions exist whether or not any financial consideration is involved in the supply of any nuclear explosive device.

6.7 The 1971 Biological Weapons Convention[8] was the first global *disarmament* treaty to outlaw the transfer of a weapon of mass destruction. Exceptionally, however, the prohibition on transfer is contained in a dedicated provision separate from the other general undertakings. Thus, under Article III, each state party 'undertakes not to transfer to any recipient whatsoever, directly or indirectly . . . any of the agents, toxins, weapons, equipment or means of delivery' set out in Article I of the Convention. The prohibition on transfer *to* any recipient means that transfer in the Biological Weapons Convention means export but not import. The importation of such weapons or other illegal items is covered by the separate prohibition on acquisition in Article I.

6.8 Each state party to the 1992 Chemical Weapons Convention[9] undertakes never under any circumstances to 'transfer, directly or indirectly, chemical weapons to anyone'.[10] Once again, the prohibition on transfer *to* any recipient means that transfer means export of chemical weapons but not import (which is similarly covered by the prohibition on acquiring chemical weapons). The prohibition on *indirect* transfer extends to outlawing the export of the parts and components of such weapons, particularly prohibited toxic chemicals and their precursors.

6.9 The 2017 Treaty on the Prohibition of Nuclear Weapons[11] draws on the language used in the NPT with only slight amendment. Thus, each state party undertakes never under any circumstances to 'transfer to any recipient whatsoever' or to '[r]eceive the transfer of or control over' nuclear weapons or other nuclear explosive devices, directly or indirectly.[12] This covers, respectively, export, and import of the prohibited weapons and devices.

6.10 UN Security Council Resolution 1540 (2004) on the non-proliferation of WMD does not define transfer, but it nonetheless regulates it explicitly. Affirming that the proliferation of nuclear, chemical, and biological weapons constitutes a threat to international peace and security, the Council decided that 'all States shall refrain from providing any form of support to non-State actors that attempt to . . . acquire [or] transfer . . . nuclear, chemical or biological weapons'.[13]

---

8 Convention on the Prohibition of the Development, Production and Stockpiling of Bacteriological (Biological) and Toxin Weapons and on their Destruction; opened for signature, 10 April 1972; entered into force, 25 March 1975.

9 Convention on the Prohibition of the Development, Production, Stockpiling and Use of Chemical Weapons and on their Destruction; adopted at Geneva, 3 September 1992; entered into force, 29 April 1997.

10 Art. I(1)(a), 1992 Chemical Weapons Convention.

11 Treaty on the Prohibition of Nuclear Weapons; adopted at New York, 7 July 2017; not yet in force.

12 Art. 1(1)(b) and (c), TPNW.

13 UN Security Council Resolution 1540, adopted on 28 April 2004, para. 1.

## The meaning of transfer in treaties governing conventional weapons

6.11    In contradistinction to treaties addressing WMD, in almost every treaty governing conventional weapons, the notion of transfer is explicitly defined (see Box 6.1). The exception is the Protocol IV on blinding laser weapons[14] annexed to the Convention on Certain Conventional Weapons (a law of armed conflict treaty).[15] Protocol IV obliges states parties to 'not transfer such weapons to any State or non-State entity' but does not define the notion of transfer.[16] In contrast, in the 1996 Amended Protocol II to the same Convention,[17] adopted one year after Protocol IV, it is specified that transfer 'involves, in addition to the physical movement of mines into or from national territory, the transfer of title to and control over the mines, but does not involve the transfer of territory containing emplaced mines'.[18]

6.12    The problem with this definition is its lack of clarity. Ambiguity results from the phrase 'in addition to'. According to one possible interpretation of the definition, to amount to transfer, there must be *both* physical movement of the weapons into or from national territory *and* transfer of title to and control over them. But the wording 'in addition to' may also be read as alternatives: under this interpretation transfer means *either* physical movement of the weapons into or from national territory, *or* transfer of title to and control over them. In this latter interpretation, the concept of transfer comprises transit, making the scope of the term broad. This is not the case with the former, which is therefore far narrower in scope.

6.13    Despite the ambiguity of this definition, it is effectively reproduced in both the 1997 Anti-Personnel Mine Ban Convention[19] and the 2008 Convention on Cluster Munitions.[20] States were well aware of the ambiguity. Indeed, in the negotiation of the Convention on Cluster Munitions, a clearer definition had been proposed during the preliminary discussions:

---

14  Protocol IV on Blinding Laser Weapons; adopted at Vienna, 13 October 1995; entered into force, 30 July 1998.
15  Convention on Prohibitions or Restrictions on the Use of Certain Conventional Weapons which may be deemed to be Excessively Injurious or to have Indiscriminate Effects; adopted at Geneva, 10 October 1980; entered into force, 2 December 1983. This instrument is usually referred to as the Convention on Certain Conventional Weapons or the Inhumane Weapons Convention.
16  Art. 1, 1995 Protocol IV on Blinding Laser Weapons.
17  Protocol on Prohibitions or Restrictions on the Use of Mines, Booby-Traps and Other Devices as amended on 3 May 1996 (Amended Protocol II); adopted at Geneva, 3 May 1996; entered into force, 3 December 1998.
18  Art. 2(15), 1996 Amended Protocol II to the Convention on Certain Conventional Weapons.
19  Art. 2(4), Convention on the Prohibition of the Use, Stockpiling, Production and Transfer of Anti-Personnel Mines and on Their Destruction; adopted at Oslo, 18 September 1997; entered into force, 1 March 1999.
20  Art. 2(8), Convention on Cluster Munitions; adopted at Dublin, 30 May 2008; entered into force, 1 August 2010.

'Transfer' means the physical movement of cluster munitions into or from national territory or the transfer of title to or control over cluster munitions, but does not include the transfer of territory containing cluster munition remnants.[21]

Removing the phrase 'in addition to' would have clarified the scope of the term. Ultimately, however, negotiating states preferred the ambiguity of the phrasing of the definitions in the 1996 Amended Protocol II and the Anti-Personnel Mine Ban Convention, and reverted to a similar wording in the text of the Convention on Cluster Munitions that was adopted.[22]

6.14    It appears that the notion of transfer in global disarmament treaties governing conventional weapons is not limited to export. This is because in both the Anti-Personnel Mine Ban Convention and the Convention on Cluster Munitions,

---

**BOX 6.1   DISARMAMENT TREATY DEFINITIONS OF TRANSFER**

'Transfer' involves, in addition to the physical movement of mines into or from national territory, the transfer of title to and control over the mines, but does not involve the transfer of territory containing emplaced mines.

*Art. 2(15), 1996 Amended Protocol II*
*to the Convention on Certain Conventional Weapons*

'Transfer' involves, in addition to the physical movement of anti-personnel mines into or from national territory, the transfer of title to and control over the mines, but does not involve the transfer of territory containing emplaced anti-personnel mines.

*Art. 2(4), Anti-Personnel Mine Ban Convention*

'Transfer' involves, in addition to the physical movement of cluster munitions into or from national territory, the transfer of title to and control over cluster munitions, but does not involve the transfer of territory containing cluster munition remnants. . . .

*Art. 2(8), Convention on Cluster Munitions*

For the purposes of this Treaty, the activities of the international trade comprise export, import, transit, trans-shipment and brokering, hereafter referred to as 'transfer'.

*Art. 2(2), Arms Trade Treaty*

---

21  See B. Docherty, 'Commentary on Article 2', in G. Nystuen and S. Casey-Maslen (ed.), *Convention on Cluster Munitions, A Commentary*, Oxford University Press, Oxford, 2010, para. 2.144.

22  Art. 2(8), 2008 Convention on Cluster Munitions.

the transfer of an unlimited number of prohibited weapons is permitted, for the purpose of stockpile destruction. This encompasses the acts of both an exporting state party and an importing state party.

6.15    In the Arms Trade Treaty, however, the definition of transfer is entirely different. Therein it is stipulated that: 'For the purposes of this Treaty, the activities of the international trade comprise export, import, transit, trans-shipment and brokering, hereafter referred to as "transfer"'.[23] This is the only explicit definition in the entire treaty.[24]

## The meaning of export

6.16    Similar to the other global disarmament treaties, export is not defined in the Arms Trade Treaty. Yet the export is subject to both obligations and prohibitions in relation to arms, munitions, and integral parts and components. Early draft texts of the Treaty did propose definitions:

> Export: the physical movement of conventional arms out of a State's territory; the transfer of title to and control over conventional arms from one State to another State, or from one State or a legal and natural person to a legal or natural person in the jurisdiction of another State.[25]
> Export (change of title, control or ownership of conventional arms).[26]

These definitions were not incorporated in the treaty text that was adopted. Although no internationally agreed definition exists of 'export', the World Customs Organization (WCO) defines 'exportation' as 'the act of taking out or causing to be taken out any goods from the Customs territory'.[27]

## Treaty prohibitions and exceptions

### The prohibition of transfer in WMD treaties

6.17    Disarmament treaties governing WMD typically prohibit all transfer of the weapons that they outlaw (see Box 6.2). With respect to nuclear weapons, the approach taken is to prohibit all transfer of any nuclear weapons and any other nuclear explosive devices, even if they are used for peaceful purposes. Following the break-up of the Soviet Union, however, nuclear weapons were left in three

---

23  Art. 2(2), 2013 Arms Trade Treaty.
24  S. Parker, 'Commentary on Article 2', in S. Casey-Maslen, A. Clapham, G. Giacca, and S. Parker, *The Arms Trade Treaty, A Commentary*, Oxford University Press, Oxford, 2016, para. 2.232.
25  Ibid., para. 2.233, citing Chair's Draft Paper on Scope (First Preparatory Committee), Annex B(1)(b); Chair's Draft Paper on Scope (Second Preparatory Committee), Annex B(1)(b).
26  Chair's Paper, 3 July 2012, §4(B)(3)(b).
27  Parker, 'Commentary on Article 2', paras. 2.234–2.235, citing WCO, *Glossary of International Customs Terms*, November 2013, p. 17, at: http://bit.ly/2Q52N9Z. The customs territory of a state is the territory over which its Customs Law operates.

of its successor states (Belarus, Kazakhstan, and Ukraine). These states transferred these weapons to the Russian Federation and became party to the NPT as non-nuclear-weapon states. The NPT recognises the valuable peaceful uses of nuclear energy. Accordingly, Article IV acknowledges the right of all states parties to the Treaty to develop nuclear energy for peaceful purposes and to benefit from international cooperation in this area.

6.18   In the Treaty on the Prohibition of Nuclear Weapons, reference is made in the preamble to the 'inalienable right' of states parties 'to develop research, production and use of nuclear energy for peaceful purposes without discrimination'.[28] While transfer is not explicitly mentioned as elements of this right, it may be considered implicit.

6.19   In the Biological Weapons Convention, the prohibition in Article I applies to 'microbial or other biological agents, or toxins whatever their origin or method of production, of types and in quantities that have no justification for prophylactic, protective or other peaceful purposes'. This means that it is not prohibited to transfer such agents or toxins where they *are* of appropriate types and quantities for prophylactic, protective, or other peaceful purposes. This exception is reinforced in Article X(1) according to which states parties 'undertake to facilitate, and have the right to participate in, the fullest possible exchange of equipment, materials, and scientific and technological information for the use of bacteriological (biological) agents and toxins for peaceful purposes'. The notion of 'exchange' encompasses, but is not limited to, transfer.

---

## BOX 6.2   TREATY PROHIBITIONS ON THE TRANSFER OF WEAPONS OF MASS DESTRUCTION

Each nuclear-weapon State Party to the Treaty undertakes not to transfer to any recipient whatsoever nuclear weapons or other nuclear explosive devices or control over such weapons or explosive devices directly, or indirectly. . . .

*Art. I, NPT*

Each State Party to this Convention undertakes not to transfer to any recipient whatsoever, directly or indirectly, . . . any of the agents, toxins, weapons, equipment or means of delivery specified in Article I. . . .

*Art. III, Biological Weapons Convention*

---

28 Twenty-first preambular paragraph to the TPNW.

> Each State Party to this Convention undertakes never under any circumstances: . . . To . . . transfer, directly or indirectly, chemical weapons to anyone. . . .
>
> *Art. I(1)(a), Chemical Weapons Convention*

> Each State Party undertakes never under any circumstances to: . . .
>
> b  Transfer to any recipient whatsoever nuclear weapons or other nuclear explosive devices or control over such weapons or explosive devices directly or indirectly;
>
> c  Receive the transfer of or control over nuclear weapons or other nuclear explosive devices directly or indirectly. . . .
>
> *Art. 1(1)(a), Treaty on the Prohibition of Nuclear Weapons*

6.20   The preamble to the Biological Weapons Convention notes the determination of the states negotiating the treaty, 'for the sake of all mankind, to exclude completely the possibility of bacteriological (biological) agents and toxins being used as weapons'.[29] In contrast, the Chemical Weapons Convention takes a slightly different approach. The prohibition of transfer applies to 'chemical weapons', which are defined as toxic chemicals and their precursors, 'except where intended for purposes not prohibited under this Convention, as long as the types and quantities are consistent with such purposes'.[30]

6.21   The Chemical Weapons Convention explicitly allows use of chemical agents for the purpose of law enforcement, including domestic riot control.[31] Thus, the transfer from one state party to another could be lawful where it concerned minimum necessary quantities of tear gas for use during a violent assembly or of pepper spray for use against violent individuals in a manner that would comply with international human rights law.

## The prohibition of transfer in conventional weapons treaties

6.22   Traditionally, the law of armed conflict and disarmament law were distinct branches of international law. Also called international humanitarian law, the former focuses on prohibition of restrictions on the use of weapons in the conduct of hostilities during armed conflicts. Thus, the formal title of the Convention on Conventional Weapons is the Convention on Prohibitions or Restrictions on the *Use* of Certain Conventional Weapons Which May Be Deemed to Be

---

29  Ninth preambular paragraph, 1971 Biological Weapons Convention.
30  Art. II(1)(a), 1992 Chemical Weapons Convention.
31  Art. II(9)(d), 1992 Chemical Weapons Convention.

Excessively Injurious or to Have Indiscriminate Effects (emphasis added). In contrast, disarmament law until the 1992 Chemical Weapons Convention typically covered the development, production, stockpiling, and transfer of weapons. In the mid-1990s, the revision of an existing Protocol to the Convention on Conventional Weapons (on mines, booby-traps, and other devices) and the addition of a new Protocol (on blinding laser weapons), this clear delimitation was broken (see Box 6.3).

---

## BOX 6.3  DISARMAMENT TREATY PROHIBITIONS ON TRANSFER OF CONVENTIONAL WEAPONS

The High Contracting Parties shall not transfer such weapons to any State or non-State entity.

*Art. 1, 1995 Protocol IV on Blinding Laser Weapons to the Convention on Certain Conventional Weapons*

In order to promote the purposes of this Protocol, each High Contracting Party:

a   undertakes not to transfer any mine the use of which is prohibited by this Protocol;

b   undertakes not to transfer any mine to any recipient other than a State or a State agency authorized to receive such transfers;

c   undertakes to exercise restraint in the transfer of any mine the use of which is restricted by this Protocol. In particular, each High Contracting Party undertakes not to transfer any anti-personnel mines to States which are not bound by this Protocol, unless the recipient State agrees to apply this Protocol; and

d   undertakes to ensure that any transfer in accordance with this Article takes place in full compliance, by both the transferring and the recipient State, with the relevant provisions of this Protocol and the applicable norms of international humanitarian law.

*Art. 8(1), 1996 Amended Protocol II to the Convention on Certain Conventional Weapons*

Each State Party undertakes never under any circumstances to:. . .

b   . . . transfer to anyone, directly or indirectly, anti-personnel mines. . . .

*Art. 1(1), Anti-Personnel Mine Ban Convention*

Each State Party undertakes never under any circumstances to:. . .

b   . . . transfer to anyone, directly or indirectly, cluster munitions. . .

*Art. 1(1), Convention on Cluster Munitions*

6.23    Protocol IV to the Convention on Conventional Weapons, adopted by states parties to the Convention in 1995, prohibited use in armed conflict of laser weapons specifically designed to blind. It also included an undertaking by states parties not to transfer such weapons 'to any State or non-State entity'. More elaborate provisions on transfer were included in 1996 in the amended Protocol II to the Convention on mines, booby-traps, and other devices. The central provision takes the same approach as in Protocol IV: where the use of a mine is prohibited by the Protocol, so too is its transfer.[32] The amended Protocol also includes an obligation not to transfer 'any mine to any recipient other than a State or a State agency authorized to receive such transfers',[33] meaning that all transfers to non-state actors are prohibited. It further requires that states parties 'exercise restraint' in transferring any mine whose use is restricted by the Protocol, especially where a recipient state is not party to the Protocol, 'unless the recipient State agrees to apply this Protocol'.[34]

6.24    Subsequent disarmament agreements to outlaw conventional weapons have, though, followed the approach taken in the Chemical Weapons Convention to prohibit use as well as development, production, stockpiling, and transfer of the weapons. The undertaking is '*never* under any circumstances' (emphasis added) to transfer the respective weapons. This is the case in both the Anti-Personnel Mine Ban Convention and the Convention on Cluster Munitions (see Box 6.3).

6.25    In fact, however, 'never' does not actually mean 'never'. In both instances, an explicit exception to the general prohibition is provided for transfer for the detection, clearance, or destruction of anti-personnel mines and cluster munitions, respectively (see Box 6.4). The number of anti-personnel mines or explosive submunitions acquired 'shall not exceed the minimum number absolutely necessary' for these purposes. The transfer of an unlimited number of either of the weapons is permitted, but for the purpose of destruction only.

---

## BOX 6.4   EXCEPTIONS TO PROHIBITIONS ON TRANSFER OF CONVENTIONAL WEAPONS

### Article 3: Exceptions

1    Notwithstanding the general obligations under Article 1, the retention or transfer of a number of antipersonnel mines for the development of and training in mine detection, mine clearance, or mine destruction techniques is permitted. The amount of such mines shall not exceed the minimum number absolutely necessary for the above-mentioned purposes.

---

32 Art. 8(1)(a), 1996 Amended Protocol II.
33 Art. 8(1)(b), 1996 Amended Protocol II.
34 Art. 8(1)(a), 1996 Amended Protocol II.

2 The transfer of anti-personnel mines for the purpose of destruction is permitted.

*Art. 3(1) and (2), Anti-Personnel Mine Ban Convention*

### Article 3: Storage and stockpile destruction

6 Notwithstanding the provisions of Article 1 of this Convention, the retention or acquisition of a limited number of cluster munitions and explosive submunitions for the development of and training in cluster munition and explosive submunition detection, clearance or destruction techniques, or for the development of cluster munition counter-measures, is permitted. The amount of explosive submunitions retained or acquired shall not exceed the minimum number absolutely necessary for these purposes.

7 Notwithstanding the provisions of Article 1 of this Convention, the transfer of cluster munitions to another State Party for the purpose of destruction, as well as for the purposes described in paragraph 6 of this Article, is permitted.

8 States Parties retaining, acquiring or transferring cluster munitions or explosive submunitions for the purposes described in paragraphs 6 and 7 of this Article shall submit a detailed report on the planned and actual use of these cluster munitions and explosive submunitions and their type, quantity and lot numbers. If cluster munitions or explosive submunitions are transferred to another State Party for these purposes, the report shall include reference to the receiving party. Such a report shall be prepared for each year during which a State Party retained, acquired or transferred cluster munitions or explosive submunitions and shall be submitted to the Secretary-General of the United Nations no later than 30 April of the following year.

*Art. 3(6)–(8), Convention on Cluster Munitions*

## Firearms Protocol

6.26 The 2001 Firearms Protocol, annexed to the United Nations Convention on Transnational Organized Crime,[35] does not cover state-to-state transfers. It seeks to prevent the illicit trafficking in firearms as well as their parts and components and ammunition. Illicit trafficking is defined as 'the import, export,

---

35 Protocol Against The Illicit Manufacturing of and Trafficking in Firearms, Their Parts and Components and Ammunition, Supplementing the United Nations Convention Against Transnational Organized Crime; adopted at New York, 31 May 2001; entered into force, 3 July 2005.

acquisition, sale, delivery, movement or transfer of firearms, their parts and components and ammunition from or across the territory of one state party to that of another if any of the states concerned does not authorise it or if the firearms are not marked in accordance with the Protocol'.[36]

## The Arms Trade Treaty regime

6.27   The Arms Trade Treaty covers all conventional weapons, albeit some provisions have narrower scopes. In certain circumstances, it prohibits unequivocally the transfer of any conventional weapon falling within the scope of the Treaty. This is the case where the transfer would violate an arms embargo adopted by the UN Security Council acting under Chapter VII of the UN Charter (see below); where it would violate international obligations under international agreements to which the state is a party; or where it has knowledge at the time of authorisation that the items would be used in the commission of genocide, crimes against humanity, or certain war crimes (see Box 6.5).

6.28   The prohibitions in Article 7 of the ATT apply only to the proposed export of a weapon, and not to the other forms of transfer, such as import or transshipment. If the proposed export has not been prohibited by the general prohibitions in Article 6, an exporting state party must assess the potential that the arms or items would contribute to or undermine peace and security. If it is determined that the arms or items would *undermine* peace and security, the export shall not be authorised. If, however, it is determined that the arms or items would *contribute to* peace and security, there must then be a further assessment of the extent to which they could be used to commit or facilitate a serious violation of international humanitarian law or international human rights law and to commit or facilitate an offence of terrorism or transnational organised crime designated under treaties to which the exporting state is a party.

6.29   If, after conducting this risk assessment and once available mitigating measures have been taken into account, the exporting state party determines that an *overriding risk* exists of *any* of these negative consequences, it shall not authorise the export. The precise meaning of 'overriding risk' is, though, debated.[37] The exporting state needs also to take into account the risk of the items being used to commit or facilitate serious acts of gender-based violence or serious acts of violence against women and children and the risk of diversion of the items.[38]

---

36 Art. 3(e), 2001 Firearms Protocol.
37 For a discussion of the controversy surrounding the meaning of 'overriding risk', see S. Casey-Maslen and A. Clapham, 'Article 7', in S. Casey-Maslen, A. Clapham, G. Giacca, and S. Parker, *The Arms Trade Treaty, A Commentary*, Oxford University Press, Oxford, 2016, paras. 7.90–7.95.
38 Art. 7(4) and 11(2), 2013 Arms Trade Treaty.

## BOX 6.5 PROHIBITIONS ON TRANSFER OF CONVENTIONAL WEAPONS IN THE ARMS TRADE TREATY

### Article 6: Prohibitions

1   A State Party shall not authorize any transfer of conventional arms covered under Article 2(1) or of items covered under Article 3 or Article 4, if the transfer would violate its obligations under measures adopted by the United Nations Security Council acting under Chapter VII of the Charter of the United Nations, in particular arms embargoes.

2   A State Party shall not authorize any transfer of conventional arms covered under Article 2(1) or of items covered under Article 3 or Article 4, if the transfer would violate its relevant international obligations under international agreements to which it is a Party, in particular those relating to the transfer of, or illicit trafficking in, conventional arms.

3   A State Party shall not authorize any transfer of conventional arms covered under Article 2(1) or of items covered under Article 3 or Article 4, if it has knowledge at the time of authorization that the arms or items would be used in the commission of genocide, crimes against humanity, grave breaches of the Geneva Conventions of 1949, attacks directed against civilian objects or civilians protected as such, or other war crimes as defined by international agreements to which it is a Party.

### Article 7: Export and Export Assessment

1   If the export is not prohibited under Article 6, each exporting State Party, prior to authorization of the export of conventional arms . . . or of items. . . under its jurisdiction and pursuant to its national control system, shall, in an objective and non-discriminatory manner, taking into account relevant factors, . . . assess the potential that the conventional arms or items:

  a   would contribute to or undermine peace and security;

  b   could be used to:

  i    commit or facilitate a serious violation of international humanitarian law;

  ii   commit or facilitate a serious violation of international human rights law;

  iii  commit or facilitate an act constituting an offence under international conventions or relating to terrorism to which the exporting State is a Party; or

> iv   commit or facilitate an act constituting an offence under international conventions or protocols relating to transnational organized crime to which the exporting State is a Party.
>
> 2   The exporting State Party shall also consider whether there are measures that could be undertaken to mitigate risks identified in (a) or (b) in paragraph 1, such as confidence-building measures or jointly developed and agreed programmes by the exporting and importing States.
>
> 3   If, after conducting this assessment and considering available mitigating measures, the exporting State Party determines that there is an overriding risk of any of the negative consequences in paragraph 1, the exporting State Party shall not authorize the export.

## UN Security Council regimes

6.30   The UN Security Council can pass resolutions that bind member states. Under Article 25 of the UN Charter, the 'Members of the United Nations agree to accept and carry out the decisions of the Security Council in accordance with the present Charter'. Article 48 provides that 'the action required to carry out the decisions of the Security Council for the maintenance of international peace and security shall be taken by all the Members of the United Nations or by some of them, as the Security Council may determine'. Article 49 further states that: 'The Members of the United Nations shall join in affording mutual assistance in carrying out the measures decided upon by the Security Council'.

### *Resolution 1540 on the proliferation of weapons of mass destruction*

6.31   In 2004, at the behest of the United States, the Security Council adopted Resolution 1540 on the proliferation of weapons of mass destruction. In the Resolution, the Council decided that 'all States shall refrain from providing any form of support to non-State actors that attempt to develop, acquire, manufacture, possess, transport, transfer or use nuclear, chemical or biological weapons and their means of delivery'.[39] The Council further decided that all States 'shall take and enforce effective measures to establish domestic controls to prevent the proliferation of nuclear, chemical, or biological weapons and their means of delivery'.[40]

6.32   These obligations encompass prohibitions on transfer, even though they clearly extend far more widely. In case of doubt, though, it is stipulated that 'none of the obligations' set out in the Resolution 'shall be interpreted so as to conflict with

---

39 UN Security Council Resolution 1540, adopted on 28 April 2004, para. 1.
40 Ibid., para. 3.

or alter the rights and obligations' of states parties to the NPT, the Chemical Weapons Convention, and the Biological Weapons Convention.[41] The 1540 Committee established pursuant to the resolution[42] supports its effective implementation. Through Resolution 1810, adopted in 2008, the Security Council urged the 1540 Committee to 'continue strengthening' its role in facilitating technical assistance, including by engaging actively in matching offers and requests for assistance.[43]

## Arms embargoes

6.33    Under Article 41 of the UN Charter, the Security Council 'may decide what measures not involving the use of armed force are to be employed to give effect to its decisions', and it may call upon the UN member states 'to apply such measures'. These measures 'may include complete or partial interruption of economic relations', which includes mandatory arms embargoes. Depending on the text of the resolution, an arms embargo prohibits the transfer of some or all weapons to the state or actor that is the subject of the resolution. For a list of mandatory arms embargoes in place as of writing, see, *supra*, paragraphs 3.15 (with respect to states) and 3.22 (with respect to non-state actors).

## Regional legal regimes

6.34    A number of legally binding regional transfer regimes have been adopted over the last two decades. The most important of these instruments are cited below.

## SADC Protocol on the Control of Firearms and Ammunition

6.35    The Southern African Development Community (SADC) Protocol on the Control of Firearms, Ammunition, and Other Related Materials was adopted in 2001 and entered into force on November 2004.[44] The Protocol prohibits 'illicit trafficking' of firearms, defining this to mean 'the import, export, acquisition, sale, delivery, movement or transfer of firearms, ammunition, and other related materials from, to, or across the territory of a State Party without the authority of State Parties concerned'.[45]

## ECOWAS Convention on Small Arms and Light Weapons

6.36    The preamble to the 2006 Economic Community of West Africa (ECOWAS) Convention notes the deep concern of its states parties 'about the

---

41  Ibid., para. 5.
42  See: http://bit.ly/2Q34BQF.
43  UN, 'About 1540 Committee: General Information', at: http://bit.ly/2RoLwJa.
44  Protocol on the Control of Firearms, Ammunition and Other Related Materials in the Southern African Development Community (SADC) Region; adopted at Gaborone, 14 August 2001; entered into force, 8 November 2004.
45  Arts. 5(1) and 1(2), 2001 SADC Firearms Protocol.

uncontrolled flow of small arms and light weapons into Africa in general and West Africa in particular', and referred to 'the need to effectively control the transfer of arms by suppliers and arms brokers'.[46] In the substantive provisions, transfer is defined very broadly as 'import, export, transit, transhipment and transport or any other movement whatsoever of small arms and light weapons, ammunition and other related materials from or through the territory of a State'.[47]

6.37    In turn, states parties are obligated to 'ban the transfer of small arms and light weapons and their manufacturing materials into their national territory or from/through their national territory'.[48] An exemption from this prohibition can be sought

> in order to meet legitimate national defence and security needs, or to partici-
> pate in peace support or other operations in accordance with the decisions
> of the United Nations, African Union, ECOWAS, or other regional or sub-
> regional body of which it is a member.[49]

A separate prohibition applies to transfers of small arms and light weapons to non-state actors unless they are 'explicitly authorised' by the importing state party.[50]

### European Union Common Position 2008/944/CFSP

6.38    European Union (EU) Common Position 2008/944/CFSP of 8 December 2008 replaced, and made binding on all EU member states, the original 1998 EU Code of Conduct on Arms Exports.[51] The Common Position sets out eight criteria for determining whether a request for export authorisation should be denied. Criterion One concerns respect for international obligations and commitments by EU member states, in particular sanctions adopted by the UN Security Council or the EU, agreements on non-proliferation and other subjects, as well as other international obligations. The EU has arms embargoes in place with respect to Belarus, China, Egypt, Eritrea, Iran, Libya, Myanmar, North Korea, Somalia, South Sudan, Sudan, Syria, Venezuela, Yemen, and Zimbabwe. It also has embargoes on non-state actors: al-Qaeda, the Taliban, and non-state actors in DR Congo, Iraq, and Lebanon.[52]

6.39    Criterion Two concerns respect for human rights in the country of final destination as well as respect by that country of international humanitarian law.

---

46  ECOWAS Convention on Small Arms and Light Weapons, Their Ammunition and Other Related Materials; adopted at Abuja, 14 June 2006; entered into force, 29 September 2009 (2006 ECOWAS Convention on Small Arms and Light Weapons).
47  Art. 1(9), 2006 ECOWAS Convention on Small Arms and Light Weapons.
48  Art. 3(1), 2006 ECOWAS Convention on Small Arms and Light Weapons.
49  Art. 4, 2006 ECOWAS Convention on Small Arms and Light Weapons.
50  Art. 3(2), 2006 ECOWAS Convention on Small Arms and Light Weapons.
51  1998 EU Code of Conduct on Arms Exports. The 2008 EU Common Position replaced and expanded the 1998 EU Code of Conduct. See Council Common Position 2008/944/CFSP of 8 December 2008 defining common rules governing control of exports of military technology and equipment, at: http://bit.ly/2SG32dt.
52  For a list of embargoes in place under European Union auspices, see, e.g., Stockholm International Peace Research Institute (SIPRI), 'SIPRI databases: Arms Embargoes', at: http://bit.ly/2qhmqR2.

Criterion Three looks at the internal situation in the country of final destination, as a function of the existence of tensions or armed conflicts. Criterion Four refers to the preservation of regional peace, security, and stability. Criterion Five addresses the national security of EU member states and of territories whose external relations are the responsibility of a member state, as well as that of friendly and allied countries.

6.40    Criterion Six looks at the behaviour of the buyer country with regard to the international community, as regards in particular its attitude to terrorism, the nature of its alliances, and respect for international law. Criterion Seven assesses the existence of a risk that the military technology or equipment will be diverted within the buyer country or re-exported under undesirable conditions. Finally, Criterion Eight concerns the compatibility of the exports of the military technology or equipment with the technical and economic capacity of the recipient country, taking into account the desirability that states should meet their legitimate security and defence needs with the least diversion of human and economic resources for armaments.

### Kinshasa Convention

6.41    The 2010 Central African Convention for the Control of Small Arms and Light Weapons (the 2010 Kinshasa Convention) follows the approach laid down in the 2006 ECOWAS Convention.[53] Under the Convention, small arms and light weapons, their ammunition, and parts and components may only be lawfully transferred where they are necessary in order to:

a    Maintain law and order, or for defence or national security purposes;
b    Participate in peacekeeping operations conducted under the aegis of the United Nations, the African Union, the Economic Community of Central African States or other regional or subregional organizations of which the State Party concerned is a member.[54]

States parties are required to prohibit any transfer of small arms and light weapons, their ammunition, and parts and components to non-state armed groups.[55]

## Politically binding regimes

### UN Disarmament Commission Guidelines

6.42    In 1991, the UN Disarmament Commission observed that: 'Arms transfers are a deeply entrenched phenomenon of contemporary international relations'.[56]

---

53  Central African Convention for the Control of Small Arms and Light Weapons, their Ammunition and all Parts and Components that can be used for their Manufacture, Repair and Assembly; adopted at Kinshasa, 30 April 2010; entered into force, 8 March 2017.

54  Art. 3(2), 2010 Kinshasa Convention.

55  Art. 4, 2010 Kinshasa Convention.

56  UN Disarmament Commission Guidelines for International Arms Transfers, endorsed by the UN General Assembly in Resolution 51/47B, adopted without a vote on 10 December 1996, para. 3.

The main Guidelines that states should 'bear in mind' in their efforts 'to control their international arms transfers', include recognising the need for transparency in arms transfers,[57] and reminds states that they 'have responsibilities in exercising restraint' as to the procurement and transfers of arms.[58] The Guidelines further observe that supplier states have a responsibility to 'seek to ensure that the quantity and level of sophistication of their arms exports do not contribute to instability and conflict in their regions or in other countries and regions or to illicit trafficking in arms'.[59] A corresponding responsibility is recalled with respect to importing states.[60] Finally, international arms transfers, the Guidelines recommend, 'should not be used as a means to interfere in the internal affairs of other States'.[61]

## *Wassenaar Arrangement documents*

6.43   The Wassenaar Arrangement on Export Controls for Conventional Arms and Dual-Use Goods and Technologies (WA) is a multilateral export control regime with 42 'Participating States'. The Arrangement seeks to promote regional and international security and stability by promoting transparency and greater responsibility in transfers of conventional arms and dual-use goods and technologies. Participating States 'seek, through their national policies, to ensure that transfers of these items do not contribute to the development or enhancement of military capabilities which undermine these goals, and are not diverted to support such capabilities'.[62]

6.44   Participating states have full discretion as to whether or not to transfer any item subject to the WA's Munition List or the List of Dual-Use Goods and Technologies:

> The decision to transfer or deny transfer of any item will be the sole responsibility of each Participating State. All measures undertaken with respect to the Arrangement will be in accordance with national legislation and policies and will be implemented on the basis of national discretion.[63]

Approximately 20 WA guidelines, elements, and procedures inform Participating States' decision-making that is based on national legislation and policies. Such guidance on the exports of conventional weapons are, for instance, the 'Elements for Objective Analysis and Advice Concerning Potentially Destabilising Accumulations of Conventional Weapons', which were adopted in 1998 and amended in 2004 and 2011; 'Best Practices for Effective Legislation on Arms Brokering',

---

57 UN Disarmament Commission Guidelines for International Arms Transfers, para. 15.
58 Ibid., para. 18.
59 Ibid., para. 20.
60 Ibid., para. 21.
61 Ibid., para. 22.
62 Wassenaar Arrangement, Initial Elements, s. I, para. I, at: http://bit.ly/2CQIE3M.
63 Ibid., s. II, para. 3.

adopted in 2003 and amended in 2016; and the 2011 'Best Practice Guidelines on Subsequent Transfer (Re-export) Controls for Conventional Weapons Systems contained in Appendix 3 to the WA Initial Elements'. Regarding dual-use items, such guidance is the 2011 'Best Practice Guidelines on Internal Compliance Programmes for Dual-Use Goods and Technologies'.

### Missile Technology Control Guidelines

6.45   The Missile Technology Control Regime (MTCR) combines the MTCR Guidelines for Sensitive Missile-Relevant Transfers and the list of dual-use items of concern, namely the Equipment, Software, and Technology Annex. The Guidelines define the purpose of the MTCR and provide the overall structure and rules to guide member states and others endorsing the Guidelines. According to the Guidelines for Sensitive Missile-Relevant Transfers,

> particular restraint will be exercised in the consideration of Category I transfers regardless of their purpose, and there will be a strong presumption to deny such transfers. Particular restraint will also be exercised in the consideration of transfers of any items in the Annex, or of any missiles (whether or not in the Annex), if the Government judges, on the basis of all available, persuasive information . . . that they are intended to be used for the delivery of weapons of mass destruction, and there will be a strong presumption to deny such transfers. Until further notice, the transfer of Category I production facilities will not be authorised.[64]

While still agreeing to exercise restraint, partners have greater flexibility in the treatment of Category II transfer applications.

6.46   The MTCR Guidelines foresee the following factors to be taken into account by states when assessing transfer applications of the items in the MTCR Annex:

A   Concerns about the proliferation of weapons of mass destruction
B   The capabilities and objectives of the missile and space programs of the recipient state
C   The significance of the transfer in terms of the potential development of delivery systems (other than manned aircraft) for weapons of mass destruction
D   The assessment of the end use of the transfers, including the relevant assurances of the recipient states. . .
E   The applicability of relevant multilateral agreements
F   The risk of controlled items falling into the hands of terrorist groups and individuals.[65]

---

64 MTCR Guidelines for Sensitive Missile-Relevant Transfers, para. 2, at: http://bit.ly/2Fehyo4.
65 Ibid., para. 3.

6.47   Any 'transfer of design and production technology directly associated with any items in the Annex will be subject to as great a degree of scrutiny and control'. In addition, 'where the transfer could contribute to a delivery system for weapons of mass destruction', states should

> authorize transfers of items in the Annex only on receipt of appropriate assurances from the government of the recipient state that: (A) the items will be used only for the purpose stated and that such use will not be modified nor the items modified or replicated without the prior consent of the Government, and (B) the items will be used only for the purpose stated and that such use will not be modified nor the items modified or replicated without the prior consent of the Government'[66]

6.48   MTCR members should notify each other of their denials of export licences for items covered by the regimes, and other members agree to consult the denying country before approving an export of the same or similar items to the same end-user. This is commonly referred to as 'no undercut' policies. States also inform each other if they have information that non-listed items are intended to contribute to delivery systems for weapons of mass destruction other than manned aircraft and commit to require an authorisation for such transfers. This is known as 'catch all control'.

## *Australia Group Guidelines*

6.49   The Australia Group coordinates national export controls on precursors of biological and chemical weapons. While the Australia Group Common Control Lists defines which items should be subject to export controls, the Guidelines for Transfers of Sensitive Chemical or Biological Items guide the states in their decision-making:

> [The] evaluation of export applications will take into account the following non-exhaustive list of factors:
>
> a  Information about proliferation and terrorism involving CBW, including any proliferation or terrorism-related activity, or about involvement in clandestine or illegal procurement activities, of the parties to the transaction;
> b  The capabilities and objectives of the chemical and biological activities of the recipient state;
> c  The significance of the transfer in terms of (1) the appropriateness of the stated end-use, including any relevant assurances submitted by the recipient state or end-user, and (2) the potential development of CBW;

---

66 Ibid., para. 5.

d   The role of distributors, brokers or other intermediaries in the transfer, including, where appropriate, their ability to provide an authenticated end-user certificate specifying both the importer and ultimate end-user of the item to be transferred, as well as the credibility of assurances that the item will reach the stated end-user;

e   The assessment of the end-use of the transfer, including whether a transfer has been previously denied to the end-user, whether the end-user has diverted for unauthorized purposes any transfer previously authorized, and, to the extent possible, whether the end-user is capable of securely handling and storing the item transferred;

f   The extent and effectiveness of the export control system in the recipient state as well as any intermediary states;

g   The applicability of relevant multilateral agreements, including the BTWC and CWC.

h   The risk of controlled items falling into the hands of terrorist groups and individuals.[67]

6.50   States commit to deny transfers 'if the Government judges, on the basis of all available, persuasive information, evaluated according to factors including those [above], 'that the controlled items are intended to be used in a chemical weapons or biological weapons program, or for CBW terrorism, or that a significant risk of diversion exists'.[68] Similarly to the MTCR, the Australia Group also foresees 'catch all controls' and 'no undercut' policies.

## *Nuclear Suppliers Group Guidelines*

6.51   The Nuclear Suppliers Group (NSG) establishes two sets of NSG Guidelines that aim 'to ensure that nuclear trade for peaceful purposes does not contribute to the proliferation of nuclear weapons or other nuclear explosive devices, and that international trade and cooperation in the nuclear field is not hindered unjustly in the process'.[69] The first set of guidelines concern nuclear transfers according to the so-called Trigger List. Trigger List items 'trigger' a requirement for International Atomic Energy Agency (IAEA) safeguards in the country of destination. The Trigger List covers fuel cycle items, technology, and software.

6.52   In the NSG Part 1 Guidelines, formal government assurances are required between the exporting and importing governments to assure that the nuclear transfer is for peaceful purposes and will not contribute to the proliferation of nuclear weapons or other nuclear explosive devices. The importing government also has to provide assurance that it will not re-transfer items, material or technology that it has

---

67 The Australia Group, Guidelines for Transfers of Sensitive Chemical or Biological Items, at: http://bit.ly/2RM4vhl.

68 Ibid.

69 Nuclear Suppliers Group, Guidelines, at: http://bit.ly/2zPrXmZ.

received to a third government without the exporting government's prior consent. There is also a requirement for physical protection measures, and an agreement to exercise particular caution in the transfer of sensitive facilities (i.e. enrichment and reprocessing facilities and equipment and technology therefor), technology and material usable for nuclear weapons or other nuclear explosive devices.[70]

6.53   The second set of guidelines applies to transfers of nuclear-related dual-use equipment, materials, software, and related technology. The NSG Part 2 Guidelines, also known as the 'Dual-Use Guidelines', were adopted in 1992 after the export control provisions then in force had not prevented one state party to the NPT (i.e. North Korea) from pursuing a clandestine nuclear weapons programme. A large part of this clandestine nuclear weapons programme effort had been to acquire dual-use items not covered by the NSG Guidelines and then use these items to build Trigger List items. According to the Guidelines, states should not authorise transfers of equipment, materials, software, or related technology: (1) for use in a non-nuclear-weapon state in a nuclear explosive activity or an unsafeguarded nuclear fuel-cycle activity, or (2) in general, when there is an unacceptable risk of diversion to such an activity, or when the transfers are contrary to the objective of averting the proliferation of nuclear weapons, or (3) when there is an unacceptable risk of diversion to acts of nuclear terrorism.[71]

6.54   Like the MTCR and Australia Group, the NSG establishes 'catch all controls' and 'no undercut' policies.

---

70 Nuclear Suppliers Group, at: http://bit.ly/2C0hVko.
71 Nuclear Suppliers Group, Guidelines for transfers of nuclear-related dual-use equipment, materials, software, and related technology (INFCIRC/254, Part 2).

# 7

# STOCKPILE DESTRUCTION

## Introduction

7.1    At the heart of disarmament is the destruction of weapons whose development, production, retention, transfer, and use – as well as stockpiling – are prohibited. Accordingly, each of the global disarmament treaties provides for stockpile destruction. In most cases, the deadline is set in terms of months or years. This is the case for the 1971 Biological Weapons Convention,[1] the 1992 Chemical Weapons Convention,[2] the 1997 Anti-Personnel Mine Ban Convention,[3] and the 2008 Convention on Cluster Munitions.[4] Exceptionally, the 2017 Treaty on the Prohibition of Nuclear Weapons[5] (not yet in force, as of writing) defers the decision as to that deadline to the first meeting of its states parties that will be held following the treaty's entry into force. Two disarmament treaties allow states parties to extend their respective deadlines: the Chemical Weapons Convention and the Convention on Cluster Munitions.

7.2    This chapter describes the relevant treaty obligations for stockpile destruction and explains the different forms of stockpile destruction techniques. Detonation

---

1    Convention on the Prohibition of the Development, Production and Stockpiling of Bacteriological (Biological) and Toxin Weapons and on Their Destruction; opened for signature at London, Moscow, and Washington, DC, 10 April 1972; entered into force, 26 March 1975.
2    Convention on the Prohibition of the Development, Production, Stockpiling and Use of Chemical Weapons and on their Destruction; adopted at Geneva, 3 September 1992; entered into force, 29 April 1997.
3    Convention on the Prohibition of the Use, Stockpiling, Production and Transfer of Anti-Personnel Mines and on their Destruction; adopted at Oslo, 18 September 1997; entered into force, 1 March 1999.
4    Convention on Cluster Munitions; adopted at Dublin, 30 May 2008; entered into force, 1 August 2010.
5    Treaty on the Prohibition of Nuclear Weapons; adopted at New York, 7 July 2017; not yet in force.

is only one option for stockpile destruction, which may not be either the cheapest or the most environmentally friendly. A particular challenge exists with respect to the components of weapons of mass destruction (WMD), especially fissile material, toxic chemicals, and bacteriological toxins.

7.3   There is no international treaty definition of a stockpile for the purposes of disarmament law. It is clear that the International Mine Action Standards (IMAS)[6] definition of 'stockpile' with respect to munitions, elaborated by the United Nations in the context of mine action, as a 'large accumulated stock of explosive ordnance'[7] is not the international legal standard. A single nuclear weapon is assuredly a stockpile, however.

## Treaty obligations, including deadlines

### Weapons of mass destruction

### Biological weapons

7.4   The first global disarmament treaty to provide for stockpile destruction was the Biological Weapons Convention, in 1971. Under Article II of the Convention, each state party 'undertakes to destroy, or to divert to peaceful purposes, as soon as possible but not later than nine months after the entry into force of the Convention, all agents, toxins, weapons, equipment, and means of delivery' outlawed in Article I (see Box 7.1). The obligation extends broadly to all such components, means, and equipment 'in its possession or under its jurisdiction or control'.

7.5   The Biological Weapons Convention entered into force in March 1975 after its ratification by 22 states, meaning that the treaty deadline for destruction was set at the end of 1975.[8] There is no possibility of extending the deadline, so states adhering to the Biological Weapons Convention since the end of 1975 should have destroyed all items in their possession or under their jurisdiction or control prior to ratification or accession.

7.6   While the Biological Weapons Convention obliges the complete destruction of all biological weapons and prohibits future production, in contrast to the later Chemical Weapons Convention, it does not provide for a specific regime of verification or enforcement. In 2001, after six years of negotiations, a proposal was

---

6   The IMAS are the standards in force for all UN mine action operations and serve as guidance to states establishing their own mine action programmes. The IMAS were initially endorsed by the UN Inter-Agency Coordination Group on Mine Action on 26 September 2001 and have since been reviewed, added to, and revised. See, e.g., 'About IMAS', at: http://bit.ly/2Q96StE.

7   IMAS 04.10: 'Glossary of mine action terms, definitions and abbreviations', 2nd Edn (May 2013), at: http://bit.ly/2Q9MPLQ.

8   If Article 2 had been drafted to say 'nine months after the entry into force of the Convention *for that state party*', this would have allowed states to adhere to the Convention and then destroy within nine months (or divert to peaceful purposes) all microbial or other biological agents or toxins and associated weapons, equipment, and means of delivery.

---

**BOX 7.1 STOCKPILE DESTRUCTION OBLIGATIONS UNDER THE BIOLOGICAL WEAPONS CONVENTION**

**Article I**

Each State Party to this Convention undertakes never in any circumstances to develop, produce, stockpile or otherwise acquire or retain:

1. microbial or other biological agents, or toxins whatever their origin or method of production, of types and in quantities that have no justification for prophylactic, protective or other peaceful purposes;
2. weapons, equipment or means of delivery designed to use such agents or toxins for hostile purposes or in armed conflict.

**Article II**

Each State Party to this Convention undertakes to destroy, or to divert to peaceful purposes, as soon as possible but not later than nine months after the entry into force of the Convention, all agents, toxins, weapons, equipment and means of delivery specified in Article I of the Convention, which are in its possession or under its jurisdiction or control. In implementing the provisions of this Article all necessary safety precautions shall be observed to protect populations and the environment.

---

presented for a legally binding protocol to the Biological Weapons Convention that would establish on-site facility visits and procedures for investigating allegations of non-compliance.[9] The United States of America objected to the protocol, however, arguing that it would be ineffective while imposing unfair burdens on the US biotechnology industry and national biological defence programmes.[10]

*Chemical weapons*

7.7    Under Article I(2) of the 1992 Chemical Weapons Convention, each state party 'undertakes to destroy chemical weapons it owns or possesses, or that are located in any place under its jurisdiction or control', in accordance with the Convention. This is a very broad formulation, encompassing not just stockpiles

---

9 J. Tucker, 'The Fifth Review Conference of the Biological and Toxin Weapons Convention', *NTI*, 1 February 2002, at http://bit.ly/2QeyNbZ.
10 ILPI, 'Biological weapons under international law', December 2016, citing Tucker, 'The Fifth Review Conference of the Biological and Toxin Weapons Convention'.

belonging to, or held by, the state party itself but also stockpiles of chemical weapons owned by another state located anywhere under the state party's jurisdiction or control. States parties make a corresponding undertaking to destroy all chemical weapons they earlier abandoned on the territory of another state party and to destroy any chemical weapons production facilities they own or possess, or that exist in any place under their jurisdiction or control.[11]

7.8    Toxic chemicals include sarin and VX (short for 'venomous agent X'), phosgene, different forms of mustard gas, and ricin. Precursors, which are chemical substances that can be used to produce toxic chemicals, consist of, for example, chlorosarin (for sarin) and methylphosphonyl difluorides (used to produce sarin and soman as a binary chemical weapon).[12] These agents must be either destroyed (if they have no legitimate peaceful purpose) or strictly controlled. But as has been seen in Syria, chlorine – not a scheduled toxic chemical – can be used as a chemical weapon. Chlorine, which is widely used to disinfect tap water, is therefore lawful to store and sell for such purposes. Even at low concentrations it can cause permanent lung damage.[13]

7.9    Chlorine was first used in chemical warfare by German forces in World War I: of the 15,000 military casualties of the 1915 gas attack on the Western Front, near Ypres (Leper), 5,000 died.[14] In Syria, a fact-finding mission of the Organisation for the Prohibition of Chemical Weapons (OPCW)[15] investigating the use of chlorine gas in June 2014 concluded that the chemical agent had been used not only in this instance but also in earlier attacks.[16] A 2015 UN Security Council resolution condemned the use of chlorine in attacks in Syria, noting that this was the 'first ever documented instance of the use of toxic chemicals as weapons within the territory of a State Party to the CWC'.[17]

---

11  Art. I(2), 1992 Chemical Weapons Convention.
12  See Chemical Weapons Convention Schedules on Chemicals, Schedules 1 and 3.
13  See, e.g., 'Syria Chlorine Attack Claims: What This Chemical Is and How It Became a Weapon', *The Conversation*, 7 September 2016, at: http://bit.ly/2zjSzvp.
14  Ibid.
15  The OPCW is established by the Chemical Weapons Convention to support and oversee the implementation of the Convention. The Convention further provides for the establishment of three subsidiary bodies to aid the three main organs of the OPCW in its work: the Scientific Advisory Board, the Advisory Body on Administrative and Financial Issues, and the Confidentiality Commission. As a subsidiary organ of the Conference of States Parties, the Confidentiality Commission's main function is to settle any disputes between states parties related to confidentiality. Independent experts mandated to assess relevant scientific and technological developments and report on such subjects to the Director-General sit on the Scientific Advisory Board. Finally, the Advisory Body on Administrative and Financial Matters advises both the OPCW Technical Secretariat and the states parties on issues relating to the OPCW programme and budgets. OPCW, 'Subsidiary Bodies', at: http://bit.ly/2PEKYBy.
16  OPCW, 'OPCW Fact Finding Mission: "Compelling Confirmation" That Chlorine Gas Used as Weapon in Syria', The Hague, 10 September 2014, at: http://bit.ly/2JzTbSe.
17  UN Security Council Resolution 2209, adopted on 6 March 2015 by 14 votes to nil, with 1 abstention (Venezuela), seventh preambular paragraph.

## BOX 7.2   DESTRUCTION OF STOCKPILED CHEMICAL WEAPONS UNDER THE CHEMICAL WEAPONS CONVENTION

### Article I

1   Each State Party to this Convention undertakes never under any circumstances:

    a   To develop, produce, otherwise acquire, stockpile or retain chemical weapons, or transfer, directly or indirectly, chemical weapons to anyone. . . .

2   Each State Party undertakes to destroy chemical weapons it owns or possesses, or that are located in any place under its jurisdiction or control, in accordance with the provisions of this Convention.

3   Each State Party undertakes to destroy all chemical weapons it abandoned on the territory of another State Party, in accordance with the provisions of this Convention.

4   Each State Party undertakes to destroy any chemical weapons production facilities it owns or possesses, or that are located in any place under its jurisdiction or control, in accordance with the provisions of this Convention.

### Article IV

1   The provisions of this Article and the detailed procedures for its implementation shall apply to all chemical weapons owned or possessed by a State Party, or that are located in any place under its jurisdiction or control, except old chemical weapons and abandoned chemical weapons to which Part IV (B) of the Verification Annex applies.

4   Each State Party shall destroy all chemical weapons specified in paragraph 1 pursuant to the Verification Annex and in accordance with the agreed rate and sequence of destruction (hereinafter referred to as 'order of destruction'). Such destruction shall begin not later than two years after this Convention enters into force for it and shall finish not later than 10 years after entry into force of this Convention. A State Party is not precluded from destroying such chemical weapons at a faster rate.

8   If a State ratifies or accedes to this Convention after the 10-year period for destruction set forth in paragraph 6, it shall destroy chemical weapons specified in paragraph 1 as soon as possible. The order of destruction and

procedures for stringent verification for such a State Party shall be determined by the Executive Council.

11 Any State Party which has on its territory chemical weapons that are owned or possessed by another State, or that are located in any place under the jurisdiction or control of another State, shall make the fullest efforts to ensure that these chemical weapons are removed from its territory not later than one year after this Convention enters into force for it.

7.10 The legal duty upon states parties to the Chemical Weapons Convention to destroy chemical weapons is detailed in Article IV of the Convention (see Box 7.2). Each state party was required to destroy its own chemical weapons, beginning within two years of the Convention's entry into force (i.e. 29 April 1997) and finishing no later than ten years after its entry into force.[18] The end date for destruction was therefore 29 April 2007. It is made explicit that a state party was allowed to destroy chemical weapons 'at a faster rate'.[19]

7.11 The Convention also, though, explicitly allowed a state party, by application made prior to 29 April 2006, to extend its treaty-mandated deadline for destruction of so-called Category 1 chemical weapons (Schedule 1 chemicals, including VX and sarin, considered the most toxic of all chemical agents). An extension of no more than five years could be granted by the OPCW Executive Council[20] for the completion of destruction of all of a state party's chemical weapons (see Box 7.3).[21] In all cases, extensive verification of compliance with the stockpile destruction obligations, including through on-site missions, is provided for in the Convention.

7.12 In fact, while some states parties were granted and respected their respective extended deadline, a problem arose as a number of them failed to meet even this prolonged time limit. Russia, for instance, had been planning to complete destruction of its chemical weapons stockpiles only by 2020, which would have been eight years after the final Convention deadline.[22] In late September 2017,

18 Art. IV(6), CWC.
19 Ibid.
20 The Council, which is the Organisation's executive organ, consists of 41 members elected by the states parties for two-year terms. The Convention requires that, in order to ensure the Council's effectiveness, it reflects the principle of equitable geographical distribution, the relative importance of the chemical industry, and political and security interests. See OPCW, 'Executive Council', at: http://bit.ly/2Pymlqi.
21 Annex to the Chemical Weapons Convention, Part IV, s. C (Destruction), para. 24.
22 See, e.g., S. Mukhopadhyay, 'Russia Plans to Completely Destroy Chemical Weapons by 2020, to Shut Down Two Facilities by November', *International Business Times*, 29 October 2015, at: http://bit.

## BOX 7.3  EXTENDING THE STOCKPILE DESTRUCTION DEADLINE UNDER THE CHEMICAL WEAPONS CONVENTION

24  If a State Party believes that it will be unable to ensure the destruction of all Category 1 chemical weapons not later than 10 years after the entry into force of this Convention, it may submit a request to the Executive Council for an extension of the deadline for completing the destruction of such chemical weapons. Such a request must be made not later than nine years after the entry into force of this Convention.

25  The request shall contain:

    a  The duration of the proposed extension;

    b  A detailed explanation of the reasons for the proposed extension; and

    c  A detailed plan for destruction during the proposed extension and the remaining portion of the original 10-year period for destruction.

26  A decision on the request shall be taken by the Conference at its next session, on the recommendation of the Executive Council. Any extension shall be the minimum necessary, but in no case shall the deadline for a State Party to complete its destruction of all chemical weapons be extended beyond 15 years after the entry into force of this Convention. The Executive Council shall set conditions for the granting of the extension, including the specific verification measures deemed necessary as well as specific actions to be taken by the State Party to overcome problems in its destruction programme. . . .

27  If an extension is granted, the State Party shall take appropriate measures to meet all subsequent deadlines.

28  The State Party shall continue to submit detailed annual plans for destruction in accordance with paragraph 29 and annual reports on the destruction of Category 1 chemical weapons in accordance with paragraph 36, until all Category 1 chemical weapons are destroyed. In addition, not later than at the end of each 90 days of the extension period, the State Party shall report to the Executive Council on its destruction activity. The Executive Council shall review progress towards completion of destruction and take the necessary measures to document this progress. . . .

*Part IV (A): Destruction of Chemical Weapons and*
*its Verification Pursuant to Article IV*

however, it announced that it had completed the destruction of the last of its 39,967 metric tons of chemical weapons. In contrast, the United States is not expected to complete destruction of its own chemical weapons stocks before 2023, 11 years after the expiry of its international legal deadline under the Convention.[23]

7.13 Any state adhering to the Chemical Weapons Convention since 29 April 2007 is obliged to destroy its own chemical weapons 'as soon as possible'. The destruction and procedures for stringent verification for such states are determined by the OPCW Executive Council.[24] Iraq, for example, which became party to the Convention in 2009, still had some stocks remaining from its chemical weapons programme that it had abandoned in the late 1980s (see Box 7.4). This included remnants of chemical weapons stored in two storage bunkers at al-Muthana. Owing to the hazardous conditions within the bunkers, Iraq was not able to conduct a detailed on-site inventory immediately after the initial declaration and destruction activities started in 2017. In November 2017 and February 2018, OPCW's Technical Secretariat confirmed that four former chemical weapons production facilities in Iraq had been completely destroyed. One former chemical weapons production facility remains subject to inspection until 2028. In March 2018, Ambassador Ahmet Üzümcü, the OPCW Director-General, congratulated Iraq on completing the destruction of its chemical weapons stockpiles.[25]

7.14 On 14 September 2013, Syria deposited its instrument of accession to the Chemical Weapons Convention, becoming a state party a month later, on 14 October. The OPCW Executive Council determined that Syria would 'complete the elimination of all chemical weapons material and equipment in the first half of 2014' and 'complete as soon as possible and in any case not later than 1 November 2013, the destruction of chemical weapons production and mixing/filling equipment'.[26] The Council's decision was endorsed by UN Security Council Resolution 2118, adopted unanimously on 27 September 2013. The 2013 Nobel Peace Prize was awarded to the OPCW 'for its extensive efforts to eliminate chemical weapons'.[27]

7.15 In early January 2016, the OPCW announced the completion of destruction of all chemical weapons declared by Syria. It reported that the need to devise

ly/2EAZS7R; see also N. Litovkin, 'Washington: Russian Chemical Weapons Will Never Threaten U.S. again', *Russia Beyond the Headlines*, 15 June 2017, at: http://bit.ly/2CXtcnm.

23 See, e.g., Associated Press, 'US Set to Destroy Thousands of Chemical Weapons at Colorado Plant', *Fox News US*, 1 September 2016, at: http://bit.ly/2CwO8R9.

24 Art. IV(8), 1992 Chemical Weapons Convention.

25 OPCW, 'OPCW Director-General Congratulates Iraq on Complete Destruction of Chemical Weapons Remnants', News release, The Hague, 13 March 2018, at: http://bit.ly/2yKbPlZ.

26 OPCW Executive Council, 'Destruction of Syrian Chemical Weapons, Decision', OPCW doc. EC-M-33/DEC.1, 27 September 2013, para. 1(d) and (e), at: http://bit.ly/2OiD0te.

27 See, e.g., UN, 'Organisation for the Prohibition of Chemical Weapons (OPCW)', at: http://bit.ly/2CXV6ij.

---

## BOX 7.4 DESTRUCTION OF CHEMICAL WEAPONS STOCKPILES IN IRAQ BY UNSCOM

UN Security Council Resolution 687 outlined an extensive plan for the disarmament of Iraq. In Paragraph 8 of the resolution, the Council decided that Iraq 'shall unconditionally accept the destruction, removal, or rendering harmless, under international supervision, of: . . . All chemical and biological weapons and all stocks of agents and all related subsystems and components and all research, development, support and manufacturing facilities related thereto'. On 19 April 1991, the Council set up the United Nations Special Commission in Iraq (UNSCOM), with the responsibility for verifying Iraq's compliance with Resolution 687 in respect of its WMD programmes.

Under UNSCOM supervision, 38,537 filled and unfilled munitions, 690 tonnes of agents, 3,000 tonnes of precursor chemicals to manufacture toxic chemical agents, and thousands of pieces of production equipment and analytical instruments were destroyed. But Iraq had removed chemical weapons, equipment, and materials from the main site of the al-Muthana state facility before the first UNSCOM inspection team arrived. Iraqi claims that it had destroyed 15,620 chemical munitions unilaterally was unverified at the time. In November 1997, UNSCOM found new evidence that Iraq had developed a production capability for VX: Iraq had obtained at least 750 tonnes of VX precursor chemicals.

*Stockholm International Peace Research Institute (SIPRI), 'Iraq: The UNSCOM Experience', Fact Sheet, October 1998, p. 3, at: http://bit.ly/2zoVbb4.*

---

a technical solution for the treatment of 'a number of cylinders in a deteriorated and hazardous condition had delayed the disposal process'.[28] The Director-General of the OPCW said:

> This process closes an important chapter in the elimination of Syria's chemical weapon programme as we continue efforts to clarify Syria's declaration and address ongoing use of toxic chemicals as weapons in that country.[29]

In June 2018, however, the OPCW's Fact-Finding Mission (FFM) confirmed that sarin had 'very likely' been used as a chemical weapon in the south of Ltamenah

---

28 OPCW, 'Destruction of Declared Syrian Chemical Weapons Completed', 4 January 2016, at: http://bit.ly/2SEbkCr.
29 Ibid.

on 24 March 2017. The FFM also concluded that chlorine was very likely used as a chemical weapon at Ltamenah Hospital and the surrounding area on 25 March 2017.[30]

7.16    As of March 2018, the OPCW stated that more than 96% of all chemical weapon stockpiles declared by possessor states had been destroyed under its verification.[31] In January 2018, the OPCW Director-General had commended the complete elimination of Libya's Category 2 chemical materials (chemical weapons, such as phosgene, which are based on chemicals other than those in Schedule 1 of the Convention). The materials had been transported to Germany for destruction at the dedicated facility operated by GEKA mbH in Munster.[32] According to the OPCW, since the Convention's entry into force in 1997 – and with its 193 states parties (as of March 2019)[33] – the Chemical Weapons Convention is the most successful disarmament treaty, eliminating an entire class of weapons of mass destruction.[34]

## Nuclear weapons

7.17    The 2017 Treaty on the Prohibition of Nuclear Weapons prohibits all stockpiling of nuclear weapons and other nuclear explosive devices but does not specify a date for their destruction (see Box 7.5). Each state party undertakes never under any circumstances to possess or stockpile any nuclear explosive devices.[35] In contrast to other global disarmament treaties,[36] it is not explicitly prohibited to 'retain' the weapons or devices banned. However, it is provided that, notwithstanding the general prohibition on stockpiling or possession, each state party that 'owns, possesses or controls nuclear weapons or other nuclear explosive devices shall immediately remove them from operational status, and destroy them as soon as possible but not later than a deadline to be determined by the first meeting of States Parties'.[37]

7.18    The stockpile destruction deadline is to be incorporated in a 'legally binding, time-bound plan for the verified and irreversible elimination of that State Party's nuclear-weapon programme, including the elimination or irreversible

---

30  OPCW, 'OPCW Confirms Use of Sarin and Chlorine in Ltamenah, Syria, on 24 and 25 March 2017', News release, 13 June 2018, at: http://bit.ly/2PCR2KX.

31  OPCW, 'OPCW Director-General Congratulates Iraq on Complete Destruction of Chemical Weapons Remnants'.

32  OPCW, 'OPCW Director-General Praises Complete Destruction of Libya's Chemical Weapon Stockpile', 11 January 2018, at: http://bit.ly/2JDWubf.

33  Israel is a signatory state while Egypt, North Korea, and South Sudan have neither signed nor acceded. See OPCW list, at: http://bit.ly/2P4fdT6.

34  OPCW, 'OPCW Director-General Praises Complete Destruction of Libya's Chemical Weapon Stockpile'.

35  Art. 1(1)(a), 2017 Treaty on the Prohibition of Nuclear Weapons.

36  The Biological and Chemical Weapons conventions, the Anti-Personnel Mine Ban Convention, and the Convention on Cluster Munitions all explicitly prohibit retention of the weapons they prohibit.

37  Art. 4(2), 2017 Treaty on the Prohibition of Nuclear Weapons.

---

## BOX 7.5 DESTRUCTION OF STOCKPILED NUCLEAR WEAPONS IN THE TREATY ON THE PROHIBITION OF NUCLEAR WEAPONS

### Article 1: Prohibitions

1 Each State Party undertakes never under any circumstances to:

    a   Develop, test, produce, manufacture, otherwise acquire, possess or stockpile nuclear weapons or other nuclear explosive devices. . . .

### Article 4: Towards the total elimination of nuclear weapons

2 Notwithstanding Article 1 (a), each State Party that owns, possesses or controls nuclear weapons or other nuclear explosive devices shall immediately remove them from operational status, and destroy them as soon as possible but not later than a deadline to be determined by the first meeting of States Parties, in accordance with a legally binding, time-bound plan for the verified and irreversible elimination of that State Party's nuclear-weapon programme, including the elimination or irreversible conversion of all nuclear-weapons-related facilities. The State Party, no later than 60 days after the entry into force of this Treaty for that State Party, shall submit this plan to the States Parties or to a competent international authority designated by the States Parties. The plan shall then be negotiated with the competent international authority, which shall submit it to the subsequent meeting of States Parties or review conference, whichever comes first, for approval in accordance with its rules of procedure.

4 Notwithstanding Article 1 (b) and (g), each State Party that has any nuclear weapons or other nuclear explosive devices in its territory or in any place under its jurisdiction or control that are owned, possessed or controlled by another State shall ensure the prompt removal of such weapons, as soon as possible but not later than a deadline to be determined by the first meeting of States Parties. Upon the removal of such weapons or other explosive devices, that State Party shall submit to the Secretary-General of the United Nations a declaration that it has fulfilled its obligations under this Article.

---

conversion of all nuclear–weapons-related facilities'.[38] The plan itself must be submitted to the other states parties no later than 60 days after a state becomes a party to the TPNW, or, alternatively, 'to a competent international authority' the states

---

38 Ibid.

parties designate. The plan must be 'negotiated with the competent international authority, which shall submit it to the subsequent meeting of States Parties or review conference, whichever comes first, for approval in accordance with its rules of procedure'.[39]

7.19    Notwithstanding the provisions in Article 1(1)(b) and (g) of the Treaty, which prohibit both transfer of nuclear weapons or other nuclear explosive devices and allowing any stationing, installation, or deployment of any such weapons or devices in its territory or at any place under its jurisdiction or control, the state party 'shall ensure the prompt removal of such weapons, as soon as possible but not later than a deadline to be determined by the first meeting of States Parties'.[40] As of writing, the Treaty had not yet entered into force and thus no date for the First Meeting of States Parties had been set.

## Conventional weapons

7.20    Two global disarmament treaties currently outlaw specific conventional weapons, one prohibiting anti-personnel mines and the other prohibiting cluster munitions. Indirectly, though, destruction provisions are also included in the 1996 Amended Protocol II[41] to the Convention on Certain Conventional Weapons.[42]

## Landmines

### The 1996 Landmine Protocol

7.21    The 1996 Amended Protocol II to the Convention on Certain Conventional Weapons (CCW) is predominantly an instrument of the law of armed conflict. But in addition to prohibiting or restricting the use of landmines, booby-traps, and other devices, it also requires that all anti-personnel mines produced before 1 January 1997 incorporate, or have attached, before their use, material or a device to provide 'a response signal equivalent to a signal from 8 grammes or more of iron in a single coherent mass'.[43] The choice of 8 grams was intended to ensure that mine detectors in widespread use would be able to detect the presence of the mine to a depth of at least 20 centimetres (below which the mine would be unlikely to detonate under the pressure of a footfall).

39  Ibid.
40  Art. 4(4), 2017 Treaty on the Prohibition of Nuclear Weapons.
41  Protocol on Prohibitions or Restrictions on the Use of Mines, Booby-Traps and Other Devices as amended on 3 May 1996 (Amended Protocol II); adopted at Geneva, 3 May 1996; entered into force, 3 December 1998.
42  Convention on Prohibitions or Restrictions on the Use of Certain Conventional Weapons Which May Be Deemed to Be Excessively Injurious or to Have Indiscriminate Effects as amended on 21 December 2001.
43  Technical Annex 2(b), 1996 Amended Protocol II.

7.22   This duty of conversion can be considered a form of stockpile destruction. If a state party is unable or unwilling to make the necessary adaptation, it may no longer use the mines and must effectively destroy them given that they may not be lawfully transferred (see Chapter 6).

## The 1997 Anti-Personnel Mine Ban Convention

7.23   The 1997 Anti-Personnel Mine Ban Convention prohibits all retention and stockpiling of anti-personnel mines and requires that they be destroyed by each state party within four years of the Convention's entry into force for it (see Box 7.6). It is not possible to extend the stockpile destruction deadline under the Convention.

7.24   In December 2017, Landmine Monitor, the research arm of the civil society International Campaign to Ban Landmines, reported that, collectively, states parties to the Convention had destroyed more than 53 million stockpiled anti-personnel mines, including more than 2.2 million in 2016.[44] Landmine Monitor noted that Belarus completed the destruction of its stockpiles in April 2017 after having been in violation since 2008 of the Convention's stockpile destruction deadline of four years.[45] Two states, though, continued to be in serious violation of their respective Convention deadlines for stockpile destruction as of writing: Greece and Ukraine. Ukraine had 4.9 million

---

**BOX 7.6   DESTRUCTION OF STOCKPILED LANDMINES IN THE ANTI-PERSONNEL MINE BAN CONVENTION**

**Article 1: General Obligations**

1   Each State Party undertakes never under any circumstances:

    b   To . . . stockpile, retain. . ., anti-personnel mines. . . .

**Article 4: Destruction of Stockpiled Anti-Personnel Mines**

Except as provided for in Article 3, each State Party undertakes to destroy or ensure the destruction of all stockpiled anti-personnel mines it owns or possesses, or that are under its jurisdiction or control, as soon as possible but not later than four years after the entry into force of this Convention for that State Party.

---

44 Landmine Monitor, 'Landmine Monitor 2017, Major Findings', at: http://bit.ly/2zhCBSc.
45 Ibid. See also: http://bit.ly/2O3gaHs.

anti-personnel mines remaining to be destroyed, while Greece had 643,267.[46] Greece's treaty deadline expired on 1 March 2008, while Ukraine had a deadline of 1 June 2010.

7.25   Landmine Monitor further reported that 31 of the 35 states not party to the Anti-Personnel Mine Ban Convention are stockpiling anti-personnel mines.[47] In 1999, it affirmed, states stockpiled about 160 million anti-personnel mines, 'but today the global total may be less than 50 million'. It observed, though, that non-state armed groups and criminal groups in Afghanistan, India, Iraq, Libya, Myanmar, Nigeria, Pakistan, Syria, Ukraine, Western Sahara, and Yemen were also believed to possess stocks.[48]

7.26   While it is not possible to extend the deadline for stockpile destruction under the Anti-Personnel Mine Ban Convention, a state party is explicitly permitted to retain 'a number' of anti-personnel mines 'for the development of and training in mine detection, mine clearance, or mine destruction techniques'.[49] It is specified, though, that the number 'shall not exceed the minimum number absolutely necessary' for those purposes.[50] Subsequently, in its report to the Third Meeting of the States Parties in Managua in 2001, the intersessional Standing Committee on the General Status and Operation of the Convention set up by the states parties recommended that 'anti-personnel mines retained for training and development purposes in accordance with Article 3 should . . . be numbered in the hundreds or thousands, and not in the tens of thousands'.[51]

## Cluster munitions

7.27   The 2008 Convention on Cluster Munitions similarly prohibits all retention and stockpiling of cluster munitions. It requires, though, that stockpiles be destroyed by each state party within eight years of the Convention's entry into force for it (see Box 7.7), instead of four years under the Anti-Personnel Mine Ban Convention. The Convention on Cluster Munitions as a whole entered into force on 1 August 2010, thus the first stockpile destruction deadlines under the Convention expired on 1 August 2018. In contrast to the Anti-Personnel Mine Ban Convention, however, it is possible to extend the stockpile destruction deadline under the

---

46 Landmine Monitor, *Landmine Monitor 2017*, International Campaign to Ban Landmines – Cluster Munition Coalition (ICBL-CMC), December 2017, p. 4. As of November 2018, Greece reported that some 440,000 stockpiled anti-personnel mines remained to be destroyed, at: http://bit.ly/2FdB2sW.

47 Landmine Monitor, 'Landmine Monitor 2017, Major Findings', at: http://bit.ly/2yKO2CC.

48 Ibid. On 6 January 2019, Geneva Call monitored the destruction by the Sahrawi Mine Action Coordination Office (SMACO) of the last 2,485 stockpiled anti-personnel mines in Western Sahara in accordance with Geneva Call's Deed of Commitment banning anti-personnel mines, signed by the Polisario Front in 2005. Geneva Call, 'Final destruction of 2,485 stockpiled anti-personnel mines in Western Sahara', 22 January 2019, at: http://bit.ly/2T3vjJX.

49 Art. 3, 1997 Anti-Personnel Mine Ban Convention.

50 Ibid.

51 See, e.g., 'Intervention of the International Committee of the Red Cross', Fifth Meeting of States Parties, Bangkok, 17 September 2003, at: http://bit.ly/2Jx4v1x.

Convention on Cluster Munitions. As of writing, no extension had been sought by a state party.

7.28   Cluster Munition Monitor, the research arm of the civil society Cluster Munition Coalition, has estimated that, prior to the start of the global effort to ban cluster munitions, 91 states stockpiled millions of cluster munitions containing more than 1 billion submunitions.[52] A total of 35 of these states have now destroyed their stockpiled cluster munitions, while eight states parties to the Convention still

---

## BOX 7.7   DESTRUCTION OF CLUSTER MUNITIONS IN THE CONVENTION ON CLUSTER MUNITIONS

### Article 1: General Obligations

1   Each State Party undertakes never under any circumstances to:

   b   Develop, produce, otherwise acquire, stockpile, retain or transfer to anyone, directly or indirectly, cluster munitions. . . .

### Article 3: Storage and stockpile destruction

1   Each State Party shall, in accordance with national regulations, separate all cluster munitions under its jurisdiction and control from munitions retained for operational use and mark them for the purpose of destruction.

2   Each State Party undertakes to destroy or ensure the destruction of all cluster munitions referred to in paragraph 1 of this Article as soon as possible but not later than eight years after the entry into force of this Convention for that State Party. Each State Party undertakes to ensure that destruction methods comply with applicable international standards for protecting public health and the environment. . . .

6   Notwithstanding the provisions of Article 1 of this Convention, the retention or acquisition of a limited number of cluster munitions and explosive submunitions for the development of and training in cluster munition and explosive submunition detection, clearance or destruction techniques, or for the development of cluster munition counter-measures, is permitted. The amount of explosive submunitions retained or acquired shall not exceed the minimum number absolutely necessary for these purposes.

---

52 Cluster Munition Monitor, *Cluster Munition Monitor 2017*, ICBL–CMC, August 2017, p. 28.

have stocks to destroy, according to the Monitor's report of August 2018.[53] As at the end of 2017, it believed that 35 states parties had destroyed 1.44 million cluster munitions and more than 177 million submunitions. This represented the destruction of 99% of the total global cluster munition stocks declared by states parties as of August 2018.[54]

---

## BOX 7.8 EXTENDING THE STOCKPILE DESTRUCTION DEADLINE UNDER THE CONVENTION ON CLUSTER MUNITIONS

### Article 3: Storage and stockpile destruction

3    If a State Party believes that it will be unable to destroy or ensure the destruction of all cluster munitions referred to in paragraph 1 of this Article within eight years of entry into force of this Convention for that State Party it may submit a request to a Meeting of States Parties or a Review Conference for an extension of the deadline for completing the destruction of such cluster munitions by a period of up to four years. A State Party may, in exceptional circumstances, request additional extensions of up to four years. The requested extensions shall not exceed the number of years strictly necessary for that State Party to complete its obligations under paragraph 2 of this Article.

4    Each request for an extension shall set out:

a    The duration of the proposed extension;

b    A detailed explanation of the proposed extension, including the financial and technical means available to or required by the State Party for the destruction of all cluster munitions referred to in paragraph 1 of this Article and, where applicable, the exceptional circumstances justifying it;

c    A plan for how and when stockpile destruction will be completed;

d    The quantity and type of cluster munitions and explosive submunitions held at the entry into force of this Convention for that State Party and any additional cluster munitions or explosive submunitions discovered after such entry into force;

e    The quantity and type of cluster munitions and explosive submunitions destroyed during the period referred to in paragraph 2 of this Article; and

---

53 Cluster Munition Monitor, *Cluster Munition Monitor 2018*, ICBL-CMC, August 2018, Major Findings, at: http://bit.ly/2JzYTDq.
54 Ibid.

> f The quantity and type of cluster munitions and explosive submunitions remaining to be destroyed during the proposed extension and the annual destruction rate expected to be achieved.
>
> 5 The Meeting of States Parties or the Review Conference shall, taking into consideration the factors referred to in paragraph 4 of this Article, assess the request and decide by a majority of votes of States Parties present and voting whether to grant the request for an extension. The States Parties may decide to grant a shorter extension than that requested and may propose benchmarks for the extension, as appropriate. A request for an extension shall be submitted a minimum of nine months prior to the Meeting of States Parties or the Review Conference at which it is to be considered.

7.29 As with the Anti-Personnel Mine Ban Convention, it is lawful to retain a 'limited number of cluster munitions and explosive submunitions for the development of and training in cluster munition and explosive submunition detection, clearance or destruction techniques, or for the development of cluster munition counter-measures'.[55] It is again specified that the number of explosive submunitions retained 'shall not exceed the minimum number absolutely necessary for these purposes'.[56]

7.30 In September 2017, at the Seventh Meeting of States Parties, Croatia, and Mexico, the Coordinators of the Working Group on Stockpile Destruction and Retention, recalled that 11 states parties had reported retaining cluster munitions and explosive submunitions for training purposes and/or the development of countermeasures in accordance with Article 3(6) of the Convention on Cluster Munitions. Of these 11 states, five reported having 'consumed' retained cluster munitions and only one declared that the number of retained munitions had not decreased in the course of 2016.[57]

7.31 Article 3 of the Convention affords each state party the possibility to request an extension of its stockpile destruction deadline for up to four years (see Box 7.8). The request must be submitted to either a meeting of states parties or a review conference.[58] A State Party may further, 'in exceptional circumstances', request additional extensions of up to four years at a time. In any event the requested extensions 'shall not exceed the number of years strictly necessary' to complete stockpile destruction.[59]

---

55 Art. 3(6), 2008 Convention on Cluster Munitions.
56 Ibid.
57 'Coordination Report: Storage and Stockpile Destruction Coordinators: Croatia and Mexico', p. 3, at: http://bit.ly/2qobXTN.
58 Art. 3(3), 2008 Convention on Cluster Munitions.
59 Ibid.

7.32    The relevant meeting of states parties or review conference deciding on the request for an extension will assess the request and decide by a majority of votes of states parties present and voting whether or not to grant it. It is possible for states parties to grant a shorter extension than the one requested and to propose 'benchmarks' that the requesting state party is called on to respect during the extension period.[60] A request for an extension must be submitted at least nine months prior to the meeting of states parties or review conference at which it is to be considered.[61]

## Destruction techniques

7.33    A variety of techniques exist to meet a state's international legal obligations for stockpile destruction. With respect to the destruction of munitions, the International Mine Action Standards (IMAS), which are non-legal but generally accepted and practiced standards, define stockpile destruction as 'the physical destructive procedure towards a continual reduction of the stockpile of explosive ordnance'.[62] Detonation is an obvious means of ensuring effective destruction of a munition. Yet this is not necessarily straightforward or inexpensive and it requires good knowledge of explosives engineering. According to the Geneva International Centre for Humanitarian Demining (GICHD):

> Options for destruction (and the associated costs) depend to a great extent on the quantity of ammunition, its condition, storage history and quality of records. Small stockpiles of poorly stored ammunition, without a complete documented history, are unlikely to be acceptable for sophisticated industrial processing.[63]

7.34    In addition, detonation may not be appropriate for certain components, especially those that are highly toxic. State practice indicates that other options exist that similarly comply with international law which, depending on the weapon, include burning, crushing, disassembly, recycling, slicing, and encasement in concrete.[64] In contrast, deep-sea dumping of munitions and explosives is unlawful, at least for states parties to the 1996 Protocol to the Convention on the Prevention of Marine Pollution by Dumping of Wastes and Other Matter (1996 London Protocol) (see Box 7.9).[65] Placing munitions in landfill sites is similarly illegitimate on the basis of environmental concerns.[66] Biological, chemical, and

---

60  Art. 3(5), 2008 Convention on Cluster Munitions.
61  Ibid.
62  IMAS 04.10: 'Glossary of mine action terms, definitions and abbreviations', 2nd Edn (May 2013), at: http://bit.ly/2AGlX0G.
63  GICHD, *A Guide to Mine Action*, 5th Edn, GICHD, Geneva, March 2014, p. 154 (hereafter, GICHD Guide to Mine Action).
64  See, e.g., ibid.
65  As at February 2019, 51 states were party to the 1996 London Protocol. See: http://bit.ly/2Fg84IQ.
66  GICHD Guide to Mine Action, p. 158.

---

**BOX 7.9  TREATY PROHIBITIONS AND
RESTRICTIONS ON DUMPING MUNITIONS AT SEA**

**1982 UN Convention on the Law of the Sea**

*Article 210: Pollution by dumping*

1   States shall adopt laws and regulations to prevent, reduce and control
pollution of the marine environment by dumping.
2   States shall take other measures as may be necessary to prevent, reduce
and control such pollution.
3   Such laws, regulations and measures shall ensure that dumping is not
carried out without the permission of the competent authorities of
States.

**1996 London Protocol**

*Article 4: Dumping of Wastes or Other Matter*

1(1) Contracting Parties shall prohibit the dumping of any wastes or other
matter. . . .

*Article 5: Incineration at Sea*

Contracting Parties shall prohibit incineration at sea of wastes or other matter.

---

nuclear material is subject to different destruction techniques than conventional
weapons.

### Biological weapons and toxins

7.35   Under Article II of the Biological Weapons Convention, in destroying biological weapons and toxins, each state party is required to observe 'all necessary
safety precautions' with a view to protecting 'populations and the environment'.
The United States began a biological weapons programme in the spring of 1943
that ran for a further 26 years. It involved weaponising biological agents such as
anthrax, tularaemia, brucellosis, Q-fever, Venezuelan equine encephalitis virus, bot-
ulism, and staphylococcal enterotoxin B.[67]

---

67 See, e.g., D.R. Franz, C.D. Parrott, and E.T. Takafuji, 'The U.S. Biological Warfare and Biological
Defense Programs', Chap. 19 in F.R. Sidell et al. (eds.), *Medical Aspects of Chemical and Biological*

7.36    In November 1969, US President Richard Nixon issued a 'Statement on Chemical and Biological Defense Policies and Programs', in which he announced an end to all US offensive biological weapons programmes:

> The United States shall renounce the use of lethal biological agents and weapons, and all other methods of biological warfare. The United States will confine its biological research to defensive measures such as immunization and safety measures.

US biological weapons stocks were destroyed over the course of the next four years. A US$12 million programme of disposal was undertaken at Pine Bluff Arsenal, where all US anti-personnel biological agents were stored, which was completed, along with the decontamination of the facilities, in May 1972.[68]

7.37    The United Kingdom's Defence Science and Technology Laboratory, better known as Porton Down, was established in 1916 to conduct research into chemical warfare. During the Cold War, between 1953 and 1976, a number of aerial release trials were carried out to help the British Government understand how a biological attack might spread across the United Kingdom.[69] In 1942, a cloud of anthrax spores was released over Gruinard Island to assess the impact. Subsequent burning of the soil and vegetation was not successful in remediating the threat, with soil samples still evidencing viable spores. In 1986, the UK government hired a contractor to decontaminate the island. The process involved saturating the soil with 280 tons of formaldehyde diluted in seawater and removing tons of topsoil. This was followed by a final formaldehyde wash. In July 1989, the government lifted travel restrictions and declared the island safe.[70]

7.38    Russia's compliance with the Biological Weapons Convention is unclear.[71] In the early 1990s, Russian President Boris Yeltsin acknowledged the existence of an inherited Soviet biological weapons programme and publicly committed Russia to establishing compliance with the Biological Weapons Convention.

---

*Warfare*, Office of the Surgeon General (Army), Falls Church, VA, 1997; E. Regis, *The Biology of Doom: The History of America's Secret Germ Warfare Project*, Henry Holt, New York, 1990, pp. 210–11; and Secretary of Defense memorandum, at: http://bit.ly/2JEHE4h.

68  T. Mangold, *Plague Wars: The Terrifying Reality of Biological Warfare*, Macmillan, New York, 1999, pp. 54–57.

69  Defence Science and Technology Laboratory, 'The Truth About Porton Down', News story, 27 June 2016, at: http://bit.ly/2Rx3Y2o.

70  See, e.g., P. Boyd, 'Anthrax Island – Inside Edition (2001)', *YouTube*, 13 December 2015, at: http://bit.ly/2F13Bvv.

71  Dr Ken Alibek, First Deputy Chief of the Soviet Biopreparat Programme from 1988 to 1992, has declared publicly that tularaemia was used by the Soviet army against German troops outside Stalingrad in late 1942. S. Hutton Siderovski, *Tularemia*, Chelsea House Publishers, Philadelphia, 2009, p. 82.

Offensive biological weapons work was prohibited in an April 1992 decree, which also required the dismantlement of the Soviet programme and pledged cooperation with the Convention framework.[72] The Russian government has since asserted that it does not still maintain a stockpile of biological weapons or engage in any illegal development or production activities. However, in its 2018 report on compliance with the BWC (and other disarmament and arms control treaties), the US Department of State declared that 'available information does not allow the United States to conclude that Russia has fulfilled its Article II obligations to destroy or divert to peaceful purposes BW items specified under Article I of its past BW program'.[73]

## Toxic chemicals

7.39   As with radioactive waste, dumping toxic chemicals at sea, particularly chemical weapons, was widely practiced in the past but is now illegal. The practice of dumping at sea is explicitly prohibited in the Chemical Weapons Convention, along with burying on land or open burning.[74] The standard method for the destruction of toxic chemical agents is closed incineration in specially designed chambers.[75]

7.40   According to one authority:

> In the decades following World War I, and even more so during and after World War II, at least four major powers disposed of massive quantities of captured, damaged, and obsolete chemical warfare . . . material by dumping them into the oceans. The jettisoned material consisted either of munitions containing chemicals (such as artillery shells, mortar rounds, or aerial

---

72 'Russia Shuns Biological Weapons', *New Scientist*, Vol. 134, No. 1882 (1992); and US Department of State, *Adherence to and Compliance with Arms Control, Nonproliferation and Disarmament Agreements and Commitments*, (Noncompliance Report), July 2010, p. 23; see NTI, 'Russia: Biological', Last updated January 2015, at: http://bit.ly/2zo5tbP.

73 US Department of State, *Adherence to and Compliance with Arms Control, Nonproliferation, and Disarmament Agreements and Commitments*, Washington, DC, April 2018, pp. 16–17.

74 According to the section dedicated to the destruction of chemical weapons that is required by Article IV of the Chemical Weapons Convention (Part IV of the Verification Annex), each state party may 'determine how it shall destroy chemical weapons, except that the following processes may not be used: dumping in any body of water, land burial or open-pit burning'. It is further stipulated that the relevant provisions of Part IV of the Verification Annex 'shall not, at the discretion of a State Party, apply to chemical weapons buried on its territory before 1 January 1977 and which remain buried, or which had been dumped at sea before 1 January 1985'. Art. III(2), 1992 Chemical Weapons Convention.

75 See, e.g., Committee on Review and Evaluation of International Technologies for the Destruction of Non-Stockpile Chemical Material and Board on Army Science and Technology, *Review of International Technologies for Destruction of Recovered Chemical Warfare Materiel*, National Research Council, United States, 2 November 2006.

bombs) or chemicals stored in large metal containers or encased in concrete. Shells and bombs were sometimes jettisoned unfettered, but more often were loaded as cargo onto ships that were sunk by opening their seacocks, by naval artillery fire, or torpedoes.[76]

Following the end of the Second World War, Germany's 65,000 tonnes of stockpiled chemical warfare munitions were ordered by the allied forces to be destroyed during the second half of 1947 as a result of the three 1945 Potsdam Conferences. Russian forces undertook the bulk of the task during the summer of 1947 using German barges and crews. The intended dump site had been outside the Faroe Islands, but ultimately the Bornholm Basin in the Baltic Sea received more than half of Germany's chemical warfare arsenal.[77]

7.41    In April 1958, the US Army disposed of 8,000 tons of mustard gas and lewisite aboard the SS *William C. Ralston*, which it scuttled.[78] Beginning in May 1964 and continuing until 1970, Operation CHASE ('Cut Holes And Sink 'Em') was a US Department of Defense programme for the disposal of unwanted munitions at sea. While most of the ships contained conventional weapons, four had chemical weapons on board. Chemical munitions were loaded onto ships to be sunk once they were at least 250 miles offshore between the coast of Florida and the Bahamas.[79] The last such operation was CHASE 10, completed in August 1970, which disposed of about 3,000 tons of nerve agent rockets encased in concrete vaults.[80]

7.42    It has been estimated that 1 million metric tons of chemical weapons lie on the ocean floor. These range from Bari Harbour in Italy, where 230 cases of exposure to sulphur mustard have been reported since 1946, to the East Coast of the United States, where sulphur mustard bombs have shown up three times in the past decade in Delaware[81]. In January 1997, the crew of a fishing vessel trawling off the Polish coast found a chunk of what looked like yellowish clay in their nets. The crew pulled it out and put it aside as they processed their catch. When they got back to port, they tossed it in a dockside trash can. The next day, crew members suffered serious burns and four men were eventually hospitalised with red, burning skin and blisters. The material was subsequently identified as a chunk of Second World

76 I. Wilkinson, 'Chemical Weapon Munitions Dumped at Sea: An Interactive Map', Middlebury Institute of International Studies at Monterey, 1 August 2017 (Updated 7 September 2017), at: http://bit.ly/2DieEyS.

77 See, e.g., 'Report on chemical munitions dumped in the Baltic Sea', Report to the 15th meeting of Helsinki Commission, Danish Environmental Protection Agency, at: http://bit.ly/2DhdDH7.

78 S. Kurak, 'Operation CHASE', *US Naval Institute Proceedings*, September 1967, pp. 40–46.

79 T. Wagner, 'Hazardous Waste: Evolution of a National Environmental Problem', *Journal of Policy History*, Vol. 16, No. 4 (2004), pp. 306–31.

80 Operation CHASE, *Global Security*, undated but accessed 1 November 2018, at: http://bit.ly/2QfeHye.

81 A. Curry, 'Chemical Weapons Dumped in the Ocean After World War II Could Threaten Waters Worldwide', *Hakai Magazine*, 11 November 2016, at: http://bit.ly/2yMRCfE

War–era sulphur mustard, frozen solid by the low temperatures on the seafloor and preserved by the below-zero winter temperatures onshore.[82]

7.43    More recently, the United States of America, among others, has opted for closed incineration. Under this process, the chemical munitions are first dismantled, resulting in three groups of component parts: the agent, the explosives, and some metal parts. Each component group is then treated separately. Agent combustion in the first chamber of the liquid incinerator at about 2,700°F and additional treatment in the afterburner (second chamber) at approximately 2,000°F leads to the 99.9999% destruction and full mineralisation of organic compounds. The generated oxides and acid gases are removed by scrubbing. The drained munitions cases and the emptied containers are decontaminated by thermal treatment.[83] In the Russian Federation, however, the main technology developed to destroy Category 1 chemical weapons stockpiles involved neutralisation of chemical agents at low temperature followed by incineration of the generated reaction mass or its bitumisation, where the residue is embedded in bitumen.[84]

### Fissile material and radioactive waste

7.44    Fissile material (e.g. uranium-233, uranium-235, and plutonium-239)[85] demands very careful disposal processes and procedures, taking into account environmental standards (see Box 7.10). In the past, however, several states regularly dumped radioactive waste in the ocean. This is despite the obligation upon every state party to the 1958 Geneva Convention on the High Seas to 'take measures to prevent pollution of the seas from the dumping of radioactive waste, taking into account any standards and regulations which may be formulated by the competent international organizations'.[86] A voluntary moratorium on dumping of low-level radioactive waste at sea was discussed in 1983 by states parties to the 1972 London Convention, but the United States voted against the proposal. The Soviet Union abstained from the vote, and continued to dump radioactive material in the Arctic seas until 1992.[87]

7.45    According to the International Atomic Energy Agency (IAEA), between 1946 (when the United States first dumped nuclear waste in the sea off California)

---

82  Ibid.

83  OPCW, 'Destruction Technologies', at: http://bit.ly/2EYuksL.

84  Ibid.

85  See, e.g., US Nuclear Regulatory Commission, 'Fissile Material', Last updated 6 July 2018, at: http://bit.ly/2CWg1SI.

86  Art. 25(1), Convention on the High Seas; adopted at Geneva, 29 April 1958; entered into force, 30 September 1962.

87  A. Lott, 'Pollution of the Marine Environment by Dumping: Legal Framework Applicable to Dumped Chemical Weapons and Nuclear Waste in the Arctic Ocean', *Nordic Environmental Law Journal*, No. 1 (2015), p. 62, at: http://bit.ly/2PD6IxN, citing J.M. Broadus and R.V. Vartanov, *The Oceans and Environmental Security: Shared U.S. and Russian Perspectives*, Island Press, Washington, DC, 1994, pp. 153 and 135.

and 1993 (when a ban on the dumping of radioactive waste was agreed under the 1972 London Convention), 14 states used ocean disposal to dispose of nuclear waste. Waste materials included liquids and solids housed in a range of containers, as well as reactor vessels with spent or damaged nuclear fuel.[88] In September 2016, the 38th Consultative Meeting of Contracting Parties to the London Convention decided to maintain the 1994 prohibition on dumping of radioactive waste at sea, although certain exempted materials may be dumped as long as they do not contain levels of radioactivity greater than de minimis concentrations as defined by the IAEA.[89] A further scientific review is required to be undertaken by February 2044.

7.46    Some of the nuclear materials declared by the United States and Russia in the 1990s as surplus to defence programmes were converted into fuel for commercial nuclear reactors. The materials involved were principally highly enriched uranium (HEU) – containing at least 20% uranium-235 – and plutonium.[90] In February 1993, the United States and Russia signed a bilateral Agreement on the Disposition of Highly Enriched Uranium Extracted from Nuclear Weapons, which provided for the United States to purchase 500 metric tons of Russian HEU over a 20-year period. This 'Megatons to Megawatts' agreement was the world's first programme for converting weapons-grade nuclear materials from dismantled nuclear warheads to commercial reactor fuel for the generation of electricity.[91] In December 2013, the two states commemorated the completion of the so-called Megatons to Megawatts Programme with the arrival in Baltimore of the last shipment of more than 500 metric tons of weapons-origin HEU down-blended from some 20,000 dismantled Russian nuclear warheads. The HEU supplied nearly 10% of all US domestic electricity over a period of 15 years.[92]

7.47    The US National Nuclear Security Administration (NNSA) has described the complex process of decommissioning US nuclear weapons in the following terms:

> Dismantling a nuclear weapon is a lengthy process that involves almost all of the facilities in NNSA's nuclear weapons complex. First, the design laboratories work with the production facilities to identify and mitigate any hazards that may arise prior to a particular weapon type being dismantled. They then

---

88 IAEA, *Inventory of radioactive waste disposals at sea*, Doc. IAEA-TECDOC-1105, August 1999, at: http://bit.ly/2AH7aTk.

89 The prohibition entered into force in 1994. See: International Maritime Organization, '38th Consultative Meeting of Contracting Parties (London Convention 1972) and 11th Meeting of Contracting Parties (London Protocol 1996), 19–23 September 2016', 23 September 2016, at: http://bit.ly/2OkZrxS.

90 Federation of American Scientists, 'Fissile Material Disposal Background', at: http://bit.ly/2SERBm7.

91 Ibid.

92 'Under U.S.-Russia Partnership, Final Shipment of Fuel Converted From 20,000 Russian Nuclear Warheads Arrives in United States and Will Be Used for U.S. Electricity', *National Nuclear Security Administration*, 11 December 2013, at: http://bit.ly/2P3ToDk.

use the unique knowledge they gained during the original design of the weapon to develop a plan to safely dismantle the weapon. Once the weapon is retired and designated for dismantlement, it is brought to the Pantex Plant . . . where the high explosives are removed from the special nuclear material, and non-nuclear components are either processed on site or are sent to other facilities within the Enterprise. The Y-12 National Security Complex . . . then dismantles the uranium components. Other non-nuclear components are sent to the Savannah River Site. . . (e.g. pressure storage devices) and the Kansas City Plant. . . (e.g. electrical components) for final processing.[93]

---

**BOX 7.10 ENVIRONMENTAL STANDARDS FOR STOCKPILE DESTRUCTION IN DISARMAMENT TREATIES**

**Biological Weapons Convention, Article II**

Each State Party to this Convention undertakes to destroy, or to divert to peaceful purposes, as soon as possible but not later than nine months after the entry into force of the Convention, all agents, toxins, weapons, equipment and means of delivery specified in Article I of the Convention, which are in its possession or under its jurisdiction or control. In implementing the provisions of this Article all necessary safety precautions shall be observed to protect populations and the environment.

**Chemical Weapons Convention, Part IV (A): Destruction of Chemical Weapons and its Verification Pursuant to Article IV**

13  Each State Party shall determine how it shall destroy chemical weapons, except that the following processes may not be used: dumping in any body of water, land burial or open-pit burning. It shall destroy chemical weapons only at specifically designated and appropriately designed and equipped facilities.

**Convention on Cluster Munitions, Article 3: Storage and stockpile destruction**

2  . . . Each State Party undertakes to ensure that destruction methods comply with applicable international standards for protecting public health and the environment.

---

93 NNSA, 'Dismantlement and Disposition', at: http://bit.ly/2RtuXM5.

7.48    More than 3,000 tons of nuclear fissile material are said to remain in the world, 'enough to create roughly 230,000 nuclear weapons, making the reduction and safe disposal of these materials key to international security'.[94] A 1992 paper by a nuclear scientist had recommended that fissile material left to be disposed of in a post-nuclear world might best be disposed of in deep boreholes.[95] But the cost of disposal, by whatever means, continues to be intimidating. One journalist noted in 2013 that 'it could cost more money and take longer to get rid of just 37.5 tons of excess, weapons-grade plutonium than it did for the Manhattan Project to produce the atomic bombs that ended World War II'.[96] The bill for the disposal of this amount is likely to be more than US$24.2 billion, and is expected to take until 2036 to complete.[97]

7.49    The safe and secure disposal of plutonium is especially challenging.[98] This has led scientists to consider increasingly bizarre proposals for ridding the planet of waste plutonium, such as sending it on a space rocket to crash into the sun. But, as has been observed, one would also have to factor in the possibility the spaceship would not make it to orbit: 'Space shuttles crash. So if you had just one crash with a space shuttle full of plutonium, that would ruin your whole day'.[99]

## Conventional munitions

### Open detonation

7.50    For conventional munitions, including anti-personnel landmines and cluster munitions, open detonation is the approach most usually adopted by a state wishing to destroy part of, or its entire stockpile. This method is used with High Explosive (HE)-filled explosive ordnance. Small quantities of another nature (e.g. smoke, pyrotechnics, and lachrymatory agents) 'can also be destroyed by inclusion in mixed stacks during large-scale demolitions'. The amounts of such other items that are included in a mixed stack must be kept down 'to a small percentage of the overall stack'.[100]

---

94 'Brief Overview of Fissile Material Reduction', University of Illinois, United States, 2018, at: http://bit.ly/2JAXHQq.

95 J. Swahn, 'The Long-Term Nuclear Explosives Predicament: The Final Disposal of Militarily Usable Fissile Material in Nuclear Waste From Nuclear Power and from the Elimination of Nuclear Weapons', Technical Peace Research Group, Institute of Physical Resource Theory, Göteborg, 1992, at: http://bit.ly/2SAiasC.

96 W. Pincus, 'The Explosive Cost of Disposing of Nuclear Weapons', *The Washington Post*, 3 July 2013, at: http://bit.ly/2qquhvs.

97 Ibid.

98 N. Wolchover, 'Why Is Plutonium More Dangerous than Uranium?', *Live Science*, 17 March 2011, at: http://bit.ly/2PCdHaj.

99 T.J. Starr, 'How to Dismantle a Nuclear Weapon', *Foxtrot Alpha*, 22 May 2017, at: http://bit.ly/2AH4sNA.

100 IMAS 11.20: 'Principles and procedures for open burning and open detonation operations', 2nd Edn, 1 January 2003 (Amendment 6, June 2013), p. 3, §6.2, at: http://bit.ly/2zotgIr.

7.51    Open detonation is likely to be the cheapest way of destroying stockpiles, notably anti-personnel mines.[101] That said,

> the shockwave caused by a detonation in a badly prepared demolition pit may not destroy all the munitions but throw some out, requiring additional EOD [explosive ordnance disposal] work in a potentially more dangerous situation (there is a possibility that some throw-outs may be armed).[102]

There is also the danger from fragmentation of the destroyed munitions, toxic smoke and fumes, and noise.[103]

7.52    Certain anti-personnel mines may not be safely destroyed using open detonation. The PFM-1 remotely deliverable anti-personnel mine, for instance, contains hydrogen chloride. A solution, according to the GICHD is to conduct 'contained detonation in a pollution control chamber', as the PFM-1 mine cannot be disassembled. 'Similar responses may be appropriate with other particular munitions'.[104]

7.53    To minimise the risks from open detonation, demolition sites should be as far away as possible from personnel and property. Sites should not be located near pipelines, power cables, or fuel storage areas. Soil should be relatively free of rocks and stones and without peat, which could burn underground. High ground reduces the effects of blast and ground shock and is also well drained, which aids digging. High ground also, though, tends to increase fragmentation range.

7.54    There should be no radio or radar transmitters in the vicinity of an open detonation site. Major demolitions are normally initiated using electric cable or radio-control systems, and as such, are vulnerable to external electro-magnetic force influence. Consequently, demolition grounds should not be situated near radar installations, radio transmitters, or near high-voltage power lines.[105]

## Open burning

7.55    Open burning is generally used with propellant, smoke, pyrotechnic, and lachrymatory (i.e. tear gas) munitions but is suitable for certain plastic-bodied anti-personnel mines. It can also be used as an alternative to detonation for certain explosives, such as trinitrotoluene (TNT) or nitroglycerine-based explosives and for gunpowder, though the IMAS caution that detonation is the cleaner method.[106]

7.56    The hazards created by burning are intense heat and light, and sometimes also toxic fumes.[107] To counter these risks, burning grounds should have no

---

101 GICHD Guide to Mine Action, p. 155.
102 Ibid.
103 IMAS 11.20: 'Principles and procedures for open burning and open detonation operations', p. 4, §7.2.
104 GICHD Guide to Mine Action, p. 159.
105 IMAS 11.20: 'Principles and procedures for open burning and open detonation operations', p. 5, §7.3.
106 Ibid., p. 4, §6.3.
107 Ibid., p. 5, §7.4.

secondary fire hazards, but should have an adequate water supply, sufficient isolation to prevent heat or fume casualties, and sandy soil with no peat. An isolated, sandy, barren area is the most suitable site, but sites near high cliffs should be avoided as rising hot-air currents can carry burning debris considerable distances.[108] The risk of blast, ground shock, or fragmentation from open burning is minimal unless the munitions burn to detonation.[109]

## Disassembly

7.57   For larger stockpiles, industrial-scale demilitarisation has 'many advantages, among them the option for mechanical disassembly'. Its major disadvantages, though, are the high capital set-up costs of design, project management, construction, and commissioning, and the significant cost and time implications that can be associated with recovery from an unplanned explosion.[110] The GICHD recalls that industrial demilitarisation was applied successfully in Albania where all anti-personnel mine stockpiles were demilitarised in the same factory where some of them had originally been produced.[111]

7.58   It may also be necessary to disassemble munitions prior to a further destruction process. This may be required in order to limit the amount of explosive that will be incinerated, as a consequence of the design of the item, or be based on the technical requirement for different components to have distinct destruction methods.[112] Available technologies include manual disassembly, mechanical disassembly, robotic disassembly, cryofracture, hydro-abrasive cutting, and microwave explosive melt-out. Each of these methods requires that exposed bare explosive be transported to the final destruction facility. The decision to opt for any particular technique is likely to be based on cost, safety, and environmental considerations, as well as the type of munitions being destroyed.[113]

7.59   Disassembly of cluster munitions may involve both extraction of submunitions from the main canister and disassembly of the submunitions themselves. Disassembly is not a complete solution to cluster munition destruction, because the explosive components require further treatment after disassembly. This may involve additional use of other techniques, such as closed incineration or cryofracture (see below).[114]

7.60   The extraction of submunitions from the main canister may be useful in allowing recovery of material for recycling. It helps to reduce the risk of throw-outs during open detonation. Disassembly of submunitions may offer additional opportunities to recover valuable materials (such as copper from shaped-charge

108 Ibid., p. 5, §7.5.
109 Ibid., p. 5, §7.4.
110 GICHD Guide to Mine Action, p. 156.
111 Ibid.
112 Ibid.
113 Ibid.
114 Ibid., p. 162.

warheads), and can increase the range of options for final disposal of energetic and inert components.[115]

7.61    The GICHD further recalls that disassembly of some former Soviet- and UK-manufactured cluster munitions, including submunitions, has been successfully implemented with the support of international mine action non-governmental organisations in several countries with relatively small stockpiles. 'This technique requires limited capital investment, but is a labour-intensive process which results in relatively slow throughput rates. The method requires semi-skilled, yet well-trained staff. Not all types of cluster munition are suitable for this technique'.[116]

## Cryofracture

7.62    Cryofracture breaks down a munition into pieces that are small enough to be destroyed by incineration. It involves use of liquid nitrogen to make the munition casing more brittle by cooling it to minus 130°C. The munition can then be shattered using mechanical shear or pressing techniques.[117] Cryofracture

> is an environmentally friendly technique with low staff requirements. It can be used for any type of munition, explosive or propellant and requires limited pre-preparation of the munition. There is no secondary waste stream, which reduces final disposal costs. In financial terms, relatively low capital investment is required for set-up costs.[118]

7.63    Cryofracture is widely used to destroy small submunitions such as the M42, M46, and M77 grenades that are dispersed by artillery cluster munitions. In such scenarios, the grenade fuses

> are cut off mechanically before the grenades are passed through a bath of liquid nitrogen to embrittle their structures. They are then crushed to expose the explosive filling and passed under a flame in an enclosed environment to ignite the explosives, which burn to extinction. The metal scrap is then separated into ferrous and non-ferrous elements.[119]

## Hydro-abrasive cutting

7.64    Hydro-abrasive cutting (slicing) uses water and abrasives at pressures ranging from 240 bar up to 1,000 bar to cut open ammunition. Among existing technologies, 'direct injection' is the preferred option, for safety reasons.[120] Hydro-abrasive

115 Ibid.
116 Ibid.
117 Ibid., p. 157.
118 Ibid.
119 Ibid., p. 162.
120 Ibid., pp. 157–58.

cutting systems need relatively few staff to operate them but can process a wide range of munitions. The GICHD affirms that the explosive safety of such systems 'is well proven' and represents a 'cost-effective method in comparison to other pre-processing methods'.[121] The major disadvantage is the high capital investment needed to procure and install the system infrastructure. Using a hydro-abrasive cutting system also produces contaminated waste water, which demands a complex filtration system to clean it.[122]

## Microwave melt-out

7.65  Microwave explosives melt-out, a technology which is under development in the United States, uses microwaves to heat up TNT-based explosive fillings. This is a 'rapid, clean technique' but with 'the major disadvantage' that it lacks the ability to control heating, which can lead to 'hot spots' forming and the filling may initiate. It is 'more energy efficient than steam melt-out systems'. Work continues on its development, as it is 'not yet a feasible production technique'.[123]

---

121 Ibid., p. 158.
122 Ibid.
123 Ibid.

# 8

# ADDRESSING THE EFFECTS OF WEAPONS

## Introduction

8.1   This chapter reviews obligations upon states parties to global disarmament treaties to address the effects of weapons they prohibit. Such measures are, most notably, the provision of assistance to victims, remedial action to destroy weapons that have been used or abandoned, and work to repair damage to the environment. The chapter also summarises treaty provisions on international cooperation and assistance that support the implementation of those obligations.

## Victim assistance

### A summary of assistance provisions in disarmament treaties

8.2   It has become increasingly common in global disarmament treaties since the 1992 Chemical Weapons Convention[1] to seek to address the needs and rights of victims to assistance. The 1971 Biological Weapons Convention[2] did not include any provisions on victim assistance, but under the Chemical Weapons Convention, if reliable information attests to the existence of victims of the use of chemical weapons 'and immediate action is indispensable', the Director-General of the Organisation for the Prohibition of Chemical Weapons (OPCW) is required to notify all the states parties and to take 'emergency measures of assistance'.[3] No obligation is, however, imposed on the states parties themselves.

---

1   Convention on the Prohibition of the Development, Production, Stockpiling and Use of Chemical Weapons and on their Destruction; adopted at Geneva, 3 September 1992; entered into force, 29 April 1997.
2   Convention on the Prohibition of the Development, Production and Stockpiling of Bacteriological (Biological) and Toxin Weapons and on their Destruction; opened for signature, 10 April 1972; entered into force, 25 March 1975.
3   Art. X(11), 1992 Chemical Weapons Convention.

8.3 The 1997 Anti-Personnel Mine Ban Convention[4] took a further step forward to address victim assistance, by imposing an obligation on each state party to 'provide assistance for the care and rehabilitation, and social and economic reintegration, of mine victims'.[5] This is limited, however, to a qualified obligation on states parties 'in a position to do so' to provide international assistance.

8.4 The most detailed obligations are contained in the 2008 Convention on Cluster Munitions.[6] Article 5 of the Convention allocates clear responsibility to each state party to 'adequately' provide age- and gender-sensitive assistance to cluster munition victims in areas under its jurisdiction or control. The required assistance includes medical care, rehabilitation, and psychological support, as well as provision for their social and economic inclusion. Article 5 also sets out in detail how a state party is to implement these obligations.

8.5 The 2013 Arms Trade Treaty[7] only addresses the needs of victims in the preamble to the Treaty, where states parties recognise 'the challenges faced by victims of armed conflict and their need for adequate care, rehabilitation and social and economic inclusion'.[8] As a commentary on that preambular paragraph observes, Norway, supported by a number of other states, had advocated a substantive provision that would encourage states parties to the Arms Trade Treaty to support the care, rehabilitation, and reintegration of victims of armed conflict or armed violence:[9]

> This preambular paragraph reflects Norway's concern for victims, but ensuring their care, rehabilitation, and reintegration is not among the substantive obligations of states parties under the ATT,[10] and the reference is limited to victims of armed conflict, even though the humanitarian goal of the treaty clearly encompasses all victims of armed violence.[11]

8.6 The 2017 Treaty on the Prohibition of Nuclear Weapons contains broad-based, substantive victim assistance provisions.[12] Drawing on language from the Convention on Cluster Munitions, Article 6(1) of the Treaty on the Prohibition of Nuclear Weapons requires states parties to provide adequate age- and gender-sensitive assistance, without discrimination, to victims of the use or testing of nuclear weapons

---

4 Convention on the Prohibition of the Use, Stockpiling, Production and Transfer of Anti-Personnel Mines and on Their Destruction; adopted at Oslo, 18 September 1997; entered into force, 1 March 1999.

5 Art. 6(3), 1997 Anti-Personnel Mine Ban Convention.

6 Convention on Cluster Munitions; adopted at Dublin, 30 May 2008; entered into force, 1 August 2010.

7 Arms Trade Treaty; adopted at the UN General Assembly in New York, 2 April 2013; entered into force, 24 December 2014.

8 Eleventh preambular paragraph to the 2013 Arms Trade Treaty.

9 S. Casey-Maslen, 'Preamble', in S. Casey-Maslen, A. Clapham, G. Giacca, and S. Parker, *The Arms Trade Treaty, A Commentary*, Oxford University Press, Oxford, 2016, para. 0.40.

10 Under s. F(1) of the Chair's Draft Paper of 24 July 2011, 'Each State Party in a position to do so, and where appropriate, may offer or receive assistance for the care and rehabilitation and social and economic reintegration of victims of armed conflict'.

11 Casey-Maslen, 'Preamble', para. 0.40.

12 Treaty on the Prohibition of Nuclear Weapons; adopted at New York, 7 July 2017; not yet in force.

under its jurisdiction. Similar to the Convention on Cluster Munitions, this assistance is to include medical care, rehabilitation, and psychological support, as well as measures to provide for the social and economic inclusion of victims.

## The definition of victims

8.7    Only exceptionally do disarmament treaties define who is to be considered a victim for the purpose of the positive obligations they incorporate. The Chemical Weapons Convention clearly limits the concept to those harmed by the *use* of chemical weapons (though the notion of harm is not itself clarified). In the Treaty on the Prohibition of Nuclear Weapons, although the relevant provision is entitled victim assistance, the word 'victim' is not even included in the text of the paragraph. It is explicit, though, that the notion encompasses those harmed by the *testing* as well as the use of nuclear weapons. The Anti-Personnel Mine Ban Convention refers to 'mine victims' in its relevant provision on assistance, indicating that assistance is not to be limited to the victims of anti-personnel mines, despite the overall scope of that treaty.

8.8    In the Convention on Cluster Munitions, however, those to be considered cluster munition victims are addressed in detail. While, in the operational provisions, victims are those directly affected by the use of cluster munitions, they are defined more broadly by the Convention to encompass individuals who have been socially marginalised or have suffered economic harm:

> all persons who have been killed or suffered physical or psychological injury, economic loss, social marginalisation or substantial impairment of the realisation of their rights caused by the use of cluster munitions. They include those persons directly impacted by cluster munitions as well as their affected families and communities.[13]

8.9    Although it is not made so explicit in the Treaty on the Prohibition of Nuclear Weapons, it is argued in a legal commentary on the Treaty that the recipients of victim assistance are also to be construed in wide terms:

> For individuals may be 'affected', directly or indirectly, by the use or testing of nuclear weapons in a number of ways beyond being personally harmed by high doses of radiation. They may be driven off land they work because of the contamination. Fertility problems may prevent them from starting a family. But if they do, genetic disorders resulting from radiation poisoning, caused by proximity to a test explosion, can be passed on to a survivor's children, grandchildren, and even great-grandchildren.[14]

---

13 Art. 2(1), 2013 Convention on Cluster Munitions.
14 S. Casey-Maslen, *The Treaty on the Prohibition of Nuclear Weapons: A Commentary*, Oxford University Press, Oxford, January 2019, para. 6.10.

8.10   Some prefer to use the term 'survivor' to victim. In the context of mine action, for instance, the term 'survivor' is widely employed with a view to minimising the risk of stigmatisation and disempowerment. In the International Mine Action Standards (IMAS), issued by the United Nations, a survivor is defined simply as 'a man, or a woman or a child who has suffered harm as a result of a mine, ERW [explosive remnants of war] or cluster munition accident'.[15]

## The nature of assistance to victims

8.11   Assistance to individual victims is substantially (though not always) weapons-specific, depending on the method of harm. It is not always successful in preventing death, even when access to the victim is achieved quickly, for instance in the case of poisoning by radiation, biological toxin, or toxic chemical agent. Irreversible brain damage may be caused to the survivors. Physical injuries by blast and fragmentation may also prove fatal, though for the survivors any limbs that are traumatically or surgically amputated may be replaced with prosthetic devices. Psychological damage, such as post-traumatic stress disorder (PTSD), is also a potential result of weapons' use.

### Nuclear weapons

8.12   Those affected by the explosion of a nuclear weapon and who survive may suffer horrific burns. Even harder to treat, though, are the effects of radiation poisoning. A person who has survived a nuclear explosion receives two doses of radiation: one during the explosion, and another from fallout, when radioactive particles float down after the explosion. According to the US Centers for Disease Control and Prevention (CDC), radiation sickness, or acute radiation syndrome (ARS), is diagnosed when a person receives more than 70 rads[16] from a source outside their body; the dose affects the whole body, or most of it, and is able to penetrate to the internal organs; and the dose is received in a short time, usually within minutes.[17]

8.13   No 'cure' exists for acute radiation syndrome, though barriers can prevent exposure and certain medications may remove some radiation from the body.[18] The treatment goals for radiation sickness are to prevent further radioactive contamination; treat life-threatening injuries, such as from burns and trauma; reduce

---

15 IMAS 04:10: "Glossary of mine action terms, definitions and abbreviations", 2nd Edn, 1 January 2003 (Amendment 6, May 2013), §3.274. But see also M. Karson, 'Why I Prefer "Victim" to "Survivor"', *Psychology Today*, Posted 30 August 2016, at: http://bit.ly/2CYR5Kw.

16 Radiation Absorbed Dose. 100 rads = 1 gray, which is employed as the International System of Units (SI) derived unit of measurement.

17 CDC, 'Acute Radiation Syndrome: A Fact Sheet for Clinicians', Last updated 23 August 2017, at: http://bit.ly/2DghnZq.

18 C. Nordqvist, 'What's to Know About Radiation Sickness?', *Medical News Today*, Last updated 15 August 2017, at: http://bit.ly/2yNeXOi.

the symptoms; and manage the pain. Decontamination involves removing as many external radioactive particles as possible to help prevent further distribution of radioactive materials and lowering the risk of internal contamination from inhalation, ingestion, or open wounds.[19]

8.14    A protein called granulocyte colony-stimulating factor, which promotes the growth of white blood cells, may counter the effect of radiation sickness on bone marrow. Severe damage to bone marrow may also demand transfusions of red blood cells or blood platelets. Potassium iodide, a non-radioactive form of iodine, may be used to fill 'vacancies' in the thyroid and prevent absorption of radioiodine. Radioiodine is eventually cleared from the body in urine. Prussian blue, a type of dye, binds to particles of caesium and thallium, which are then excreted in faeces. This treatment speeds up the elimination of the radioactive particles and reduces the amount of radiation cells may absorb. Diethylenetriamine pentaacetic acid (DTPA) binds to particles of plutonium, americium, and curium, which then pass out of the body in urine, thereby reducing the amount of radiation absorbed.[20]

8.15    A 2016 publication by the International Law and Policy Institute (ILPI) and the United Nations Institute for Disarmament Research (UNIDIR) affirmed that the detonation of a nuclear weapon affects women and men differently, 'both in terms of the biological impacts of ionizing radiation and gender-specific impacts'. Its research suggests that women are often the most affected in terms of their psychological health, their displacement, social stigma, and discrimination.[21] In addition, pregnant women exposed to high doses of ionising radiation are at risk of harm to their children, including malformations and mental retardation. The risk of spontaneous abortion and stillbirth is also heightened if pregnant women are exposed to a certain level of radiation.[22]

## Chemical weapons

8.16    The nature of assistance to the direct victims of the use of chemical weapons will depend on the chemical agent that has been used. In seeking to resolve the Moscow theatre siege in 2002, when Chechen separatists took around 1,000 people hostage demanding an end to the conflict in Chechnya, Russian Special Forces pumped in a narcotic gas to the auditorium. While the exact composition of this gas has never been made public, it is widely believed to be a derivative of fentanyl, a powerful anaesthetic opioid.[23] The standard treatment for an opioid overdose is the

---

19 Mayo Clinic, 'Radiation Sickness', 2018, at: http://bit.ly/2JzaoLI.

20 Ibid.

21 J. Borrie, A. Guro Dimmen, T. Graff Hugo, C. Waszink, and K. Egeland, *Gender, Development and Nuclear Weapons: Shared Goals, Shared Concerns*, ILPI & UNIDIR, 2016, p. 11, at: http://bit.ly/2PFgIGI.

22 Ibid., p. 12.

23 See, e.g., European Court of Human Rights, *Finogenov and Others v. Russia*, Judgment, 20 December 2011 (as rendered final on 4 June 2012), para. 109.

drug Naloxone, which blocks or reverses the effects of opioid medication, including extreme drowsiness, slowed breathing, or loss of consciousness.[24]

8.17 More recently, five people in the United Kingdom – one a former Russian intelligence operative – were poisoned in 2018 as a result of exposure to the toxic chemical, Novichok, one of whom died as a result.[25] The standard treatment for those exposed to a nerve agent is to administer two antidotes, atropine and pralidoxime, while providing 'supportive' care for essential cardiac and respiratory functions during the time taken for the toxins to leave the body.[26] Novichok agents are reported to produce more permanent injury, even following appropriate nerve agent antidote treatment.[27]

8.18 The thirtieth of November each year is the annual Day of Remembrance for all the victims of chemical warfare. On 30 November 2017, a ceremony was held in the Ypres (Leper) room at the OPCW's Headquarters. The room is named after the site in Belgium of the first large-scale chemical weapons attack in April 1915. In his remarks to the ceremony on 30 November 2017, the OPCW Director-General said:

> The suffering of the victims underscores the importance of keeping the international norm against the use of chemical weapons strong and abiding. It is incumbent upon us to redouble our efforts to realise the vision of the Convention and to show zero tolerance for any use of chemical weapons anywhere.[28]

8.19 In 2011, the Conference of States Parties to the CWC decided to establish a trust fund for the victims of chemical weapons and an International Support Network for Victims of Chemical Weapons. The resolution encouraged states parties 'in a position to do so' to actively support the Network and to provide medical treatment to the victims of chemical weapons in their countries.[29]

8.20 With respect to biological weapons, victims of biological warfare might be given antibiotics orally (pills) or intravenously, even before the specific agent is identified. There are already protective vaccines available for anthrax, botulinum toxin, tularaemia, plague, Q fever, and smallpox. Immune protection against ricin and staphylococcal toxins may also be possible in the near future.[30]

24 'Naloxone', *Drugs.com*, September 2017, at: http://bit.ly/2JxMBeP.
25 In September 2018, the British Crown Prosecution Service publicly announced that they were charging in absentia two Russian nationals. See, e.g., M. Bennetts, 'Russia Asks Britain for Help in Identifying Novichok Suspects', *The Guardian*, 7 September 2018, at: https://bit.ly/2O38W5F.
26 C. Milmo, 'Novichok Nerve Agent Makes Treatment of Soviet Spy and Daughter "Very Difficult", Expert', *News*, 12 March 2018, at: http://bit.ly/2JzZDbV.
27 'Novichok Agent', *Science Direct*, 2018, at: http://bit.ly/2qpSGBj.
28 OPCW, 'OPCW Honours All Victims of Chemical Warfare During Remembrance Day', 30 November 2017, at: http://bit.ly/2JysPju.
29 'Decision: The Establishment of the International Support Network for Victims of Chemical Weapons and the Establishment of a Voluntary Trust Fund for This Purpose', Doc. C-16/DEC.13, 2 December 2011, at: http://bit.ly/2CYXuW4.
30 'Biological Warfare Treatment', *WebMD*, 2018, at: http://bit.ly/2P2y0hA.

## Victims of mines and cluster munitions

8.21    The nature of assistance to those injured by anti-personnel mines, cluster munition remnants (e.g. explosive submunitions), and other explosive remnants of war has strong similarities. The particularity of blast anti-personnel mines, however, is that the person who detonates the mine will always suffer traumatic amputation of at least one foot and often also one or both legs. Multiple surgical interventions are needed, along with delayed primary closure of the wounded stump (to enable an artificial limb to be fitted). But combined with a prolonged rehabilitative process – usually including the fitting of one or more prosthetic limbs – physical rehabilitation can, however, enable a mine victim to successfully reintegrate into his or her community.

8.22    For any victims of weapons, there may be psycho-social impacts as well as physical consequences. For, as the Geneva International Centre for Humanitarian Demining (GICHD) has observed:

> Although physical wounds caused by mines and other explosive remnants of war are often horrific, psychological and social impacts are also significant. Difficulties in relationships and daily functioning can be considerable and the survivor may face social stigmatisation, rejection and unemployment. These negative consequences affect survivors in different ways. Both boys and girls may drop out of school as a result of an accident and may find it difficult to get married later in life. Adults who are no longer able to generate income for their families often experience frustration and depression.[31]

---

### BOX 8.1    PROVISIONS ON VICTIM ASSISTANCE IN DISARMAMENT TREATIES

#### Chemical Weapons Convention, Article X: Assistance and Protection against Chemical Weapons

11    If the information available from the ongoing investigation or other reliable sources would give sufficient proof that there are victims of use of chemical weapons and immediate action is indispensable, the Director-General shall notify all States Parties and shall take emergency measures of assistance, using the resources the Conference has placed at his disposal for such contingencies. The Director-General shall keep the Executive Council informed of actions undertaken pursuant to this paragraph.

---

31 GICHD, *A Guide to Mine Action*, 5th Edn, Geneva, March 2014, p. 189.

## Anti-Personnel Mine Ban Convention, Article 6:
## International Cooperation and Assistance

3   Each State Party in a position to do so shall provide assistance for the care and rehabilitation, and social and economic reintegration, of mine victims and for mine awareness programs. . . .

## Convention on Cluster Munitions, Article 5:
## Victim Assistance

1   Each State Party with respect to cluster munition victims in areas under its jurisdiction or control shall, in accordance with applicable international humanitarian and human rights law, adequately provide age- and gender-sensitive assistance, including medical care, rehabilitation and psychological support, as well as provide for their social and economic inclusion. Each State Party shall make every effort to collect reliable relevant data with respect to cluster munition victims.

2   In fulfilling its obligations under paragraph 1 of this Article each State Party shall:

   a   Assess the needs of cluster munition victims;
   b   Develop, implement and enforce any necessary national laws and policies;
   c   Develop a national plan and budget, including timeframes to carry out these activities, with a view to incorporating them within the existing national disability, development and human rights frameworks and mechanisms, while respecting the specific role and contribution of relevant actors;
   d   Take steps to mobilise national and international resources;
   e   Not discriminate against or among cluster munition victims, or between cluster munition victims and those who have suffered injuries or disabilities from other causes; differences in treatment should be based only on medical, rehabilitative, psychological or socio-economic needs;
   f   Closely consult with and actively involve cluster munition victims and their representative organisations;
   g   Designate a focal point within the government for coordination of matters relating to the implementation of this Article; and
   h   Strive to incorporate relevant guidelines and good practices including in the areas of medical care, rehabilitation and psychological support, as well as social and economic inclusion.

> ### Treaty on the Prohibition of Nuclear Weapons, Article 6: Victim Assistance and Environmental Remediation
>
> 1   Each State Party shall, with respect to individuals under its jurisdiction who are affected by the use or testing of nuclear weapons, in accordance with applicable international humanitarian and human rights law, adequately provide age- and gender-sensitive assistance, without discrimination, including medical care, rehabilitation and psychological support, as well as provide for their social and economic inclusion.

## Clearance of munitions

8.22   Several global disarmament treaties require that munitions that have been used be cleared from the affected areas and destroyed. This is not the case under either the Biological Weapons Convention or the Chemical Weapons Convention, which only require destruction of stockpiles. However, clearance continues today in Belgium and France of unexploded or abandoned shells containing chlorine or mustard gas used in the First World War. It is estimated that 1 in 20 shells fired during that conflict contained a chemical agent, meaning some 50 million of the 1 billion munitions fired were chemical weapons.[32]

### Clearance of anti-personnel mines

8.23   Article 5 of the APMBC requires that all emplaced anti-personnel mines in areas under the jurisdiction or control of a state party be cleared and destroyed within ten years of that state becoming party to the Convention. However, states parties that are unable to meet the ten-year deadline are entitled to ask for one or more extension periods of up to ten years at a time. The requests are submitted in advance of the forthcoming meeting of states parties or review conference. They are then discussed by key stakeholders, including a group of states parties before being considered formally by the meeting or conference. While extensions to the Article 5 were supposed to be exceptional, they have proved to be common.

8.24   The international non-governmental organisation (NGO), Norwegian People's Aid, publishes an annual report on progress in mine clearance around the world, called *Clearing the Mines*. Its 2017 edition reported that, as at the end of 2016,

---

32 See, e.g., R. Albright, *Clean-up of Chemical and Explosive Munitions: Location, Identification and Environmental Remediation*, William Andrew, Oxford, 2011, p. 120; A. Hall, 'The Iron Harvest: Meet the Soldiers Tasked with Clearing Hundreds of Tonnes of Deadly World War I Shells and Mines from Beneath Flanders' Fields', *Daily Mail*, 10 November 2013, at: http://bit.ly/2qpk6qY.

59 states and 3 territories[33] were still contaminated with anti-personnel mines over a total global area of less than 2,000 km². Algeria completed mine clearance in December 2016, the most heavily mined state to have done so since the entry into force of the APMBC in 1999. But in 2016 and 2017, new use of anti-personnel mines of an improvised nature, especially those made and laid by Islamic State in Iraq and Syria, had added extensive mine contamination for the first time in more than a decade.[34]

8.25  The key to efficient mine clearance is high-quality survey. A combination of non-technical and technical survey is employed to identify the location and extent of areas with contamination. Non-technical survey focuses on the gathering of information from records, interviews, and observation from a safe area. Technical survey uses full clearance techniques, normally in lanes penetrating into a suspected mined area, to try and identify the start of the mine contamination (or outer perimeter of the mine belt, if they have been laid by appropriately trained, regular armed forces).

8.26  Clearance generally uses one of three techniques: manual, animal, or mechanical. As the GICHD notes:

> Manual mine clearance methods have not changed significantly since World War II. Techniques continue to rely on a deminer working along a marked lane using a metal detector, prodder, rake or an excavation kit until a suspicious object is encountered. Although these methods often mean relatively slow progress, they are widespread and popular in mine action programmes, in recognition of the very high levels of confidence associated with the land they release. Some organisations involved in manual clearance choose not to use alternative methods and assets.[35]

Modern detectors are usually based around the principle of magnetic induction, and are able to filter out signals from 'unwanted' metallic compounds in the soil. Some also feature ground penetrating radar (GPR).[36] Rakes are used for excavation and mine detection in sandy beaches, deserts, and other soft terrains without significant root systems, thick undergrowth, or stones.[37] Daily clearance output for a

---

33  Afghanistan, Angola, Argentina, Armenia, Azerbaijan, Bosnia and Herzegovina, Cambodia, Cameroon, Chad, Chile, China, Colombia, Croatia, Cuba, Cyprus, the Democratic Republic of Congo, Ecuador, Egypt, Eritrea, Ethiopia, Georgia, India, Iran, Iraq, Israel, Jordan, Kyrgyzstan, Lao PDR, Lebanon, Libya, Mauritania, Morocco, Myanmar, Niger, Nigeria, North Korea, Oman, Pakistan, Palau, Palestine, Peru, Russia, Senegal, Serbia, Somalia, South Korea, South Sudan, Sri Lanka, Sudan, Syria, Tajikistan, Thailand, Turkey, Ukraine, Uzbekistan, the United Kingdom, Vietnam, Yemen, and Zimbabwe; and Kosovo, Nagorno-Karabakh, and Western Sahara. Mauritania declared completion of its clearance obligations at the 2018 Meeting of States Parties.

34  Mine Action Review, *Clearing the Mines 2017*, Norwegian People's Aid, 2017, p. 1, at: http://bit.ly/2RvZCs5.

35  GICHD, *A Guide to Mine Action*, 5th Edn, p. 134.

36  Ibid., p. 135.

37  Ibid., p. 136.

single deminer is between 5 square metres and 150 square metres,[38] with an average of about 20 square metres a day.

8.27   Once a mine has been identified, it is either destroyed in situ or moved to a safe place for demolition (typically at the end of each working day).[39] Thus, a mine may be cleared without its destruction (meaning it could be re-used later), which explains why the Anti-Personnel Mine Ban Convention obligates states parties to destroy them, rather than merely to clear them.[40]

8.28   Animals used in clearance operations are generally mine detection dogs, although giant African pouched rats are also used. An animal detector system (ADS) uses trained animals to detect odours from specific vapours associated with the explosive or other components of mines and munitions. Explosive detection animals can detect mines with a low metal content, deep buried anti-vehicle mines, and mines buried in areas with a high metal contamination.[41] ADS can be faster and more cost-effective than manual demining detector methods. Daily progress has been recorded from 300 square metres to 2,000 square metres.[42] Of course, once a mine has been detected, a manual deminer is still required to clear and destroy it.

8.29   As the GICHD observes, mechanical systems can be 'highly cost-effective components in a demining programme, accelerating the progress of other assets, through removing vegetation and tripwires and breaking up soil. They can perform important functions in technical survey and, in some cases, can be used as a primary clearance method'.[43] The most common types of machines used in demining operations are equipped with flails, sifters, tillers, and rollers.[44]

8.30   Flails are machines on the front of which are attached chains with hammers, which are rotated using a horizontal shaft. The hammers impact or dig through the ground, resulting in the detonation or fragmentation of near-surface mines. The rotation of the shaft is adjusted to determine the digging depth.[45] Tillers function similar to flails:

> They use a rotating drum fitted with hardened chisels or teeth on its circumference to help dig or bite through the ground. The length of the chisel controls the clearance depth. A flexible knee joint helps increase the degree of freedom of the chisels and absorb most shocks. However, by doing so, the productivity of the tillers is reduced. Tillers use large, powerful engines and tend to be heavy

---

38 Ibid., p. 137.

39 Ibid., pp. 134–35.

40 Compare this with Article 10(1) of the 1996 Amended Protocol II to the Convention on Certain Conventional Weapons, which provides that: 'Without delay after the cessation of active hostilities, all minefields, mined areas, mines, booby-traps and other devices shall be cleared, removed, destroyed or maintained'.

41 GICHD, *A Guide to Mine Action*, 5th Edn, p. 138.

42 Ibid., p. 139.

43 Ibid.

44 Ibid.

45 A. Juneja, 'Flail Technology in Demining', *Journal of Conventional Weapons Destruction*, Vol. 20, No. 2 (July 2016), at: http://bit.ly/2zjCeXs.

and difficult to maneuver. Tillers can be coupled with flails to destroy mines more reliably. They have been used in Bosnia and Herzegovina and Croatia.[46]

A mine roller is a device that is attached to a tank or armoured vehicle with the aim of confirming (to a high degree of confidence) that no mines are present in a particular area. Mine rollers have several heavy wheels and can have short projecting steel grinders. These grinders allow a higher ground pressure, ensuring the explosion of pressure-activated devices, such as mines.[47]

---

### BOX 8.2 CLEARANCE AND DESTRUCTION PROVISIONS IN GLOBAL DISARMAMENT TREATIES

**1996 Amended Protocol II to the Convention on Certain Conventional Weapons, Article 10: Removal of minefields, mined areas, mines, booby-traps and other devices and international cooperation**

1   Without delay after the cessation of active hostilities, all minefields, mined areas, mines, booby-traps and other devices shall be cleared, removed, destroyed or maintained in accordance with Article 3 and paragraph 2 of Article 5 of this Protocol.

**Anti-Personnel Mine Ban Convention, Article 5: Destruction of anti-personnel mines in mined areas**

1   Each State Party undertakes to destroy or ensure the destruction of all anti-personnel mines in mined areas under its jurisdiction or control, as soon as possible but not later than ten years after the entry into force of this Convention for that State Party.

**Convention on Cluster Munitions, Article 4: Clearance and destruction of cluster munition remnants and risk reduction education**

1   Each State Party undertakes to clear and destroy, or ensure the clearance and destruction of, cluster munition remnants located in cluster munition contaminated areas under its jurisdiction or control, as follows:

(a)   Where cluster munition remnants are located in areas under its jurisdiction or control at the date of entry into force of this Convention

---

46 Ibid.
47 Armtrac Ltd., "The Benefits and Uses of a Mine Roller", 4 October 2017, at: http://bit.ly/2PwgEt5.

for that State Party, such clearance and destruction shall be completed as soon as possible but not later than ten years from that
date;

(b)  Where, after entry into force of this Convention for that State Party,
cluster munitions have become cluster munition remnants located in
areas under its jurisdiction or control, such clearance and destruction
must be completed as soon as possible but not later than ten years
after the end of the active hostilities during which such cluster munitions became cluster munition remnants. . . .

## Clearance of cluster munition remnants

8.31  The techniques for clearance of cluster munition remnants depend on which
type of remnants is to be destroyed. Under the Convention on Cluster Munitions,
cluster munition remnants are defined as failed cluster munitions, abandoned cluster munitions, unexploded submunitions, and unexploded bomblets.[48] Where the
remnants are abandoned cluster munitions, meaning that they have not been used,
they are akin to stockpiles and would need to be addressed in the same way as other
cluster munition stockpiles. Failed cluster munitions are those that have been fired,
dropped, or launched but where the submunitions have not been dispersed from
their container or dispenser.[49]

8.32  Abandoned or failed cluster munitions are relatively exceptional in terms
of contamination. By far the greater problem comes from unexploded submunitions or bomblets.[50] As at July 2018, according to Mine Action Review, 27 states
and 3 other areas were contaminated with cluster munition remnants.[51] In contrast
to mine clearance, areas contaminated with unexploded submunitions or bomblets are often cleared from the inside out, whereby a clearance operator enters the
contaminated area and seeks to identify the centre of the strike and then clears
outwards to cover the 'footprint' (the area covered by a single cluster munition
strike). A typical footprint may cover 5,000 square metres to 10,000 square metres
in an oval shape.

48  Art. 2(7), 2008 Convention on Cluster Munitions.
49  Art. 2(4), 2008 Convention on Cluster Munitions.
50  Art. 2(13) and (15), 2008 Convention on Cluster Munitions. Note that the only difference between
    submunitions and bomblets is that bomblets are dropped from canisters that are fixed to the wings
    of an aircraft.
51  Afghanistan, Angola, Azerbaijan, Bosnia and Herzegovina, Cambodia, Chad, Chile, Croatia, the Dem-
    ocratic Republic of Congo, Georgia, Germany, Iran, Iraq, Lao PDR, Lebanon, Libya, Montenegro,
    Serbia, Somalia, South Sudan, Sudan, Syria, Tajikistan, Ukraine, the United Kingdom, Vietnam, and
    Yemen; and Kosovo, Nagorno-Karabakh, and Western Sahara. Mine Action Review, *Clearing Cluster
    Munition Remnants 2018*, Norwegian People's Aid, August 2018, p. 1, at: https://bit.ly/2O3ApnP.

8.33    In 2017, a total of more than 153,000 submunitions were destroyed by clearance operations around the world from some 95 square kilometres of contaminated area. As in previous years, in 2017 the largest area of clearance of cluster munition remnants took place in Laos, the world's most heavily contaminated state. In fact, more than one third of total recorded global clearance was conducted there.[52] In accordance with Article 4 of the CCM (see Box 8.1), each state has a deadline of 10 years to complete survey and clearance of all cluster munition remnants in areas under its jurisdiction or control upon becoming party to the Convention. Those that cannot meet the deadline may seek an extension of up to five years at a time. The first Article 4 deadlines were expiring on 1 August 2020.

## Environmental remediation

### *Irradiated soil*

8.34    Environmental remediation is costly, hazardous, and highly challenging. This is evidenced by two major experiences, one in Spain and the second on the Marshall Islands. On 17 January 1966, during refuelling operations, a United States B-52 bomber carrying four nuclear weapons collided with a military refuelling aircraft and crashed near Palomares, a village on the Mediterranean Sea in Andalucía in Spain. When two of the four weapons hit the ground, the high explosive they contained detonated, releasing three kilograms of radioactive plutonium that spread out over two square kilometres of land.[53] Shortly after the accident, the United States shipped 1,700 tonnes (approximately 1,200 cubic metres) of contaminated earth to South Carolina, after which the incident was largely forgotten. Concern was revived by tests in the 1990s that revealed high levels of americium, a decay product of plutonium, and further tests showed that 50,000 cubic metres of earth were still contaminated.[54] Today, parts of the town are still off limits due to the continued existence of waste.[55]

8.35    There is no agreed standard for environmental remediation of former nuclear test sites. In the context of the testing on the Marshall Islands, the Marshall Islands government proposed adopting the national guidance

---

52  Ibid., p. 3.
53  M. Gonzalez, 'Trump Presidency Will Force Renegotiation of Palomares Nuclear Clean-Up', *El País*, 27 January 2017, at: http://bit.ly/2Ak8iMH.
54  S. Burgen, 'US to Clean Up Spanish Radioactive Site 49 Years After Plane Crash', *The Guardian*, 19 October 2015, at: http://bit.ly/2D0mXz4.
55  J. Gerrard, 'Deputy for Almeria Criticises Government on Palomares Nuclear Cleanup', *Euro Weekly*, 16 February 2018, at: http://bit.ly/2OGnjRx. In August 2018, Senator Richard Blumenthal introduced the Palomares Veterans Act of 2018, a bill to ensure that U.S. veterans exposed to plutonium in the clean-up of the 1966 Palomares disaster would finally receive Department of Veterans Affairs 'disability benefits'. Senator Blumenthal '73 Introduces Bill for Veterans Affected by 1966 Nuclear Disaster', Yale Law School, 29 August 2018, at: http://bit.ly/2CnEVcL.

established by the US Environmental Protection Agency (EPA) for the clean-up of radioactive contamination at 'Superfund' sites in the United States.[56] This limits annual exposure at such sites after clean-up to 15 millirems of radiation above natural background levels from all sources. The US Department of Energy used a 100-millirem[57] standard for the clean-up in past efforts in the Marshall Islands.[58]

8.36   Between 1948 and 1958, 43 nuclear tests were conducted on Enewetak Atoll, part of the Marshall Islands, which are located between Hawaii and the Philippines. This included 'Ivy Mike', the first hydrogen bomb ever tested, on 1 November 1952. 'Four islands were entirely vaporized; only deep blue radioactive craters in the ocean remained'.[59] In the early 1970s, the Enewetak islanders threatened legal action if they were not able to return to their home. In 1972, the US government agreed to clean up the atoll in a joint project by the Atomic Energy Commission (now the Department of Energy) and the Department of Defense.[60]

8.37   The greatest problem, according to Department of Energy reports, was Runit, a 75-acre island on which 11 nuclear tests were conducted in 1958. At the north of the island, a 300-foot-wide crater was designated 'a special problem' because of 'high subsurface contamination' from pulverised plutonium. Government scientists believed that other islands might be rendered habitable, but that Runit would always be too toxic. US government officials decided to collect radioactive debris from the other islands and simply dump it into the Runit crater, then to cap it with a thick concrete dome.[61] It has been estimated that 85,000 cubic metres of radioactive material was collected and dumped in this way.[62]

8.38   In early 2018, however, there was growing concern about the fate of the dome. When it was built in the late 1970s, climate change and sea level rise were not a factor, so the site was built right next to the shore on the ocean side of the island. Subsequently, however, storm surges have driven sea water across some of the atolls and the water is penetrating the underside of the dome, because to save money, the interior was not lined with concrete as had been planned. Added to that, a 2013 US Department of Energy report had already warned that the

---

56 T. Lum *et al.*, 'Republic of the Marshall Islands Changed Circumstances Petition to Congress', *CRS Report for Congress*, Updated 16 May 2005, p. 4, at: http://bit.ly/2JbjOfU. Superfund sites are those hazardous waste sites being addressed by the US Superfund programme.

57 The rem (Roentgen equivalent man) is the unit of radiation dosage applied to humans. It is defined as the dosage in rads that will cause the same amount of biological injury as one rad of X-rays or gamma rays.

58 Lum *et al.*, 'Republic of the Marshall Islands Changed Circumstances Petition to Congress', p. 5.

59 D. Philipps, 'Troops Who Cleaned Up Radioactive Islands Can't Get Medical Care', *The New York Times*, 28 January 2017, at: http://bit.ly/2CxYfFh.

60 Ibid.

61 Ibid.

62 M. Willacy, 'It Was Supposed to Be a Trip to Paradise, Instead It Sealed Their Fate', *ABC News* (Australia), Updated 28 November 2017, at: http://bit.ly/2PaZKA1.

dome could be smashed apart by the increased ferocity of typhoons. If this were to occur, large quantities of radioactive material would seep into the surrounding waters.[63]

---

## BOX 8.3   ENVIRONMENTAL REMEDIATION PROVISIONS IN GLOBAL DISARMAMENT TREATIES

### Treaty on the Prohibition of Nuclear Weapons, Article 6: Victim Assistance and Environmental Remediation

2   Each State Party, with respect to areas under its jurisdiction or control contaminated as a result of activities related to the testing or use of nuclear weapons or other nuclear explosive devices, shall take necessary and appropriate measures towards the environmental remediation of areas so contaminated.

### Anti-Personnel Mine Ban Convention, Article 5: Destruction of anti-personnel mines in mined areas

3   If a State Party believes that it will be unable to destroy or ensure the destruction of all anti-personnel mines referred to in paragraph 1 within that time period, it may submit a request to a Meeting of the States Parties or a Review Conference for an extension of the deadline for completing the destruction of such anti-personnel mines, for a period of up to ten years.

4   Each request shall contain: . . . c) The humanitarian, social, economic, and environmental implications of the extension. . . .

### Convention on Cluster Munitions, Article 4: Clearance and destruction of cluster munition remnants and risk reduction education

6   A request for an extension shall be submitted to a Meeting of States Parties or a Review Conference prior to the expiry of the time period referred to in paragraph 1 of this Article for that State Party. Each request shall be submitted a minimum of nine months prior to the Meeting of States Parties or Review Conference at which it is to be considered. Each request shall set out:

h   The humanitarian, social, economic and environmental implications of the proposed extension. . . .

---

63 A. Wernick, 'Seawater Is Infiltrating a Nuclear Waste Dump on a Remote Pacific Atoll', *Public Radio International*, 19 February 2018, at: http://bit.ly/2S5NVd3.

8.39    As Mark Willacy, an Australian journalist who visited the islands, reported, the Marshall Islands government would like to see the United States take responsibility for what it sees as a United States problem. In 1986, however, the US government concluded an agreement with the Marshall Islands whereby the islands would take over running its own affairs in return for a final payment of some US$150 million.[64]

## Soil contaminated with Agent Orange

8.40    Agent Orange, a chemical agent the composition of which includes dioxin, was widely deployed by United States forces in Vietnam in the 1960s and early 1970s to destroy forests and cause tree leaves to fall off to deprive the Viet Cong of cover. Over a decade of the conflict in south-east Asia, the United States sprayed about 20 million gallons of Agent Orange and other herbicides in Cambodia, the Lao People's Democratic Republic, and Vietnam. The action halted when scientists commissioned by the US Department of Agriculture reported concerns that dioxin showed 'a significant potential to increase birth defects'. By the time the spraying stopped, Agent Orange and other herbicides had destroyed 2 million hectares of forest and cropland.[65]

8.41    Five decades later, the United States began a joint programme with the Vietnamese government to clean up the dioxin 'hot spots' it left behind. In 2012, a US$100 million experimental procedure to eliminate a dioxin 'hot spot' in Da Nang at an airbase was the beginning of a vast environmental clean-up. Most dioxin has dissipated over the years, as it breaks down in sunlight or clings to soil particles and is washed away in rainwater.[66] However, three major hot spots were identified where Agent Orange was stored, and another 25 or so potential hot spots exist across the country, mostly on and around former US military installations.[67]

8.42    The clean-up process involves preventing access to contaminated areas building constructing fences and other barriers to protect the local population

64  The Compact of Free Association, enacted in 1986, governs the economic and strategic relationships between the United States and the Marshall Islands. The Agreement granted US$150 million as part of a 'full and final settlement' of legal claims against the US Government, but provided for possible additional compensation, if loss or damages to persons or property arose or were discovered that could not reasonably have been identified as of the effective date of the agreement, and if such injuries rendered the Provisions of the Compact 'manifestly inadequate'. T. Lum *et al.*, 'Republic of the Marshall Islands Changed Circumstances Petition to Congress', CRS Report for Congress, Updated 16 May 2005, Summary, at: http://bit.ly/2JbjOfU.

65  T. Fuller, '4 Decades on, U.S. Starts Cleanup of Agent Orange in Vietnam', *The New York Times*, 9 August 2012, at: http://bit.ly/2Qd7H4J.

66  The Aspen Institute, 'Clean Up Efforts', August 2011, at: http://bit.ly/2EYoOGr.

67  D. Malloy, 'U.S. Helping Defuse Vietnam's Dioxin Hot Spots Blamed on Agent Orange', *The Washington Post*, 8 April 2016, at: http://bit.ly/2RwjnzJ.

from further exposure. Containment measures such as concrete caps, filtration systems, and sediment traps prevent dioxin from being transported to secondary sites such as ponds and streams, and from there up the food chain to people.[68] The contaminated soils are cleaned of dioxin by US companies by stripping away the soil and taking it away to subject it to extreme heat, which renders the dioxin harmless.[69]

## International cooperation and assistance

8.43  To support treaty implementation and compliance, global disarmament treaties since the Chemical Weapons Convention foresee measures of international cooperation and assistance, typically in a dedicated article (see Box 8.4). International cooperation and assistance often covers technical, material, and financial assistance by other states, including support to victim assistance, clearance of used or abandoned munitions, and environmental remediation. The CWC foresees a distinct voluntary trust fund to this end.

8.44  The Arms Trade Treaty explicitly specifies in the context of international assistance: legal and legislative assistance, institutional capacity-building, stockpile management as well as disarmament, demobilisation, and reintegration (DDR), model legislation, and effective practices for implementation. It is often stipulated that assistance may be provided, inter alia, through the United Nations system, international, regional, or national organisations or institutions, the International Committee of the Red Cross, national Red Cross and Red Crescent societies and their International Federation, NGOs, or on a bilateral basis.

---

### BOX 8.4  INTERNATIONAL COOPERATION AND ASSISTANCE PROVISIONS IN GLOBAL DISARMAMENT TREATIES

#### Biological Weapons Convention, Article V

The States Parties to this Convention undertake to consult one another and to cooperate in solving any problems which may arise in relation to the objective of, or in the application of the provisions of, the Convention. Consultation and cooperation pursuant to this Article may also be undertaken through appropriate international procedures within the framework of the United Nations and in accordance with its Charter.

---

68  The Aspen Institute, 'Clean Up Efforts'.
69  'Cleaning Up Agent Orange', *Deutsche Welle*, 10 August 2012, at: http://bit.ly/2JxU79y.

## Chemical Weapons Convention, Article X: Assistance and Protection against Chemical Weapons

7   Each State Party undertakes to provide assistance through the Organization [OPCW] and to this end to elect to take one or more of the following measures:

    a   To contribute to the voluntary fund for assistance to be established by the Conference at its first session;

    b   To conclude, if possible not later than 180 days after this Convention enters into force for it, agreements with the Organization concerning the procurement, upon demand, of assistance;

    c   To declare, not later than 180 days after this Convention enters into force for it, the kind of assistance it might provide in response to an appeal by the Organization. If, however, a State Party subsequently is unable to provide the assistance envisaged in its declaration, it is still under the obligation to provide assistance in accordance with this paragraph.

## Anti-Personnel Mine Ban Convention, Article 6: International cooperation and assistance

3   Each State Party in a position to do so shall provide assistance for the care and rehabilitation, and social and economic reintegration, of mine victims and for mine awareness programmes.

4   Each State Party in a position to do so shall provide assistance for mine clearance and related activities.

## Convention on Cluster Munitions, Article 6: International cooperation and assistance

2   Each State Party in a position to do so shall provide technical, material and financial assistance to States Parties affected by cluster munitions, aimed at the implementation of the obligations of this Convention.

4   . . . [E]ach State Party in a position to do so shall provide assistance for clearance and destruction of cluster munition remnants. . . .

7   Each State Party in a position to do so shall provide assistance for the implementation of the obligations referred to in Article 5 of this Convention to adequately provide age- and gender-sensitive assistance, including medical care, rehabilitation and psychological support, as well as provide for social and economic inclusion of cluster munition victims.

**Treaty on the Prohibition of Nuclear Weapons,
Article 7: International cooperation and assistance**

1    Each State Party shall cooperate with other States Parties to facilitate the implementation of this Treaty.

3    Each State Party in a position to do so shall provide technical, material and financial assistance to States Parties affected by nuclear-weapons use or testing. . . .

4    Each State Party in a position to do so shall provide assistance for the victims of the use or testing of nuclear weapons or other nuclear explosive devices.

# 9

# REPORTING, VERIFICATION, AND COMPLIANCE

## Introduction

9.1 This chapter discusses the range of confidence-building measures, review mechanisms, verification, and other measures that promote compliance with disarmament treaties. These include initial and annual reporting obligations, meetings of states parties, as well as, in certain circumstances, treaty secretariats and even compulsory fact-finding and compliance mechanisms. Beyond the state-based systems foreseen in treaties, the chapter also references the unofficial civil-society monitoring initiatives that assess state compliance with their international disarmament obligations.

9.2 A number of key terms that appear in this chapter, while widely employed, are the subject of markedly different understandings by key stakeholders. The most contentious of these are 'verification' and 'compliance'. Verification is best understood as the means by which it is confirmed whether a state is respecting the provisions of a treaty to which it is party (or other agreement that it has endorsed).[1] This involves, especially, on-site inspections of weapons production or storage facilities and installations where the weapons have been deployed. With respect to alleged use of a weapon, the term 'investigation' is more common than 'verification'.[2] In certain circumstances, such an investigation may be carried out by means of a fact-finding mission.

---

1 According to the United States (US) Department of Defense (DoD), verification means, in 'arms control, any action, including inspection, detection, and identification, taken to ascertain compliance with agreed measures'. *DoD Dictionary of Military and Associated Terms*, September 2018, p. 245.

2 That said, in the 1992 Chemical Weapons Convention, the part of the treaty that addresses 'Investigations in cases of alleged use of chemical weapons' is contained in its 'Verification Annex'. Convention on the Prohibition of the Development, Production, Stockpiling and Use of Chemical Weapons and on their Destruction; adopted at Geneva, 3 September 1992; entered into force, 29 April 1997, Verification Annex, Part XI.

9.3    Compliance means respect by a state for the terms of a treaty to which it is party (or other instrument that it has endorsed). Thus, for example, in the 1972 Anti-Ballistic Missile Treaty (ABM Treaty),[3] it is stipulated that 'for the purpose of providing assurance of compliance with the provisions of this Treaty, each Party shall use national technical means of verification at its disposal in a manner consistent with generally recognized principles of international law'.[4] Compliance measures mean those actions that are taken by others to ensure respect with such a treaty or agreement, especially when a state is found to have violated its obligations. Thus, for example, Article XII of the 1992 Chemical Weapons Convention concerns 'measures to redress a situation and to ensure compliance, including sanctions'. Therein it is stipulated that 'the Conference [of the states parties] shall take the necessary measures, as set forth in paragraphs 2, 3 and 4, to ensure compliance with this Convention and to redress and remedy any situation which contravenes the provisions of this Convention'.[5]

9.4    The notion of confidence-building measures (CBMs) is less disputed: it is generally accepted that the term means measures, especially of transparency, and which may be of a voluntary or binding nature, that promote confidence among others[6] that the terms of a treaty or other instrument are being respected and implemented. Sometimes, verification itself is described as a form of CBM. In January 2018, for instance, the United Nations (UN) Secretary-General told the UN Security Council that 'effective verification mechanisms have proven to be some of the most successful and enduring types of confidence-building measures'.[7]

## Global disarmament treaties' reporting obligations

### Biological Weapons Convention

9.5    Reporting by states parties on progress in implementing their international legal obligations is a staple of disarmament treaties. The 1971 Biological Weapons Convention[8] is thus exceptional in that it does not require either an initial declaration or annual reporting. This would prove to be an error of omission. Already at the First Review Conference in 1980, states parties decided to call for details of

3    Treaty Between the United States of America and the Union of Soviet Socialist Republics on the Limitation of Anti-Ballistic Missile Systems (ABM Treaty); signed at Moscow, 26 May 1972; entered into force, 3 October 1972; United States' withdrawal, 2002.
4    Art. XII(1), ABM Treaty.
5    Art. XII(1), 1992 Chemical Weapons Convention.
6    This is, of course, particularly the other state party to a bilateral disarmament treaty or other states parties in the case of a multilateral agreement.
7    UN, 'Confidence-Building Measures Supporting Arms Control Extremely Critical, Secretary-General Tells Security Council Meeting on Non-proliferation', UN doc. SG/SM/18858-SC/13167-DC/3755, 18 January 2018, at: http://bit.ly/2P8opWw.
8    Convention on the Prohibition of the Development, Production and Stockpiling of Bacteriological (Biological) and Toxin Weapons and on their Destruction; opened for signature, 10 April 1972; entered into force, 25 March 1975.

national implementation measures to be provided to the United Nations. At the Convention's Second Review Conference in 1986, states parties agreed upon a further set of CBMs 'in order to prevent or reduce the occurrence of ambiguities, doubts, and suspicions and in order to improve international co-operation in the field of peaceful biological activities'. These CBMs were expanded upon by the Convention's Third Review Conference in 1991.[9]

9.6    Under the agreements, the states parties to the Biological Weapons Convention undertook to provide annual reports, using agreed forms, on research centres and laboratories; vaccine production facilities; national biological defence research and development programmes; past activities in biological research and development programmes; outbreaks of infectious diseases and similar occurrences caused by toxins; and on legislation, regulations and other measures.[10] The UN Secretary-General has noted, however, that 'unfortunately, participation has been less than satisfactory, with fewer than half of all States Parties regularly providing information'.[11] On this basis, the Arms Control Association believes that the measures have proved 'largely unsuccessful' thus far.[12] Indeed, it continues to be disputed among states whether the CBMs are even legally binding or are merely voluntary in nature.

### *Chemical Weapons Convention*

9.7    Compliance with the detailed – and legally binding – reporting obligations under the 1992 Chemical Weapons Convention has been at a higher level.[13] States are obligated to make an initial declaration within 30 days of becoming party to the Convention in which they, inter alia, declare whether they own or possess any chemical weapons, or whether chemical weapons are located in any place under their jurisdiction or control (and provide detail on any such weapons).[14] Declarations on stockpiles are broken down into three categories:

- Category 1: nerve agents, including VX and sarin
- Category 2: other chemical weapons, such as phosgene
- Category 3: Unfilled munitions, devices, and equipment designed specifically to employ chemical weapons.[15]

The lists of chemicals to be declared are not exhaustive.

---

9 UN Office for Disarmament Affairs (UNODA), 'Biological Weapons: The Biological Weapons Convention', at: http://bit.ly/2DiQkgi.

10 Ibid.

11 UN, 'Confidence-Building Measures Supporting Arms Control Extremely Critical, Secretary-General Tells Security Council Meeting on Non-proliferation', UN doc. SG/SM/18858-SC/13167-DC/3755, 18 January 2018.

12 'The Biological Weapons Convention (BWC) At A Glance', *Fact Sheet*, Arms Control Association, Last updated September 2018, at: http://bit.ly/2AHFVbg.

13 Convention on the Prohibition of the Development, Production, Stockpiling and Use of Chemical Weapons and on their Destruction; adopted at Geneva, 3 September 1992; entered into force, 29 April 1997.

14 Art. III(1)(a), 1992 Chemical Weapons Convention.

15 D. Kimball, 'The Chemical Weapons Convention (BWC) At A Glance', Fact Sheet, Arms Control Association, Last updated June 2018, at: http://bit.ly/2JzR3tv.

9.8    States parties are further required to report on all chemical weapons production facilities on their territory since January 1946; plans for the destruction of
all weapons and facilities; all transfers of chemical weapons or production equipment since January 1946; and all riot-control agents in their possession.[16] Information regarding the implementation of plans for destruction of chemical weapons
must be submitted each year to the Technical Secretariat of the Organisation for the
Prohibition of Chemical Weapons (OPCW), specifying the quantities of chemical weapons destroyed the previous year 'at each destruction facility'.[17] The relevant provision further stipulates that, if 'appropriate', the 'reasons for not meeting
destruction goals should be stated'.[18]

## Anti-Personnel Mine Ban Convention

9.9    There are also detailed reporting requirements under the 1997 Anti-Personnel Mine Ban Convention.[19] Article 7 on transparency measures obligates
each state to make an initial declaration within six months of becoming party
to the Convention and then to update the report for each calendar year by
30 April the following year.[20] A detailed set of reporting requirements cover
most of the obligations upon states parties under the Convention, including
the following:

- National implementation measures;
- The total number of stockpiled anti-personnel mines;
- The location of all mined areas under their jurisdiction or control that contain,
  or are suspected to contain, anti-personnel mines along with details on the
  types and quantities of anti-personnel mines therein;
- The types and quantities of anti-personnel mines retained or transferred in
  connection with mine clearance or destruction;
- Programmes for the de-commissioning of anti-personnel mine production
  facilities;
- Progress in the destruction of stockpiled and emplaced anti-personnel mines
  (including the location of destruction sites and the relevant safety and environmental standards).

9.10    The list does not include any information on support for mine victim
assistance − domestically or internationally − or details of annual mine casualties,

16  Art. III(1)(a), (c), and (e), 1992 Chemical Weapons Convention.
17  The Technical Secretariat of the OPCW assists the Conference of the States Parties and the Execu-
    tive Council in the performance of their functions.
18  1992 Chemical Weapons Convention, Annex, Part IV (A) (Destruction of Chemical Weapons and its
    Verification Pursuant to Article IV), para. 36.
19  Convention on the Prohibition of the Use, Stockpiling, Production and Transfer of Anti-Personnel
    Mines and on their Destruction; adopted at Oslo, 18 September 1997; entered into force, 1
    March 1999.
20  Art. 7(1) and (2), Anti-Personnel Mine Ban Convention.

though many states parties have volunteered such information in their annual reports. Moreover, states parties adopted a Guide to Reporting at the Fourteenth Meeting of States Parties recommending that such information be provided systematically. Arguably, the most serious omission is of an obligation to detail the estimated size of mined areas and progress in releasing suspected or confirmed mined areas. This is because the number of mines in an area tells little of the impact inflicted on nearby communities or the clearance challenge that remains, while the number of destroyed mines similarly reflects poorly the rate of progress by a state party towards its Article 5 clearance deadline under the Convention. Increasingly, though, affected states are including such information in their annual reports, and the Guide to Reporting mentioned above similarly recommends that it be provided systematically.[21]

## Convention on Cluster Munitions

9.11 Some of the lessons from implementation of the Anti-Personnel Mine Ban Convention were able to be incorporated in the transparency measures demanded of states parties to the 2008 Convention on Cluster Munitions.[22] The information sought in the Convention on Cluster Munitions in relation to the survey, clearance, and destruction of cluster munition remnants (required by Article 4 of the Convention) is thus materially broader than its predecessor treaty, encompassing the size as well as the location of all cluster munition-contaminated areas under an affected state party's jurisdiction or control. Similarly, required reporting on the progress of clearance and destruction programmes comprehends details on the size and the location of the contaminated areas cleared each previous calendar year.[23]

9.12 Article 7 of the Convention on Cluster Munitions also obligates each state party to report annually on the implementation of its obligations to provide adequate victim assistance and on its efforts 'to collect reliable relevant data with respect to cluster munition victims'.[24] It is a further requirement that the amounts, types, and destinations of international cooperation and assistance provided in accordance with Article 6 of the Convention be included in annual reporting.[25]

---

21 The Maputo Action Plan, adopted by states parties at the Convention's Third Review Conference stipulates that:

> Each State Party with ongoing mine clearance obligations will undertake all reasonable efforts to quantify and qualify its remaining implementation challenge as soon as possible, and report this information through its Article 7 transparency report by 30 April 2015 and annually thereafter. This information should identify the precise perimeters and locations, to the extent possible, of all areas under its jurisdiction or control that contain anti-personnel mines and therefore require clearance, and that are suspected to contain anti-personnel mines and therefore require further survey.

Maputo Action Plan, adopted 27 June 2014, Third Review Conference of the Anti-Personnel Mine Ban Convention, Maputo, para. 8, at: http://bit.ly/2RvDC0u. See the *Guide to Reporting* under the Anti-Personnel Mine Ban Convention of October 2015, at: http://bit.ly/2F4IDJ3.

22 Convention on Cluster Munitions; adopted at Dublin, 30 May 2008; entered into force, 1 August 2010.

23 Art. 7(1)(h) and (i), 2008 Convention on Cluster Munitions.

24 Art. 7(1)(k), 2008 Convention on Cluster Munitions.

25 Art. 7(1)(n), 2008 Convention on Cluster Munitions.

## *Treaty on the Prohibition of Nuclear Weapons*

9.13   The reporting requirements under the 2017 Treaty on the Prohibition of Nuclear Weapons[26] (not yet in force, as on 1 March 2019) are minimal. Each state must make an initial declaration to the UN Secretary-General within 30 days of becoming party to the Treaty.[27] The declaration must first report on whether the state owned, possessed, or controlled any nuclear explosive devices in the past, but eliminated its nuclear-weapon programme before becoming party to the Treaty.[28] The state must further declare whether it owns, possesses, or controls any nuclear explosive devices (as at the date it became a party).[29] Finally, the state party must declare whether there are any nuclear explosive devices in any place under its jurisdiction or control that are owned, possessed, or controlled by another state.[30]

9.14   As of writing, only one state had made the requisite Article 2 declaration. When it deposited its instrument of accession to the Treaty in early September 2018, the Cook Islands declared that:

a    . . . it does not own, possess, or control nuclear weapons or nuclear explosive devices, neither does it have a nuclear-weapon programme or nuclear-weapons-related facilities in its territory or in any place under its jurisdiction or control;

b    notwithstanding Article 1 (a), . . . that it does not own, possess, or control any nuclear weapons or other nuclear explosive devices;

c    notwithstanding Article 1 (g), . . . that there are no nuclear weapons or other nuclear explosive devices in its territory or in any place under its jurisdiction or control that are owned, possessed or controlled by another State.[31]

9.15   If, as is the case with the Cook Islands, the declaration by a state party on each of these three issues is in the negative, meaning it has never had nuclear weapons itself and does not, upon becoming party to the Treaty on the Prohibition of Nuclear Weapons, have foreign nuclear weapons anywhere on sovereign territory or on territory it controls, that is the effective end of its reporting obligations. There is thus no annual reporting obligation as exists under the other global disarmament treaties. Even for states that once had nuclear weapons but destroyed them before becoming party to the Treaty on the Prohibition of Nuclear Weapons, they will have no further reporting obligations as it will be for the 'competent international authority' designated by states parties to verify the 'irreversible elimination of its nuclear-weapon programme' to report to the other states parties.[32] Since states

---

26  Treaty on the Prohibition of Nuclear Weapons; adopted at New York, 7 July 2017; not yet in force.
27  Art. 2(1), 2017 Treaty on the Prohibition of Nuclear Weapons.
28  Art. 2(1)(a), 2017 Treaty on the Prohibition of Nuclear Weapons.
29  Art. 2(1)(b), 2017 Treaty on the Prohibition of Nuclear Weapons.
30  Art. 2(1)(c), 2017 Treaty on the Prohibition of Nuclear Weapons.
31  Declaration available on the UN Treaty Section website, at: http://bit.ly/2DjbN8I.
32  Art. 4(1), 2017 Treaty on the Prohibition of Nuclear Weapons.

parties have committed to not acquire new nuclear weapons, there is no need for new reporting at any later stage.

9.16    In contrast, those states parties that either have their own nuclear explosive devices, or host those of another state on their territory, are obligated to submit a report to each meeting of states parties and each review conference on the progress made towards the implementation of its obligations.[33] These are, namely, to destroy the weapons and eliminate its nuclear-weapons programme, or to have the foreign state remove the weapons within a deadline to be set by the first meeting of states parties. In each case, the state party must submit a declaration of compliance to the UN Secretary-General at the end of the process.[34]

## Other instruments' reporting and information exchange

### Arms Trade Treaty

9.17    Reporting under the 2013 Arms Trade Treaty[35] is addressed in its Article 13. Each state party must provide an initial report to the Treaty Secretariat on the implementation measures it has taken, which include 'national laws, national control lists and other regulations and administrative measures'. The report must be updated on any new measures 'when appropriate'.[36]

9.18    With respect to weapons transfers, states parties are required to report annually, by 31 May of the following year, on *either* its authorised exports and imports *or* its actual exports and imports of conventional arms within the scope of the Treaty. The reports do not need to be made publicly available, although most states parties do so. There is no corresponding reporting obligation concerning ammunition or integral parts and components.[37]

### UN Register of Conventional Weapons

9.19    The UN Register of Conventional Weapons (UNROCA) was established in 1991 within the United Nations to foster transparency in international arms transfers, thereby aiming at building confidence between countries and enabling preventive diplomacy. The UNROCA requests countries to report on their exports and imports of seven categories of major weapons systems which are deemed the most offensive ones, namely:

Category I – Battle tanks
Category II – Armoured combat vehicles

---

33  Art. 4(5), 2017 Treaty on the Prohibition of Nuclear Weapons.
34  Art. 4(3) and (4), 2017 Treaty on the Prohibition of Nuclear Weapons.
35  Arms Trade Treaty; adopted at the UN General Assembly in New York, 2 April 2013; entered into force, 24 December 2014.
36  Art. 13(1), 2013 Arms Trade Treaty.
37  Art. 13(3), 2013 Arms Trade Treaty.

Category III – Large-calibre artillery system
Category IV – Combat aircraft and unmanned combat aerial vehicles (UCAV)
Category V – Attack helicopters
Category VI – Warships
Category VII – Missiles and missile launchers.

9.20   Furthermore, states can report on exports and imports of small arms and light weapons (SALW), military holdings, procurement through national production as well as relevant policies and national legislation. At the time of writing, the UNROCA has received reports from more than 170 states.[38] A consistent challenge to the UNROCA remains that a wide spectrum of conventional weapons, including the most modern weapons systems, are not covered.

## UN Programme of Action on Small Arms and Light Weapons

9.21   The 2001 UN Programme of Action on Small Arms and Light Weapons (PoA) foresees biannual reporting on a diverse range of implementation measures undertaken at the national level: (1) national coordination agencies; (2) national point of contacts; (3) legislations, regulations, administrative procedures; (4) law enforcement/criminalisation; (5) stockpile management and security; (6) collection and disposal; (7) export controls; (8) brokering; (9) marking, record keeping and tracing; (10) disarmament, demobilisation and reintegration (DDR); and (11) awareness raising. In addition, states report on measures undertaken at the regional and global level, such as international cooperation and assistance and information exchanged with other states.[39] The states' reports are publicly available on the webpage of the UN Office of Disarmament Affairs.[40]

## Wassenaar Arrangement

9.22   The Wassenaar Arrangement (WA) foresees general information exchange 'on risks associated with transfers of conventional arms and dual-use goods and technologies in order to consider, where necessary, the scope for co-ordinating national control policies to combat these risks'.[41] Participating States also agree to exchange information on regions they consider relevant to the purposes of the Arrangement. Any information exchanged remains confidential. The 2015 Elements for the Effective Fulfilment of National Reporting Requirements illustrate processes and procedures already utilised by some in fulfilling their reporting requirements.

---

38 United Nations Register of Conventional Arms, at: http://bit.ly/2C0NRFv.
39 Report on implementation of the United Nations Programme of Action to Prevent, Combat and Eradicate the Illicit Trade in Small Arms and Light Weapons in All Its Aspects, Reporting Template.
40 Retrievable at: http://bit.ly/2RGqfLG.
41 Wassenaar Arrangement, Initial Elements, s. IV, at: http://bit.ly/2CQIE3M.

9.23 Regarding arms transfer decisions, participating states exchange information every six months on deliveries to non-participating states of conventional arms set forth in Appendix 3 of the WA Initial Elements, derived from the categories of the UN Register of Conventional Arms. The information should include the quantity and the name of the recipient state and, except in the category of missiles and missile launchers, details of model and type.[42]

9.24 With regard to dual-use goods and technology, states notify licences denied to non-participants where the reasons for denial are relevant to the purposes of the WA. They also notify all denials regarding dual-use items towards non-participating states on an aggregate basis, twice per year. Furthermore, for items in the Sensitive List and Very Sensitive List, participating states notify, on an individual basis, all licences denied pursuant to the purposes of the WA to non-participating states and notify licences issued or transfers made to non-participants, on an aggregate basis, twice per year.[43]

### Nuclear Suppliers Group

9.25 Similarly to the Australia Group and the Missile Technology Control Regime (MTCR),[44] the Nuclear Suppliers Group (NSG) participants exchange information in writing on an intersessional basis. Moreover, they report regularly in the NSG's Consultative Group, Information Exchange Meeting, and Plenary. Information exchange includes notifications of export denials that have been issued as a result of national decisions not to authorise transfers of dual-use equipment or technology. This information exchange allows that NSG participants do not approve transfers of such items without first consulting with the government that issued the notification.

### Hague Code of Conduct against Ballistic Missile Proliferation

9.26 The 2002 Hague Code of Conduct against Ballistic Missile Proliferation (HCoC) establishes transparency and confidence-building instruments complementary to the MTCR. Member states commit to provide information with regard to ballistic missile systems and expandable space launch vehicles. States exchange pre-launch notifications on their ballistic missile and space launch vehicle launches and test flights. These notifications include such information as the generic class of the ballistic missile or space Launch vehicle, the planned launch notification window, the launch area and the planned direction. Furthermore, they provide annual information on of their respective policies and land (test-) launch sites as well as on the number and generic class of ballistic missile systems and space launch vehicles

---

42 Ibid., s. VI.

43 Ibid., s. V.

44 For information exchange related to ballistic missile systems, see the 2002 International Code of Conduct against Ballistic Missile Proliferation (HCoC).

launched during the preceding year. States are encouraged to consider inviting international observers to their land (test-) launch sites.[45]

## Vienna Document

9.27   The 2011 Vienna Document establishes politically binding confidence- and security-building measures (CSBMs) to increase openness and transparency concerning military activities conducted inside the Organization for Security and Co-operation in Europe (OSCE)'s zone of application, i.e. all territory, surrounding sea areas and air space of the European and Central Asian participating States. The Vienna Document foresees a variety of information exchange.

9.28   The 'Annual Exchange of Military Information (AEMI)' establishes exchange of information on command organisation, location, personnel strength, and major conventional weapon and equipment systems of active combat forces. The activities under 'Defense Planning' serve for exchanging information on defence policy, force planning, budgets, procurements, and calendars. 'Risk Reduction' is a mechanism for consultation and cooperation through notifications and meetings regarding unusual military activities. 'Prior Notification of Certain Military Activities (CMA)' requires that at least 42 days advance notice should be given to other states for CMA exceeding one of the following thresholds: 9,000 troops, 250 tanks, 500 armoured combat vehicles, or 250 pieces of artillery. Information exchange according to 'Annual calendars' concerns prior notification of military activities planned for the subsequent calendar year.[46] These forms of information exchange among OSCE member states seek to diffuse misunderstandings, misperceptions, and miscalculations as well as to prevent 'surprises' regarding arms procurement and military activities.

## Treaty on Conventional Armed Forces in Europe

9.29   The 1990 Treaty on Conventional Armed Forces in Europe (CFE Treaty)[47] is the major cornerstone of conventional arms control in Europe. While its main purpose is to limit deployments of conventional weapons and forces to its zone of application, its Protocol on Notification and Exchange establishes a broad spectrum of exchange of information between states parties on:

- The structure of land forces and air and air defence aviation forces within the area of application;
- The overall holdings in each category of conventional armaments and equipment limited by the Treaty;

---

45 The International Code of Conduct against Ballistic Missile Proliferation, at: http://bit.ly/2PrAsO9.

46 OSCE Vienna Document 2011 on Confidence- and Security-building Measures.

47 Treaty on Conventional Armed Forces in Europe (CFE Treaty); signed, 19 November 1990; entered into force, 17 July 1992.

- The location, numbers, and types of conventional armaments and equipment in service with the conventional armed forces;
- The location and numbers of battle tanks, armoured combat vehicles, artillery, combat aircraft and attack helicopters within the area of application but not in service with conventional armed forces;
- Objects of verification and declared sites;
- Location of sites from which conventional armaments and equipment have been withdrawn;
- Changes in organisational structures or force levels;
- Entry into and removal from service with the conventional armed forces of conventional armaments and equipment limited by the Treaty;
- Entry into and exit from the area of application of conventional armaments and equipment limited by the Treaty in service with the conventional armed forces; and
- Conventional armaments and equipment in transit through the area of application.[48]

9.30    Most importantly, annual reports on the actual location of tanks, armoured combat vehicles and artillery must be issued when they are different from their designated peacetime location. Furthermore, quarterly reports must detail by territory the actual location of tanks, armoured combat vehicles, and artillery as well as the total number of combat aircraft and attack helicopters in the entire treaty area. Changes of more than 30 tanks, 30 armoured combat vehicles, or ten artillery pieces on a state's territory as well as any increase by 18 or more combat aircraft or attack helicopters in a country's holdings in the Treaty area of application must be notified to all states parties.[49]

## Implementation support mechanisms

9.31    A range of means and mechanisms are established by the global disarmament treaties – or subsequently instituted by the states parties to those treaties – to promote and support their effective implementation. Two are particularly common: a treaty secretariat (sometimes termed an implementation support unit or ISU) and regular meetings of the states parties, whether annually, biannually, or through less frequent review conferences. The ISU does not have a formal analysis or examination role under the applicable treaties or agreements; these tasks, which are left to the states parties themselves, are often exercised during or in connection with a meeting of states parties.

---

48 Protocol on Notification and Exchange to the Treaty on Conventional Armed Forces in Europe (CFE Treaty); signed, 19 November 1990; entered into force, 17 July 1992.
49 D. Kimball and K. Reif, 'The Conventional Armed Forces in Europe (CFE) Treaty and the Adapted CFE Treaty at a Glance', *Fact Sheet*, Arms Control Association, August 2012, at: http://bit.ly/2SqD1i6.

## *Secretariats and implementation support units*

### *OPCW*

9.32   By far the most elaborate institutional mechanism set up to promote and support implementation of a global disarmament treaty is the OPCW. Created by the Chemical Weapons Convention itself to 'achieve' the Convention's 'object and purpose', it is tasked 'to ensure the implementation of its provisions, including those for international verification of compliance with it, and to provide a forum for consultation and cooperation among States Parties'.[50] This includes, since a decision by the Conference of States Parties in June 2018, the competence to identify the user of chemical weapons where it is alleged that they have been used by or on the territory of a state party.[51] The resolution by the Conference called upon the Secretariat to put in place arrangements

> to identify the perpetrators of the use of chemical weapons in the Syrian Arab Republic by identifying and reporting on all information potentially relevant to the origin of those chemical weapons in those instances in which the OPCW Fact-Finding Mission determines or has determined that use or likely use occurred, and cases for which the OPCW-UN Joint Investigative Mechanism has not issued a report.[52]

The OPCW's role in the verification of alleged use of chemical weapons in or by a state party is discussed further below.

9.33   All states parties to the Chemical Weapons Convention are members of the OPCW,[53] which was awarded the Nobel Peace Prize in 2013 'for its extensive efforts to eliminate chemical weapons'.[54] The OPCW's headquarters are in The Hague,[55] where it has its Technical Secretariat.[56] The Organisation is governed by

---

50  Art. VIII(1), 1992 Chemical Weapons Convention.

51  On 27 June 2018, the Fourth Special Session of the Conference of the States Parties to the Chemical Weapons Convention adopted a decision on addressing the threat from chemical weapons use. The decision brought forward by the United Kingdom and supported by 30 countries (Albania, Australia, Belgium, Bulgaria, Canada, Denmark, Estonia, Finland, France, Georgia, Germany, Iceland, Ireland, Japan, Latvia, Lithuania, Luxembourg, Malta, the Netherlands, New Zealand, Norway, Poland, Portugal, Republic of Moldova, Romania, Slovakia, Slovenia, Sweden, Turkey, and the United States of America), was adopted with 106 states parties present and voting, of whom 82 voted in favour and 24 voted against.

52  OPCW, 'CWC Conference of the States Parties Adopts Decision Addressing the Threat from Chemical Weapons Use', News release, The Hague, 27 June 2018, at: http://bit.ly/2P3gA4u.

53  Art. VIII(2), 1992 Chemical Weapons Convention.

54  See: OPCW, 'Nobel Peace Prize', at: http://bit.ly/2CX0VfH.

55  Art. VIII(3), 1992 Chemical Weapons Convention.

56  The Technical Secretariat of the OPCW assists the Conference of the States Parties and the Executive Council in the performance of their functions. The specific functions of the Technical Secretariat are listed in Article VIII(38) and (39) of the Convention.

an Executive Council of 41 states chosen according to a detail formula set out in the Convention.[57] Its relationship with the UN is regulated by an agreement adopted by the UN General Assembly in September 2001.[58]

## Anti-Personnel Mine Ban Convention

9.34   In concluding the Anti-Personnel Mine Ban Convention in 1997, states parties had elected not to create a secretariat for the Convention. Relying on the good will of states to bolster the relatively limited support provided by the United Nations, though, swiftly proved to be challenging. Therefore, at the Third Meeting of States Parties in 2001, it was decided to create an Implementation Support Unit (ISU), which is hosted by the Geneva International Centre for Humanitarian Demining (GICHD) in Geneva.

9.35   The decision not to provide for the creation of a secretariat in the Convention itself has also proved problematic. Costs are not automatically allocated, pro rata, from the states parties on an assessed basis, so the ISU must rely on voluntary contributions from states. On 6 September 2011, a revised agreement governing the relationship between the ISU and the GICHD was signed by the president of the Tenth Meeting of States Parties and the Director of the Centre.[59]

9.36   The scope of the activities undertaken by the ISU is defined by the 'Directive by the States Parties to the Implementation Support Unit', which was adopted at the Tenth Meeting of States Parties in 2010. This mandate stipulates that the ISU shall, in support of the states parties to the Anti-Personnel Mine Ban Convention:

a   Prepare, support and carry out follow-up activities from formal and informal meetings under the Convention including Meetings of the States Parties, Review Conferences, Amendment Conferences, intersessional meetings, Standing Committees, the Coordinating Committee, and the Article 5 Extension Request Analysing Group.

b   Provide substantive and other support to the President, President-Designate, Co-Chairs, and Co-Rapporteurs in their work related to all such meetings.

c   Provide advice and technical support to States Parties on the implementation and universalization, including on the Sponsorship Programme, of the Convention.

d   communication and information regarding the Convention towards States not Party and the public.

---

57 The mandate of the Council is set out Article VIII(32) of the Convention. Regional groups are represented on the Council in accordance with the following formula stipulated in the Convention: Africa – nine members; Asia – nine members; Eastern Europe – five members; Latin America and the Caribbean – seven members; Western Europe and other states – ten members; and one further state party, designated on a rotating basis, from Asia or Latin America and the Caribbean. Art. VIII(23), 1992 Chemical Weapons Convention. The Council's current composition is listed at: http://bit.ly/2yOhJ5X.

58 In the United Nations System, the OPCW is classified as a 'Related Organization' and, as is the case with the IAEA, it reports to the UN Security Council and the UN General Assembly.

59 See ISU, 'Implementation Support Unit: Overview', at: http://bit.ly/2RvGWJ7.

e    Keep records of formal and informal meetings under the Convention, and communicate, as appropriate, the decisions and priorities resulting from such meetings to States Parties and other stakeholders.

f    Liaise, and coordinate as appropriate, with relevant international organisations that participate in the work of the Convention, including the ICBL [International Campaign to Ban Landmines], the ICRC, the UN, and the GICHD.[60]

## Convention on Cluster Munitions

9.37    Notwithstanding the challenges posed by the lack of a formally constituted secretariat in the context of the Anti-Personnel Mine Ban Convention, in negotiating the Convention on Cluster Munitions a decade later states again chose not to establish an ISU under the Convention itself. Again, however, states parties subsequently decided to create an Implementation Support Unit, which would be hosted by the GICHD, under an agreement signed in 2014.[61] The ISU was formally established in May 2015 in Geneva. Based on the decisions taken at the relevant meeting of states parties, the Unit has a mandate to:

*    Provide technical support and advice to the Presidency in all aspects of its role and mandate in leading the work of the Convention;
*    Provide support to all States Parties through the Convention's implementation machinery and office holders, as well as to the Sponsorship Programme and the thematic working groups;
*    Provide advice and technical support to individual States Parties through the development of a resource base of relevant expertise and practices on the implementation of the Convention;
*    Prepare for and keep records of formal and informal meetings under the Convention and other relevant knowledge products, expertise and information pertaining to the implementation of the Convention;
*    Facilitate communication amongst States Parties and other relevant actors, cooperate and coordinate amongst these and maintain public relations including efforts to promote universalization and other work of the Convention;
*    Serve as an interface between the States Parties and the international community on issues related to the implementation of the CCM.[62]

---

60 See, e.g., 'Draft Implementation Support Unit 2014 work plan and budget', Submitted by the Director of the Implementation Support Unit and endorsed by the Coordinating Committee on 1 November 2013, Doc. APLC/MSP.13/2013/3, 8 November 2013, para. 2.

61 The decision was taken at the Second Meeting of States Parties in Beirut in 2011. 'Agreement between the States Parties to the Convention on Cluster Munitions and the Geneva International Centre for Humanitarian Demining on the Hosting of the Implementation Support Unit for the Convention', Document submitted by the President of the Fourth Meeting of States Parties, Doc. CCM/MSP/2014/INF/1, 31 July 2014, at: http://bit.ly/2P2StTs.

62 ISU, 'Mandate', at: http://bit.ly/2OlvA8I.

## Biological Weapons Convention

9.38   The Biological Weapons Convention also had made no provision for an ISU, but in 2006 the Convention's Sixth Review Conference decided to establish an Implementation Support Unit for the Convention within the Geneva branch of the UN Office for Disarmament Affairs (UNODA). The ISU, which is funded by assessed contributions, is given a five-year mandate by each successive review conference. Thus, in 2011, the Seventh Review Conference renewed the mandate of the ISU until the Eighth Review Conference in 2016. In turn, the Eighth Review Conference renewed the ISU's mandate until the Convention's Ninth Review Conference in 2021. The Seventh Review Conference also added new tasks for the Unit to undertake.[63]

9.39   The ISU of the Biological Weapons Convention, which was officially launched on 20 August 2007, provides the following services and support:

- Administrative support and assistance
- National implementation support and assistance
- Support and assistance for confidence-building measures
- Support and assistance for obtaining universality
- Administration of the database for assistance requests and offers, and facilitation of associated exchanges of information; and
- Support for states parties' efforts to implement the decisions and recommendations of review conferences.[64]

## Arms Trade Treaty

9.40   In a break from the bulk of practice, the states negotiating the Arms Trade Treaty decided from the outset that a secretariat would be needed to support its implementation and decided to establish it under the terms of the Treaty itself.[65] According to the relevant provision, the Secretariat, which is responsible to the states parties, is required to undertake the following responsibilities:

a   Receive, make available and distribute the reports as mandated by the Treaty
b   Maintain and make available to States Parties the list of national points of contact
c   Facilitate the matching of offers of and requests for assistance for Treaty implementation and promote international cooperation as requested
d   Facilitate the work of the Conference of States Parties, including making arrangements and providing the necessary services for meetings under this Treaty; and
e   Perform other duties as decided by the Conferences of States Parties.[66]

---

63 UN Office at Geneva, 'The Biological Weapons Convention: Implementation Support Unit', at: http://bit.ly/2AIKUIM.
64 Ibid.
65 Art. 18, 2013 Arms Trade Treaty.
66 Art. 18(3), 2013 Arms Trade Treaty. See the Secretariat's homepage for the treaty, at: http://bit.ly/2CZalar.

The Arms Trade Treaty Secretariat, which is funded by assessed contributions, is located in Geneva.

## UN Office for Disarmament Affairs

9.41   The UN Secretary-General, namely the UN Office for Disarmament Affairs (UNODA), in certain cases undertakes the role of administrative support to disarmament instruments similar to that of implementation support units. While the CCW is supported by UNODA's branch in Geneva, the UN Secretariat in New York manages aspects of the 2001 UN Programme of Action on Small Arms and Light Weapons (PoA).[67] Despite calls for an independent secretariat by a small number of states negotiating the Treaty on the Prohibition of Nuclear Weapons, the decision was taken not to establish one under the Treaty. The UN Secretary-General is entrusted with ensuring the performance of many of the tasks that a secretariat would otherwise perform, such as convening the meetings of states parties and review conferences.

## *Meetings of states parties and review conferences*

9.42   In the case of each global disarmament treaty, the states parties meet regularly to discuss issues relating to the status and operation of the treaty. This meeting is effectively the primary decision-making treaty body in every case. Under the Chemical Weapons Convention, however, considerable responsibility is devolved to the Executive Council of the OPCW.

## *Biological Weapons Convention*

9.43   The Biological Weapons Convention is unusual in that it did not foresee regular (annual or biennial) meetings of states parties, only five-yearly review conferences. Thus, Article XII of the Convention required that five years after the Convention's entry into force (or earlier if requested by a majority of states parties), a conference of states parties would be held in Geneva to

> review the operation of the Convention, with a view to assuring that the purposes of the preamble and the provisions of the Convention, including the provisions concerning negotiations on chemical weapons, are being realised. Such review shall take into account any new scientific and technological developments relevant to the Convention.

9.44   This first review conference duly took place in Geneva on 3–21 March 1980. The conference decided that the Second Review Conference would

---

67 Programme of Action to Prevent, Combat and Eradicate the Illicit Trade in Small Arms and Light Weapons in All Its Aspects; adopted at the United Nations Conference on the Illicit Trade in Small Arms and Light Weapons in All Its Aspects, New York, 20 July 2001, at: http://bit.ly/2qsN4qe.

take place five years later (in practice, it turned out to be six). Thereafter, subsequent review conferences have been held every five years (though the Fifth Review Conference, which was suspended in December 2001 following a bitter dispute on possible verification measures and mechanisms, reconvened in 2002). As of writing, the most recent review conference was the eighth, held in 2016.

9.45    But even though meetings of states parties were not foreseen in the Biological Weapons Convention, a number have been convened at the request of states parties. The First Meeting of States Parties, held in 2003, addressed two issues: the adoption of necessary national measures to implement the prohibitions set out in the Convention, including the enactment of penal legislation; and national mechanisms to establish and maintain the security and oversight of pathogenic microorganisms and toxins.[68]

9.46    A second meeting was held the following year. The Second Meeting of States Parties discussed strengthening institutional efforts and mechanisms for the surveillance, detection, diagnosis, and combating of infectious diseases affecting humans, animals, and plants; and the enhancing of international capabilities for responding to, investigating, and mitigating the effects of cases of alleged use of biological weapons or suspicious outbreaks of disease. Further meetings of states parties have been held in most years since then, serving among other things as preparation for the next review conference.

### Chemical Weapons Convention

9.47    The Conference of the States Parties to the Chemical Weapons Convention is the OPCW's 'principal organ';[69] one of the Organisation's three main organs, along with the Executive Council (generally, in practice, the most important body) and the Technical Secretariat.[70] The Conference is held annually, unless otherwise agreed by the states parties.[71] Decision-making on substantive issues is to be decided by two-thirds majority if efforts at consensus have been exhausted.[72]

9.48    The specific activities to be undertaken by the Conference, which are listed in the Chemical Weapons Convention[73] (see Box 9.1), include the following:

- Taking measures necessary to ensure compliance with the Convention
- Deciding on the programme and budget and the scale of the financial contributions to be paid by states parties
- Approving the Organisation's annual report
- Electing the members of the Executive Council
- Appointing the Director-General

---

68 Implementation Support Unit, 'Biological Weapons Convention: Background Information', 2012, p. 4, at: http://bit.ly/2OnCJ8m.
69 Art.VIII(19), 1992 Chemical Weapons Convention.
70 Art.VIII(4), 1992 Chemical Weapons Convention.
71 Art.VIII(11), 1992 Chemical Weapons Convention.
72 Art.VIII(18), 1992 Chemical Weapons Convention.
73 Art.VIII(21), 1992 Chemical Weapons Convention.

- Fostering international cooperation for peaceful purposes in the field of chemical activities; and
- Reviewing scientific and technological developments that could affect the Convention.[74]

---

## BOX 9.1  THE CONFERENCE OF STATES PARTIES TO THE CHEMICAL WEAPONS CONVENTION

The Conference shall:

a    Consider and adopt at its regular sessions the report, programme and budget of the Organization, submitted by the Executive Council, as well as consider other reports;

b    Decide on the scale of financial contributions to be paid by States Parties in accordance with paragraph 7;

c    Elect the members of the Executive Council;

d    Appoint the Director-General of the Technical Secretariat (hereinafter referred to as 'the Director-General');

e    Approve the rules of procedure of the Executive Council submitted by the latter;

f    Establish such subsidiary organs as it finds necessary for the exercise of its functions in accordance with this Convention;

g    Foster international cooperation for peaceful purposes in the field of chemical activities;

h    Review scientific and technological developments that could affect the operation of this Convention and, in this context, direct the Director-General to establish a Scientific Advisory Board to enable him, in the performance of his functions, to render specialized advice in areas of science and technology relevant to this Convention, to the Conference, the Executive Council or States Parties. The Scientific Advisory Board shall be composed of independent experts appointed in accordance with terms of reference adopted by the Conference;

i    Consider and approve at its first session any draft agreements, provisions and guidelines developed by the Preparatory Commission;

j    Establish at its first session the voluntary fund for assistance in accordance with Article X;

k    Take the necessary measures to ensure compliance with this Convention and to redress and remedy any situation which contravenes the provisions of this Convention, in accordance with Article XII.

*Article VIII(21), Chemical Weapons Convention*

---

74 OPCW, 'About the Conference of the States Parties', at: http://bit.ly/2yPBj1H.

9.49 The Convention obliges the Conference to establish two subsidiary bodies: the Commission for the Settlement of Disputes related to Confidentiality and the Scientific Advisory Board. In addition, the Conference has used its authority to establish further subsidiary organs (committees). The Advisory Board for Education and Outreach,[75] which 'will offer practical advice and proposals on education and outreach strategies, approaches, and tools, and develop a portfolio of activities in line with global trends', met for the first time in 2016.[76]

9.50 The Convention also foresees the convening of regular review conferences in order to 'undertake reviews of the operation' of the Convention, taking into account 'any relevant scientific and technological developments'.[77] Three such conferences have been held to date, on a five-yearly basis: in 2003, 2008, and 2013. The Third Review Conference concluded with a political declaration in which states parties reiterated their 'deep concern' that chemical weapons might have been used in the Syrian Arab Republic, underlining that 'the use of chemical weapons by anyone under any circumstances would be reprehensible and completely contrary to the legal norms and standards of the international community'.[78] The fourth review conference was held in The Hague on 19–23 November 2018.

## Anti-Personnel Mine Ban Convention

9.51 The Anti-Personnel Mine Ban Convention included provision for regular (currently annual) meetings of states parties and five-yearly review conferences. The First Meeting of States Parties was held in Maputo in 1999 following the entry into force of the Convention. The third review conference, which took place in 2014, was also held there. The meetings of states parties are given an indicative, not exhaustive list of tasks. In sum, these are to consider 'any matter with regard to the application or implementation of the Convention', which encompasses:

- The operation and status of the Convention
- Matters arising from the transparency reports submitted by states parties
- International cooperation and assistance
- Technologies for the clearance of anti-personnel mines
- Compliance issues
- Decisions on clearance extension requests.

75 OPCW Conference of the States Parties, Decision: 'Establishment of an Advisory Board on Education and Outreach', Twentieth Session, Decision C-20/DEC.9, 3 December 2015, at: http://bit.ly/2CZpubR.

76 OPCW, 'First Advisory Board on Education and Outreach Meets as Next Step in Evolution of OPCW', 29 April 2016, at: http://bit.ly/2AJzKU1.

77 Art.VIII(22), 1992 Chemical Weapons Convention.

78 OPCW, 'Third Review Conference Concludes with Consensus Final Document and Political Declaration', Press release, 19 April 2013, at: http://bit.ly/2RxZAjp.

When issues of particular concern arise – typically relating to use of anti-personnel mines – a final declaration can be issued by the meeting.

9.52   To support the annual meetings, states parties decided early in the life of the Convention to create an intersessional work programme. The programme was created at the First Meeting of States Parties in Maputo in May 1999. Initially, there were five standing committees, each meeting twice between the annual meetings of states parties. These were subsequently streamlined into four committees meeting in a single week: general status and operation; mine clearance; stockpile destruction; and victim assistance. At the Third Review Conference in Maputo in 2014, states parties agreed to maintain the informal intersessional meetings each year, but to shorten them to two days in total.

9.53   The intersessional 'Standing Committee' meetings have proved to be a critical element in reviewing the implementation of the Convention, a forum where the bulk of the substantive discussions have taken place. As with all meetings of the Convention, NGOs have participated actively. The meetings remain informal, at least in the sense that no binding decisions are taken, but declarations of completion of clearance and destruction of emplaced mines are frequently delivered during the Committee meetings. The Fourth Review Conference in Oslo in 2019 was expected to assess whether the intersessional work programme would continue and, if so, in which form.

9.54   Review conferences are governed by Article 12 of the Convention. They have been held every five years since 2004: the minimum interval allowed by this provision. Their purpose is fourfold: to review the operation and status of the Convention (a task also allocated to the meetings of states parties); to consider the need for further meetings of states parties (and the interval between them); to take decisions on requests for Article 5 extensions on clearance and destruction of emplaced mines; and to adopt, 'if necessary', in the final report conclusions related to the implementation of the Convention.

## Convention on Cluster Munitions

9.55   A broadly similar approach to that taken under the APMBC has been employed in the case of the Convention on Cluster Munitions, combining annual meetings of states parties and five-yearly review conferences. An intersessional work programme was instituted by the First Meeting of States Parties but was ended by the First Review Conference in Dubrovnik in 2015. After some discussion, that Conference ultimately decided to maintain the frequency of the meetings of states parties as annual rather than moving to biennial events.

9.56   The role of the meetings of states parties is set out in Article 11 of the Convention on Cluster Munitions (see Box 9.2). As with the Anti-Personnel Mine Ban Convention, the purpose is to consider 'any matter with regard to the application or implementation' of the Convention, but here the Convention on Cluster Munitions annual meetings are also explicitly given the power, 'where necessary', to 'take decisions' in respect of any such issue. These issues include the operation and status of the Convention; issues arising from the transparency reports submitted by states parties; international cooperation and assistance; technologies for the clearance of cluster munition remnants; disputes and compliance issues; and requests for extension to the deadlines for the destruction of cluster munition stockpiles (under Article 3) and of cluster munition remnants (under Article 4).

9.57 Article 12 of the Convention on Cluster Munitions provides for review conferences, which can be held every five years or more (but not at intervals of less than five years). As mentioned above, the Convention's First Review Conference of the CCM was held in Dubrovnik in 2015. The Second Review Conference was being convened in 2020 in Geneva under the presidency of Switzerland. The purpose of each Review Conference is to review the operation and status of the Convention; to consider the need for, and interval between, meetings of states parties; and to take decisions on request by states parties for extensions to their deadlines for the destruction of cluster munition stockpiles and of cluster munition remnants.

## Arms Trade Treaty

9.58 Under Article 17 of the ATT, a Conference of States Parties was to be convened within one year of the entry into force of the Treaty 'and thereafter at such other times as may be decided by the Conference of States Parties'. The First Conference of States Parties was held at Cancun in Mexico in August 2015.

---

### BOX 9.2 THE MEETINGS OF STATES PARTIES TO THE CONVENTION ON CLUSTER MUNITIONS

1 The States Parties shall meet regularly in order to consider and, where necessary, take decisions in respect of any matter with regard to the application or implementation of this Convention, including:

a The operation and status of this Convention;

b Matters arising from the reports submitted under the provisions of this Convention;

c International cooperation and assistance in accordance with Article 6 of this Convention;

d The development of technologies to clear cluster munition remnants;

e Submissions of States Parties under Articles 8 and 10 of this Convention; and

f Submissions of States Parties as provided for in Articles 3 and 4 of this Convention.

*Article 11(1), Convention on Cluster Munitions*

The Conference decided to hold the next 'session' of the Conference of States Parties the following year,[79] a practice that has so far been repeated by each session.

9.59    The mandate of the Conference of States Parties is broad. The list given in the Treaty is exhaustive, not illustrative, and mandatory. Thus, the Conference of States Parties shall:

- Review the implementation of the Treaty, 'including developments in the field of conventional arms'
- Consider and adopt recommendations regarding the Treaty's implementation and operation, 'in particular the promotion of its universality'
- Consider proposed amendments to the Treaty
- Consider issues arising from the interpretation of the Treaty
- Consider and decide the tasks and budget of the Treaty Secretariat
- Consider the establishment of 'any subsidiary bodies as may be necessary to improve the functioning' of the Treaty; and
- Perform 'any other function consistent' with the Treaty.[80]

9.60    Extraordinary meetings of the Conference of States Parties will be held at 'such other times as may be deemed necessary by the Conference of States Parties, or at the written request of any State Party[,] provided that this request is supported by at least two-thirds of the States Parties'.[81] One such extraordinary meeting was convened in preparation for the first meeting of the Conference of States Parties in Cancun. There is no provision for the organisation of review conferences under the ATT.

## Treaty on the Prohibition of Nuclear Weapons

9.61    The 2017 Treaty on the Prohibition of Nuclear Weapons had not yet entered into force as on 1 March 2019. Article 8 provides for regular meetings of states parties, the first of which will be held within one year of the entry into force of the Treaty. Subsequent meetings will be convened every two years unless the states parties otherwise agree, with a review conference to be held after five years and then every six years thereafter. Extraordinary meetings of states parties will be convened if one third of the states parties support a written request by any state party.

9.62    The scope of work of these meetings is broad, with the meetings of states parties effectively mandated to consider any matters 'pursuant to and consistent

79 'First Conference of States Parties, Cancun, Mexico, 24–27 August 2015, Final Report', Doc. ATT/CSP1/2015/6, 27 August 2015, para. 39, at: http://bit.ly/2zp0mrM.
80 Art. 17(4), 2013 Arms Trade Treaty.
81 Art. 17(5), 2013 Arms Trade Treaty.

## BOX 9.3 AMENDMENT OF SELECTED GLOBAL DISARMAMENT TREATIES

### Biological Weapons Convention, Article XI

Any State Party may propose amendments to this Convention. Amendments shall enter into force for each State Party accepting the amendments upon their acceptance by a majority of the States Parties to the Convention and thereafter for each remaining State Party on the date of acceptance by it.

### Chemical Weapons Convention, Article XV

1   Any State Party may propose amendments to this Convention. Any State Party may also propose changes, as specified in paragraph 4, to the Annexes of this Convention. Proposals for amendments shall be subject to the procedures in paragraphs 2 and 3. . . .

2   The text of a proposed amendment shall be submitted to the Director-General for circulation to all States Parties and to the Depositary. The proposed amendment shall be considered only by an Amendment Conference. Such an Amendment Conference shall be convened if one third or more of the States Parties notify the Director-General not later than 30 days after its circulation that they support further consideration of the proposal. The Amendment Conference shall be held immediately following a regular session of the Conference unless the requesting States Parties ask for an earlier meeting. In no case shall an Amendment Conference be held less than 60 days after the circulation of the proposed amendment.

3   Amendments shall enter into force for all States Parties 30 days after deposit of the instruments of ratification or acceptance by all the States Parties referred to under subparagraph (b) below:

   a   When adopted by the Amendment Conference by a positive vote of a majority of all States Parties with no State Party casting a negative vote; and

   b   Ratified or accepted by all those States Parties casting a positive vote at the Amendment Conference.

### Anti-Personnel Mine Ban Convention, Article 13

1   At any time after the entry into of this Convention any State Party may propose amendments to this Convention. Any proposal for an amendment

shall be communicated to the Depositary, who shall circulate it to all States Parties and shall seek their views on whether an Amendment Conference should to convened to consider the proposal. If a majority of the States Parties notify the Depositary no later than 30 days after its circulation that support further consideration of the proposal, the Depositary shall convene an Amendment Conference to which all States Parties shall be invited.

2  States not parties to this Convention, the United Nations, other relevant regional organizations, the International Committee of the Red Cross and relevant non-governmental organizations or institutions may be invited to attend in accordance with the agreed Rules of Procedure.

3  The Amendment Conference shall be held immediately following a Meeting of the States Parties or a Review Conference unless a majority of the States Parties agree that it be held earlier.

4  Any amendment to this convention shall be adopted by a two thirds of the state parties present and voting at the Amendment Conference. The Depositary shall communicate any amendment so adopted to the States Parties.

5  An amendment to this convention shall enter into force for all states parties to this convention which have accepted it, upon the deposit with the Depositary of instruments of acceptance by a majority of States Parties. Thereafter it shall enter into force for any remaining State Party on the date of deposit of its instrument of acceptance.

with the provisions of' the Treaty, including its status and implementation. Under Article 4, the first meeting of states parties is explicitly obligated to set the deadlines for the destruction of a state party's nuclear explosive devices and for the removal of a foreign state's nuclear weapons from any area under the jurisdiction or control of a state party.

9.63   There is also provision in disarmament law treaties for their amendment. The procedures for amendment, and for their application to states parties, differ substantively from treaty to treaty, as set out in Box 9.3.

## Verification

9.64   The general principles of international law require that states enter into international treaties in good faith, intending to abide by their obligations. However, as Jozef Goldblat has pointed out, 'when such vital matters as national security are involved, special assurances are needed that the parties will not engage in violating or circumventing their contracted commitments'.[82] Suzanne Massie, a Swiss writer, famously taught US President Ronald Reagan the Russian proverb, 'Доверяй, но проверяй', which means 'Trust, but verify'.[83] President Reagan would go on to use this proverb often in the context of discussions on nuclear disarmament with the Soviet Union.

9.65   Verification relates primarily to the development, production, stockpiling, or transfer of a weapon. The process of verification begins with the collection of information from the concerned state regarding the implementation of the parties' obligations.

> The correctness of this information is usually checked, and the performance of states is monitored by off-site and on-site inspection as well as observation of forces, weapons or activities covered by the agreement. Inspections can be conducted either in a systematic manner – continuously or periodically – or ad hoc, as decided by the verifying body, or upon challenge, as a result of specific demand.[84]

9.66   The extent to which global disarmament treaties incorporate such detailed verification, though, varies substantially. By far the most sophisticated mechanism is set out in the Chemical Weapons Convention, and relates to the destruction of chemical weapon stockpiles and the de-commissioning of production facilities. In contrast, the Biological Weapons Convention contains no detailed verification provisions, although it is possible to seek UN Security Council approval for an investigation.[85] The following sections describe selected important mechanisms for assessing progress in stockpile destruction, whether production facilities have been destroyed or converted, and whether weapons have been used in violation of a state's international legal obligations.

### Investigating alleged use

9.67   A critical concern is where one state believes that another state has used a weapon in violation of international law, in particular a disarmament or law of armed conflict treaty to which they are both party. A range of mechanisms exist to verify alleged use, as discussed below.

---

82 J. Goldblat, *Arms Control: The New Guide to Negotiations and Agreements*, Sage, Thousand Oaks, CA, 2002, p. 309.

83 See her webpage at: http://bit.ly/2CZa5s9.

84 Goldblat, *Arms Control: The New Guide to Negotiations and Agreements*, p. 310.

85 Under the 1971 Biological Weapons Convention, any state party which finds that any other state party is in violation of its obligations under the Convention 'may lodge a complaint' with the UN Security Council. Art. VI(1), 1971 Biological Weapons Convention. Each state party to the Convention

> undertakes to co-operate in carrying out any investigation which the Security Council may initiate, in accordance with the provisions of the Charter of the United Nations, on the basis of the complaint received by the Council. The Security Council shall inform the States Parties to the Convention of the results of the investigation.
>
> *Art. VI(2), 1971 Biological Weapons Convention.*

## Biological and chemical weapons

### The Biological Weapons Convention

9.68    The Biological Weapons Convention does not have a verification mechanism built in to the treaty architecture although it is possible to engage the UN Security Council to investigate alleged violations of the Convention. This is tricky with respect to use, though, given that use of biological weapons is not directly and explicitly prohibited by the Convention. Nonetheless, by virtue of Article VI, any state party to the Biological Weapons Convention that

> finds that any other State Party is acting in breach of obligations deriving from the provisions of the Convention may lodge a complaint with the Security Council of the United Nations. Such a complaint should include all possible evidence confirming its validity, as well as a request for its consideration by the Security Council.[86]

9.69    Each state party to the Biological Weapons Convention

> undertakes to co-operate in carrying out any investigation which the Security Council may initiate, in accordance with the provisions of the Charter of the United Nations, on the basis of the complaint received by the Council. The Security Council shall inform the States Parties to the Convention of the results of the investigation.[87]

### The UN Secretary-General's Mechanism

9.70    In the late 1980s, following use of chemical weapons by Iraq both against Iran and against the Kurds at Halabja, the UN Secretary-General elaborated a mechanism to allow him to investigate alleged use of biological or chemical weapons. The Secretary-General's Mechanism (SGM), first set out in a UN General Assembly Resolution in 1987[88] was reaffirmed the following year by UN Security Council Resolution 620. It was further endorsed by the Assembly in its Resolution 45/57, adopted without a vote on 4 December 1990. In this resolution, the Assembly:

> Endorse[d] the proposals of the group of qualified experts established in pursuance of its resolution 42/37 C of 30 November 1987 concerning technical guidelines and procedures to guide the Secretary-General in the conduct of timely and efficient investigation of the reports of use of chemical and bacteriological (biological) or toxin weapons...[89]

---

86  Art.VI(1), 1971 Biological Weapons Convention.
87  Art.VI(2), 1971 Biological Weapons Convention.
88  UN General Assembly Resolution 42/37C of 30 November 1987.
89  UN General Assembly Resolution 45/57, adopted without a vote on 4 December 1990, para. 3.

9.71   The Assembly further noted

> the continuing significance of the Security Council decision to consider immediately, taking into account the investigations of the Secretary-General, appropriate and effective measures in accordance with the Charter of the United Nations, should there be any future use of chemical weapons in violation of international law.[90]

9.72   The SGM, which predates the adoption of the Chemical Weapons Convention, involves the conduct of a prompt investigation by the UN Secretary-General in response to allegations brought to his attention concerning the possible use of biological or chemical weapons. Triggered by a request from any UN member state, the Secretary-General is authorised to launch an investigation, including dispatching a fact-finding team to the site of the alleged incident and to report on the findings to all UN member states. As UNODA reports, the purpose is 'to ascertain in an objective and scientific manner facts of alleged violations of the 1925 Geneva Protocol, which bans the use of chemical and biological weapons, or other relevant rules of customary international law'.[91]

9.73   The Mechanism was first used in 1992 in both Azerbaijan and Mozambique. More recently, it was applied in Syria in 2013 prior to the Syrian Arab Republic becoming a state party to the CWC. The mission dispatched by the Secretary-General concluded that:

> On the basis of the evidence obtained during our investigation of the Ghouta incident, the conclusion is that, on 21 August 2013, chemical weapons have been used in the ongoing conflict between the parties in the Syrian Arab Republic, also against civilians, including children, on a relatively large scale.

In particular, the mission found 'clear and convincing evidence that surface-to-surface rockets containing the nerve agent Sarin were used in Ein Tarma, Moadamiyah, and Zamalka in the Ghouta area of Damascus'.[92]

9.74   The SGM has not yet been used with respect to alleged use of biological weapons. In 2004, however, at the Second Meeting of States Parties to the BWC, the states parties recognised that the SGM 'represents an international institutional mechanism for investigating cases of alleged use of biological or toxin weapons'.[93]

---

90 Ibid., para. 4.

91 UNODA, 'Secretary-General's Mechanism for Investigation of Alleged Use of Chemical and Biological Weapons', at: http://bit.ly/2Qlfz4x.

92 UN Mission to Investigate Allegations of the Use of Chemical Weapons in the Syrian Arab Republic, 'Report on Allegations of the Use of Chemical Weapons in the Ghouta Area of Damascus on 21 August 2013', UN docs. A/67/997 and S/2013/553, 16 September 2013, paras. 27–28.

93 BWC Implementation Support Unit, 'Biological Weapons Convention: Background Information', 2012, p. 5.

## The OPCW

9.75    The OPCW has its own mechanism for investigating alleged use by any state party to the Chemical Weapons Convention. In response to persistent allegations of chemical weapon attacks in Syria, the OPCW Fact Finding Mission (FFM) was set up in 2014 'to establish facts surrounding allegations of the use of toxic chemicals, reportedly chlorine, for hostile purposes in the Syrian Arab Republic'. The FFM is required to study available information relating to allegations of use of chemical weapons in Syria, including information provided by the Syrian Arab Republic and others. In 2015, the OPCW Executive Council and the UN Security Council endorsed the continual operation of the FFM.[94]

9.76    The FFM confirmed that chemical weapons had been used in Syria. The FFM's findings were the basis for the work of the OPCW-UN Joint Investigative Mechanism, an independent body established by the UN Security Council in its Resolution 2235 of 7 August 2015. The purpose of the Joint Investigative Mechanism was to identify the perpetrators of the chemical weapon attacks confirmed by the FFM, but the mandate of the Mechanism expired in December 2017 and was not renewed, following objections from the Russian Federation.[95] As of writing, however, the work of the FFM was continuing.

## Anti-personnel mines

## The Anti-Personnel Mine Ban Convention

9.77    Alleged use of conventional weapons has also been the subject of a range of fact-finding mechanisms. The Anti-Personnel Mine Ban Convention has an elaborate fact-finding mechanism incorporated into its architecture (see Box 9.4), but this has never been used, despite allegations of use levelled at a number of states parties (and one acknowledged instance of use).[96] The emphasis is on 'co-operative compliance', which avoids 'naming and shaming'. This has its advantages, but also its shortcomings, and helps to explain the critical role that the civil society reports by Landmine Monitor also plays.

9.78    With respect to non-state actors, a particular mechanism has been established for armed groups that sign the Deed of Commitment on Anti-Personnel Mines established by Geneva Call, an international NGO based in Geneva. In

---

94 OPCW, 'Syria and the OPCW: The Fact-Finding Mission (FFM)', at: http://bit.ly/2JyRRPo.
95 Ibid.
96 Landmine Monitor, the civil society monitoring body led by Human Rights Watch with respect to use of mines, noted in its 2014 report that Yemen admitted a violation of the prohibition on use, which occurred in 2011. In addition, a number of allegations of mine use in previous years by the armed forces of South Sudan (in 2013 and 2011), Sudan (in 2011), Turkey (from 2009), and Cambodia-Thailand (2008 and 2009) remain unresolved and warrant ongoing attention and resolution by those governments and other States Parties. *Landmine Monitor 2014*, at: *http://bit.ly/2AK02FO*.

## BOX 9.4 FACT-FINDING UNDER ARTICLE 8 OF THE ANTI-PERSONNEL MINE BAN CONVENTION

1 The States Parties agree to consult and cooperate with each other regarding the implementation of the provisions of this Convention, and to work together in a spirit of cooperation to facilitate compliance by States Parties with their obligations under this Convention.

2 If one or more States Parties wish to clarify and seek to resolve questions relating to compliance with the provisions of this Convention by another State Party, it may submit, through the Secretary-General of the United Nations, a Request for Clarification of that matter to that State Party. Such a request shall be accompanied by all appropriate information. . . .

7 All States Parties shall cooperate fully with the Meeting of the States Parties or the Special Meeting of the States Parties in the fulfilment of its review of the matter, including any fact-finding missions that are authorized in accordance with paragraph 8.

8 If further clarification is required, the Meeting of the States Parties or the Special Meeting of the States Parties shall authorize a fact-finding mission and decide on its mandate by a majority of States Parties present and voting. . . .

10 Upon receiving a request from the Meeting of the States Parties or a Special Meeting of the States Parties, the Secretary-General of the United Nations shall, after consultations with the requested State Party, appoint the members of the mission, including its leader. Nationals of States Parties requesting the fact-finding mission or directly affected by it shall not be appointed to the mission. The members of the fact-finding mission shall enjoy privileges and immunities under Article VI of the Convention on the Privileges and Immunities of the United Nations, adopted on 13 February 1946.

11 Upon at least 72 hours' notice, the members of the fact-finding mission shall arrive in the territory of the requested State Party at the earliest opportunity. The requested State Party . . . shall be responsible for ensuring the security of the mission to the maximum extent possible while they are on territory under its control.

12 Without prejudice to the sovereignty of the requested State Party, the fact-finding mission may bring into the territory of the requested State Party the necessary equipment which shall be used exclusively for gathering information on the alleged compliance issue. . . .

13 The requested State Party shall make all efforts to ensure that the fact-finding mission is given the opportunity to speak with all relevant persons

who may be able to provide information related to the alleged compliance issue.

14   The requested State Party shall grant access for the fact-finding mission to all areas and installations under its control where facts relevant to the compliance issue could be expected to be collected. This shall be subject to any arrangements that the requested State Party considers necessary for: a) The protection of sensitive equipment, information and areas; b) The protection of any constitutional obligations the requested State Party may have with regard to proprietary rights, searches and seizures, or other constitutional rights; or c) The physical protection and safety of the members of the fact-finding mission. . . .

15   The fact-finding mission may remain in the territory of the State Party concerned for no more than 14 days, and at any particular site no more than 7 days, unless otherwise agreed.

17   The fact-finding mission shall report, through the Secretary-General of the United Nations, to the Meeting of the States Parties or the Special Meeting of the States Parties the results of its findings.

2009, Geneva Call conducted a fact-finding mission in 2009 to the Philippines to verify alleged use of anti-personnel mines. In a summary of the report, made public in 2010, the organisation confirmed that anti-personnel mines had been used on the southern island of Mindanao but it did not confirm, beyond reasonable doubt, that the Moro Islamic Liberation Front (MILF) had been responsible. In 2000, the MILF had signed the Deed of Commitment for Adherence to a Total Ban on Anti-Personnel Mines and for Cooperation in Mine Action.[97]

## UN Commissions of Inquiry

9.79   UN Commissions of Inquiry, typically established by the Human Rights Council, have served to identify unlawful use of both conventional weapons and weapons of mass destruction. Thus, for instance, the Independent International Commission of Inquiry on the Syrian Arab Republic was established on 22 August 2011 by the Human Rights Council. In March 2017, the Commission reported the indiscriminate presence of anti-personnel mines, improvised explosive

97 Geneva Call, 'Investigation in the Philippines Finds Evidence of AP Mine Use; MILF Responsibility Not Established', 26 March 2010, at: http://bit.ly/2CZugpN.

devices, and booby-traps in civilian areas captured from Islamic State by the Kurdish People's Protection Units (YPG) or the Syrian Democratic Forces. Locally produced mines of an improvised nature 'continue to be laid' by Islamic State 'with devastating effect', it said.[98]

### Verifying stockpile destruction and non-production

9.80 The OPCW is also responsible for verifying the destruction of chemical weapon stockpiles and their non-production by states parties to the Chemical Weapons Convention. The Convention establishes on-site activities to generate confidence in states parties' compliance. These include routine inspections of chemical weapons-related facilities and chemical industry facilities to verify the content of declarations and to confirm that activities are consistent with the Convention obligations. Challenge inspections can be conducted at any facility or location in states parties to clarify questions of possible non-compliance. To prevent abuse of this measure, however, the Executive Council may decide by a three-quarters majority vote to stop a challenge inspection from going forward.

9.81 There is no equivalent mechanism for the Biological Weapons Convention, which has led to concern that stockpiles have been maintained by a number of states parties, including Russia. The Arms Control Association, for instance, claims that the Convention has been 'flagrantly violated in the past'.[99] The Soviet Union, it says, maintained an enormous offensive biological weapons programme after ratifying the Convention. The Russian Federation says that the biological weapons programme has been terminated. Iraq violated its commitments as a signatory state with its biological weapons programme, which was uncovered by the United Nations Special Commission in Iraq (UNSCOM) after the Gulf War. According to the Stockholm International Peace Research Institute (SIPRI), Iraq may have produced up to 10 billion doses of anthrax, botulinum toxin, and aflatoxin. Anthrax, a highly infectious bacterium, and botulinum toxin, one of the most toxic substances known to man, are among the most likely candidates for biological weapon agents.[100] Iraq subsequently became a state party to the Convention.

9.82 In 2001, the United States had blocked the establishment of a verification mechanism for the Biological Weapons Convention, arguing that it could be used for commercial espionage while being ineffective in preventing or detecting violations.[101] The monitoring regime contained in a draft Protocol,

---

98 'Human Rights Abuses and International Humanitarian Law Violations in the Syrian Arab Republic, 21 July 2016–28 February 2017', Conference room paper of the Independent International Commission of Inquiry on the Syrian Arab Republic, UN doc. A/HRC/34/CRP.3, 10 March 2017, para. 90.

99 'The Biological Weapons Convention (BWC) At A Glance', Arms Control Association, Last updated 21 February 2018, at: http://bit.ly/2QipoAa.

100 SIPRI, 'Iraq: The UNSCOM Experience', *Fact Sheet*, October 1998, p. 3, at: http://bit.ly/2zoVbb4.

101 In October 2017, Russian President Vladimir Putin suggested that tissue samples sought as part of a US Air Force medical research programme on arthritis might be intended for research on genetic weapons. This programme, the United States asserts, 'consists of legitimate medical

elaborated in the 1990s, had three basic elements: mandatory declarations of dual-capable activities and facilities; routine visits to declared facilities, without specific evidence of a treaty violation; and short-notice challenge investigations, requested by a state party, of a suspect facility, an alleged use of biological weapons, or a suspicious outbreak of disease, so as to address concerns about possible non-compliance.[102]

## Verifying compliance with prohibitions on nuclear weapons

### Comprehensive safeguards agreements

9.83    Preventing the proliferation of nuclear weapons is a major objective of the international community. Verifying this work has been entrusted, in particular, to the International Atomic Energy Agency (IAEA), which was established in 1957. Through a set of technical measures, known as safeguards, the IAEA endeavours to verify that non-nuclear-weapon states are honouring their international legal obligations to use nuclear material and technology only for peaceful purposes.[103] States accept these measures through the conclusion of safeguards agreements. The objective of IAEA safeguards is to 'deter the spread of nuclear weapons by the early detection of the misuse of nuclear material or technology'.[104] Verification measures include on-site inspections, visits, and ongoing monitoring and evaluation.[105]

9.84    Each non-nuclear-weapon state party to the 1968 Treaty on the Non-Proliferation of Nuclear Weapons (NPT)[106] is obligated to conclude a safeguards agreement with the IAEA. This is required in order to verify the respect of that state's NPT duties 'with a view to preventing diversion of nuclear energy from peaceful uses to nuclear weapons or other nuclear explosive devices'.[107] Such a safeguards agreement must concern 'source or special fissionable material whether it is being produced, processed or used in any principal nuclear facility or is outside any such facility'.[108] Further, the requisite safeguards must be applied on all such material that is being used in peaceful nuclear activities on any territory under the state's jurisdiction or control.[109]

research that does not violate the BWC'. US Department of State, *Adherence to and Compliance with Arms Control, Nonproliferation, and Disarmament Agreements and Commitments*, Washington, DC, April 2018, p. 6.

102 NTI, 'Biological Weapons Convention (BWC) Compliance Protocol', 1 August 2001, at: http://bit.ly/2AJ6DjM.

103 IAEA, 'Safeguards and verification', 2017, at: http://bit.ly/2CWbUa2.

104 IAEA, 'Basics of IAEA safeguards', 2017, at: http://bit.ly/2Ctxrps.

105 IAEA, 'IAEA safeguards overview', 2017, at: http://bit.ly/2q2kJGL.

106 Treaty on the Non-Proliferation of Nuclear Weapons; opened for signature at London, Moscow, and Washington, DC, 1 July 1968; entered into force, 5 March 1970.

107 Art. III(1), NPT.

108 Ibid.

109 Ibid.

9.85 At the end of 2017, the IAEA had safeguards agreements in force with 182 states.[110] The IAEA concludes three types of safeguards agreements:[111] comprehensive safeguards agreements with non-nuclear-weapon states parties to the NPT; 'voluntary offer' safeguards agreements with each of the five nuclear-weapon states parties to the NPT recognised under that Treaty; and item-specific safeguards agreements with states not party to the NPT.[112] Of the 185 non-nuclear-weapon states parties to the NPT (excluding the Democratic People's Republic of Korea),[113] the IAEA has, to date, concluded comprehensive safeguards agreements with 174. Some 100 of these states have also concluded small quantities protocols[114] to their comprehensive safeguards agreements.[115]

9.86 The IAEA carries out different types of on-site inspections and visits under comprehensive safeguards agreements. Routine inspections are the type most frequently used. These may be carried out according to a set schedule or may be 'of an unannounced or short-notice character'. Ad hoc inspections are typically conducted to verify a state's reports of its nuclear material or of nuclear material being transferred by one state to another. The Agency's right to carry out routine inspections under comprehensive safeguards agreements is limited to those locations within a nuclear facility, or other locations containing nuclear material, through which nuclear material is expected to flow. These are known as strategic points.[116]

9.87 Special inspections may be carried out in certain circumstances. The IAEA is authorised to carry out special inspections if it considers that information from a particular state is not adequate. Finally, safeguards visits may be made to declared facilities to verify design information pertaining to safeguards. For example, such visits may be carried out during construction to determine the completeness of the declared design information or during a facility decommissioning, to confirm that sensitive equipment was rendered unusable.[117] Activities that IAEA inspectors perform during and in connection with on-site inspections of, or visits to, facilities may include auditing the facility's accounting and operating records

---

110 IAEA, 'Safeguards implementation in 2017: Helping prevent the spread of nuclear weapons', 2018, at: http://bit.ly/2R39468.

111 IAEA, 'Safeguards legal framework', 2017, at: http://bit.ly/2END7h9.

112 Safeguards are implemented in three states not party to the NPT – India, Israel, and Pakistan – on the basis of item-specific agreements they have concluded with the IAEA. IAEA, 'Safeguards agreements', 2017, at: http://bit.ly/2AmFDXc.

113 Four UN member states are states not party: India, Israel, Pakistan, and South Sudan. The Cook Islands and Niue, which are neither UN member states nor UN observer states (but are considered states by the UN Secretary-General), are said to consider themselves bound by its provisions by virtue of New Zealand being a party to the NPT. R. Avenhaus, V. Kremenyuk, and G. Sjöstedt, *Containing the Atom*, Lexington Books, Lexington, KY, 2002, p. 123.

114 As the name suggests, these protocols are for states with very limited quantities of nuclear material. The purpose of an 'SQP' is to reduce the burden of safeguards implementation for states with little or no nuclear activities, while retaining the integrity of the safeguards system. IAEA, *Safeguards implementation guide for states with small quantities protocols*, Vienna, 2016, at: http://bit.ly/2yriOjC.

115 IAEA, 'Safeguards agreements', 2017.

116 IAEA, 'IAEA safeguards overview', 2017.

117 Ibid.

and comparing these records with the state's reports to the Agency; verifying the inventory of nuclear material and any changes to it; taking environmental samples; and applying 'containment and surveillance' measures, such as seal application or the installation of surveillance equipment.[118]

### IAEA Additional Protocol

9.88   The Additional Protocol is a binding agreement with the IAEA granting the Agency additional inspection authority to that provided in safeguards agreements. A principal aim is to enable the IAEA inspectorate to provide assurance about the accuracy and completeness of declared activities and the absence of undeclared activities. Under the Protocol, the IAEA is granted expanded rights of access to both information and sites.[119] As of September 2018, 133 states had an Additional Protocol in force with the IAEA.[120] The Protocol was developed following the failure of the IAEA to identify Iraq's clandestine nuclear-weapons programme under the comprehensive safeguards agreement.[121]

9.89   Article 3(1) of the Treaty on the Prohibition of Nuclear Weapons stipulates that the obligations to maintain existing safeguards agreements are 'without prejudice to any additional relevant instruments that it may adopt in the future'. This language reflects the inability of the negotiating states to agree that the Treaty should require each state party to either conclude or maintain an IAEA Additional Protocol in every case.

### Monitoring nuclear test explosions: The CTBTO monitoring system

9.90   The verification regime of the 1996 Comprehensive Nuclear-Test-Ban Treaty (CTBT)[122] is designed to detect any nuclear explosion conducted underground, underwater, or in the atmosphere. Although the CTBT is not in force, the Preparatory Commission for the Comprehensive Nuclear-Test-Ban Treaty Organization (CTBTO) has an International Monitoring System that consists of 321 monitoring stations and 16 laboratories worldwide. Seismic, hydro-acoustic, and infrasound stations monitor the situation underground, in the oceans, and in the atmosphere, respectively. Radionuclide stations detect radioactive debris from atmospheric explosions or which are vented by underground or underwater nuclear explosions.[123]

---

118 Ibid.
119 Ibid.
120 IAEA, 'Status of the additional protocol: Status as of 24 September 2018', at: http://bit.ly/2OnV1Xc.
121 See, e.g., T. Findlay, 'Looking Back: The Additional Protocol', *Arms Control Today*, 1 November 2007, at: http://bit.ly/2CZIEyj.
122 Comprehensive Nuclear-Test-Ban Treaty; adopted at the UN General Assembly in New York, 10 September 1996; not yet in force.
123 CTBTO, 'Overview of the Verification Regime', at: http://bit.ly/2q2V7cV.

9.91    On 3 September 2017, Lassina Zerbo, Executive Secretary of the CTBTO announced in a press release that the Organization's monitoring stations 'picked up an unusual seismic event' in the Democratic People's Republic of Korea (DPRK) that morning:

> If confirmed as a nuclear test, this act would indicate that the DPRK's nuclear programme is advancing rapidly. It constitutes yet another breach of the universally accepted norm against nuclear testing; a norm that has been respected by all countries but one since 1996. It also underlines yet again the urgent need for the international community to act on putting in place a legally binding ban on nuclear testing once and for all. I urge the DPRK to refrain from further nuclear testing and to join the 183 States Signatories who have signed the Comprehensive Nuclear-Test-Ban Treaty (CTBT). I sincerely hope that this will serve as the final wake-up call to the international community to outlaw all nuclear testing by bringing the CTBT into force.[124]

### Verifying compliance with limitations of conventional weapons

9.92    The Treaty on Conventional Armed Forces in Europe (CFE Treaty) foresees inspections for a state party to verify compliance with the treaty's numerical limitations of conventional armed forces, namely on-site inspections, challenge inspections and on-site monitoring of destruction by other states parties. While states parties have the unconstrained right to monitor the process of destruction, states may refuse challenge inspections, however. The CFE Treaty does not enable permanent inspections. By 1995, the end of the CFE Treaty's reduction period, the states parties completed and verified the destruction or conversion of more than 52,000 battle tanks, armoured combat vehicles, artillery pieces, combat aircraft and attack helicopters. In addition, they have conducted over 4,000 on-site inspections.[125]

9.93    The 2011 Vienna Document establishes continuous verification activities among OSCE member states. The Vienna Document invites states to visit air bases and demonstrations of new major weapon systems or equipment as well as facilitates contacts between members of the armed forces, such as through joint trainings and academic exchanges. Moreover, it calls for observation of Certain Military Activities (CMA) by inviting all OSCE states to

---

124 CTBTO, 'CTBTO Executive Secretary Lassina Zerbo on the Unusual Seismic Event Detected in the Democratic People's Republic of Korea', Press release, Vienna, 3 September 2017, at: http://bit.ly/2CU6A72.
125 D. Kimball and K. Reif, 'The Conventional Armed Forces in Europe (CFE) Treaty and the Adapted CFE Treaty at a Glance', *Fact Sheet*, Arms Control Association, August 2012, at: http://bit.ly/2SqD1i6.

observe Certain Military Activities exceeding the thresholds of 13,000 troops, 300 tanks, 500 armoured combat vehicles or 250 pieces of artillery.

9.94 Compliance and verification measures under the Vienna Document consist of on-site inspections and evaluation visits which allow the confirmation of the accuracy of information exchanged. States can be inspected by other states 36 hours after request for inspection for maximum 48 hours by a team of four inspectors. The inspection concerns a specified area that is notified before arrival to which there is no refusal by the host state possible. States within the zone of application are subject to three inspections per year. With regard to evaluations, states are subject to up to a maximum of 15 evaluation visits per year depending on the size of military structure reported. While the request is issued five days in advance, the visit by three team members can only last 12 hours. The visit concerns a single formation or unit that may be unavailable. Furthermore, access to sensitive facilities and equipment must not be provided.[126]

## Compliance measures

9.95 A range of measures exist to redress a situation of non-compliance, as summarised in this section. These include sanctions, referral of a dispute as to application of the provisions of a treaty to the International Court of Justice, or referral of a compliance issue to the UN General Assembly. In more serious cases, referral of a compliance issue to the UN Security Council is foreseen.

## Biological Weapons Convention

9.96 Under the 1971 Biological Weapons Convention, any state party which finds that any other state party is in violation of its obligations under the Convention 'may lodge a complaint' with the UN Security Council.[127] The complaint 'should include all possible evidence confirming its validity, as well as a request for its consideration by the Security Council'. Each State Party to this Convention undertakes to co-operate in carrying out any investigation which the Security Council may initiate, in accordance with the provisions of the Charter of the United Nations, on the basis of the complaint received by the Council. The Security Council shall inform the States Parties to the Convention of the results of the investigation.

## Chemical Weapons Convention

9.97 In the Chemical Weapons Convention, Article XII concerns 'measures to redress a situation and to ensure compliance, including sanctions'. As the text of

---

126 OSCE Vienna Document 2011 on Confidence- and Security-building Measures.
127 Art. VI(1), 1971 Biological Weapons Convention.

the provision evidences (see Box 9.5), a state party's rights and privileges under the Convention may be restricted or suspended if it fails to comply with a request by the Executive Council to address a problem with compliance. In cases of particular gravity, the Conference of States Parties is obligated to bring the issue 'to the attention' of the UN General Assembly and the UN Security Council.[128]

9.98  Distinct from, but closely related to Article XII is the provision on dispute settlement in Article XIV. It is specified in paragraph 6 of Article XIV that the article is 'without prejudice' to Article IX on consultations with respect to implementation and fact-finding or to the provisions on measures to redress a situation and to ensure compliance, including sanctions in Article XII. Article XIV requires that disputes about the application of the Convention be settled in accordance with its provisions 'and in conformity with the provisions of the Charter of the United Nations'.[129]

---

**BOX 9.5  MEASURES TO REDRESS A SITUATION AND TO ENSURE COMPLIANCE, INCLUDING SANCTIONS**

1   The Conference shall take the necessary measures, as set forth in paragraphs 2, 3 and 4, to ensure compliance with this Convention and to redress and remedy any situation which contravenes the provisions of this Convention. In considering action pursuant to this paragraph, the Conference shall take into account all information and recommendations on the issues submitted by the Executive Council.

2   In cases where a State Party has been requested by the Executive Council to take measures to redress a situation raising problems with regard to its compliance, and where the State Party fails to fulfil the request within the specified time, the Conference may, inter alia, upon the recommendation of the Executive Council, restrict or suspend the State Party's rights and privileges under this Convention until it undertakes the necessary action to conform with its obligations under this Convention.

3   In cases where serious damage to the object and purpose of this Convention may result from activities prohibited under this Convention, in particular by Article I, the Conference may recommend collective measures to States Parties in conformity with international law.

4   The Conference shall, in cases of particular gravity, bring the issue, including relevant information and conclusions, to the attention of the United Nations General Assembly and the United Nations Security Council.

*Article XII, Chemical Weapons Convention*

---

128  Art. XII(2) and (4), 1992 Chemical Weapons Convention.
129  Art. XIV(1), 1992 Chemical Weapons Convention.

9.99   When a dispute arises between two or more states parties, or between one or more states parties and the OPCW, the parties concerned must consult together 'with a view to the expeditious settlement of the dispute by negotiation or by other peaceful means of the parties' choice, including recourse to appropriate organs of this Convention and, by mutual consent, referral to the International Court of Justice in conformity with the Statute of the Court'.[130] In addition, the Conference of States Parties and the Executive Council of the OPCW are 'separately empowered', subject to UN General Assembly authorisation, to request the ICJ 'to give an advisory opinion on any legal question arising within the scope' of the activities of the OPCW.[131]

## Anti-Personnel Mine Ban Convention

9.100   In the Anti-Personnel Mine Ban Convention, two separate articles address compliance issues: Article 8 on facilitation and clarification of compliance, and Article 10 on the settlement of disputes. Under Article 8, a meeting of states parties 'may request the requested State Party to take measures to address the compliance issue within a specified period of time. The requested State Party shall report on all measures taken in response to this request'.[132] It is further stipulated that a meeting of states parties 'may suggest to the States Parties concerned ways and means to further clarify or resolve the matter under consideration, including the initiation of appropriate procedures in conformity with international law'.[133] To date, this has not occurred.

9.101   Under Article 10, states parties are required to 'consult and cooperate with each other' with a view to settling 'any dispute that may arise' with regard to the 'application' of the Convention.[134] Each state party may bring any such dispute before a meeting of states parties.[135] It is specified that the article 'is without prejudice' to the provisions of the Convention on facilitation and clarification of compliance in Article 8.[136]

## Convention on Cluster Munitions

9.102   The 2008 Convention on Cluster Munitions has broadly similar provisions on compliance measures to those included in the Anti-Personnel Mine Ban Convention. Article 8 on the facilitation and clarification of compliance, though, has a number of more generic rules than its predecessor, stipulating that a meeting of

---

130  Art. XIV(2), 1992 Chemical Weapons Convention.
131  Art. XIV(5), 1992 Chemical Weapons Convention.
132  Art. 8(18), Anti-Personnel Mine Ban Convention.
133  Art. 8(19), Anti-Personnel Mine Ban Convention.
134  Art. 10(1), Anti-Personnel Mine Ban Convention.
135  Ibid.
136  Art. 10(3), Anti-Personnel Mine Ban Convention.

states parties 'may decide to adopt . . . general procedures or specific mechanisms for clarification of compliance, including facts, and resolution of instances of non-compliance with the provisions of this Convention as it deems appropriate'.[137] Article 10(1) of the Convention provides that when a dispute arises between two or more states parties relating to its application, the states parties concerned 'shall consult together with a view to the expeditious settlement of the dispute by negotiation or by other peaceful means of their choice, including recourse to the Meeting of States Parties and referral to the International Court of Justice in conformity with the Statute of the Court'.[138]

## Treaty on the Prohibition of Nuclear Weapons

9.103    The 2017 Treaty on the Prohibition of Nuclear Weapons does not have specific compliance provisions but it does incorporate an article on dispute settlement. Under Article 11(1), when a 'dispute arises between two or more States Parties relating to the interpretation or application of this Treaty, the parties concerned shall consult together with a view to the settlement of the dispute by negotiation or by other peaceful means of the parties' choice in accordance with Article 33 of the Charter of the United Nations'. Article 33 of the Charter concerns the pacific settlement of disputes. It requires that, 'first of all', the parties to any dispute whose continuance 'is likely to endanger the maintenance of international peace and security' to 'seek a solution by negotiation, enquiry, mediation, conciliation, arbitration, judicial settlement, resort to regional agencies or arrangements, or other peaceful means of their own choice'.[139] It is further stated that the UN Security Council 'shall, when it deems necessary, call upon the parties to settle their dispute by such means'.[140]

---

137  Art. 8(6), 2008 Convention on Cluster Munitions.
138  Art. 10(1), 2008 Convention on Cluster Munitions.
139  Art. 33(1), UN Charter.
140  Art. 33(2), UN Charter.

# 10

# DISARMAMENT, DEMOBILISATION, AND REINTEGRATION (DDR)

## Introduction

10.1   Since the 1980s, disarmament, demobilisation, and reintegration (DDR) activities (also termed 'micro-disarmament') have been important components in efforts to stabilise conflict-affected societies as well as to facilitate their longer-term development. In a note on DDR to the United Nations (UN) General Assembly, the UN Secretary-General defined the disarmament element of the DDR process as:

> the collection, documentation, control and disposal of small arms, ammunition, explosives and light and heavy weapons of combatants and often also of the civilian population. Disarmament also includes the development of responsible arms management programmes.[1]

10.2   As discussed in this chapter, four 'generations' of DDR have been identified over the past three decades to reflect significant changes in approach and methodology. First- and second-generation programmes were typically incorporated in a peace agreement, marking a post-conflict enterprise that brought together former warring parties in a common process of disarmament. Second-generation DDR broadened the focus beyond the fighters to encompass also peacebuilding in affected communities. Third-generation DDR began to operate programmes during armed conflict, rendering the process more complex as well as more dangerous.

10.3   Today, however, in some countries DDR now focuses less on the disarmament aspect and more on deradicalisation of individuals. Thus, originally conceived of as a means to reconcile parties to a longstanding armed conflict, reduce

---

1   UN Secretary-General, 'Disarmament, demobilization and reintegration', 2 March 2006, UN doc. 60/705.

the availability of weapons, and support post-conflict peacebuilding, increasingly such initiatives and programmes are being conducted while hostilities persist, and sometimes overtly as part of a national counterterrorism strategy. It remains to be seen what the consequences of such a loss of neutrality may be.

10.4   The notion of micro-disarmament recalls the link between DDR and the broader problem of small arms and light weapons. Indeed, the UN Programme of Action on Small Arms and Light Weapons (PoA), adopted in 2001,[2] explicitly calls for the development and implementation at national level, 'where possible', of 'effective' DDR programmes, 'including the effective collection, control, storage and destruction of small arms and light weapons, particularly in post-conflict situations'.[3] At global level, the PoA encourages the disarmament and demobilisation of former fighters and their subsequent reintegration into civilian life, 'particularly in post-conflict situations'. This may include the provision of support for the 'effective disposition . . . of collected small arms and light weapons'.[4] More and more, though, at the least in fourth-generation DDR, potential beneficiaries are asked to come in without their weapons. Thereby, the authorities are seeking to avoid traps and ambushes. They are asked to denounce other members of the group, with disarmament relegated to a level of secondary importance.

10.5   DDR is not treaty-based, nor is it otherwise codified by international law. It is only directly subject to politically binding guidelines, especially in the context of the Integrated DDR Standards (IDDRS) issued by the United Nations, along with resolutions and presidential statements emanating from the UN Security Council.[5] That said, international human rights law, international criminal law, and the law of armed conflict are all relevant to DDR as there exist duties on states under these bodies of international law to prosecute those who have

2   Programme of Action to Prevent, Combat and Eradicate the Illicit Trade in Small Arms and Light Weapons in All Its Aspects; adopted at the United Nations Conference on the Illicit Trade in Small Arms and Light Weapons in All Its Aspects, New York, 20 July 2001, at: http://bit.ly/2qsN4qe.

3   Ibid., para. 21.

4   Ibid., para. 34.

5   In 2006, for example, a Security Council Presidential Statement underlined the 'crucial importance' of the DDR of ex-combatants,

> taking into account the special needs of child soldiers and women, and encourage[d] the international community to work in close partnership with the countries concerned. It further affirms the need to find lasting solutions to the problem of youth unemployment in order to prevent the recruitment of such youth by illegal armed groups.

Presidential Statement S/PRST/2006/38 on Peace consolidation in West Africa, 9 August 2006, at: http://bit.ly/2ALR8rD. More recently, in Resolution 2423 (2018), the Council urged the government of Mali to implement the Agreement on Peace and Reconciliation by, inter alia, progress in the cantonment and DDR processes,

> as well as in an inclusive and consensual security sector reform, with a view to the progressive redeployment of the reconstituted and reformed defence and security forces in Mali, through the registration of all combatants eligible to the DDR process by the end of 2018.

UN Security Council Resolution 2423, 28 June 2018, para. 3.

committed crimes under international law, such as war crimes[6] or extrajudicial executions.[7] With a view to building or consolidating peace, DDR is typically eschewing the investigation and prosecution of individual programme beneficiaries, some of whom may have been responsible for such crimes.

## Four generations of DDR

10.6    Modern DDR began as part of peace agreements in El Salvador and Guatemala in the Americas, and Mozambique, Namibia, and South Africa in post-apartheid southern Africa in the late 1980s and early 1990s. As longstanding conflicts were being brought to an end, the issue of what to do with the many fighters that had participated in the fighting was debated. Most of the fighters were men, but some were children and others were women, rendering reintegration a major challenge. A chief concern in a post-conflict environment is preventing the resumption of hostilities. DDR programmes are said to reduce the risk of conflict recurring by reducing the availability of weapons, geographically dispersing former fighters and disrupting their social networks, providing former fighters with economic opportunities unrelated to conflict, building confidence between former warring parties, including restructuring the military, and helping governments to realise peace dividends.[8]

---

6    For a discussion of the duty to investigate violations of the law of armed conflict, see ICRC Customary International Humanitarian Law Study, Rule 158 (Prosecution of War Crimes): 'States must investigate war crimes allegedly committed by their nationals or armed forces, or on their territory . . . They must also investigate other war crimes over which they have jurisdiction and, if appropriate, prosecute the suspects'. In the case of grave breaches of the 1949 Geneva Conventions (which are committed in international armed conflict only), the exercise of universal jurisdiction is mandatory. See the 1949 Geneva Convention I, Art. 49; 1949 Geneva Convention II, Art. 50; 1949 Geneva Convention III, Art. 129; 1949 Geneva Convention Art. 146; and the 1977 Additional Protocol I (applicable to international armed conflict), Art. 85; and see also the Basic Principles and Guidelines on the Right to a Remedy and Reparation for Victims of Gross Violations of International Human Rights Law and Serious Violations of International Humanitarian Law, UN General Assembly Resolution 60/147, 21 March 2006; Report of the UN Special Rapporteur on extrajudicial, summary or arbitrary executions, UN doc. A/68/382 13 September 2013, para. 101. See also, e.g., Report of the UN Special Rapporteur on the Promotion and Protection of Human Rights and Fundamental Freedoms While Countering Terrorism, UN doc. A/68/389, 18 September 2013, para. 42.

7    As the Minnesota Protocol on the Investigation of Potentially Unlawful Death recalls, 'Where an investigation reveals evidence that a death was caused unlawfully, the State must ensure that identified perpetrators are prosecuted and, where appropriate, punished through a judicial process', Minnesota Protocol on the Investigation of Potentially Unlawful Death (2016), Office of the UN High Commissioner for Human Rights, 2017, para. 9(c), citing UN Basic Principles and Guidelines on the Right to Remedy and Reparation; Updated Set of Principles for the Protection and Promotion of Human Rights through Action to Combat Impunity, Principle 4; and Art. 2(3), 1966 International Covenant on Civil and Political Rights.

8    J. Schulhofer-Wohl and N. Sambanis, *Disarmament, Demobilization, and Reintegration Programs: An Assessment*, Research Report, Folke Bernadotte Academy, Sweden, 2010, para. 15, at: http://bit.ly/2QhLEdk.

### First-generation DDR

10.7   The approach generally taken by the United Nations in early DDR programmes was to house fighters in camps ('cantonment') and then demobilise them in a formal process. Most were given basic vocational training and dispatched with a small quantity of cash and some basic tools with a view to their successful reintegration into community life. A small number might be invited to join armed forces of national unity. While, as two experts report, these early DDR programmes were 'far from perfect', they were conducted 'with military-like precision'.[9]

10.8   One of the early 'first-generation' DDR programmes was in Guatemala. The internal armed conflict between the security forces and the URNG (Guatemalan National Revolutionary Unity), which lasted from 1960 to 1996, involved hundreds of massacres of ethnic minorities as part of the military's 'scorched earth' policy. Between 1981 and 1983, as many as 1 in 20 of the entire Ixil population may have been killed.[10] This led to a clamour for justice as well as peace. Balancing these two essential elements is a principal challenge in any DDR programme, as prosecutions may remove a realistic possibility of DDR and vice versa.

10.9   The conflict ended in late December 1996, when the government and the URNG signed the last of 12 peace accords, ushering in a formal official cease-fire.[11] In addition to seeking to address many longstanding social and economic issues, the Peace Accords also set the terms for the DDR of the former non-state fighters. This included vocational training for agriculture, construction, or small business management.[12] As is often the case, however, in addition to the men who formed the bulk of the fighting forces, significant numbers of both women and children participated actively in the conflict in Guatemala. A 2007 report by a research institute concluded that the character of the DDR process itself in Guatemala influenced its success among women: the female fighters who opted for collective reintegration were in general more socially active than those who reintegrated individually, as the cooperatives offered many possibilities for social activity and participation and as these women also had arrangements to look after their children.[13] The report called

---

9  R. Muggah and C. O'Donnell, 'Next Generation Disarmament, Demobilization and Reintegration', *Stability: International Journal of Security and Development*, Vol. 4, No. 1 (2015), at: http://bit.ly/2JHCVyN.

10  Guatemala Human Rights Commission, 'Genocide in the Ixil Triangle', 2011, at: http://bit.ly/2PKKz0N.

11  Secretaria de la Paz, *Acuerdos de Paz*, Guatemala City, 2012; see R. Janzen, 'Guatemalan Ex-Combatant Perspectives on Reintegration: A Grounded Theory', *The Qualitative Report*, Vol. 19, Art. 41 (2014), p. 2, at: http://bit.ly/2RypS57.

12  W. Hauge and B. Thoresen, *El destino de los ex-combatientes en Guatemala: Obstaculizadores o agentes de cambio?* [In English: 'The fate of the former fighters in Guatemala: Obstacles or agents of change?'], North-South Institute, Guatemala City, 2007, p. 23.

13  W. Hauge, 'The Demobilization and Political Participation of Female Fighters in Guatemala', Report to the Norwegian Ministry of Foreign Affairs, International Peace Research Institute, Oslo (PRIO), Oslo, March 2007.

for DDR processes to incorporate longer transition periods, especially in the case of protracted armed conflict.

## The development of international standards for DDR

10.10   Experiences and lessons learned from what became known as 'first-generation' DDR were the basis for the 2006 IDDRS issued by the United Nations. The standards were a response to the fragmentation and inconsistency of the UN approach to DDR across different countries.[14] The IDDRS are currently incorporated in 25 modules and three sub-modules,[15] though, as of writing, the standards were in the process of being revised. Collectively, they serve to guide the planning, implementation, and evaluation of DDR programmes.

10.11   A specific module in the IDDRS is directed to women and DDR.[16] In 2000, UN Security Council Resolution 1325 on women, peace, and security, adopted after the DDR programme in Guatemala, had called for the 'different needs of female and male ex-combatants . . . and the needs of their dependants' to be considered in planning. It was, though, observed that women 'are almost never included in the planning or implementation of DDR' despite their increasing involvement in combat or association with armed groups and forces in other roles.[17] The module further observes that:

> A strict 'one man, one gun' eligibility requirement for DDR, or an eligibility test based on proficiency in handling weapons, may exclude many women and girls from entry into DDR programmes. The narrow definition of who qualifies as a 'combatant' has been motivated to a certain extent by budgetary considerations, and this has meant that DDR planners have often overlooked or inadequately attended to the needs of a large group of people participating in and associated with armed groups and forces. However, these same people also present potential security concerns that might complicate DDR.[18]

10.12   Recalling similar challenges that existed in Guatemala, Mozambique, and others on how to treat former child fighters, the issue of children and DDR is considered in a further specific module in the IDDRS. Therein it is stated that 'child DDR is not the same as that for adults. Rather, it is a specific process with its own requirements, several of which are fundamentally different from adult demobilization programmes'.[19] Further, in his 2006 report to the

---

14  UN, IDDRS 1.10: 'Introduction to the IDDRS', 2006 (Rev'd Edn, 2014), p. 2.
15  At: http://bit.ly/2PIePJk.
16  IDDRS 5.10: 'Women, Gender and DDR'.
17  UN, IDDRS 5.10: 'Women, Gender and DDR', 2006, p. 1.
18  Ibid., p. 10.
19  UN, IDDRS Module 5:30: 'Children and DDR', 2006, p. 1, at: http://bit.ly/2Ff5DZh.

UN General Assembly on DDR, the UN Secretary-General called for efforts to be made to ensure that the DDR of children was 'not contingent' on adult DDR 'or the conclusion of broader security sector reform and power sharing negotiations'.[20] At the same time, the IDDRS caution that: 'There is no simple formula for the DDR of children that can be routinely applied in all circumstances, so each programme needs to be context-specific and developed and managed in order to be sustainable'.[21] The challenge, the Standards observe, 'is to encourage girls and boys to benefit from DDR programmes while avoiding any damaging effects'.[22]

10.13    In fact, as has been the case with women, operational practice has largely been to exclude children (at least those under 15 years of age) from formal DDR processes. Instead, the focus has been on ensuring that children released from armed forces and armed groups following advocacy and negotiation are swiftly tracked into mainstream rehabilitation and reintegration similar to the way programmes would support other conflict-affected children. This option is partially recognised in the Optional Protocol to the 1989 Convention on the Rights of the Child (CRC), which provides that: 'States Parties shall take all feasible measures to ensure that persons within their jurisdiction recruited or used in hostilities contrary to the present Protocol are demobilized or otherwise released from service'.[23]

10.14    While this approach reflects a certain logic, it may also create frustration, particularly among older children who may wish to receive the benefits of reintegration that their elder colleagues enjoy. Thus, a further distinct IDDRS module addresses youth, which concerns children from the age of 15 (and adults up to the age of 24). As the module recognises, youth 'fall between the legal categories of child and adult, and their needs are not necessarily well served by programmes designed for mature adults or very young children'.[24]

10.15    Warning of the dangers of failure for the success of a fragile peace, the module calls for DDR programmes to 'analyse and deal with the reasons why young people join armed forces and groups', with a view to providing 'the type of DDR assistance that would make them feel secure'.[25] A further challenge is the need to coordinate youth DDR programmes with those for children and adults 'in order to deal with the particular needs of this "in-between" group and make sure that people who started out as child soldiers but are now over 18

20 'Disarmament, Demobilization and Reintegration: Report of the Secretary-General', UN doc. A/60/705, 2 March 2006, para. 9(k).

21 Ibid., p. 2.

22 Ibid., p. 8.

23 Art. 6(1), Optional Protocol to the Convention on the Rights of the Child on the involvement of children in armed conflict; adopted and opened for signature by UN General Assembly Resolution 54/263 of 25 May 2000; entered into force, 12 February 2002.

24 UN, IDDRS Module 5.20: 'Youth and DDR', 2006, p. 1, at: http://bit.ly/2OqGMke.

25 Ibid., p. 3.

receive proper support'.[26] But while the current module is relatively strong on analysis and theory, it offers relatively little in terms of programming guidance.

## Second-generation DDR

10.16   A second generation of DDR had already begun to emerge in the 2000s, while the IDDRS were in the process of being completed. This new, more sophisticated approach saw adaptation occurring 'in line with the evolution of global peace, security, and development agendas'.[27] The features of this new generation reflected a broadening of focus from 'a narrow preoccupation' with the demobilisation and reintegration of former fighters to the far more expansive – and expensive – goals of building the conditions for sustainable peace.[28] This second wave of DDR programmes, which was especially common following conflicts in the Balkans, South-East Asia, and West and Central Africa, was expected to 'contain and reduce multiple forms of violence, while also neutralizing spoilers, building bridges with communities, and contributing to legacy public goods'.[29] The DDR agenda was becoming increasingly ambitious.

10.17   Central to both first- and second-generation DDR, however, was the disarmament of former fighters. The IDDRS describe disarmament, 'generally understood as the "act of reducing or depriving of arms"', as 'the first step' in a DDR process.[30] The UN further affirms that the disarmament component of a DDR programme 'should usually' comprise four main phases: information collection and operational planning; weapons collection or retrieval operations; stockpile management; and destruction.[31]

10.18   Although controversial (for fear, sometimes justified, that it generates renewed arms procurement and trading), financial and other incentives have often been given in exchange for the handing in of weapons. Based on an analysis of DDR programmes through 2008, one academic has argued that swapping weapons for cash seemed to work in some places, but not in others 'where the possession of arms and their use is accepted as a cultural value'. To avoid the risk of fraud and illegal diversion of funds, he suggested that non-liquid incentives such as supermarket vouchers can be handed out during the weapons collection phase of DDR. 'Others have recommended "weapons-for-development" schemes and the strengthening of cultural norms against the possession and use of weapons as an answer to this

---

26 Ibid., p. 4.
27 Muggah and O'Donnell, 'Next Generation Disarmament, Demobilization and Reintegration'.
28 R. Muggah, 'No Magic Bullet: A Critical Perspective on Disarmament, Demobilization and Reintegration (DDR) and Weapons Reduction in Post-Conflict Contexts', *The Commonwealth Journal of International Affairs*, 2005, at: http://bit.ly/2QiMV3V.
29 Muggah and O'Donnell, 'Next Generation Disarmament, Demobilization and Reintegration'.
30 UN, IDDRS Module 4.10: 'Disarmament', p. 1, at: http://bit.ly/2SKrGt9.
31 Ibid.

problem'.[32] It is further argued that communities 'should be made aware of the importance of small arms collection and control following the end of formal disarmament programs'.[33]

10.19   As the IDDRS observe, in the past, fighters have been allowed to enter a DDR programme

> if they can submit the required amount of ammunition. This system is open to abuse, however, as ammunition is easy to hand out to non-combatant supporters, who can then enter a programme for the personal or political gain of the one who gave them the ammunition. The handing over of ammunition, unless it is also a self-contained system (such as mines, grenades, surface-to-air missiles or certain anti-tank rocket launchers), should therefore not be a sufficient criterion for entry.[34]

The IDDRS requires that the physical destruction of weapons be approached as a separate issue from the destruction of ammunition and explosives. For the destruction of the latter, the Standards refer to the International Mine Action Standards (IMAS) issued also by the United Nations, especially IMAS 11.10.[35]

## Third-generation DDR

10.20   While DDR programmes were becoming more sophisticated, they remained steadfastly a post-conflict undertaking wherein former fighters were generally prepared and willing to lay down their arms. As time went on, however, and certain conflicts became protracted, so-called third-generation DDR emerged. The particularities of this new generation, which has taken root since the beginning of the 2010s, is that it is implemented during ongoing armed hostilities, with a view to promoting peace. Muggah and O'Donnell give the example of the Democratic Republic of Congo (DRC), where some 20,000 members of the Forces Démocratiques de Libération du Rwanda (FDLR) were sent back to Rwanda between 2000 and 2010 (including many children), leaving some 2,000 FDLR fighters who continued to 'ravage' the east of the DRC. With respect to these hard-core elements 'a new kind of forceful DDR was initiated in the context of "robust peacekeeping" operations in 2012'.[36]

10.21   It is possible to see these experiences during armed conflict as marking a turning point in DDR. The fundamental concept of DDR has evolved from post-conflict programming by consent, implemented with a view to *building* peace,

---

32 W.A. Knight, 'Disarmament, Demobilization, and Reintegration and Post-Conflict Peacebuilding in Africa: An Overview', *African Security*, Vol. 1 (2008), pp. 24–52, at 51, at: http://bit.ly/2QgCHkn.

33 Ibid.

34 UN, IDDRS Module 4.10: 'Disarmament', p. 16, §8.4.3.

35 IMAS 11.10: Guide for the destruction of stockpiled anti-personnel mines, 2nd Edn, 1 January 2003 (as amended through June 2013).

36 Muggah and O'Donnell, 'Next Generation Disarmament, Demobilization and Reintegration'.

to a new, more coercive form of programming that was implemented during hostilities with the aim of *achieving* peace. Thus, in the Central African Republic, Libya, Mali, the Niger Delta, and Yemen, DDR was being 'reconceived' in the shape of 'dynamic political processes' instead of 'stand-alone or one-off enterprises'. Therein, this new way of working is 'connected in complex ways to peace negotiations and robust peace operations, justice, and security sector reform, and peace- and state-building'.[37]

10.22   This new environment for DDR programming brings with it obvious challenges. Thus, as Munive and Stepputat observe, sensitivities run especially high during ongoing conflict, with trust correspondingly low. They recall that in Afghanistan, for instance, the International Security Assistance Force (ISAF) team working on DDR issues was carefully instructed (with original emphasis):

> If fighters are to be removed from the battlefield it is critical that reintegration is NEVER seen or profiled to them as an act of 'Surrender'. The terms 'Surrender' and 'Laying down of weapons' should NEVER be used in any conversation, discussion or reference.[38]

10.23   The first phase of DDR in Afghanistan, which followed the United States' intervention in Afghanistan after the 9/11 attacks, claimed significant successes. According to one report, by January 2005 more than 30,000 of an estimated 60,000 members of Afghan militia forces had been disarmed since the beginning of the DDR process in 2003. In addition, more than 90 per cent of all heavy weapons in Afghanistan had reportedly been collected.[39] But success was not sustained, and the Taliban insurgency grew in strength and extent over the following decade. By 2015, it was being argued by one commentator that four international programmes designed to disarm, demobilise, and reintegrate militias in Afghanistan since 2001 had 'largely failed'. The programmes

> have instead largely reinforced existing power relations. Perhaps their gravest impact has been to deepen patterns of political exclusion that underlie much of the violence that have driven support for the insurgency.[40]

One criticism is that Western powers have tended to use DDR programmes and language in Afghanistan to demobilise 'specific armed groups for perceived short-term political or security gains while rearming and protecting others'.[41]

---

37  Ibid.
38  J. Munive and F. Stepputat, 'Rethinking Disarmament, Demobilization and Reintegration Programs', *Stability: International Journal of Security & Development*, Vol. 4, No. 1 (2015), pp. 1–13, at 5, at: http://bit.ly/2zpX6MJ.
39  'DDR – Disarmament, Demobilization and Reintegration', *Global Security*, Last updated 17 August 2012, at: http://bit.ly/2Qd4O3Y.
40  D. Derksen, 'The Politics of Disarmament and Rearmament in Afghanistan', United States Institute of Peace, 20 May 2015, at: http://bit.ly/2JCTKKX.
41  Ibid.

## *Fourth-generation DDRR*

10.24    The danger of DDR becoming politically slanted is increasing. Arguably, in an era marked by terrorism and counterterrorism operations, a fourth generation of programming is now emerging. In this new version of DDR, disengagement and disassociation are largely replacing disarmament and demobilisation. Weapons collection is no longer a primary aim of the programme, replaced by measures designed to encourage defections from the ranks of a terrorist group. Hand-in-hand with this amended focus is the importance of reconciliation, to ensure former terrorists can safely reintegrate into communities, leading to a new abbreviation of DDRR (Disengagement, Disassociation, Reintegration, and Reconciliation). Nowhere is this more starkly illustrated than in the Lake Chad Basin. DDRR describes more accurately the actions emerging to tackle the ongoing threat from Boko Haram[42] and a splinter group, the Islamic State in West Africa, in their campaign of terror across Cameroon, Chad, Niger, and especially the north-east of Nigeria, whence Boko Haram emerged in 2009.[43]

10.25    Boko Haram has been identified at the international level as a terrorist group and subject to sanctions. In May 2014, the UN Security Council's Al-Qaida Sanctions Committee approved the addition of Boko Haram to its list of individuals and entities subject to targeted financial sanctions and arms embargo, as set out in Security Council Resolution 2083.[44] As a result of the listing by the Sanctions Committee, any individual or entity that provides financial or material support to Boko Haram, including by providing arms or recruits, is itself eligible to be added to the Al-Qaida Sanctions List and subject to the sanctions measures.[45]

10.26    Boko Haram had already been designated by the United States (US) Department of State in November 2013 as a Foreign Terrorist Organization[46] and

---

42 The popular name for the group translates as 'Western education is harmful', while the full title is Jama'atu Ahlis Sunna Lidda'awati wal-Jihad – 'People Committed to the Prophet's Teachings for Propagation and Jihad'. A split occurred in 2017, leading to two Boko Haram factions operating in the Lake Chad Basin. See, e.g., Reuters, 'Boko Haram Split Creates Two Deadly Forces', *Voice of America*, 4 August 2017, at: http://bit.ly/2DlWtbw.

43 The conflict with Boko Haram erupted after what was reportedly an extrajudicial execution by the Nigerian police of the group's spiritual leader, Muslim cleric Mohammed Yusuf, in 2009. Yusuf had formed the group in 2002 in Maiduguri, the capital of Borno state in north-east Nigeria, establishing a mosque and an Islamic school to which many poor Muslim families from across Nigeria as well as neighbouring countries sent their children. BBC, 'Who are Nigeria's Boko Haram Islamist group?', 24 November 2016, at: http://bit.ly/2F3mqhG. The group came to prominence, first locally and then nationally, following a series of armed attacks on police stations and other government buildings. See, e.g., J. Ford, 'The origins of Boko Haram', *The National Interest*, 6 June 2014, p. 2, at: http://bit.ly/2F0vmo3; and M. Smith, 'Explaining Nigeria's Boko Haram & Its Violent Insurgency', *Fact Sheet, Africa Check*, 22 September 2014 (Last updated 31 July 2017), at: http://bit.ly/2ALwB6j.

44 UN Security Council Resolution 2083 (2012), adopted under Chapter VII of the UN Charter, para. 1.

45 UN, 'Security Council Al-Qaida Sanctions Committee Adds Boko Haram to Its Sanctions List', Press release, UN doc. SC/11410, 22 May 2014.

46 See: US Department of State, 'Foreign Terrorist Organizations', at: http://bit.ly/2Opq1Wz.

a Specially Designated Global Terrorist. On 3 June 2014, following the decision by the United Nations, the European Union (EU) announced it too had imposed sanctions on Boko Haram as an al-Qaeda-linked terrorist group.[47] The decision subjects the organisation as well as any individuals or entities that support them financially or materially to sanctions, including an arms embargo, asset freeze, and a travel ban.[48] The various sanctions measures complicate significantly the funding and delivery of any DDR programme.

10.27   Nigeria has made political space for a DDRR programme, understanding that not everyone should be – or indeed realistically can be – successfully prosecuted and incarcerated. At the end of March 2017, the UN Security Council adopted Resolution 2349, in which it urged Lake Chad Basin governments to implement consistent policies to promote defections from Boko Haram, to deradicalise and reintegrate those who had already defected, and to ensure there was no impunity for those responsible for terrorist attacks.[49]

10.28   As of writing, relevant policy and programmatic initiatives were also being elaborated in Nigeria's neighbours, albeit a little sporadically. But some have focused on reinforcing judicial sanction for Boko Haram associates, including children, leaving little or no space for DDRR. In Niger, for instance, trials conducted in camera of around 1,000 suspected Boko Haram fighters began in early 2017 on charges of criminal conspiracy for terrorism. The defendants were Malians, Nigerians, and Nigeriens. Niger's Attorney General told the press that convictions and acquittals of terrorist suspects had already occurred with sentences of between three and nine years' imprisonment for the convicted.[50] Back in December 2016, however, following an initiative by the governor of Diffa region, the Nigerien Minister of the Interior made a surprise public announcement that repentant Boko Haram associates would be given the opportunity to hand themselves in to the authorities and accept a deradicalisation programme rather than be prosecuted.[51] In addition, if someone in a terrorist group defects and prevents an attack and informs on other members, he may be given immunity from prosecution (and not even directed to a DDRR programme).

10.29   In contrast, in Cameroon, the 2014 Anti-Terrorism Law[52] prescribes the mandatory death penalty for any person who commits, or threatens to commit, an act likely to cause death, injury, or material damage where there is intent to intimidate the public or disrupt the functioning of public services.[53] In early 2016,

---

47 AFP/PTI, 'EU Adds Nigeria's Boko Haram to Blacklisted Terror Groups', Brussels, 3 June 2014.
48 E. Benari, 'EU Imposes Sanctions on Boko Haram', *Arutz Sheva*, 3 June 2014.
49 UN Security Council Resolution 2349; adopted by consensus on 31 March 2017, para. 31.
50 AFP, 'Niger: discrets procès d'un millier de militants de Boko Haram', *RTBF*, 10 March 2017, at: http://bit.ly/2JAYMrh.
51 E. Brackley, 'West Africa: The Region in Niger Quietly Piloting a Boko Haram Amnesty', *AllAfrica*, 20 April 2017, at: http://bit.ly/2OoSTyu.
52 Law No. 2014/028 of 23 December 2014 on the suppression of acts of terrorism.
53 S. 2(1), 2014 Anti-Terrorism Law. Section 16 of the Law, however, stipulates that prosecution 'shall be waived' for any person who, after agreeing with another to commit an act of terrorism, reports the

Cameroon sentenced 89 Boko Haram fighters to death[54] and many trials have taken place since then.[55] Currently, very little space appears to be available at all for DDRR in Cameroon. The apparent determination to prosecute and convict all adult Boko Haram associates is likely to further exacerbate overcrowding in Cameroon's prisons without encouraging low-level or ancillary Boko Haram associates to defect and thereby further weaken the group.

10.30    Chad has similarly taken a repressive approach to its threat from Boko Haram. In early August 2015, following a series of attacks, Chad adopted a new anti-terrorism law.[56] As in Cameroon, the mandatory death penalty is imposed on any person who commits, finances, recruits, or trains people to participate in, acts of terrorism.[57] The law reintroduced the death penalty just six months after the government had proposed its abolition. Lesser terrorist offences are punishable with life imprisonment.[58] Where national laws and policies are repressive, the space for DDR and DDRR is substantially reduced.

---

plan to a public official; uses 'all means' to help prevent the commission of the offence; and helps to identify his or her co-offenders or accomplices.

54 BBC, 'Cameroon Sentences 89 Boko Haram Fighters to Death', 17 March 2016, at: http://bit. ly/2PJyZ64.

55 Despite requiring the pronouncement of the death penalty for many offences, Cameroon is an "abolitionist" state, meaning that there is a de facto moratorium on the execution of a death sentence.

56 Law 034/PR/2015, adopted on 5 August 2015.

57 Arts. 14–17 and 25, Law 034/PR/2015.

58 Art. 24, Law 034/PR/2015.

# OUTLOOK

According to an old Danish proverb, it is difficult to predict, especially the future. This applies to any branch of international law, let alone disarmament, where the law oftentimes plays 'catch-up' with new technological developments. For the foreseeable future, the existing disarmament institutions may continue to struggle to agree upon new regulations governing weapons of mass destruction. Competing interests and high stakes among the 197 states that can adhere to global disarmament treaties based on the current 'all states' formula makes consensus very hard to achieve in a diplomatic conference. The logjam in the Conference on Disarmament (which has only 65 members from the total of 197 states) is testament to the challenges. While maintaining the consensus approach typically leads to stalemate and impasse, the conclusion of treaties without consensus, however, undermines efforts to achieve universalisation.

Over the last 25 years, three instruments have been adopted by vote, namely the Comprehensive Nuclear-Test-Ban Treaty (CTBT) in 1996[1] and the Arms Trade Treaty in 2013,[2] both in the United Nations (UN) General Assembly, and most recently in 2017, the Treaty on the Prohibition of Nuclear Weapons.[3] The consensus approach within the United Nations meant that the Anti-Personnel Mine Ban Convention[4] and the Convention on Cluster Munitions[5] were concluded in ad hoc diplomatic

---

1   Comprehensive Nuclear-Test-Ban Treaty; adopted at New York, 10 September 1996; not yet in force
2   Arms Trade Treaty; adopted at New York, 2 April 2013; entered into force, 24 December 2014.
3   Treaty on the Prohibition of Nuclear Weapons; adopted at New York, 7 July 2017.
4   Convention on the Prohibition of the Use, Stockpiling, Production and Transfer of Anti-Personnel Mines and on their Destruction; adopted at Oslo, 18 September 1997; entered into force, 1 March 1999.
5   Convention on Cluster Munitions; adopted at Dublin, 30 May 2008; entered into force, 1 August 2010.

conferences (in 1997 and 2008, respectively), both of which were convened outside UN auspices. The Convention on Certain Conventional Weapons[6] – which adopts new legally binding rules by consensus – last adopted a total prohibition on the use of a weapon (blinding laser weapons) more than 20 years ago, in 1995.[7]

Weapons and weapons systems on the horizon that may demand regulation by disarmament treaty include artificial intelligence systems that take the human out of the decision-making on targeting and firing, as well as techniques for the enhancement of the capacities of humans when serving as soldiers. Offensive cyber operations are already influencing the conduct of hostilities; this is only likely to increase in the coming years. Added into the mix of armaments must be three-dimensional printers capable of producing weapons, which take that ability out of states and private corporations and put it in the hands of individuals. Separately, armed groups, particularly but not only Islamic State in both Iraq and Syria, have made and used large numbers of improvised anti-personnel mines. Thousands have been killed by these groups, which are only indirectly concerned by global disarmament treaties whose prohibitions focus on the behaviour of states.

Further challenges to international disarmament law remain the universalisation and implementation of existing treaties. With the exception of the Biological Weapons Convention[8] and Chemical Weapons Convention,[9] all global disarmament treaties are far from universal and do not encompass the majority of great powers. Most global disarmament treaties led to policy changes among states parties. Yet state compliance and implementation is not guaranteed as some have been accused of continued development of chemical and biological weapons. Moreover, we may be witnessing the birth of a new nuclear arms race between the United States, Russia, and China.

International disarmament efforts, however, have always been incremental. Fragmentation in international legal treaty-making for disarmament may lead to the conclusion of more bilateral or plurilateral agreements that are elaborated directly between affected and concerned parties rather than global multilateral treaties negotiated and adopted through and at the United Nations. While the

6  Convention on Prohibitions or Restrictions on the Use of Certain Conventional Weapons Which May Be Deemed to Be Excessively Injurious or to Have Indiscriminate Effects; adopted at Geneva, 3 May 1996; entered into force, 3 December 1998.

7  Protocol IV on Blinding Laser Weapons); adopted at Vienna, 13 October 1995; entered into force, 30 July 1998. The Amended Protocol II in 1996 only included limited prohibitions on anti-personnel mines while Protocol V deals with post-conflict clean-up of unexploded ordnance and abandoned explosive ordnance.

8  Convention on the Prohibition of the Development, Production and Stockpiling of Bacteriological (Biological) and Toxin Weapons and on Their Destruction; opened for signature at London, Moscow, and Washington, DC, 10 April 1972; entered into force, 26 March 1975.

9  Convention on the Prohibition of the Development, Production, Stockpiling and Use of Chemical Weapons and on their Destruction; adopted at Geneva, 3 September 1992; entered into force, 29 April 1997.

international disarmament architecture is flexible for evolving in such a manner, coherence between instruments is critical. Moreover, given the manifold challenges regarding disarmament, continuous dedication is necessary. A former UN Secretary-General had observed that the world is 'over-armed' while peace 'is underfunded'. Indeed, disarmament is a question of commitment.

# BIBLIOGRAPHY

## Books and monographs

Albright, R., *Clean-up of Chemical and Explosive Munitions: Location, Identification and Environmental Remediation*, William Andrew, Oxford, 2011.

Avenhaus, R., V. Kremenyuk, and G. Sjöstedt, *Containing the Atom*, Lexington Books, United States, 2002.

Best, G., *War and Law Since 1945*, Clarendon Press, Oxford, 2002.

Boothby, W., *Weapons and the Law of Armed Conflict*, 2nd Edn, Oxford University Press, Oxford, 2016.

Broadus, J.M. and R.V. Vartanov, *The Oceans and Environmental Security: Shared U.S. and Russian Perspectives*, Island Press, Washington, DC, 1994.

Brownlie, I., *International Law and the Use of Force by States*, Oxford University Press, Oxford, 1963.

Casey-Maslen, S. (ed.), *Weapons Under International Human Rights Law*, Cambridge University Press, Cambridge, 2014.

Casey-Maslen, S. (ed.), *The War Report: Armed Conflict in 2013*, Oxford University Press, Oxford, 2014.

Casey-Maslen, S., with S. Haines, *Hague Law Interpreted: The Conduct of Hostilities Under the Law of Armed Conflict*, Hart, Oxford, 2018.

Casey-Maslen, S., *The Treaty on the Prohibition of Nuclear Weapons: A Commentary*, Oxford University Press, Oxford, January 2019.

Casey-Maslen, S., A. Clapham, G. Giacca, and S. Parker, *The Arms Trade Treaty, A Commentary*, Oxford University Press, Oxford, 2016.

Casey-Maslen, S., M. Homayounnejad, H. Stauffer, and N. Weizmann, *Drones and Other Unmanned Weapons Systems Under International Law*, Brill, Boston, MA, August 2018.

Clapham, A., *Brierly's Law of Nations*, 7th Edn, Oxford University Press, Oxford, 2012.

Clapham, A. and P. Gaeta (eds.), *The Oxford Handbook of International Law in Armed Conflict*, Oxford University Press, Oxford, 2014.

Crawford, J., *Brownlie's Principles of Public International Law*, 8th Edn, Oxford University Press, Oxford, 2012.

Dinstein, Y., *The Conduct of Hostilities under the Law of International Armed Conflict*, 2nd Edn, Cambridge University Press, Cambridge, 2010.

Dinstein, Y., *War, Aggression and Self-Defence*, 5th Edn, Cambridge University Press, Cambridge, 2017.

Evans, M.D. (ed.), *International Law*, 4th Edn, Oxford University Press, Oxford, 2014.

French Ministry of Defence, *Manuel de Droit des Conflits Armés*, Paris, 2012.

Goldblat, J., *Arms Control: The New Guide to Negotiations and Agreements*, Sage, Thousand Oaks, CA, 2002.

Gray, C., *International Law and the Use of Force*, 4th Edn, Oxford University Press, Oxford, 2018.

Hutton Siderovski, S., *Tularemia*, Chelsea House Publishers, Philadelphia, 2009.

Kierulf, J., *Disarmament under International Law*, Djof Publishing, Denmark, 2017.

Kroenig, M., *Logic of American Nuclear Strategy: Why Strategic Superiority Matters*, Oxford University Press, Oxford, 2018.

Krutzsch, W. and R. Trapp, *A Commentary on the Chemical Weapons Convention*, Martinus Nijhoff, The Netherlands, 1994.

Mangold, T., *Plague Wars: The Terrifying Reality of Biological Warfare*, Macmillan, New York, 1999.

Maslen, S., *Commentary on the 1997 Anti-Personnel Mine Ban Convention*, Oxford University Press, Oxford, 2003.

Nystuen, G. and S. Casey-Maslen (eds.), *The Convention on Cluster Munitions: A Commentary*, Oxford University Press, Oxford, 2010.

Nystuen, G., S. Casey-Maslen, and A. Golden Bersagel (eds.), *Nuclear Weapons Under International Law*, Cambridge University Press, Cambridge, 2014.

*P5 Glossary of Key Nuclear Terms*, Atomic Energy Press, Beijing, 2015.

Pictet, J., *Development and Principles of International Humanitarian Law*, Martinus Nijhoff, Geneva, 1985.

Regis, E., *The Biology of Doom: The History of America's Secret Germ Warfare Project*, Henry Holt, New York, 1990.

Shaw, M.N., *International Law*, 8th Edn, Cambridge University Press, Cambridge, 2017.

Sidell, F.R. et al. (eds.), *Medical Aspects of Chemical and Biological Warfare*, Office of the Surgeon General (Army), Falls Church, VA, 1997.

Stürchler, N., *The Threat of Force in International Law*, Cambridge University Press, Cambridge, 2007.

United Kingdom Ministry of Defence, *The Manual of the Law of Armed Conflict*, Oxford University Press, Oxford, 2005.

Weller, M. (ed.), *The Oxford Handbook of the Use of Force in International Law*, Oxford University Press, Oxford, 2015.

## Articles, reports, and online materials

'1907 Second Hague Peace Conference', *Global Security*, at: https://bit.ly/2P1gERD.

Abbott, K. and D. Snidal, 'Hard and Soft Law in International Governance', *International Organization*, Vol. 54, No. 3 (2000), pp. 421–56.

'Anglo-German Naval Agreement', *Encyclopaedia Britannica*, at: https://bit.ly/2PwjxXA.

'Arms Manufacturers and the Public', *Foreign Affairs*, Vol. 12, No. 4 (July 1934), at: https://fam.ag/2QGvOsk.

The Aspen Institute, 'Clean Up Efforts', August 2011, at: http://bit.ly/2EYoOGr.

Baker, B., 'Hague Peace Conferences (1899 and 1907)', *Max Planck Encyclopedia of Public International Law*, at: https://bit.ly/1Vl5Rv5.

Benari, E., 'EU Imposes Sanctions on Boko Haram', *Arutz Sheva*, 3 June 2014.

'Biological Warfare Treatment', *WebMD*, 2018, at: http://bit.ly/2P2y0hA.

Borrie, J. and T. Caughley, 'Viewing Weapons Through a Humanitarian Lens: From Cluster Munitions to Nukes?', *Irish Studies in International Affairs*, Vol. 25 (2014), pp. 23–43.

Borrie, J., A. Guro Dimmen, T. Graff Hugo, C. Waszink, and K. Egeland, *Gender, Development and Nuclear Weapons: Shared Goals, Shared Concerns*, ILPI & UNIDIR, 2016, at: http://bit.ly/2PFgIGI.

Boyd, P., 'Anthrax Island – Inside Edition (2001)', *YouTube*, 13 December 2015, at: http://bit.ly/2F13Bvv.

Boyle, K. and S. Simonsen, 'Human Security, Human Rights and Disarmament', *Disarmament Forum*, No. 3 (2004), at: http://bit.ly/2RjrW0U.

'Brief Overview of Fissile Material Reduction', University of Illinois, United States, 2018, at: http://bit.ly/2JAXHQq.

Burr, W., 'The Making of the Nuclear Suppliers Group, 1974–1976', Wilson Center, 16 April 2014, at: http://bit.ly/2Avpsa0.

Carpenter, C., 'Vetting the Advocacy Agenda: Network Centrality and the Paradox of Weapons Norms', *International Organization*, Vol. 65, No. 1 (2011), pp. 69–102.

Cluster Munition Monitor, *Cluster Munition Monitor 2017*, ICBL-CMC, August 2017.

Cluster Munition Monitor, *Cluster Munition Monitor 2018*, ICBL-CMC, August 2018.

Committee on Review and Evaluation of International Technologies for the Destruction of Non-Stockpile Chemical Material and Board on Army Science and Technology, *Review of International Technologies for Destruction of Recovered Chemical Warfare Material*, National Research Council, United States, 2 November 2006.

Coupland, R.M. and R. Russbach, 'Victims of Antipersonnel Mines: What Is Being Done?' *Medicine & Global Survival*, Vol. 1 (1994).

CTBTO, 'CTBTO Executive Secretary Lassina Zerbo on the Unusual Seismic Event Detected in the Democratic People's Republic of Korea', Press release, Vienna, 3 September 2017, at: http://bit.ly/2CU6A72.

CTBTO, 'Overview of the Verification Regime', at: http://bit.ly/2q2V7cV.

CTBTO Preparatory Commission, 'General Overview of the Effects of Nuclear Testing', at: http://bit.ly/2OmfMCu.

Curry, A., 'Chemical Weapons Dumped in the Ocean After World War II Could Threaten Waters Worldwide', *Hakai Magazine*, 11 November 2016, at: http://bit.ly/2yMRCfE.

Davenport, K., 'The Missile Technology Control Regime at a Glance', *Fact Sheet*, at: http://bit.ly/2yLAOFV.

'DDR – Disarmament, Demobilization and Reintegration', *Global Security*, Last updated 17 August 2012, at: http://bit.ly/2Qd4O3Y.

Derksen, D., 'The Politics of Disarmament and Rearmament in Afghanistan', United States Institute of Peace, 20 May 2015, at: http://bit.ly/2JCTKKX.

Federation of American Scientists, 'Fissile Material Disposal Background', at: http://bit.ly/2SERBm7.

Fenwick, C.G., 'The Denunciation of the Disarmament Clauses of the Treaty of Versailles', *The American Journal of International Law*, Vol. 29, No. 4 (October 1935), pp. 675–78.

Finaud, M., '"Humanitarian Disarmament": Powerful New Paradigm or Naive Utopia?' Research Series No. 21/17, Geneva Centre for Security Policy (GCSP), Geneva, at: http://bit.ly/2zc4n2q.

Findlay, T., 'Looking Back: The Additional Protocol', *Arms Control Today*, 1 November 2007, at: http://bit.ly/2CZIEyj.

Ford, J., 'The Origins of Boko Haram', *The National Interest*, 6 June 2014, at: http://bit. ly/2F0vmo3.

Geneva *Call*, 'Investigation in the Philippines Finds Evidence of AP Mine Use; MILF Responsibility Not Established', 26 March 2010, at: http://bit.ly/2CZugpN.

Geneva International Centre for Humanitarian Demining, *A Guide to Mine Action*, 5th Edn, GICHD, Geneva, 2014.

Gerrard, J., 'Deputy for Almeria Criticises Government on Palomares Nuclear Cleanup', *Euro Weekly*, 16 February 2018, at: http://bit.ly/2OGnjRx.

Gill, A., 'Taking the Path of Delegitimization to Nuclear Disarmament', Working Paper, Centre for a New American Security, Stanford, April 2009, at: http://bit.ly/2OZg8UX

Guatemala Human Rights Commission, 'Genocide in the Ixil Triangle', 2011, at: http://bit. ly/2PKKz0N.

Haines, S., 'War at Sea: Nineteenth-Century Laws for Twenty-First Century Wars?', *International Review of the Red Cross*, Vol. 98, No. 2 (2016), pp. 419–47.

Hall, A., 'The Iron Harvest: Meet the Soldiers Tasked with Clearing Hundreds of Tonnes of Deadly World War I Shells and Mines from Beneath Flanders' Fields', *Daily Mail*, 10 November 2013, at: http://bit.ly/2qpk6qY.

Hauge, W., 'The Demobilization and Political Participation of Female Fighters in Guatemala', *Report to the Norwegian Ministry of Foreign Affairs*, International Peace Research Institute, Oslo (PRIO), Oslo, March 2007.

Hauge, W. and B. Thoresen, *El destino de los ex-combatientes en Guatemala: Obstaculizadores o agentes de cambio?* North-South Institute, Guatemala City, 2007.

Hayashi, N., 'The Role and Importance of the Hague Conferences: A Historical Perspective', *UNIDIR*, Geneva, 2017, at: https://bit.ly/2Pw7LMC.

Holquist, P., 'The Russian Empire as a "Civilized State": International Law as Principle and Practice in Imperial Russia, 1874–1878', *National Council for Eurasian and East European Research*, 2004, at: https://bit.ly/2RKyIxK.

ICRC, 'Stopping the Landmines Epidemic: From Negotiation to Action', 1 July 1996, at: http://bit.ly/2qgo7hq.

ICRC, 'Intervention of the International Committee of the Red Cross', *Fifth Meeting of States Parties*, Bangkok, 17 September 2003, at: http://bit.ly/2Jx4v1x.

ICRC, *Guide to the Legal Review of New Weapons, Means and Methods of Warfare*, ICRC, Geneva, 2006.

ICRC, 'How Is the Term "Armed Conflict" Defined in International Humanitarian Law?' *ICRC Opinion Paper*, March 2008, at: http://bit.ly/2CLr9Sc.

ICRC, 'The ICRC and weapon bearers', 29 October 2010, at: http://bit.ly/2q8Maiq.

ILPI, 'Biological Weapons Under International Law', December 2016.

Implementation Support Unit, 'Biological Weapons Convention: Background Information', 2012, at: http://bit.ly/2OnCJ8m.

Institute of Physics, 'A Brief History of Space', at: http://bit.ly/2Rbsdmk.

International Committee of the Red Cross (ICRC), '1976 Convention on the Prohibition of Military or any Hostile Use of Environmental Modification Techniques', *Fact Sheet*, ICRC, Geneva, January 2003.

International Maritime Organization, '38th Consultative Meeting of Contracting Parties (London Convention 1972) and 11th Meeting of Contracting Parties (London Protocol 1996), 19–23 September 2016', 23 September 2016, at: http://bit.ly/2OkZrxS.

Janzen, R., 'Guatemalan Ex-Combatant Perspectives on Reintegration: A Grounded Theory', *The Qualitative Report*, Vol. 19, Art. 41 (2014), at: http://bit.ly/2RypS57.

Jervis, R., 'Cooperation Under the Security Dilemma', *World Politics*, Vol. 30, No. 2 (January 1978), pp. 167–214.

Jevglevskaja, N., 'St Petersburg, 1868: First International Agreement Prohibiting the Use of Certain Weapons', *Online Atlas on the History of Humanitarianism and Human Rights*, at: https://bit.ly/2yecw7c.

Juneja, A., 'Flail Technology in Demining', *Journal of Conventional Weapons Destruction*, Vol. 20, No. 2 (July 2016), at: http://bit.ly/2zjCeXs.

Karson, M., 'Why I Prefer "Victim" to "Survivor"', *Psychology Today*, Posted 30 August 2016, at: http://bit.ly/2CYR5Kw.

Kimball, D., 'The Chemical Weapons Convention (BWC) at a Glance', *Fact Sheet*, Arms Control Association, at: http://bit.ly/2JzR3tv.

Kimball, D., 'The Intermediate-Range Nuclear Forces (INF) Treaty at a Glance', *Fact Sheet*, Arms Control Association, at: http://bit.ly/2EzzzPf.

Kimball, D., 'The Open Skies Treaty at a Glance', *Fact Sheet*, Arms Control Association, Updated October 2012, at: http://bit.ly/2G7AmYD.

Kimball, D. and K. Reif, 'The Anti-Ballistic Missile (ABM) Treaty at a Glance', *Fact Sheet*, Arms Control Association, August 2012, at: http://bit.ly/2PmA8jN.

Kimball, D. and K. Reif, 'The Conventional Armed Forces in Europe (CFE) Treaty and the Adapted CFE Treaty at a Glance', *Fact Sheet*, Arms Control Association, August 2012, at: http://bit.ly/2SqD1i6.

Kirgis, F.L., 'North Korea's Withdrawal from the Nuclear Nonproliferation Treaty', *Insights*, Vol. 8, No. 2 (24 January 2003), at: http://bit.ly/2D6Iru8.

Knight, W.A., 'Disarmament, Demobilization, and Reintegration and Post-Conflict Peacebuilding in Africa: An Overview', *African Security*, Vol. 1 (2008), pp. 24–52, at: http://bit.ly/2QgCHkn.

Kohen, M. and B. Schramm, 'General Principles of Law', *Oxford Bibliographies*, at: https://bit.ly/2BwybtD.

Kurak, S., 'Operation CHASE', *US Naval Institute Proceedings*, September 1967, pp. 40–46.

Landmine Monitor, *Landmine Monitor 2017*, International Campaign to Ban Landmines – Cluster Munition Coalition (ICBL-CMC), December 2017.

Lieber, K.A., 'Grasping the Technological Peace: The Offense-Defense Balance and International Security', *International Security*, Vol. 25, No. 1 (Summer 2000), pp. 71–104.

Litovkin, N., 'Washington: Russian Chemical Weapons Will Never Threaten U.S. Again', *Russia Beyond the Headlines*, 15 June 2017, at: http://bit.ly/2CXtcnm.

Lott, A., 'Pollution of the Marine Environment by Dumping: Legal Framework Applicable to Dumped Chemical Weapons and Nuclear Waste in the Arctic Ocean', *Nordic Environmental Law Journal*, 2015, No. 1, at: http://bit.ly/2PD6IxN.

Lum, T. et al., 'Republic of the Marshall Islands Changed Circumstances Petition to Congress', CRS Report for Congress, Updated 16 May 2005, at: http://bit.ly/2JbjOfU.

Majumdar, D., 'Novator 9M729: The Russian Missile that Broke INF Treaty's Back?' *The National Interest*, 7 December 2017, at: http://bit.ly/2P7C3bI.

Makhijani, A., 'A Readiness to Harm: The Health Effects of Nuclear Weapons Complexes', *Arms Control Today*, 1 July 2005, at: http://bit.ly/2zkUgso.

McClelland, J., 'The Review of Weapons in Accordance with Article 36 of Additional Protocol 1', *International Review of the Red Cross*, Vol. 850 (2003), p. 397.

Mine Action Review, *Clearing the Mines 2017*, Norwegian People's Aid, 2017, at: http://bit.ly/2RvZCs5.

Mine Action Review, *Clearing Cluster Munition Remnants 2018*, Norwegian People's Aid, August 2018, at: https://bit.ly/2O3ApnP.

Muggah, R., 'No Magic Bullet: A Critical Perspective on Disarmament, Demobilization and Reintegration (DDR) and Weapons Reduction in Post-Conflict Contexts', *The Commonwealth Journal of International Affairs*, 2005, at: http://bit.ly/2QiMV3V.

Muggah, R. and C. O'Donnell, 'Next Generation Disarmament, Demobilization and Reintegration', *Stability: International Journal of Security and Development*, Vol. 4, No. 1 (2015), at: http://bit.ly/2JHCVyN.

Mukhopadhyay, S., 'Russia Plans to Completely Destroy Chemical Weapons by 2020, to Shut Down Two Facilities by November', *International Business Times*, 29 October 2015, at: http://bit.ly/2EAZS7R.

Munive, J. and F. Stepputat, 'Rethinking Disarmament, Demobilization and Reintegration Programs', *Stability: International Journal of Security & Development*, Vol. 4, No. 1 (2015), at: http://bit.ly/2zpX6MJ.

NATO, 'Arms Control, Disarmament and Non-Proliferation in NATO', at: https://bit.ly/2ND8I41.

*NATO's Comprehensive, Strategic-Level Policy for Preventing the Proliferation of Weapons of Mass Destruction (WMD) and Defending Against Chemical, Biological, Radiological and Nuclear (CBRN) Threats*, 1 September 2009, at: http://bit.ly/2OcxY1c.

Nexon, D.H., 'The Balance of Power in the Balance', *World Politics*, Vol. 61, No. 2 (2009), pp. 330–59.

Nordqvist, C. 'What's to Know About Radiation Sickness?' *Medical News Today*, Last updated 15 August 2017, at: http://bit.ly/2yNeXOi.

'Novichok Agent', *Science Direct*, 2018, at: http://bit.ly/2qpSGBj.

NTI, 'Biological Weapons Convention (BWC) Compliance Protocol', 1 August 2001, at: http://bit.ly/2AJ6DjM.

NTI, 'Conference on Disarmament (CD)', at: http://bit.ly/2z7BxjN.

NTI, 'Russia: Biological', at: http://bit.ly/2zo5tbP.

NTI, 'Treaty on Conventional Armed Forces in Europe (CFE)', at: http://bit.ly/2qhmQXy.

Nuclear Suppliers Group, *Guidelines for Transfers of Nuclear-Related Dual-Use Equipment, Materials, Software, and Related Technology* (INFCIRC/254, Part 2).

Oestern, G. (ed.), *Nuclear Weapons Ban Monitor*, Norwegian People's Aid, New York, October 2018, at: http://bit.ly/2Q1eOgA.

'Operation CHASE', *Global Security*, at: http://bit.ly/2QfeHye.

OSCE, 'Ensuring Military Transparency – The Vienna Document', at: http://bit.ly/2F0YTOz

Panda, A., 'The Uncertain Future of the INF Treaty', *Council on Foreign Relations*, 25 October 2017, at: http://bit.ly/2Q0Y9tz.

Paris, R., 'Human Security: Paradigm Shift or Hot Air?' *International Security*, Vol. 26, No. 2 (Fall 2001), pp. 87–102.

*A Prohibition on Nuclear Weapons: A Guide to the Issues*, UN Institute for Disarmament Research (UNIDIR) and International Law and Policy Institute (ILPI), Geneva, February 2016.

'Russia Shuns Biological Weapons', *New Scientist*, Vol. 134, No. 1882 (1992).

Schelling, T., *Arms and Influence*, Yale University Press, New Haven, 1966.

Schulhofer-Wohl, J. and N. Sambanis, *Disarmament, Demobilization, and Reintegration Programs: An Assessment*, Research Report, Folke Bernadotte Academy, Sweden, 2010, at: http://bit.ly/2QhLEdk.

Shaffer, G.C., M.A. Gregory, and M. Pollack, 'Hard vs. Soft Law: Alternatives, Complements, and Antagonists in International Governance', *Minnesota Law Review*, Vol. 94 (June 2009), pp. 706–99.

SIPRI, 'Iraq: The UNSCOM Experience', *Fact Sheet*, October 1998, p. 3, at: http://bit.ly/2zoVbb4.

Smith, M., 'Explaining Nigeria's Boko Haram & Its Violent Insurgency', *Fact Sheet*, Africa Check, 22 September 2014 (Last updated 31 July 2017), at: http://bit.ly/2ALwB6j.

Starr, T.J., 'How to Dismantle a Nuclear Weapon', *Foxtrot Alpha*, 22 May 2017, at: http://bit.ly/2AH4sNA.

Stockholm International Peace Research Institute (SIPRI), 'SIPRI Databases: Arms Embargoes', undated but accessed 28 October 2018, at: http://bit.ly/2qhmqR2.

Swahn, J., 'The Long-Term Nuclear Explosives Predicament: The Final Disposal of Militarily Usable Fissile Material in Nuclear Waste from Nuclear Power and from the Elimination of Nuclear Weapons', Technical Peace Research Group, Institute of Physical Resource Theory, Göteborg, 1992, at: http://bit.ly/2SAiasC.

'Syria Chlorine Attack Claims: What This Chemical Is and How It Became a Weapon', *The Conversation*, 7 September 2016, at: http://bit.ly/2zjSzvp.

'Timeline of Syrian Chemical Weapons Activity, 2012–2018', Arms Control Association, at: http://bit.ly/2Sqa5Xv.

Tucker, J., 'The Fifth Review Conference of the Biological and Toxin Weapons Convention', *NTI*, 1 February 2002, at: http://bit.ly/2QeyNbZ.

'Under U.S.-Russia Partnership, Final Shipment of Fuel Converted from 20,000 Russian Nuclear Warheads Arrives in United States and Will Be Used for U.S. Electricity', National Nuclear Security Administration, 11 December 2013, at: http://bit.ly/2P3ToDk.

United States Department of Defense, *Field Manual 3–3 – Chemical and Biological Contamination Avoidance*, 1992.

United States Department of Defense, *Dictionary of Military Terms*, as amended through 31 October 2009.

United States Department of Defense, *Nuclear Posture Review*, February 2018, at: http://bit.ly/2AzQ4Hb.

United States *Department of Defense Dictionary of Military and Associated Terms*, September 2018, at: http://bit.ly/2qbOvcj.

United States Department of State, 'Antarctic Treaty', Bureau of Arms Control, Verification and Compliance, undated but accessed 1 January 2018, at: http://bit.ly/2QkjYEQ.

United States Department of State, *Adherence to and Compliance with Arms Control, Nonproliferation, and Disarmament Agreements and Commitments*, Washington, DC, April 2018.

United States Department of State, 'Treaty Between The United States of America and The Union of Soviet Socialist Republics on the Limitation of Anti-Ballistic Missile Systems (ABM Treaty)', at: https://bit.ly/2IVgl5m.

United States Department of State, Office of the Historian, 'Rush-Bagot Pact, 1817 and Convention of 1818', *Milestones in the History of U.S. Foreign Relations*, at: https://bit.ly/2mdwHh5.

United States Department of State, Office of the Historian, 'The Washington Naval Conference, 1921–1922', *Milestones in the History of U.S. Foreign Relations*, at: https://bit.ly/1qCET1o.

United States Nuclear Regulatory Commission, 'Fissile Material', at: http://bit.ly/2CWg1SI.

*Uppsala Conflict Data Program*, Department of Peace and Conflict Research, Uppsala University, Sweden, at: http://bit.ly/2z7GTLV.

Vité, S., 'Typology of Armed Conflicts in International Humanitarian Law: Legal Concepts and Actual Situations', *International Review of the Red Cross*, Vol. 91, No. 873 (March 2009), pp. 69–94.

Wagner, T., 'Hazardous Waste: Evolution of a National Environmental Problem', *Journal of Policy History*, Vol. 16, No. 4 (2004), pp. 306–31.

Wernick, A., 'Seawater Is Infiltrating a Nuclear Waste Dump on a Remote Pacific Atoll', *Public Radio International*, 19 February 2018, at: http://bit.ly/2S5NVd3.

Wilkinson, I., 'Chemical Weapon Munitions Dumped at Sea: An Interactive Map', Middlebury Institute of International Studies at Monterey, 1 August 2017 (Updated 7 September 2017), at: http://bit.ly/2DieEyS.

Wolchover, N., 'Why Is Plutonium More Dangerous than Uranium?' *Live Science*, 17 March 2011, at: http://bit.ly/2PCdHaj.

## European Court of Human Rights

*Finogenov and others v. Russia*, Judgment, 20 December 2011 (as rendered final on 4 June 2012).

## International Atomic Energy Agency materials

'Basics of IAEA safeguards', 2017, at: http://bit.ly/2Ctxrps.
'IAEA safeguards overview', 2017, at: http://bit.ly/2q2kJGL.
Inventory of radioactive waste disposals at sea, Doc. IAEA-TECDOC-1105, August 1999, at: http://bit.ly/2AH7aTk.
'Safeguards agreements', 2017, at: http://bit.ly/2AmFDXc.
'Safeguards and verification', 2017, at: http://bit.ly/2CWbUa2.
'Safeguards implementation in 2017: Helping prevent the spread of nuclear weapons', 2018, at: http://bit.ly/2R39468.
'Safeguards legal framework', 2017, at: http://bit.ly/2END7h9.
Safeguards implementation guide for states with small quantities protocols, Vienna, 2016, at: http://bit.ly/2yriOjC.
'Status of the additional protocol: Status as of 24 September 2018', at: http://bit.ly/2OnV1Xc.

## International Criminal Court

'Elements of crimes', UN doc. PCNICC/2000/1/Add.2 (2000).

## International Criminal Tribunal for the former Yugoslavia

Application and Proposed Amicus Curiae Brief Concerning the 15 April 2011 Trial Chamber Judgment and Requesting that the Appeals Chamber Reconsider the Findings of Unlawful Artillery Attacks during Operation Storm.
Prosecutor v. Gotovina and Markač.
Prosecutor v. Haradinaj.
Prosecutor v. Mile Mrkšić, Miroslav Radić, and Veselin Šljivančin.
Prosecutor v. Tadić (aka 'Dule').

## Organisation for the Prohibition of Nuclear Weapons

'About the Conference of the States Parties', at: http://bit.ly/2yPBj1H.
Conference of the States Parties, Decision: 'Establishment of an Advisory Board on Education and Outreach', Twentieth Session, Decision C-20/DEC.9, 3 December 2015, at: http://bit.ly/2CZpubR.
'CWC Conference of the States Parties Adopts Decision Addressing the Threat from Chemical Weapons Use', News release, The Hague, 27 June 2018, at: http://bit.ly/2P3gA4u.
'Decision: The Establishment of the International Support Network for Victims of Chemical Weapons and the Establishment of a Voluntary Trust Fund for this purpose', Doc. C-16/DEC.13, 2 December 2011, at: http://bit.ly/2CYXuW4.

'Destruction of Declared Syrian Chemical Weapons Completed', 4 January 2016, at: http://bit.ly/2SEbkCr.

'Executive Council', at: http://bit.ly/2Pymlqi.

Executive Council, 'Destruction of Syrian Chemical Weapons, Decision', OPCW doc. EC-M-33/DEC.1, 27 September 2013, at: http://bit.ly/2OiD0te.

'First Advisory Board on Education and Outreach Meets as Next Step in Evolution of OPCW', 29 April 2016, at: http://bit.ly/2AJzKU1.

'OPCW Confirms Use of Sarin and Chlorine in Ltamenah, Syria, on 24 and 25 March 2017', News release, 13 June 2018, at: http://bit.ly/2PCR2KX.

'OPCW Director-General Congratulates Iraq on Complete Destruction of Chemical Weapons Remnants', News release, The Hague, 13 March 2018, at: http://bit.ly/2yKbPlZ.

'OPCW Director-General Praises Complete Destruction of Libya's Chemical Weapon Stockpile', 11 January 2018, at: http://bit.ly/2JDWubf.

'OPCW Fact Finding Mission: "Compelling Confirmation" That Chlorine Gas Used as Weapon in Syria', The Hague, 10 September 2014, at: http://bit.ly/2JzTbSe.

'OPCW Fact-Finding Mission Confirms Likely Use of Chlorine in Saraqib, Syria', Press release, 16 May 2018, at: http://bit.ly/2Roqw5r.

'OPCW Honours All Victims of Chemical Warfare During Remembrance Day', 30 November 2017, at: http://bit.ly/2JysPju.

'Subsidiary Bodies', at: http://bit.ly/2PEKYBy.

'Syria and the OPCW: The Fact-Finding Mission (FFM)', at: http://bit.ly/2JyRRPo.

'Third Review Conference Concludes with Consensus Final Document and Political Declaration', Press release, 19 April 2013, at: http://bit.ly/2RxZAjp.

## United Nations documents and resolutions

### General Assembly resolutions

Resolution 1(I).

Resolution S-10/2: Final Document of the Tenth Special Session of the Assembly, 30 June 1978.

Resolution 1665 (XVI).

Resolution 42/37C.

Resolution 45/57.

Resolution 72/38.

## International Court of Justice

Case Concerning Military and Paramilitary Activities in and against Nicaragua (Nicaragua v. United States of America), Judgment (Merits), 27 June 1986.

Legality of the Threat or Use of Nuclear Weapons, Advisory Opinion, 8 July 1996.

North Sea Continental Shelf Cases (Germany/Denmark and Germany/The Netherlands), Judgment, 20 February 1969.

*Nuclear Tests Case (New Zealand v. France)*, Judgment, 20 December 1974.

## International DDR Standards

IDDRS Module 1.10: 'Introduction to the IDDRS', 2006 (Rev'd Edn, 2014).

IDDRS Module 4.10: 'Disarmament'.

IDDRS Module 5.10: 'Women, Gender and DDR', 2006.
IDDRS Module 5.20: 'Youth and DDR', 2006.
IDDRS Module 5:30: 'Children and DDR', 2006.

## International Mine Action Standards

IMAS 04.10: 'Glossary of mine action terms, definitions and abbreviations', 2nd Edn (May 2013).
IMAS 11.10: Guide for the destruction of stockpiled anti-personnel mines, 2nd Edn, 1 January 2003 (as amended through June 2013).
IMAS 11.20: 'Principles and procedures for open burning and open detonation operations', 2nd Edn, 1 January 2003 (Amendment 6, June 2013).

## Press releases

'Confidence-Building Measures Supporting Arms Control Extremely Critical, Secretary-General Tells Security Council Meeting on Non-proliferation', UN doc. SG/SM/18858-SC/13167-DC/3755, 18 January 2018, at: http://bit.ly/2P8opWw.
'Human Cost of Illicit Flow of Small Arms, Light Weapons Stressed in Security Council Debate', UN doc. SC/11889, 13 May 2015, at: http://bit.ly/2PYACJF.
'Security Council Al-Qaida Sanctions Committee Adds Boko Haram to Its Sanctions List', Press release, UN doc. SC/11410, 22 May 2014.

## Reports and guidelines

'Disarmament, Demobilization and Reintegration: Report of the Secretary-General', UN doc. A/60/705, 2 March 2006.
'First Conference of States Parties to the Arms Trade Treaty, Cancun, Mexico, 24–27 August 2015, Final Report', Doc. ATT/CSP1/2015/6, 27 August 2015, at: http://bit.ly/2zp0mrM.
Minnesota Protocol on the Investigation of Potentially Unlawful Death (2016), Office of the UN High Commissioner for Human Rights, 2017.
Report of the Conventional Armaments Commission, UN doc. S/C.3/32/Rev.1, 18 August 1948.
'Report of the Panel of Governmental Experts on Small Arms', Annex to UN doc. A/52/298, 27 August 1997, para. 26, at: http://bit.ly/2ORrUQX.
Report of the UN Special Rapporteur on Extrajudicial, Summary or Arbitrary Executions, UN doc. A/68/382 13 September 2013.
Report of the UN Special Rapporteur on the Promotion and Protection of Human Rights and Fundamental Freedoms While Countering Terrorism, UN doc. A/68/389, 18 September 2013.
Report on Implementation of the United Nations Programme of Action to Prevent, Combat and Eradicate the Illicit Trade in Small Arms and Light Weapons in All Its Aspects.
'Small Arms and Light Weapons, Report of the Secretary-General', UN doc. S/2015/289, 27 April 2015.
'United Nations Military Staff Committee', at: http://bit.ly/2EQaDTM.
UN Development Programme (UNDP), *Human Development Report, New Dimensions of Human Security*, at: http://bit.ly/2D9fOfL.

UN Disarmament Commission, 'Guidelines for International Arms Transfers in the Context of General Assembly Resolution 46/36 H of 6 December 1991: Report of the Disarmament Commission', UN General Assembly, UN doc. A/51/42, 1996.

UN Mission to Investigate Allegations of the Use of Chemical Weapons in the Syrian Arab Republic, 'Report on Allegations of the Use of Chemical Weapons in the Ghouta Area of Damascus on 21 August 2013', UN docs. A/67/997 and S/2013/553, 16 September 2013, paras. 27–28.

UN Office for Disarmament Affairs (UNODA), 'Biological Weapons: The Biological Weapons Convention', at: http://bit.ly/2DiQkgi.

UN Office for Disarmament Affairs (UNODA), 'The Conference on Disarmament and Negative Security Assurances', Fact Sheet, July 2017, at: http://bit.ly/2SI9VL0.

UNODA, 'Secretary-General's Mechanism for Investigation of Alleged Use of Chemical and Biological Weapons', at: http://bit.ly/2Qlfz4x.

UN Office at Geneva (UNOG), 'The Convention on Certain Conventional Weapons', at: http://bit.ly/2O9InuF.

UNOG, 'The Biological Weapons Convention: Implementation Support Unit', at: http://bit.ly/2AIKUIM.

UN Register of Conventional Arms, at: http://bit.ly/2C0NRFv.

UN Secretary General, 'Disarmament, Demobilization and Reintegration', 2 March 2006, UN doc. 60/705.

## Security Council resolutions

Resolution 661 (1990).
Resolution 733 (1992).
Resolution 984 (1995).
Resolution 1390 (2002).
Resolution 1493 (2003).
Resolution 1540 (2004).
Resolution 1556 (2004).
Resolution 1718 (2006).
Resolution 1701 (2006).
Resolution 1737 (2006).
Resolution 1907 (2009).
Resolution 1970 (2011).
Resolution 2083 (2012).
Resolution 2117 (2013).
Resolution 2127 (2013).
Resolution 2209 (2015).
Resolution 2216 (2015).
Resolution 2349 (2017).
Resolution 2423 (2018).
Resolution 2428 (2018).

## Press articles

AFP, 'Niger: discrets procès d'un millier de militants de Boko Haram', *RTBF*, 10 March 2017, at: http://bit.ly/2JAYMrh.

*AFP/PTI*, 'EU Adds Nigeria's Boko Haram to Blacklisted Terror Groups', Brussels, 3 June 2014.

Almukhtar, S., 'Most Chemical Attacks in Syria Get Little Attention: Here Are 34 Confirmed Cases', *The New York Times*, 13 April 2018, at: http://bit.ly/2Q3c2rl.

Associated Press, 'US Set to Destroy Thousands of Chemical Weapons at Colorado Plant', *Fox News US*, 1 September 2016, at: http://bit.ly/2CwO8R9.

BBC, 'Cameroon Sentences 89 Boko Haram Fighters to Death', 17 March 2016, at: http://bit.ly/2PJyZ64.

BBC, 'Russia Nuclear Treaty: Gorbachev Warns Trump Plan Will Undermine Disarmament', 21 October 2018, at: https://bbc.in/2ODVAkt.

BBC, 'Who Are Nigeria's Boko Haram Islamist Group?' 24 November 2016, at: http://bit.ly/2F3mqhG.

Bennetts, M., 'Russia Asks Britain for Help in Identifying Novichok Suspects', *The Guardian*, 7 September 2018, at: https://bit.ly/2O38W5F.

Brackley, E., 'West Africa: The Region in Niger Quietly Piloting a Boko Haram Amnesty', *AllAfrica*, 20 April 2017, at: http://bit.ly/2OoSTyu.

Burgen, S., 'US to Clean Up Spanish Radioactive Site 49 Years After Plane Crash', *The Guardian*, 19 October 2015, at: http://bit.ly/2D0mXz4.

'Cleaning up Agent Orange', *Deutsche Welle*, 10 August 2012, at: http://bit.ly/2JxU79y.

Fuller, T., '4 Decades on, U.S. Starts Cleanup of Agent Orange in Vietnam', *The New York Times*, 9 August 2012, at: http://bit.ly/2Qd7H4J.

Gonzalez, M., 'Trump Presidency Will Force Renegotiation of Palomares Nuclear Clean-Up', *El País*, 27 January 2017, at: http://bit.ly/2Ak8iMH.

Malloy, D., 'U.S. Helping Defuse Vietnam's Dioxin Hot Spots Blamed on Agent Orange', *The Washington Post*, 8 April 2016, at: http://bit.ly/2RwjnzJ.

Philipps, D., 'Troops Who Cleaned Up Radioactive Islands Can't Get Medical Care', *The New York Times*, 28 January 2017, at: http://bit.ly/2CxYfFh.

Pincus, W., 'The Explosive Cost of Disposing of Nuclear Weapons', *The Washington Post*, 3 July 2013, at: http://bit.ly/2qquhvs.

'Putin: Unilateral US Withdrawal from ABM Treaty Pushing Russia Toward New Arms Race', *RT*, 19 June 2015, at: http://bit.ly/2OTOt7V.

Reuters, 'Boko Haram Split Creates Two Deadly Forces', *Voice of America*, 4 August 2017, at: http://bit.ly/2DlWtbw.

Willacy, M., 'It Was Supposed to Be a Trip to Paradise, Instead It Sealed Their Fate', *ABC News* (Australia), at: http://bit.ly/2PaZKA1.

# ANNEXES

## Annex 1

### Graphical overview of disarmament-related treaties and instruments

This graph clusters disarmament-related treaties and instruments according to categories of weapons, themes and measures to provide a general overview of international disarmament law.

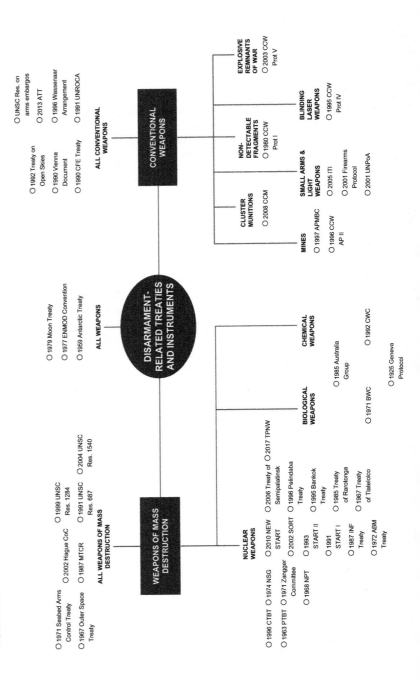

# Annex 2

## *Table of disarmament-related treaties and instruments*

| ALL WEAPONS | | |
|---|---|---|
| YEAR OF ADOPTION | FULL TITLE | SHORT TITLE/ABBREVIATION |
| MULTILATERAL INSTRUMENTS | | |
| 1959 | The Antarctic Treaty | The Antarctic Treaty |
| 1967 | Treaty on Principles Governing the Activities of States in the Exploration and Use of Outer Space, Including the Moon and other Celestial Bodies | Outer Space Treaty |
| 1971 | Treaty on the Prohibition of the Emplacement of Nuclear Weapons and other Weapons of Mass Destruction on the Seabed and the Ocean Floor and in the Subsoil thereof | Seabed Treaty |
| 1977 | Convention on the Prohibition of Military or any Hostile Use of Environment Modification Techniques | ENMOD Convention |
| 1979 | Agreement Governing the Activities of States on the Moon and Other Celestial Bodies | Moon Treaty |
| 1996 | Protocol to Convention on the Prevention of Marine Pollution by Dumping of Wastes and Other Matter | London Protocol |

| WEAPONS OF MASS DESTRUCTION | | |
|---|---|---|
| YEAR OF ADOPTION | FULL TITLE | SHORT TITLE/ABBREVIATION |
| 1. ALL WEAPONS OF MASS DESTRUCTION | | |
| 1987 | Missile Technology Control Regime | MTCR |
| 1991 | United Nations Special Commission on Iraq (UNSCOM) | UNSCR 687 |
| 1999 | United Nations Monitoring, Verification, and Inspection Commission (on Iraq) (UNMOVIC) | UNSCR 1284 |
| 2002 | The Hague Code of Conduct against Ballistic Missile Proliferation | HCoC |
| 2004 | United Nations Security Council Resolution 1540 (2004) on the Non-Proliferation of Weapons of Mass Destruction | UNSCR 1540 |

*(Continued)*

| YEAR OF ADOPTION | FULL TITLE | SHORT TITLE/ABBREVIATION |
|---|---|---|
| 2. NUCLEAR WEAPONS/NUCLEAR ENERGY | | |
| 2.1. BILATERAL INSTRUMENTS | | |
| 2.1.1. USA – USSR/RUSSIAN FEDERATION | | |
| 1972 | Treaty between the USA and the USSR on the Limitation of Anti-Ballistic Missile Systems | ABM Treaty |
| 1987 | Treaty between the USA and the USSR on the Elimination of their Intermediate-Range and Shorter-Range Missiles | INF Treaty |
| 1991 | Treaty between the USA and the USSR on the Reduction and Limitation of Strategic Offensive Arms | START I |
| 1993 | Treaty between the USA and the Russian Federation on further Reductions and Limitation of Strategic Offensive Arms | START II |
| 2002 | Treaty between the USA and the Russian Federation on Strategic Offensive Reductions | SORT or Moscow Treaty |
| 2010 | Treaty between the USA and the Russian Federation on Measures for the Further Reduction and Limitation of Strategic Offensive Arms | New START |
| 2.2. MULTILATERAL INSTRUMENTS | | |
| 1963 | Treaty banning Nuclear Weapons Tests in the Atmosphere, in Outer Space and under Water | PTBT |
| 1968 | Treaty on the Non-Proliferation of Nuclear Weapons | NPT |
| 1971 | Non-Proliferation Treaty Exporters' Committee Trigger List | Zangger Committee |
| 1974 | Nuclear Suppliers Group Guidelines | NSG |
| 1996 | Comprehensive Nuclear Test Ban Treaty | CTBT |
| 2017 | Treaty on the Prohibition of Nuclear Weapons | TPNW |
| 2.3. REGIONAL INSTRUMENTS | | |
| 2.3.1. AFRICA | | |
| 1996 | African Nuclear-Weapon-Free Zone Treaty (and Additional Protocols) | Pelindaba Treaty |

| YEAR OF ADOPTION | FULL TITLE | SHORT TITLE/ABBREVIATION |
|---|---|---|
| | 2.3.2.  AMERICAS | |
| 1967 | Treaty on a Nuclear-Weapon-Free Zone in Latin America and the Caribbean (and Additional Protocols) | Tlatelolco Treaty |
| | 2.3.3.  ASIA-PACIFIC | |
| 1985 | South Pacific Nuclear-Weapon Free Zone Treaty (and Additional Protocols) | Rarotonga Treaty |
| 1995 | Southeast Asian Nuclear-Weapon-Free Zone Treaty (and Additional Protocols) | Bangkok Treaty |
| 2006 | Central Asian Nuclear-Weapon-Free-Zone Treaty (and Additional Protocols) | Semipalatinsk Treaty |
| | 3.  BIOLOGICAL WEAPONS | |
| | MULTILATERAL INSTRUMENTS | |
| 1971 | Convention on the Prohibition of the Development, Production, and Stockpiling of Bacteriological (Biological) Weapons and Toxin Weapons and on their Destruction | BWC |
| | 4.  CHEMICAL WEAPONS | |
| | MULTILATERAL INSTRUMENTS | |
| 1992 | Convention on the prohibition of the development, production, stockpiling and use of chemical weapons and on their destruction | CWC |
| | 5.  BIOLOGICAL AND CHEMICAL WEAPONS | |
| | MULTILATERAL INSTRUMENTS | |
| 1925 | Protocol for the prohibition of the use in war of asphyxiating, poisonous or other gases, and of bacteriological methods of warfare | Geneva Protocol |
| 1984 | Australia Group Guidelines | AG |

| | CONVENTIONAL WEAPONS | |
|---|---|---|
| YEAR OF ADOPTION | FULL TITLE | SHORT TITLE/ABBREVIATION |
| | 1.  ALL CONVENTIONAL WEAPONS | |
| | MULTILATERAL INSTRUMENTS | |
| | UNSC Res. on Arms Embargos (see paras. 3.15, 3.22, and 6.33 of the Guide) | |

(*Continued*)

| YEAR OF ADOPTION | FULL TITLE | SHORT TITLE/ABBREVIATION |
|---|---|---|
| 1991 | United Nations Register of Conventional Arms | UNROCA |
| 1996 | Wassenaar Arrangement on Export Controls for Conventional Arms and Dual-Use Goods and Technologies (Control Lists) | Wassenaar Arrangement |
| 2003 | Protocol V to the CCW on Explosive Remnants of War | CCW Protocol V |
| 2013 | The Arms Trade Treaty | ATT |
| | REGIONAL INSTRUMENTS | |
| | EUROPE | |
| 1990 | Treaty on Conventional Armed Forces in Europe | CFE Treaty |
| 1990 | Vienna Document of the Negotiations on Confidence- and Security-Building Measures | Vienna Document |
| 1992 | Treaty on Open Skies | Open Skies Treaty |
| | 2. MINES | |
| | MULTILATERAL INSTRUMENTS | |
| 1981/1996 | Amended Protocol II to the CCW on Prohibitions or Restrictions on the Use of Mines, Booby-Traps and other Devices | CCW Protocol II |
| 1997 | Convention on the Prohibition of the Use, Stockpiling, Production, and Transfer of Anti-Personnel Mines and on their Destruction | Anti-Personnel or Mine Ban Convention |
| | 3. CLUSTER MUNITION | |
| | MULTILATERAL INSTRUMENTS | |
| 2008 | Convention on Cluster Munitions | CCM |
| | 4. NON-DETECTABLE FRAGMENTS | |
| | MULTILATERAL INSTRUMENTS | |
| 1980 | Protocol I to the CCW on Non-Detectable Fragments | CCW Protocol I |
| | 5. BLINDING LASER WAEPONS | |
| | MULTILATERAL INSTRUMENTS | |
| 1996 | Amended Protocol II to the CCW on Prohibitions or Restrictions on the Use of Mines, Booby-Traps and other Devices | Amended Protocol II |

# Annex 3

## *Disarmament-related institutions, think tanks and training centres*

| No | INTERGOVERNMENTAL INSTITUTIONS |
|---|---|
| 1 | Anti-Personnel Mine Ban Convention Implementation Support Unit (APMBC ISU) |
| 2 | Arms Trade Treaty (ATT) Secretariat |
| 3 | Australia Group (AG) Secretariat |
| 4 | Biological Weapons Convention Implementation Support Unit (BWC ISU) |
| 5 | Convention on Cluster Munitions Implementation Support Unit (CCM ISU) |
| 6 | Hague Code of Conduct against Ballistic Missile Proliferation (HCoC) Executive Secretariat (Austrian Ministry for Europe, Integration and Foreign Affairs) |
| 7 | International Atomic Energy Agency (IAEA) |
| 8 | Missile Technology Control Regime (MTCR) Point of Contact (French Ministry for Europe and Foreign Affairs) |
| 9 | Nuclear Suppliers Group (NSG) Point of Contact (The Permanent Mission of Japan to the International Organisations in Vienna) |
| 10 | Organisation for the Prohibition of Chemical Weapons (OPCW) |
| 11 | Organization for Security and Co-operation in Europe (OSCE) |
| 12 | United Nations Office for Disarmament Affairs (UNODA) |
| 13 | Wassenaar Arrangement Secretariat |

| No | THINK TANKS AND TRAINING CENTRES |
|---|---|
| 1 | Arab Institute for Security Studies (ACSIS) |
| 2 | Arms Control Association (ACA) |
| 3 | Belfer Center for Science and International Affairs |
| 4 | British American Security Information Council (BASIC) |
| 5 | Brookings Institution |
| 6 | Carnegie Endowment for International Peace (CEIP) |
| 7 | Center for Arms Control and Non-Proliferation (CACNP) |
| 8 | Center for International Cooperation (NYU-CIC) |
| 9 | Center for Strategic and International Studies (CSIS) |
| 10 | Centre for Nuclear Non-Proliferation and Disarmament (CNND) |
| 11 | Chatham House |
| 12 | Council on Foreign Relations (CFR) |
| 13 | European Union Institute for Security Studies (EUISS) |
| 14 | European Union Non-Proliferation and Disarmament Consortium |
| 15 | European Leadership Network (ELN) |
| 16 | Federation of American Scientists (FAS) |
| 17 | *Fondation pour la recherche stratégique* (FRS) |
| 18 | Geneva Centre for Security Policy (GCSP) |
| 19 | Geneva Disarmament Platform (GDP) |
| 20 | German Institute for International and Security Affairs (SWP) |
| 21 | Institute for Peace Research and Security Policy, Hamburg (IFSH) |

(*Continued*)

| No | THINK TANKS AND TRAINING CENTRES |
|----|----------------------------------|
| 22 | *Institut des Relations Internationales et Stratégiques* (IRIS) |
| 23 | *Institut français des relations internationales* (IFRI) |
| 24 | International Institute for Strategic Studies (IISS) |
| 25 | *Istituto Affari Internazionali* (IAI) |
| 26 | James Martin Center for Nonproliferation Studies (CNS) |
| 27 | NATO Defence College (NDC) |
| 28 | Nuclear Threat Initiative (NTI) |
| 29 | Peace Research Institute Oslo (PRIO) |
| 30 | PIR Center Moscow |
| 31 | RAND Corporation |
| 32 | Royal United Services Institute for Defence and Security Studies (RUSI) |
| 33 | Small Arms Survey (SAS) |
| 34 | Stimson Center |
| 35 | Stockholm International Peace Research Institute (SIPRI) |
| 36 | United Nations Institute for Disarmament Research (UNIDIR) |
| 37 | Vienna Center on Disarmament and Non-Proliferation (VCDNP) |
| 38 | Wilton Park |

# GLOSSARY OF ABBREVIATIONS AND ACRONYMS

| | |
|---|---|
| **ABM Treaty** | 1972 Anti-Ballistic Missile Treaty |
| **APMBC** | 1997 Anti-Personnel Mine Ban Convention |
| **CANWFZ** | 2006 Treaty on a Nuclear-Weapon-Free Zone in Central Asia |
| **CSBM** | Confidence and security-building measure |
| **CTBT** | 1996 Comprehensive Nuclear-Test-Ban Treaty |
| **DDR** | disarmament, demobilisation, and reintegration |
| **ENMOD** | 1976 Convention on the Prohibition of Military or Any Other Hostile Use of Environmental Modification Techniques |
| **ICJ** | International Court of Justice |
| **ICRC** | International Committee of the Red Cross |
| **IDDRS** | Integrated DDR Standards |
| **IHL** | international humanitarian law |
| **INF Treaty** | 1987 Intermediate-Range Nuclear Forces Treaty |
| **JCPOA** | 2015 Joint Comprehensive Plan of Action |
| **MTCR** | 1987 Missile Technology Control Regime |
| **NATO** | North Atlantic Treaty Organization |
| **New START** | 2010 New Strategic Arms Reduction Treaty |
| **NPT** | 1968 Treaty on the Non-Proliferation of Nuclear Weapons |
| **OHCHR** | Office of the UN High Commissioner for Human Rights |
| **OSCE** | Organization for Security and Co-operation in Europe |
| **PoA** | 2001 UN Programme of Action on Small Arms and Light Weapons |
| **PTBT** | Partial Nuclear-Test-Ban Treaty |
| **SALT** | Strategic Arms Limitation Talks |
| **SALT I** | Strategic Arms Limitation Treaty I |
| **SALT II** | Strategic Arms Limitation Treaty II |
| **SALW** | small arms and light weapons |

| | |
|---|---|
| **SORT** | 2002 Strategic Offensive Reductions Treaty |
| **START I** | 1991 Strategic Arms Reduction Treaty I |
| **START II** | 1993 Strategic Arms Reduction Treaty II |
| **TPNW** | 2017 Treaty on the Prohibition of Nuclear Weapons |
| **UN** | United Nations |
| **UNICEF** | United Nations Children's Fund |
| **US** | United States of America |
| **WMD** | weapon of mass destruction |

# INDEX